THE ENDURING QUESTIONS OF POLITICS

SECOND EDITION

edited by

WERNER FELD

ALAN T. LEONHARD

WALTER W. TOXEY, JR.

Department of Political Science
Louisiana State University in New Orleans

PRENTICE-HALL, INC., Englewood Cliffs, New Jersey

Library of Congress Cataloging in Publication Data

FELD, WERNER J   comp.
    The enduring questions of politics.

    Includes bibliographical references.
    1. Political science—Addresses, essays,
lectures. I. Leonhard, Alan T., joint comp.
II. Toxey, Walter W., joint comp. III. Title.
JA66.F4 1974   320′.08   73-13549
ISBN 0-13-277327-9

Printed in the United States of America

10 9 8 7 6 5 4 3 2 1

PRENTICE-HALL INTERNATIONAL, INC., London
PRENTICE-HALL OF AUSTRALIA, PTY. LTD., Sydney
PRENTICE-HALL OF CANADA, LTD., Toronto
PRENTICE-HALL OF INDIA PRIVATE LIMITED, New Delhi
PRENTICE-HALL OF JAPAN, INC., Tokyo

CONTENTS

7   THE INTERNATIONAL SOCIETY   252

FOREWORD

As we observed in the Preface to the first edition of this book, the immediate question in the reader's mind is apt to be, "Why another readings book for the introductory course in political science?" The editors of this volume reply that it is an attempt at innovation. Several years of teaching this course to freshman students have convinced us that there is a need for thought-provoking commentary in a book of readings in order to give coherence to what appears too often to be a mass of unrelated bits and pieces. We feel that entering freshmen should not be overburdened with materials that they will have difficulty in digesting. The consequence is often rejection of the entire book by the students, regardless of how excellent some of the selections may be. For this reason it seemed to us better to offer fewer readings and to introduce selections for each chapter with comments designed to evoke the student's interest in the subject matter and to place the selections in the context of discussion. Through this technique we hope to arouse the student's curiosity sufficiently to induce him to read the selections with alacrity and care. If we succeed in this objective, we will have made a significant contribution to the student's learning process. In this second edition we have added a comparative note—*Point and Counterpoint*—for each chapter, which, in most cases, will pose contradictory statements concerning a major question covered in the chapter. This contrasting of viewpoints at the outset will also serve to stimulate the student's curiosity.

The choice of readings was also crucial, of course, and had to take into consideration the prospective readers. In most cases the entering freshman has had only limited contact with the many-splendored, as well as much-maligned, thing called politics. In high school the student became only slightly acquainted with politics in his civics course, which concentrated primarily on the basic processes of federal and state government. At home, he may have heard his father occasionally discuss forthcoming elections or various activities at city hall. His third source of knowledge about politics may have been the daily newspapers, provided he had the time to cast a glance or two at the more serious parts of the news.

The level of knowledge freshmen are likely to have with respect to politics is one consideration upon which we have based our choice of readings. Another consideration was the fact that the introductory political science course or perhaps a course in American Government may be the only one in this field that a nongovernment major may take throughout his undergraduate college career. Since we believe that enlightened citizenship requires a degree of familiarity with some of the fundamental issues of politics our selections needed to stimulate interest in, and sharpen the student's judgment on, current political events.

To meet these requirements, we have concentrated on what may best be called the *enduring questions of politics*. Throughout the ages certain issues of politics have been persistent subjects of writing and discussion. For example, standards of public morality and the scope of official powers were actively debated questions 2500 years ago, and this debate continues today. Generally political theorists feel that questions about freedom, equality, dictatorship, authority, government under law, as well as other topics treated in this volume, warrant continual exploration. Knowledge of the past, as Thucydides said, is essential to those who seek to know the future, and those who write the history of their own times also write of and for all times. Hence a number of selections come from the pens of writers who have lived during periods ranging from ancient Greece to the nineteenth century. It is refreshing to discover that many of these authors, highly respected now as then, wrote in a simple and clear way. The opportunity to read works by Aristotle, John Locke, J. S. Mill, James Madison, Adam Smith, and other great authors provides the beginning student with excellent vehicles for recognizing the intricate and absorbing nature of politics.

Besides the selections taken from the formal treatises and essays of political theorists, past and present, we have included a number of excerpts from the landmark decisions of the Supreme Court of the United States. The addition of examples of judicial reasoning in the practical determination of disputes, and examples of the objectives of working political groups furnishes a connecting element between theory and practice.

In the choice of the readings we have given high priority to readability, clarity, and interest, but equally important were the pertinent insights that a particular selection could provide for the understanding of the subject matter. Although we have attempted to avoid the inclusion of materials already presented in other books of readings, certain classics had to have their place in our volume. We have abridged those materials which seemed to be unduly long, but we have taken care not to cut out any passages necessary to a full understanding of the author's arguments.

Having stressed issues rather than structure and functions, we hope to have contributed to the stimulation of controversy. If the entering freshman were first exposed to a labyrinth of structures and a confusing array of functions, his enthusiasm for one of the most dynamic disciplines in the social sciences might well wane quickly. Memorizing materials is likely to be deadly for the introductory course in politics. On the other hand, prodding freshmen into thinking about issues and drawing them into active dialogue in the spirit of Socrates could produce a very meaningful learning experience. This is the aim of our book.

The volume is divided into seven chapters. The first chapter examines the nature of politics and discusses briefly the variety of viewpoints that various writers have taken in defining politics. In the second chapter the sources of authority are investigated and the types and patterns of authority described. Chapter 3 examines the varying forms of dictatorships that have existed throughout the ages and probes into the essential features of this type of governmental system, whether in ancient times or in contemporary China. The fourth chapter spotlights the concepts of freedom and equality, indicating the various meanings and limitations involved in these terms. In the fifth chapter we try to determine the essential features of constitutionalism and its relationship to democracy. Chapter 6 examines the interrelationships between the economic and the political orders and discusses the swings of the pendulum between *laissez-faire* philosophy and government intervention in the economy. Finally, in Chapter 7 we explore the relations among nation-states including the birth and possible slow demise of the modern state, as well as movement toward international organization and eventually, perhaps, toward world government.

Although, as we have noted earlier, the readings in the different chapters are preceded by explanatory and transitional comments, we have not taken a doctrinaire stand on any of the issues examined in this book. This, of course, does not mean that our general commitment to democratic government may not have colored our observations. But whatever this coloration, it should not prevent any instructor from using our book as collateral reading with any text for the introductory course in political science. On the other hand, we believe that this volume can also be used alone as a core work; we feel that such use may be especially appropriate in courses constructed around large lecture sections divided into weekly discussion groups.

We owe special thanks to Mr. Milton McGowen, Political Science Editor of Prentice-Hall, for his suggested improvements to this edition. We also would like to express our thanks to our colleagues Professors Lyle A. Downing, Charles D. Hadley, and Robert B. Thigpen for reading the manuscript and offering most valuable comments. Mr. Stuart Carroll, one of our graduate students, has also given us new ideas about the book as it will be viewed by the students and for these we are duly grateful. Last but not least we owe our deepest gratitude to Mrs. Janet A. Davis for her preparation of the index, editorial comments on the manuscript, and the typing of the many drafts of the manuscript.

THE EDITORS

New Orleans, Louisiana

THE ENDURING
QUESTIONS
OF
POLITICS

THE NATURE OF POLITICS

1

POINT

A "realistic" view.

The study of politics is the study of influence and the influential. The influential are those who get the most of what there is to get. Those who get the most are *elite;* the rest are *mass.**

As a discipline, Political Science is the study of the shaping and sharing of power.†

COUNTERPOINT

A view with moral overtones.

The essence of politics lies in [the] fundamental freedom of man in society to *master his own fate* by political means. Hence, politics also rests on the fundamental purposes of man in a social setting. It has to do with the *preservation (or creation) of the community of human beings* in which he wants to live. Politics involves the *basic human values,* religious or ideological, which furnish the goals and principles he sets for himself.‡

---

* Reprinted by permission of the World Publishing Company from *Politics: Who Gets What, When and How?* by Harold Lasswell; p. 13. Copyright © 1958 by Meridian Books.

† From Harold D. Lasswell and Abraham Kaplan, *Power and Society* (New Haven, Conn.: Yale University Press, 1950), pp. 240–41, by permission of the author and the publisher.

‡ From Peter H. Merkl, *Political Continuity and Change* (New York: Harper & Row, 1967), p. 10, by permission of the author and the publisher.

When we read the definition of politics on the left, we are apt to be struck by its breadth—which kind of influence and what use of power?—as well as by its cynicism. It conjures up the satisfaction of narrowly based interests of the elites and the benign neglect of the aspirations of the masses. While in many respects it may reflect down-to-earth realism, it does not fulfill our moral expectations. On the other hand, the concept of politics expressed by Professor Merkl has moral overtones inasmuch as it emphasizes the needs of the Community and the strengthening of basic human values. It seems to lift politics out of the morass and attribute to it goals whose attainment benefits all members of the society rather than a small number of individuals.

The question regarding the distinctive feature or features that permit an activity to be called "political" has been pondered by political thinkers and philosophers since the time of ancient Greece. But despite these efforts, no definite agreement has been reached on the nature of politics. Aristotle, the Greek philosopher who lived in the fourth century before Christ, devoted some of his fertile thoughts and writings to elucidating the term "political." His concepts are much closer to those expressed by Merkl than the definitions of Lasswell and Kaplan. Our first selection provides us with the basic thoughts of Aristotle. The scenario for the Aristotelian concepts is the relatively small city-state, a number of which covered ancient Greece. The term for the city-state is a Greek word, "polis," from which the term "politics" is derived. Aristotle regarded the *polis* as one of the main associations found in society, all created "for the purpose of attaining some good." The *polis*, however, was distinguished by being the "most sovereign and inclusive association"; the term "sovereign" suggests that authority was an essential ingredient of the *polis*, which Aristotle called the "political" association. Politics, therefore, was related to the exercise of authority. Since, according to Aristotle, the basic objective of the political association or the *polis* was the promotion of the common good, the proper kind of authority was that exercised in the common interest. We find, therefore, a clear similarity between Aristotle's and Merkl's notions of politics.

THE POLITICAL ASSOCIATION

ARISTOTLE

§ 1. Observation shows us, first, that every polis [or state] is a species of association, and, secondly, that all associations are instituted for the purpose of attaining some good—for all men do all their acts with a view to achieving something which is, in their view, a good. We may therefore hold [on the basis of what we actually observe] that all associations aim at some good; and we may also hold that the particular association which is the most sovereign of all, and includes all the rest, will pursue this aim most. . . . This most sovereign and inclusive association is the polis, as it is called, or the political association.

§ 2. It is a mistake to believe that the "statesman" [the *politikos,* who handles the affairs of a political association] is the same as the monarch of a kingdom, or the manager of a household, or the master of a number of slaves. Those who hold this view consider that each of these persons differs from the others not with a difference of kind, but [merely with a difference of degree, and] according to the number, or the paucity, of the persons with whom he deals. On this view a man who is concerned with few persons is a master: one who is concerned with more is the manager of a household: one who is concerned with still more is a "statesman," or a monarch. This view abolishes any real difference between a large household and a small polis; and it also réduces the difference between the "statesman" and the monarch to the one fact that the latter has an uncontrolled and sole authority, while the former exercises his authority in conformity with the rules imposed by the art of statesmanship and as one who rules and is ruled in turn. But this is a view which cannot be accepted as correct. . . .

§ 3. Our point will be made clear if we proceed to consider the matter according to our normal method of analysis. Just as, in all other fields, a compound should be analysed until we reach its simple and uncompounded elements (or, in other words, the smallest atoms of the whole which it constitutes), so we must also consider analytically the

From The Politics of Aristotle, *translated by Ernest Barker (Oxford: The Clarendon Press, 1948), pp. 1–8, by permission of The Clarendon Press, Oxford.*

elements of which a polis is composed. We shall then gain a better insight into the difference from one another of the persons and associations just mentioned; and we shall also be in a position to discover whether it is possible to attain a systematic view of the general issues involved. . . .

All associations are in the nature of parts of the political association. Men journey together with a view to some particular advantage, and by way of providing some particular thing needed for the purposes of life; and similarly the political association seems to have come together originally, and to continue in existence, for the sake of the *general* advantage which it brings. (*Ethics*, VIII, c. ix, § 4).

. . . The first form of association naturally instituted for the satisfaction of daily recurrent needs is thus the family; and the members of the family are accordingly termed by Charondas "associates of the bread-chest," as they are also termed by Epimenides the Cretan "associates of the manager." The next form of association—which is also the *first* to be formed from more households than one, and for the satisfaction of something more than daily recurrent needs—is the village. § 6. The most natural form of the village appears to be that of a colony or offshoot from a family; and some have thus called the members of the village by the name of "sucklings of the same milk," or, again, of "sons and the sons of sons". . . . This, it may be noted, is the reason why each Greek polis was originally ruled—as the peoples of the barbarian world still are—by kings. They were formed of persons who were already monarchically governed . . . [and] households are always monarchically governed by the eldest of the kin, just as villages, when they are offshoots from the household, are similarly governed in virtue of the kinship between their members. . . . The fact that men generally were governed by kings in ancient times, and that some still continue to be governed in that way, is the reason that leads us all to assert that the gods are also governed by a king. We make the lives of the gods in the likeness of our own—as we also make their shapes. . . .

§ 8. When we come to the final and perfect association, formed from a number of villages, we have already reached the polis—an association which may be said to have reached the height of full self-sufficiency; or rather [to speak more exactly] we may say that while it *grows* for the sake of mere life [and is so far, and at that stage, still short of full self-sufficiency], it *exists* [when once it is fully grown] for the sake of a good life [and is therefore fully self-sufficient].

Because it is the completion of associations existing by nature, every polis exists by nature, having itself the same quality as the earlier associations from which it grew. . . . § 9. Again [and this is a second reason for regarding the state as natural] the end, or final cause, is the best. Now self-sufficiency [which it is the object of the state to bring about] is the end, and so the best; [and on this it follows that the state brings about the best, and is therefore natural, since nature always aims at bringing about the best].

From these considerations it is evident that the polis belongs to the class of things that exist by nature, and that man is by nature an animal intended to live in a polis. . . .

§ 10. . . . The reason why man is a being meant for political association, in a higher degree than bees or other gregarious animals can ever associate, is evident. Nature, according to our theory, makes nothing in vain; and man alone of the animals is furnished with the faculty of language. § 11. The mere making of sounds serves to indicate pleasure and pain, and is thus a faculty that belongs to animals in general: their nature enables them to attain the point at which they have perceptions of pleasure and pain, and can signify those perceptions to one another. But language serves to declare what is advantageous and what is the reverse, and it therefore serves to declare what is just and what is unjust. § 12. It is the peculiarity of man, in comparison with the rest of the animal world, that he alone possesses a perception of good and evil, of the just and the unjust, and of other similar qualities: and it is association in [a common perception of] these things which makes a family and a polis.

We may now proceed to add that [though the individual and the family are prior in the order of time] the polis is prior in the order of nature to the family and the individual. § 13. The reason for this is that the whole is necessarily prior [in nature] to the part. If the whole body be destroyed, there will not be a foot or a hand. . . .

§ 14. We thus see that the polis exists by nature and that it is prior to the individual. . . . Not being self-sufficient when they are isolated, all individuals are so many parts all equally depending on the whole [which alone can bring about self-sufficiency]. The man who is isolated— who is unable to share in the benefits of political association, or has no need to share because he is already self-sufficient—is no part of the polis, and must therefore be either a beast or a god. § 15. [Man is thus intended by nature to be a part of a political whole, and] there is therefore an immanent impulse in all men towards an association of this order. But the man who first *constructed* such an association was none the less the greatest of benefactors. Man, when perfected, is the best of animals; but if he be isolated from law and justice he is the worst of all. § 16. Injustice is all the graver when it is armed injustice; and man is furnished from birth with arms [such as, for instance, language] which are intended to serve the purposes of moral prudence and virtue, but which may be used in preference for opposite ends. . . . Justice [which is his salvation] belongs to the polis; for justice, which is the determination of what is just, is an ordering of the political association.

In our second selection Aristotle discusses the classification of constitutions. If the constitutions were directed toward the pursuit of the common interest, they were the "right" constitutions regardless of whether the One, the Few, or the Many made up the ruling authority. On the other side were the "wrong" or "perverted" constitutions under which the ruling authorities would be enabled to attain primarily their selfish interests.

CONSTITUTIONS AND THEIR CLASSIFICATION

ARISTOTLE

§ 1. Citizenship has now been defined and determined.[1] We have next to consider the subject of constitutions. Is there a single type, or are there a number of types? If there are a number of types, what are these types; how many of them are there; and how do they differ? A constitution (or polity) may be defined as "the organization of a polis, in respect of its offices generally but especially in respect of that particular office

From The Politics of Aristotle, *translated by Ernest Barker (Oxford: The Clarendon Press, 1948), pp. 127–31, by permission of The Clarendon Press, Oxford.*

---

[1] In the first two sections of c. I of this book Aristotle had begun by raising the question "What is a polis?" In order to answer that question, he found it first necessary to ask (following his analytic method of resolving a compound into its elements), "What is the member of a polis, or, in other words, the citizen?" The first five chapters have fully discussed that question. We might now expect him to return to the previous question, "What is a polis?" But that question has already been answered in the course of the discussion of the other question (cf. the definition of the polis in c. I, § 12); and Aristotle now turns to a different question, "What is a *politeia,* or constitution?" This is a question which logically follows on the discussion of citizenship. Since citizenship is participation in office, and since participation in office is regulated by the constitution, a discussion of the *polites* necessarily leads to a discussion of the *politeia.*

which is sovereign in all issues." The civic body [the *politeuma* [2] or body of persons established in power by the polity] is everywhere the sovereign of the state; in fact the civic body is the polity (or constitution) itself. § 2. In democratic states, for example, the people [or *dēmos*] is sovereign: in oligarchies, on the other hand, the few [or *oligoi*] have that position; and this difference of the sovereign bodies is the reason why we say that the two types of constitution differ—as we may equally apply the same reasoning to other types besides these.

[It is thus evident that there are a number of types of constitution, but before we discuss their nature] we must first ascertain two things—the nature of the end for which the state exists, and the various kinds of authority to which men and their associations are subject. § 3. So far as the first of these things is concerned, it has already been stated, in our first book (where we were concerned with the management of the household and the control of slaves), that "man is an animal impelled by his nature to live in a polis." A *natural impulse* is thus one reason why men desire to live a social life even when they stand in no need of mutual succour; but they are also drawn together by a *common interest,* in proportion as each attains a share in good life [through the union of all in a form of political association].[3] § 4. The good life is the chief end, both for the community as a whole and for each of us individually. But men also come together, and form and maintain political associations, merely for the sake of life,[4] for perhaps there is some element of the good even in the simple act of living, so long as the evils of existence

---

[2] The civic body, or *politeuma,* acts as the deliberative, and as such is the supreme authority or sovereign. Aristotle, as Newman remarks in his note, "proves that the constitution is especially an ordering of the supreme authority by showing that the supreme authority is decisive of the character of the constitution, from which it follows that the main business of the constitution is to fix the supreme authority."

[3] Aristotle here suggests two ends for which the state, as an association, exists— (1) the end of providing satisfaction for a natural impulse, which exists and acts even apart from interest, and (2) the end of providing satisfaction for a common interest. This common interest, it should be noted, is not only or mainly economic: it is an interest in the attainment of a *good* (rather than a comfortable) life: and it requires for its satisfaction those institutions, such as a system of justice, which are necessary to such a life. It is this common interest in the attainment of a good life which is the chief end served by the state.

[4] In the previous section Aristotle has distinguished "social life" and "good life." Here he introduces a third factor—the factor of "life" itself, independently of its being "social" or "good." The state or polis is connected with all three factors: it satisfies men's impulse towards a social life (which may exist apart from any need of mutual succour); it gives men a share in the good life which is their common interest; but it also helps men simply to live—and life itself is a thing of value. Compare Book I, c. II, § 8.

do not preponderate too heavily. § 5. It is an evident fact that most men cling hard enough to life to be willing to endure a good deal of suffering, which implies that life has in it a sort of healthy happiness and a natural quality of pleasure.

[So far of the end for which the state exists. As regards the second question,] it is easy enough to distinguish the various kinds of rule of authority of which men commonly speak; and indeed we have often had occasion to define them ourselves in works intended for the general public. § 6. The rule of a master is one kind; and here, though there is really a common interest which unites the natural master and the natural slave, the fact remains that the rule is primarily exercised with a view to the master's interest, and only incidentally with a view to that of the slave, who must be preserved in existence if the rule itself is to remain. § 7. Rule over wife and children, and over the household generally, is a second kind of rule, which we have called by the name of household management. Here the rule is either exercised in the interest of the ruled or for the attainment of some advantage common to both ruler and ruled. Essentially it is exercised in the interest of the ruled, as is also plainly the case with other arts besides that of ruling, such as medicine and gymnastics—though an art may incidentally be exercised for the benefit of its practitioner, and there is nothing to prevent (say) a trainer from becoming occasionally a member of the class he instructs, in the same sort of way as a steersman is always one of the crew. § 8. Thus a trainer or steersman primarily considers the good of those who are subject to his authority; but when he becomes one of them personally, he incidentally shares in the benefit of that good—the steersman thus being also a member of the crew, and the trainer (though still a trainer) becoming also a member of the class which he instructs.

§ 9. This principle also applies to a third kind of rule—that exercised by the holders of political office. When the constitution of a state is constructed on the principle that its members are equals and peers, the citizens think it proper that they should hold office by turns [which implies that the office of ruler is primarily intended for the benefit of the ruled and is therefore a duty to be undertaken by each in turn, though incidentally the ruler shares in the general benefit by virtue of being himself a member of the citizen body]. At any rate this is the natural system, and the system which used to be followed in the days when men believed that they ought to serve by turns, and each assumed that others would take over the duty of considering his benefit, just as he had himself, during his term of office, considered the interest of others. § 10. To-day the case is altered. Moved by the profits to be derived from office and the handling of public property, men want to hold office continuously. It is as if the holders of office were sick men, who got the benefit of permanent health [by being permanently in office]: at any rate their ardour for office is just what it would be if that were the case. § 11. The conclusion which follows is clear. Those constitutions which consider the common interest are *right* constitutions, judged by the standard of absolute justice. Those constitutions which consider only the personal interest of the rulers are all *wrong* constitutions, or *perversions* of the right forms. Such perverted forms are despotic [i.e. calculated on the model of the rule of a master, or "despotēs," over slaves]; whereas the polis is an association of freemen.

Note on the basis of Aristotle's classification of constitutions:

This preliminary classification of constitutions into the two *genera* of right and wrong, or normal and perverted, is based on the principle that political rule, by virtue of its specific nature, is essentially for the benefit of the ruled. That is the principle of absolute justice in regard to the proper use of political power; and it is a principle which squares with what has been said above, in § 4, about the main end of the polis—that it is a *common* interest, which, as such, is for the benefit not of a section, but of each and all. Aristotle has thus concluded in this chapter (partly from what has been said in §§ 2–5 about the end of the polis, and partly from what has been said in §§ 5–10 about the specific nature of political rule, or rule over a political association of freemen, as contrasted with other forms of rule) that the fundamental principle to be followed in a polis, and therefore in its *politeia* or constitution, is the principle of the holding of office for the common interest of all the members, and particularly for the interest of the ruled, who are nearly the whole of the members. That principle separates the right constitutions which follow it from the wrong which contravene it.

The Diversity of "Political" Activities

When we attempt to decide in our own minds what the nature of politics is, it may be best to let our thoughts wander and seek to determine which actions and situations we normally associate with politics. If we do this, many different ideas will obviously come to mind. Clearly, elections to local, state, and federal offices are in the realm of politics. The various efforts made in support of the nomination and election of a certain individual, whether carried out through the mass media or by personal contact, are accepted by us as part of politics. We also realize that at times the proverbial "smoke-filled room" in a hotel during a party convention may play a more important role in the nomination of an individual than the desires of the public at large and that the manipulation of facts can have a bearing on the outcome of an election. While in such cases we may mutter something about "dirty politics," we recognize nevertheless that these facts are part and parcel of the political game. When it comes to the making of laws and ordinances on the local, state, and federal levels, we are at times painfully aware that special interest groups exercise more influence on the content of legislation than does the average voter. And since the subjects of legislation may range far and wide, a great variety of economic groups, church bodies, veterans' organizations, and other groups in society may be involved in bringing pressure to bear on the outcome of legislative battles. Of course, all of us are members of one or another group and sometimes of several groups, and therefore we may benefit indirectly from the efforts made by the leadership of some of these organizations.

The administration of laws and ordinances also produces certain actions on the part of the population which we regard as political. For example, dairy farmers seeking higher milk prices from an administrative agency authorized to regulate these prices may apply pressure by withholding milk from the market. A nightclub owner whose establishment the authorities threaten to close because he is presenting a risqué show may attempt to prevent this by promising financial support to the district attorney and the sheriff in future elections. While we accept, as a normal part of politics, the provision of financial support for a candidate to defray the expenses of his election campaign, there are moral and legal boundaries to such practices.

Finally, politics may even invade the judicial process. Subtle influence can be exerted on a court through the use of special publicity regarding certain features of a case before the judges. We do not suggest that the judges will necessarily succumb to the influence exerted nor that our faith in the impartiality of the judicial system is misplaced. We simply want to point out that, depending on the motives and purpose of an endeavor to influence the court, an attempt may be labeled political.

This brief survey of activities which we customarily associate with the term "politics" is obviously far from exhaustive. But even limited as it is, it suggests that a great diversity of activities may fall under this classification. It also suggests that authority and rule are important elements in any characterization of politics and it is obvious that the exercise of authority and rule carries with it the possession of power. With this in mind, a number of political thinkers, both historically and contemporarily, have used as the chief criterion for the definition of politics the accumulation and exercise of power wherever it is found. For example, Niccolo Machiavelli stated in his famous work *The Prince,* published in 1513, that "A wise prince must rely on what is in *his* power and not on what is in the power of others."

The contemporary thinkers Harold D. Lasswell and Abraham Kaplan declare that "*a political act* is one performed in power perspectives" and consider a *"political movement"* to be a "continuing political act performed by an aggregate of persons in a power perspective. . . ." A similarly broad view of politics is taken by Robert Dahl, who defines a political system as "any persistent pattern of human relationships that involves, to a significant extent, power, rule, or authority." * Dahl admits that with his definition many organization not ordinarily regarded as "political" fall under this classification: private clubs, business firms, labor unions, religious organizations, civic groups, primitive tribes, clans, and perhaps even families. Of course, some of these organizations may on occasion act "politically" also under more restrictive criteria such as those to be discussed later. However, under the Dahl definition, they are engaged in politics simply because they have an internal "government." To give the reader a greater insight into the implications of these rather broad views of politics, short excerpts from the book by Professors Lasswell and Kaplan, *Power and Society,* and from an essay by C. Wright Mills, "The Structure of Power in American Society," follow.

PROCESS

HAROLD D. LASSWELL / ABRAHAM KAPLAN

Political Acts, Movements, and Cycles

A *political act* is one performed in power perspectives; a *political movement* is a continuing political act performed by an aggregate of persons in a power perspective of elaborated identifications, demands, and expectations.

We conclude our discussion of the political process, as we began, with a consideraion of the *act* as the unit of which this process—and, indeed, all interpersonal relations—are composed. Like other acts, the political act passes through phases of "impulse," "subjectivity," and "expression." Conduct is goal-directed and hence implicates values; the impulsive phase of the act is constituted by the needs of or initial striving for those values. . . .

A political movement is most simply characterized as a collective

Reprinted from Harold D. Lasswell and Abraham Kaplan, Power *and* Society *(New Haven, Conn.: Yale University Press, 1950), pp. 240–41, by permission of the publisher.*

---

* Robert Dahl, *Modern Political Analysis* (Englewood Cliffs, N.J.: Prentice-Hall, 1963), p. 6.

political act so conceived. It is performed by a large number of persons, exhibiting varying degrees of solidarity and organization (so that it is a wider concept than "a political act of a group"); engaged in a continuing pattern of practices (so that a single election is not a movement, though the campaign leading up to and including it may constitute one); and in a perspective which does not antecedently limit the goals, plans, and participants (so that a movement may change its direction or composition without losing its identity).[1]

As with the individual act, a political movement originates in a situation of need or tension. Insecurity and frustration (or contrariwise, highly indulgent expectations) produce a stress toward action. Initially, the experiences on which this stress is based are individual and private. Gradually, they are related to the experiences of others, and the private malaise or sense of unrealized opportunity ("if only things were different!") acquires a vaguely social formulation. . . .

THE STRUCTURE OF POWER IN AMERICAN SOCIETY

C. WRIGHT MILLS

Power has to do with whatever decisions men make about the arrangements under which they live, and about the events which make up the history of their times. Events that are beyond human decision do happen; social arrangements do change without benefit of explicit de-

From Power, Politics and People: The Collected Essays of C. Wright Mills, *edited by Irving Louis Horowitz, pp. 23–38. Copyright © 1963 by the Estate of C. Wright Mills. Reprinted by permission of Oxford University Press, Inc.*

---

[1] Since an act is defined as political in terms of its perspectives, its characterization as such may vary with changing observational standpoints. Thus a movement may appear to its participants as purely religious, say, and to outsiders as definitely political. The definition selected here takes the standpoint of the actor himself, and classifies the act as political only if power enters significantly into the perspectives of the actor as end or means for the act. Other definitions might emphasize the likelihood of later occurrence of such perspectives, or power consequences independent of perspective, and so on.

cision. But in so far as such decisions are made, the problem of who is involved in making them is the basic problem of power. In so far as they could be made but are not, the problem becomes who fails to make them?

We cannot today merely assume that in the last resort men must always be governed by their own consent. For among the means of power which now prevail is the power to manage and to manipulate the consent of men. That we do not know the limits of such power, and that we hope it does have limits, does not remove the fact that much power today is successfully employed without the sanction of the reason or the conscience of the obedient.

Surely nowadays we need not argue that, in the last resort, coercion is the "final" form of power. But then, we are by no means constantly at the last resort. Authority (power that is justified by the beliefs of the voluntarily obedient) and manipulation (power that is wielded unbeknown to the powerless)—must also be considered, along with coercion. In fact, the three types must be sorted out whenever we think about power.

In the modern world, we must bear in mind, power is often not so authoritative as it seemed to be in the medieval epoch: ideas which justify rulers no longer seem so necessary to their exercise of power. At least for many of the great decisions of our time—especially those of an international sort—mass "persuasion" has not been "necessary," the fact is simply accomplished. Furthermore, such ideas as are available to the powerful are often neither taken up nor used by them. Such ideologies usually arise as a response to an effective debunking of power; in the United States such opposition has not been effective enough recently to create the felt need for new ideologies of rule.

There has, in fact, come about a situation in which many who have lost faith in prevailing loyalties have not acquired new ones, and so pay no attention to politics of any kind. They are not radical, not liberal, not conservative, not reactionary. They are inactionary. They are out of it. If we accept the Greeks' definition of the idiot as an altogether private man, then we must conclude that many American citizens are now idiots. And I should not be surprised, although I do not know, if there were not some such idiots even in Germany. This—and I use the word with care—this spiritual condition seems to me the key to many modern troubles of political intellectuals, as well as the key to much political bewilderment in modern society. Intellectual "conviction" and moral "belief" are not necessary, in either the rulers or the ruled, for a ruling power to persist and even to flourish. So far as the role of ideologies is concerned, their frequent absences and the prevalence of mass indifference are surely two of the major political facts about the western societies today.

How large a role any explicit decisions do play in the making of history is itself an historical problem. For how large that role may be depends very much upon the means of power that are available at any given time in any given society. In some societies, the innumerable actions of innumerable men modify their milieux, and so gradually modify the structure itself. These modifications—the course of history—go on behind the backs of men. History is drift, although in total "men make it." Thus, innumerable entrepreneurs and innumerable consumers by ten-thousand decisions per minute may shape and re-shape the free-market economy. Perhaps this was the chief kind of limitation Marx had in mind when he wrote, in *The 18th Brumaire,* that "Men make their own history, but they do not make it just as they please; they do not make it under circumstances chosen by themselves. . . ."

But in other societies—certainly in the United States and in the Soviet Union today—a few men may be so placed within the structure that by their decisions they modify the milieux of many other men, and in fact nowadays the structural conditions under which most men live. Such elites of power also make history under circumstances not chosen altogether by themselves, yet compared with other men, and compared with other periods of world history, these circumstances do indeed seem less limiting.

I should contend that "men are free to make history," but that some men are indeed much freer than others. For such freedom requires access to the means of decision and of power by which history can now be made. It has not always been so made; but in the later phases of the modern epoch it is. It is with reference to this epoch that I am contending that if men do not make history, they tend increasingly to become the utensils of history-makers as well as the mere objects of history.

The history of modern society may readily be understood as the story of the enlargement and the centralization of the means of power—in economic, in political, and in military institutions. The rise of industrial society has involved these developments in the means of economic production. The rise of the nation-state has involved similar developments in the means of violence and in those of political administration.

In the western societies, such transformations have generally occurred gradually, and many cultural traditions have restrained and shaped them. In most of the Soviet societies, they are happening very rapidly indeed and without the great discourse of western civilization, without the Renaissance and without the Reformation, which so greatly strengthened and gave political focus to the idea of freedom. In those societies, the enlargement and the coordination of all the means of power has occurred more brutally, and from the beginning under tightly centralized authority. But in both types, the means of power have now become international in scope and similar in form. To be sure, each of them has its own ups and downs; neither is as yet absolute; how they run differs quite sharply.

Yet so great is the reach of the means of violence, and so great the economy required to produce and support them, that we have in the immediate past witnessed the consolidation of these two world centers, either of which dwarfs the power of Ancient Rome. As we pay attention to the awesome means of power now available to quite small groups of men we come to realize that Caesar could do less with Rome than Napoleon with France; Napoleon less with France than Lenin with Russia. But what was Caesar's power at its height compared with the power of the changing inner circles of Soviet Russia and the temporary administrations of the United States? We come to realize—indeed they continually remind us—how a few men have access to the means by which in a few days continents can be turned into thermonuclear wastelands. That the facilities of power are so enormously enlarged and so decisively centralized surely means that the powers of quite small groups of men, which we may call elites, are now of literally inhuman consequence.

My concern here is not with the international scene but with the United States in the middle of the twentieth century. I must emphasize "in the middle of the twentieth century" because in our attempt to understand any society we come upon images which have been drawn from its past and which often confuse our attempt to confront its present reality. That is one minor reason why history is the shank of any social science: we must study it if only to rid ourselves of it. In the United States, there are indeed many such images and usually they have to do with the first half of the nineteenth century. At that time the economic facilities of the United States were very widely dispersed and subject to little or to no central authority.

The state watched in the night but was without decisive voice in the day.

One man meant one rifle and the militia were without centralized orders.

Any American, as old-fashioned as I, can only agree with R. H. Tawney that "Whatever the future may contain, the past has shown no more excellent social order than that in which the mass of the people were the masters of the holdings which they ploughed and the tools with which they worked, and could boast . . . 'It is a quietness to a man's mind to live upon his own and to know his heir certain!' "

But then we must immediately add: all that is of the past and of little relevance to our understanding of the United States today. Within this society three broad levels of power may now be distinguished. I shall begin at the top and move downward.

The power to make decisions of national and international consequence is now so clearly seated in political, military, and economic institutions that other areas of society seem off to the side and, on occasion, readily subordinated to these. The scattered institutions of religion, education and family are increasingly shaped by the big three, in which history-making decisions now regularly occur. Behind this fact there is all the push and drive of a fabulous technology; for these three institutional orders have incorporated this technology and now guide it, even as it shapes and paces their development.

As each has assumed its modern shape, its effects upon the other two have become greater, and the traffic between the three has increased. There is no longer, on the one hand, an economy, and, on the other, a political order, containing a military establishment unimportant to politics and to money-making. There is a political economy numerously linked with military order and decision. This triangle of power is now structural fact, and it is the key to any understanding of the higher circles in America today. For as each of these domains has coincided with the others, as decisions in each have become broader, the leading men of each—the high military, the corporation executives, the political directorate—have tended to come together to form the power elite of America.

The political order, once composed of several dozen states with a weak federal-center, has become an executive apparatus which has taken up into itself many powers previously scattered, legislative as well as administrative, and which now reaches into all parts of the social structure. The long-time tendency of business and government to become more closely connected has since World War II reached a new point of explicitness. Neither can now be seen clearly as a distinct world. The growth of executive government does not mean merely the "enlargement of government" as some kind of autonomous bureaucracy: under American conditions, it has meant the ascendency of the corporation man into political eminence. Already during the New Deal, such men had joined the political directorate; as of World War II they came to dominate it. Long involved with government, now they have moved into quite full direction of the economy of the war effort and of the post-war era.

The economy, once a great scatter of small productive units in somewhat automatic balance, has become internally dominated by a few hundred corporations, administratively and politically interrelated, which together hold the keys to economic decision. This economy is at once a permanent-war economy and a private-corporation economy. The most important relations of the corporation to the state now rest on the coincidence between military and corporate interests, as defined by the military and the corporate rich, and accepted by politicians and public. Within the elite as a whole, this coincidence of military domain and corporate realm strengthens both of them and further subordinates the merely political man. Not the party politician, but the corporation executive, is now more likely to sit with the military to answer the question: what is to be done?

The military order, once a slim establishment in a context of civilian distrust, has become the largest and most expensive feature of government; behind smiling public relations, it has all the grim and clumsy efficiency of a great and sprawling bureaucracy. The high military have gained decisive political and economic relevance. The seemingly permanent military threat places a premium upon them and virtually all political and economic actions are now judged in terms of military definitions of reality: the higher military have ascended to a firm position within the power elite of our time.

In part at least this is a result of an historical fact, pivotal for the years since 1939: the attention of the elite has shifted from domestic problems—centered in the 'thirties around slump—to international problems—centered in the 'forties and 'fifties around war. By long historical usage, the government of the United States has been shaped by domestic clash and balance; it does not have suitable agencies and traditions for the democratic handling of international affairs. In considerable part, it is in this vacuum that the power elite has grown.

(i) To understand the unity of this power elite, we must pay attention to the psychology of its several members in their respective milieux. In so far as the power elite is composed of men of similar origin and education, of similar career and style of life, their unity may be said to rest upon the fact that they are of similar social type, and to lead to the fact of their easy intermingling. This kind of unity reaches its frothier apex in the sharing of that prestige which is to be had in the world of the celebrity. It achieves a more solid culmination in the fact of the interchangeability of positions between the three dominant institutional orders. It is revealed by considerable traffic of personnel within and between these three, as well as by the rise of specialized go-betweens as in the new style high-level lobbying.

(ii) Behind such psychological and social unity are the structure and the mechanics of those institutional hierarchies over which the political directorate, the corporate rich, and the high military now preside. How each of these hierarchies is shaped and what relations it has with the others determine in large part the relations of their rulers. Were these hierarchies scattered and disjointed, then their respective elites might tend to be scattered and disjointed; but if they have many interconnections and points of coinciding interest, then their elites tend to form a coherent kind of grouping. The unity of the elite is not a simple reflection of the unity of institutions, but men and institutions are always related; that is why we must understand the elite today in connection with such institutional trends as the development of a permanent-war establishment, alongside a privately incorporated economy, inside a virtual political vacuum. For the men at the top have been selected and formed by such institutional trends.

(iii) Their unity, however, does not rest solely upon psychological similarity and social intermingling, nor entirely upon the structural blending of commanding positions and common interests. At times it is the unity of a more explicit co-ordination.

To say that these higher circles are increasingly co-ordinated, that this is *one* basis of their unity, and that at times—as during open war—such coordination is quite wilful, is not to say that the co-ordination is total or continuous, or even that it is very sure-footed. Much less is it to say that the power elite has emerged as the realization of a plot. Its rise cannot be adequately explained in any psychological terms.

Yet we must remember that institutional trends may be defined as opportunities by those who occupy the command posts. Once such opportunities are recognized, men may avail themselves of them. Certain types of men from each of these three areas, more far-sighted than others, have actively promoted the liaison even before it took its truly modern shape. Now more have come to see that their several interests can more easily be realized if they work together, in informal as well as in formal ways, and accordingly they have done so.

The idea of the power elite is of course an interpretation. It rests upon and it enables us to make sense of major institutional trends, the social similarities and psychological affinities of the men at the top. But the idea is also based upon what has been happening on the middle and lower levels of power, to which I now turn.

There are of course other interpretations of the American system of power. The most usual is that it is a moving balance of many competing interests. The image of balance, at least in America, is derived from the idea of the economic market: in the nineteenth century, the balance was thought to occur between a great scatter of individuals and enterprises; in the twentieth century, it is thought to occur between great interest blocs. In both views, the politician is the key man of power because he is the broker of many conflicting powers.

I believe that the balance and the compromise in American society—the "countervailing powers" and the "veto groups," of parties and associations, of strata and unions—must now be seen as having mainly to do with the middle levels of power. It is these middle levels that the political journalist and the scholar of politics are most likely to understand and to write about—if only because, being mainly middle class themselves, they are closer to them. Moreover these levels provide the noisy content of most "political" news and gossip; the images of these levels are more or less in accord with the folklore of how democracy works; and, if the master-image of balance is accepted, many intellectuals, especially in their current patrioteering, are readily able to satisfy such political optimism as they wish to feel. Accordingly, liberal interpretations of what is happening in the United States are now virtually the only interpretations that are widely distributed.

But to believe that the power system reflects a balancing society is, I think, to confuse the present era with earlier times, and to confuse its top and bottom with its middle levels.

By the top levels, as distinguished from the middle, I intend to refer, first of all, to the scope of the decisions that are made. At the top today, these decisions have to do with all the issues of war and peace. They have also to do with slump and poverty which are now so very much problems of international scope. I intend also to refer to whether or not the groups that struggle politically have a chance to gain the positions from which such top decisions are made, and indeed whether their members do usually hope for such top national command. Most of the competing interests which make up the clang and clash of American politics are strictly concerned with their slice of the existing pie. Labor unions, for example, certainly have no policies of an international sort other than those which given unions adopt for the strict economic protection of their members. Neither do farm organizations. The actions of such middle-level powers may indeed have consequence for top-level policy; certainly at time they hamper these policies. But they are not truly concerned with them, which means of course that their influence tends to be quite irresponsible.

The facts of the middle levels may in part be understood in terms of the rise of the power elite. The expanded and centralized and interlocked hierarchies over which the power elite preside have encroached upon the old balance and relegated it to the middle level. But there are also independent developments of the middle levels. These, it seems to me, are better understood as an affair of entrenched and provincial demands than as a center of national decision. As such, the middle level often seems much more of a stalemate than a moving balance.

(i) The middle level of politics is not a forum in which there are debated the big decisions of national and international life. Such debate is not carried on by nationally responsible parties representing and clarifying alternative policies. There are no such parties in the United States. More and more, fundamental issues never come to any point of decision before the Congress, much less before the electorate in party campaigns. In the case of Formosa, in the spring of 1955 the Congress abdicated all debate concerning events and decisions which surely bordered on war. The same is largely true of the 1957 crisis in the Middle East. Such decisions now regularly by-pass the Congress, and are never clearly focused issues for public decision.

The American political campaign distracts attention from national and international issues, but that is not to say that there are no issues in these campaigns. In each district and state, issues are set up and watched by organized interests of sovereign local importance. The professional politician is of course a party politician, and the two parties are semifeudal organizations: they trade patronage and other favors for votes and for protection. The differences between them, so far as national issues are concerned, are very narrow and very mixed up. Often each seems to be fifty parties, one to each state; and accordingly, the politician as campaigner and as Congressman is not concerned with national party lines, if any are discernible. Often he is not subject to any effective national party discipline. He speaks for the interests of his own constituency, and he is concerned with national issues only in so far as they affect the interests effectively organized there, and hence his chances of re-election. That is why, when he does speak of national matters, the result is so often such an empty rhetoric. Seated in his sovereign locality, the politician is not at the national summit. He is on and of the middle levels of power.

(ii) Politics is not an arena in which free and independent organizations truly connect the lower and middle levels of society with the top levels of decision. Such organizations are not an effective and major part of American life today. As more people are drawn into the political arena, their associations become mass in scale, and the power of the individual becomes dependent upon them; to the extent that they are effective, they have become larger, and to that extent they have become less accessible to the influence of the individual. This is a central fact about associations in any mass society: it is of most consequence for political parties and for trade unions.

In the 'thirties, it often seemed that labor would become an insurgent power independent of corporation and state. Organized labor was then emerging for the first time on an American scale, and the only political sense of direction it needed was the slogan, "organize the unorganized." Now without the mandate of the slump, labor remains without political direction. Instead of economic and political struggles it has become deeply entangled in administrative routines with both corporation and state. One of its major functions, as a vested interest of the new society, is the regulation of such irregular tendencies as may occur among the rank and file.

There is nothing, it seems to me, in the make-up of the current labor leadership to allow us to expect that it can or that it will lead, rather than merely react. In so far as it fights at all it fights over a share of the goods of a single way of life and not over that way of life itself. The typical labor leader in the U.S.A. today is better understood as an adaptive creature of the main business drift than as an independent actor in a truly national context.

(iii) The idea that this society is a balance of powers requires us to assume that the units in balance are of more or less equal power and that they are truly independent of one another. These assumptions have rested, it seems clear, upon the historical importance of a large and independent middle class. In the latter nineteenth century and during the Progressive Era, such a class of farmers and small businessmen fought politically—and lost—their last struggle for a paramount role in national decision. Even then, their aspirations seemed bound to their own imagined past.

This old, independent middle class has of course declined. On the most generous count, it is now 40 per cent of the total middle class (at most 20 per cent of the total labor force). Moreover, it has become politically as well as economically dependent upon the state, most notably in the case of the subsidized farmer.

The *new* middle class of white-collar employees is certainly not the political pivot of any balancing society. It is in no way politically unified. Its unions, such as they are, often serve merely to incorporate it as hanger-on of the labor interest. For a considerable period, the old middle class *was* an independent base of power; the new middle class cannot be. Political freedom and economic security *were* anchored in small and independent properties; they are not anchored in the worlds of the white-collar job. Scattered property holders were economically united by more or less free markets; the jobs of the new middle class are integrated by corporate authority. Economically, the white-collar classes are in the same condition as wage workers; politically, they are in a worse condition, for they are not organized. They are no vanguard of historic change; they are at best a rear-guard of the welfare state.

The agrarian revolt of the 'nineties, the small-business revolt that has been more or less continuous since the 'eighties, the labor revolt of the 'thirties—each of these has failed as an independent movement which could countervail against the powers that be; they have failed as politically autonomous third parties. But they have succeeded, in varying degree, as interests vested in the expanded corporation and state; they have succeeded as parochial interests seated in particular districts, in local divisions of the two parties, and in the Congress. What they would become, in short, are well-established features of the *middle* levels of balancing power, on which we may now observe all those strata and interests which in the course of American history have been defeated in their bids for top power or which have never made such bids.

Fifty years ago many observers thought of the American state as a mask behind which an invisible government operated. But nowadays, much of what was called the old lobby, visible or invisible, is part of the quite visible government. The "governmentalization of the lobby" has proceeded in both the legislative and the executive domain, as well as between them. The executive bureaucracy becomes not only the center of decision but also the arena within which major conflicts of power are resolved or denied resolution. "Administration" replaces electoral politics; the maneuvering of cliques (which include leading Senators as well as civil servants) replaces the open clash of parties.

The shift of corporation men into the political directorate has accelerated the decline of the politicians in the Congress to the middle levels of power; the formation of the power elite rests in part upon this relegation. It rests also upon the semiorganized stalemate of the interests of sovereign localities, into which the legislative function has so largely fallen; upon the virtually complete absence of a civil service that is a politically neutral but politically relevant, depository of brain-power and executive skill; and it rests upon the increased official secrecy behind which great decisions are made without benefit of public or even of Congressional debate.

There is one last belief upon which liberal observers everywhere base their interpretations and rest their hopes. That is the idea of the public and the associated idea of public opinion. Conservative thinkers, since the French Revolution, have of course Viewed With Alarm the rise of the public, which they have usually called the masses, or something to that effect. "The populace is sovereign," wrote Gustave LeBon, "and the tide of barbarism mounts." But surely those who have supposed the masses to be well on their way to triumph are mistaken. In our time, the influence of publics or of masses within political life is in fact decreasing, and such influence as on occasion they do have tends, to an unknown but increasing degree, to be guided by the means of mass communication.

In a society of publics, discussion is the ascendant means of communication and the mass media, if they exist, simply enlarge and animate this discussion, linking one face-to-face public with the discussions of another. In a mass society, the dominant type of communication is the formal media, and publics become mere markets for these media: the "public" of a radio program consists of all those exposed to it. When we try to look upon the United States today as a society of publics, we realize that it has moved a considerable distance along the road to the mass society.

In official circles, the very term, "the public," has come to have a phantom meaning, which dramatically reveals its eclipse. The deciding elite can identify some of those who clamor publicly as "Labor," others as "Business," still others as "Farmer." But these are not the public. "The public" consists of the unidentified and the nonpartisan in a world of defined and partisan interests. In this faint echo of the classic notion, the public is composed of these remnants of the old and new middle classes whose interests are not explicitly defined, organized, or clamorous. In a curious adaptation, "the public" often becomes, in administrative fact, "the disengaged expert," who, although never so well informed, has never taken a clear-cut and public stand on controversial issues. He is the "public" member of the board, the commission, the committee. What "the public" stands for, accordingly, is often a vagueness of policy (called "open-mindedness"), a lack of involvement in public affairs (known as "reasonableness"), and a professional disinterest (known as "tolerance").

All this is indeed far removed from the eighteenth-century idea of the public of public opinion. The idea parallels the economic idea of the magical market. Here is the market composed for freely competing entrepreneurs; there is the public composed of circles of people in discussion. As price is the result of anonymous, equally weighted, bargaining individuals, so public opinion is the result of each man's having thought things out for himself and then contributing his voice to the great chorus. To be sure, some may have more influence on the state of opinion than others, but no one group monopolizes the discussion, or by itself determines the opinions that prevail.

In this classic image, the people are presented with problems. They

discuss them. They formulate viewpoints. These viewpoints are organized, and they compete. One viewpoint "wins out." Then the people
act on this view, or their representatives are instructed to act it out, and
this they promptly do.

Such are the images of democracy which are still used as working
justifications of power in America. We must now recognize this description as more fairy tale than a useful approximation. The issues that now
shape man's fate are neither raised nor decided by any public at large.
The idea of a society that is at bottom composed of publics is not a
matter of fact; it is the proclamation of an ideal, and as well the assertion of a legitimation masquerading as fact.

I cannot here describe the several great forces within American
society as well as elsewhere which have been at work in the debilitation
of the public. I want only to remind you that publics, like free associations, can be deliberately and suddenly smashed, or they can more slowly
wither away. But whether smashed in a week or withered in a generation, the demise of the public must be seen in connection with the rise
of centralized organizations, with all their new means of power, including those of the mass media of distraction. These, we now know, often
seem to expropriate the rationality and the will of the terrorized or—as
the case may be—the voluntarily indifferent society of masses. In the
more democratic process of indifference the remnants of such publics as
remain may only occasionally be intimidated by fanatics in search of
"disloyalty." But regardless of that, they lose their will for decision because they do not possess the instruments for decision; they lose their
sense of political belonging because they do not belong; they lose their
political will because they see no way to realize it.

The political structure of a modern democratic state requires that
such a public as is projected by democratic theorists not only exist but
that it be the very forum within which a politics of real issues is enacted.

It requires a civil service that is firmly linked with the world of
knowledge and sensibility, and which is composed of skilled men who,
in their careers and in their aspirations, are truly independent of any
private, which is to say, corporation, interests.

It requires nationally responsible parties which debate openly and
clearly the issues which the nation, and indeed the world, now so rigidly
confronts.

It requires an intelligentsia, inside as well as outside the universities, who carry on the big discourse of the western world, and whose
work is relevant to and influential among parties and movements and
publics.

And it certainly requires, as a fact of power, that there be free association standing between families and smaller communities and pub-

lics, on the one hand, and the state, the military, the corporation, on the other. For unless these do exist, there are no vehicles for reasoned opinion, no instruments for the rational exertion of public will.

Such democratic formations are not now ascendant in the power structure of the United States, and accordingly the men of decision are not men selected and formed by careers within such associations and by their performance before such publics. The top of modern American society is increasingly unified, and often seems wilfully coordinated: at the top there has emerged an elite whose power probably exceeds that of any small group of men in world history. The middle levels are often a drifting set of stalemated forces: the middle does not link the bottom with the top. The bottom of this society is politically fragmented, and as a passive fact, increasingly powerless: at the bottom there is emerging a mass society.

These developments, I believe, can be correctly understood neither in terms of the liberal nor the Marxian interpretation of politics and history. Both these ways of thought arose as guidelines to reflection about a type of society which does not now exist in the United States. We confront there a new kind of social structure, which embodies elements and tendencies of all modern society, but in which they have assumed a more naked and flamboyant prominence.

That does not mean that we must give up the ideals of these classic political expectations. I believe that both have been concerned with the problem of rationality and of freedom: liberalism, with freedom and rationality as supreme facts about the individual; Marxism, as supreme facts about man's role in the political making of history. What I have said here, I suppose, may be taken as an attempt to make evident why the ideas of freedom and of rationality now so often seem so ambiguous in the new society of the United States of America.

Pluralism

While today most scholars acknowledge that powerful elites are extremely influential in determining public policies, it is also recognized that multiple elites compete with each other and that in democratic societies voters can exercise meaningful choices bearing on the power position of different elites. The multiple system of *competing* elites, i.e., the competition between business, labor, governmental, and other elite groups, is seen as containing in itself the mechanism of checking different elites from abusing their power or oppressing the individual. This is the underlying notion of pluralism, a term frequently found in political science literature. Scholars who consider pluralism as a key factor in explaining the working of politics stress the fragmentation of power in a society and the influence of public opinion and elections on the behavior of elites. They hope that with multiple elites bargaining about the formulation and implementation of public policy, each in its own areas of interest, the power of diverse groups and institutions in society will roughly balance out, thus making the emergence of power monopoly unlikely.*

The concept of pluralism based on the existence and interaction of multiple elites presumes that as modern industrial societies become more differentiated in their occupational and economic composition, elites proliferate and their elite status is founded on their attainment of professional skills. The proliferation is caused by four main processes: the growth of population, the growth of occupational specialization, the growth of bureaucracy, and the growth of moral diversity. The proliferation and partial autonomy of elites, their differences in composition, recruitment, and moral outlooks reduce the likelihood of one all-powerful elite emerging. Moreover, these elites examine critically each other's actions and decisions, thereby checking each other's power and limiting the abuse of power.†

According to the preceding concept of pluralism, the public interest is represented in the United States by a political elite consisting of the President, his Cabinet, Senators, and Representatives. The economic elite is only one of several elites and has to compete with the others for benefits and resources emanating from the government. Although on occasion one elite may dominate the others, this is an exception because no single elite in our complex society can undertake or even designate the numerous social tasks performed by others. Each elite is thus subordinate in areas outside its speciality, and none is likely to be able to determine the patterns of selection and recruitment for the rest. Finally, no elite can preempt moral leadership because each elite develops its own notions of what is just and right.‡

Some scholars have broadened the concept of pluralism by focusing on "groups" in general rather than only on elite groupings. Groups, which are defined as consisting of two or more interacting people, are seen as structures of power because they concentrate human resources for the achievement of specific purposes and therefore serve the realization of important social values and aspirations held by individuals in society. Groups constitute the great link between individuals and the State and operate with a varying mixture of

---

* Cf. Thomas R. Dye and L. Harmon Zeigler, *The Irony of Democracy* (Belmont, Calif.: Wadsworth, 1970), pp. 14–18.

† Cf. Suzanne Keller, *Beyond the Ruling Class* (New York: Random House, 1968), pp. 65, 83, 273, 274.

‡ *Ibid.*, pp. 96–99, 125–27.

ideology and self-interest. They seek to attain their goals through strong internal organization which can concentrate power and through the exercise of predominating influence when encountering the pursuit of goals by other groups.*

For the group-oriented pluralists, the State is also a group since it concentrates power for the achievement of given purposes. However—and here we find a fundamentally Aristotelian notion—the State differs from other groups inasmuch as it stands above other groups. In view of this position, it establishes for the other groups the rules of permissible behavior and enforces these rules. It is within the limits of behavior permitted by the State that groups seek to influence to their advantage the content of rules, laws, administrative orders, and the interpretations of regulations made by officials of the State (lawmakers, administrators, and judges). Although the efforts of the groups in the pursuit of their goals may cause internal power struggles among the officials of the State and sometimes coalitions of officials with particular groups outside the State, the basic function of the State is to serve as an umpire in overseeing the struggle among groups and to ensure that the rules set by the State are followed. Moreover, the interests of those who are unrepresented in groups are to be presented by the State. As a consequence, the manifold groups are seen as being in some kind of equilibrium inasmuch as none can continually dominate the decisions of the State and all are subject to a potential veto by other groups.

A Variety of Definitions of Politics

It would not serve a useful purpose within the scope of this book to delve into all the definitions that contemporary political scientists have elaborated to describe the nature of politics. Let us mention only a few in summary manner. Some scholars have used concern with legal government as the main criterion for determining what falls under the classification of politics, while others have focused on the notion of struggle among groups or even individuals pursuing conflicting objectives on public issues. Still others have felt that politics must involve activities but not necessarily struggles regarding a public issue, with the latter term to be interpreted in such a way that it pertains not only to actions by government, but also to actions by private organizations (i.e., large business corporations or labor unions) that affect the public at large. Finally, increasing attention has been paid during the last few years to a focus on the system of interactions in a society that arises out of or is con-

---

* Cf. Earl Latham, The Group Basis of Politics (New York: Octagon Books, 1965), pp. 1–54. See also Robert A. Dahl, Who Governs? (New Haven, Conn.: Yale University Press, 1961), and David Truman, The Governmental Process (New York: Knopf, 1951).

cerned with the making of authoritative or binding decisions. These decisions may provide benefits for the members of the society, such as social security or access to public works, or subject them to "deprivations" such as taxes or a jail sentence.* In the politically developed countries of the world a major source of these decisions is the branches of government—the legislatures, the executive and administrative agencies, or the courts. Elections of all kinds are also authoritative decisions for both the voters and the candidates. In a developing country in Africa such decisions may emanate from the tribal chief or the witch doctor. This approach is adaptable to political systems all over the world but lacks usefulness for international politics where, as we will see later, the sovereign nation-state does not consider itself bound by any higher authority and the factor of naked power plays a predominant role.

This brief survey of the different conceptions regarding the nature of politics suggests that each conception has somewhat different implications for the object of our inquiry. Each definition brings to the surface a different set of problems and provides special insights and emphases. None appears to offer fully clear-cut conclusions as to what the actual nature of politics is, and therefore we would not consider ourselves justified in marking any of these conceptions as either right or wrong. Perhaps politics as a major area of human and social behavior is too complex and variegated to be subsumed under a brief theoretical definition.

Politics and Voting

Despite our reluctance to insist on the truth and correctness of one of the several definitions of politics we have discussed, we do not want to leave the impression that only the "influential" and "powerful" as described in the preceding selection determine the nature and shape of governmental decisions and public policies. At least in democratic systems of government, history has shown again and again and the "pluralists" recognize that access and influence over the governmental decision-makers by the "powerful few" can be counteracted by the ballot box and other means of politics by those often called the "powerless." Such efforts have been especially successful when the Aristotelian principles of the promotion of the common good and the exercise of authority in the common interest had been severely violated by the politics of the "influential." What can be done to remedy such a situation and how you as a young citizen can participate in the corrective process are the topics of our next selection, which shows the importance of voting in the formulation and structure of public policy.

---

* See David Easton, A Framework for Political Analysis (Englewood Cliffs, N.J.: Prentice-Hall, 1965), p. 50.

POLITICAL STAKES OF YOUNG VOTERS

WILLIAM C. MITCHELL

This current generation of young people is more acutely aware of the impact of government and public policy on people, and on themselves in particular, than any previous generation. Many aspects of their lives contribute to their awareness. A highly unpopular war, fought for the most part by the young, has called attention to the impact of government as has no other event in this century. The often repressive measures taken by government or its agents to control newly emerging lifestyles has revealed the awesome power of governmental surveillance and control over citizens. . . .

To change public policies in these areas, individuals have several available alternatives. Activists have called for revolution; for rapid change through violent means. This [selection] suggests that there is another, less disruptive means to change—the exercise of voting power. Although the vote is only one available resource of influence, it *is* a resource; it has the major advantage of being among the most honored, legitimate, and inexpensive means of changing governments and their policies.

Social Position and Interests

Young people have some special concerns; they occupy a peculiar role or position in our society. Young voters should be clear about their current positions. For the most part, they have low incomes, have had little political power, and are chiefly concerned with earning a livelihood or preparing themselves for career and family life while having as much enjoyment as possible. They are likely to be highly mobile yet are subject to considerable authority. They have more free time and fewer

From *William C. Mitchell,* Why Vote? *(Chicago: Markham Publishing Company, 1971),* pp. 8–10, 19–23. Reprinted by permission of Rand McNally College Publishing Company, Chicago.

financial burdens than most working adults, and their consumption habits differ from those of the rest of society. Their taxes are apt to be much lower and yet more burdensome (if they are unmarried) than those of adults working full time. . . . While a young voter's position is apt to be unique in some areas, all experience certain problems in common and therefore share certain interests.

No group in current society has greater potential for idealism or more freedom to express and implement that idealism. Most young men and women have not retreated into cynicism nor have they experienced many incentives to be corrupt. With their idealism, they have unusual opportunities for much fuller participation in political activities than they will ever have again. College students, in particular, have the liberty to take time off from studies to engage in politics actively. They are not tied to an eight-hour-a-day job and they are free of many of the inhibitions and obstacles that life presents to older people and many minority group members. Perhaps for those reasons many politicians have sought unpaid young people to work in their campaigns.

But ideals are of little use unless they can be achieved, at least to some degree. Politics demands both idealism and practicality. The youthful voter who wishes to support and even stimulate idealistic candidates to run for public office must confront the resistance of some and the apathy of many. To overcome both requires intelligence, inspiration, and hard work. The young have these capacities and the opportunity to be politically effective. . . .

College Students and Local Government

Local government has not been a prime interest among college students during recent years if, indeed, it has ever been of much concern. Radicals have generally tended to feel that local governments deal with unimportant, everyday matters and only the federal government is concerned with the big emotional issues of "survival." Most have felt that anyone who occupies himself with these pedestrian issues is either wasting his time or is, himself, pedestrian. All this is changing as students discover that local officials have enormous discretion over policies of immediate concern in their daily lives. As the right to vote in local and state elections is rapidly being extended, the incentives to influence and even elect local officials must, necessarily, increase. Students who are adversely affected by local policies will have no one to blame but themselves if they abstain from participation.

Local officials are in a powerful position to do good to or to inflict harm on students. Most local governments have been of special import during the past several years of nearly daily confrontations in many college and university towns. . . .

Whether officials pursue hard or soft policies with regard to youth-oriented activities differs greatly among states and local communities. Possession (not sale) of marijuana, for example, entails prison sentences of but a few months in some states—several years in many others—and can bring life imprisonment in Texas. Police surveillance on campuses varies from one campus to another just as the degree of that attention varies. The extent to which local officials intervene in campus affairs will be vitally affected by students themselves as they decide whether or not to participate in local politics.

If students can vote where they attend school they will be exceedingly influential wherever students constitute at least a substantial minority of the electorate. In some college towns they outnumber townspeople by 2 or 3 to one. The possibilities of affecting local policies and electing officials is partially determined by the size and activism of the student group. Since many large schools are located in small towns the possibilities for significant control are considerable. Students outnumber the locals as is the case in such diverse places as Pullman, Washington, with Western Washington's 14,000 students and Pullman's 6,000 local citizens, and Penn State where students (26,000) outnumber locals (12,500) by more than 2 to 1. Ann Arbor's 55,000 townspeople "confront" 36,000 students. Madison's 115,000 local residents have approximately 35,000 university students in their midst.

A police chief whose superiors are selected by students is likely to behave in very different ways from one whose superiors are not. Besides having the power to make life miserable, local governments are in a position to add to the happiness of young students. Their policies on such matters as political demonstrations, local recreational facilities, liquor licenses, child care centers, public transportation, pollution control, low cost housing and rent controls, and traffic laws can be crucial for the student who must spend at least four years of his life in their jurisdictions. So apparently trivial a matter as wading in public fountains has become a hot issue in many small provincial towns and even cities. Local politics may be "where it's at" during the 1970s. Students with identifiable interests could control some college cities mentioned and others on the basis of superior numbers. But first, residency laws must be liberalized, and that action depends upon the actions of state legislatures and probably the Supreme Court. At present these requirements range from only 90 days in California, New York, New Jersey, and Pennsylvania to two years in Mississippi. . . .

Where It's at for Black Voters

The Black revolution for increased money, power, status, and general well-being has a lengthy history of tragedy and disappointment. The more recent phases, however, suggest that a much better day is in the offing. Contributors to the growing power of the black movement have been many people and countless tactics, including violence. It is becoming increasingly clear that the blacks can make and are making effective use of the vote. Civil rights legislation during the past decade has been of considerable value in helping blacks gain political recognition. Blacks should continue to vote and to vote in greater numbers and with greater frequency. Because blacks constitute about 11 percent (23 million) of the U.S. population they constitute a powerful voting bloc. How powerful this bloc can be depends on their size in different constituencies. The precise relationship will be discussed below.

When black voters attend the polls they can elect officials of their own color and convictions, as is demonstrated by some recent election results.[1] In 1960, there were fewer than 200 black officials. In June, 1968, an estimated 1,126 blacks were holding elective public office; by late 1970 there were 1,769 or an increase of more than 1,500 since 1960. Black officials are most numerous in the South and most numerous on school boards (451) and city councils (650). Black political positions also comprise a U.S. Senatorship (Edward W. Brooke of Massachusetts); 12 Congressional seats; 33 State Senatorships; 172 State Representatives; 64 mayorships including those of Gary, Indiana, and Cleveland, Ohio; and 144 judgeships. There will be more like Carl Stokes, Charles Evers, and Richard D. Hatcher. In 1970 Wilson C. Riles, a black educator, defeated the well-known Max Rafferty for the office of Superintendent of Education in California.

Increasing numbers of blacks who hold high appointive national offices include Supreme Court Justice Thurgood Marshall. The U.S. Civil Service Commission has reported that Negroes held 311,376 civil service jobs in 1962 and by 1969 had increased that number to 426,917.[2] These jobs include all levels from the lowest paid to the highest paid positions. More recently, black employment in the federal government increased while total federal employment was declining.

---

[1] "Black Public Officials," *CQ Guide to Current American Government* (Washington, D.C.: Congressional Quarterly, Inc., Spring 1971), pp. 26–31.

[2] "Negroes in Federal Jobs: Moving Upward," *U.S. News and World Report,* May 25, 1970, p. 68.

VOTING DILEMMAS AND THE LOGIC OF CHOICE

WILLIAM C. MITCHELL

Although having vote power is now a fact, to exercise that power poses a dilemma in choice, at least for the voter who wishes to make the most of his vote. It would be foolish not to recognize the inherent dilemmas confronting a voter who, approaching the polls for the first time, wants to do good for himself, his generation, and the nation. . . . Most of them confront all voters, but some are of special interest for the first-time, youthful voter.

Conventional voting studies by political scientists tell us that most voters are (1) not well informed, (2) apathetic if not cynical, (3) inclined to vote as their parents did, (4) inclined to vote as members of their social groupings previously have, and (5) inclined to be somewhat less than rational in their decision processes and their choices. Although evidence in favor of the first four generalizations is often highly impressive and persuasive, voters need not behave in these ways. Certainly this should not be true of students, who have acquired a vast social consciousness during the past decade and who are daily involved in intense emotional and intellectual experiences as students and young adults. If anyone has the opportunity and capacity to become intelligent voters it is today's 18 to 20 year old. The problems of choice and the decision processes should be well within his grasp.

A Small Investment in the Tools of Choice

While the dilemmas of choice can sometimes be anguishing experiences they are subject to analysis. We cannot, by analysis, guarantee that we will make the *best* choices, but clearly we can improve our choices and the process we use to make choices. First, we need to know what we must decide, how to go about discovering alternatives, and how to con-

Reprinted from William C. Mitchell, Why Vote? (Chicago: Markham Publishing Co., 1971), pp. 29–46. Reprinted by permission of Rand McNally College Publishing Company, Chicago.

sider their comparative worth. . . . To do a job right requires tools; this small investment in the tools of choice has considerable payoff for those who master the next few pages. The costs of the investment are not great, but they do entail some degree of abstraction and a certain amount of logical rigor. Abstraction of particulars is a necessity since we cannot treat each election or each set of candidates as a unique instance; the generalized advice here is suitable for most elections. Our concern, therefore, is with the acquisition of some basic tools that can be applied to a wide variety of election choices—ranging from purely local referenda to the major, critical Presidential elections that may occur only once in a generation.

The outline of choice presented here is easily summarized. (1) Voting is a form of political action involving individual choices. At minimum, these choices pertain to such mundane matters as deciding whether to register and vote and for whom to vote. (2) Advice concerns the principles a voter should employ in answering these questions. Each voter must make his own estimates of the personal and social costs and benefits stemming from his choices and of the probabilities of success or impact his vote will have on the electoral outcomes. . . . (3) The objective of this discussion is to increase the voter's capacity to handle these problems for himself as circumstances change. We begin with some reflections on the question of whether voting is worthwhile. . . .

Is Voting Worthwhile?

The answer to this question is *yès,* with the qualification that anyone's personal influence in any large arena is apt to be small. The new voter must not blithely assume that utopia has now arrived and that anything, and everything, he wants will be immediately forthcoming. With 140 million potential voters, a single voter's influence cannot, in itself, be impressive. In the 1968 Presidential election there were 73.2 million voters. Still, every vote counts: the following pages will explain how much and under which conditions.

Voting is important in a number of ways. First, those who do not vote are, in effect, voting; they have decided *not* to support any of the competitors. Nonvoting can influence and has influenced many elections, especially close ones. Many elections are won by fewer than 1 percent of those casting ballots. We have had fourteen Presidents who won by less than popular majorities; in two cases the candidates (Tilden, 1876 and Cleveland, 1888) won the general election but lost the battle of the Electoral College. Twenty-one of our Presidential elections have been won by such small margins that a shift of not more than 1 percent could have changed the outcomes.[1]

A second factor in voting is the differential weights or importance of votes in different elections and districts. The influence of any voter is partially dependent on the size of the constituency in which he votes. For example, in senatorial contests all the voters choose the same number of senators (two) but the variance in the size of the voting population is enormous. Each senator from New York obviously represents many more citizens than do the Senators from Alaska or Nevada. Since all senators have the same voting power—one vote—each of their constituents might be said to have varying vote power or influence on public policy even though the magnitude of those differences may not appear very significant to a voter in New York or Nevada.

A third factor determining whether a vote is consequential depends to some extent upon the voter's *own* evaluation of his own action. A voter may consider his participation in the political life of the nation as rewarding in itself; voting makes him feel good. Or, he may consider voting his sacred duty; violation of that duty makes him feel guilty. Many Americans do treat voting merely as a duty, while many more apparently feel good because they voted. The first group may become defensive and apologetic whenever they fail in these responsibilities. The others may derive satisfaction in the act of demonstrating their loyalties or allegiance to the nation and its heritage. Still others take some sporting pride in supporting their party and/or its candidates. Still others— perhaps less numerous—derive pleasure from the thought that they might influence the actual outcome of a close race.

Various bits of scholarly research on voting behavior and national loyalties—the "civic culture"—suggest that these rewards are not merely fanciful; in fact, at least one major cross-national study of five nations shows that fully 85 percent of Americans are extremely proud of their political institutions and do feel satisfaction when going to the polls.[2] Only 12 percent claimed "they never enjoy, never get angry, and never feel contempt during campaigns."[3] In fact, most citizens do have a sense of political involvement even when they do not vote.

Aside from these psychic rewards, the most important reason for voting is *the expectation of some tangible returns in the way of more*

---

[1] Neal R. Pierce, *The People's President* (New York: Simon and Schuster, 1968), pp. 317–21.

[2] Gabriel A. Almond and Sidney Verba, *The Civic Culture* (Princeton, N.J.: Princeton University Press, 1963), p. 146.

[3] *Ibid.*

favorable policies supporting or advancing one's way of life or ideals. In short, the outcome of the election will make a difference for him—at least, he expects that it will do so. The significance a national election may have for each voter differs in terms of both the contents of policies and actions as well as the magnitude of policy differences. Although this difference will be minimal for some voters, for others the expected gains or losses may be material and considerable.

For still others the difference may, in fact, be zero; those voters are totally indifferent about who wins and about the subsequent policy outcomes. They may view all candidates and parties as equally bad or equally good. In this case, one obvious course of action is not to vote. Another is to support still another candidate, either by write-in or in preparation for a future election. But it is an obvious fact that the outcomes of national elections are a matter of indifference to countless citizens. Daily life is not always measurably affected by election results, and, in our system, those who vote for the loser are not excluded from the normal services of government. About all we can and ought to do with doubtful persons is attempt to persuade them that their low estimates of electoral outcomes are erroneous. . . .

Can My Vote Influence the Electoral Outcome?

While it is necessary to demonstrate that expected electoral payoffs either maximize gains or minimize losses, these calculations are hardly sufficient inducements to vote. A voter should also be convinced that his vote will have some impact on deciding the outcome. The obvious facts of political life are such that many voters find this possibility very unrealistic; nevertheless, at least 60–63 percent of the eligible voters have been turning out for Presidential elections since 1952 and over 90 percent of certain groups vote in those elections. Surely not all who voted have been convinced that their votes were inconsequential or that the outcomes were unimportant, nor have those who stayed at home been motivated by their rational decision that the elections were unimportant or that their chances of deciding the outcomes approached zero. Many did not vote because they were denied the opportunity to implement their voting decisions. Unduly stringent registration and residency requirements, plus literacy tests, have been responsible for much abstention. One famous pollster, Elmo Roper, has estimated that nearly 20 million citizens could not vote in 1960.[4] In other words, nearly 20 per-

---

[4] Reported in James D. Barber, *Citizen Politics* (Chicago: Markham Publishing Co., 1969), p. 6.

cent were unable to cast ballots. Slightly over 80 percent of the voting population did vote, suggesting that most citizens view voting as worthwhile.

The "Costs" of Voting

Everything of value has its cost or price, and voting is no exception. The voter pays in real costs other than money: the parties pay money costs to acquire his vote. The young voter about to consider exercising his choice must ask himself whether the act of voting is worthwhile; in asking this question he must estimate not only what he hopes to achieve or stands to lose and the chances of their outcome, but he must also decide how much his action will cost. The cost of voting is not as easy to determine as the price of a commodity on the market; no price tags can be found. Nevertheless, the costs include the amount of time consumed in registering and actually attending the polls on election day, the costs of transportation, and, above all, the amounts of time and energy spent in becoming better informed before voting. These are real costs even though they cannot be readily summed in a dollar and cents figure. They are also "opportunity costs"; time and energy devoted to political activity could have been allocated to other, nonpolitical tasks and pleasures. Thus, since time is a finite quantity the term "opportunity" means foregone opportunities; generally one cannot simultaneously perform political and nonpolitical activities. This is the case even if political activities are also pleasurable. A choice must be made under most conditions. Occasionally a person may engage in private or public political activities as his first concern, but reap some complementary beneficial side effects. For example, by attending a political party rally one might meet some interesting members of the opposite sex. . . .

If voting has variable costs, how can one decide how much to spend? The answer to this question is simple in a formal sense. It is exceedingly difficult in the practical sense of deciding whether and how far one should travel to the polls, how much time should be spent in the voting booth, and how much time and intellectual energy should be devoted to becoming better informed about the issues, the candidates' positions, the importance of the election, and the probabilities of being influential. The simplest formal answer to the question is *continue devoting resources to the task as long as the incremental gain is greater than the incremental costs sustained or incurred by the expenditure of resources. When the expected marginal benefits are equalled by the expected marginal costs the voter should put a halt to his efforts.* The total cost of voting consists of both certain relatively fixed items, such as the amount of time spent in actually attending the election, and a set of variable costs largely incurred in gathering and interpreting information prior to a decision on whether and how to vote. Total costs rise as more resources are devoted to the informational process. They continue to rise as more activity or resources are devoted to voting preparation. During this period, total benefits to be derived from increased preparation increase, but most likely at a decreasing rate. The rational voter should cease his search for more useful information at the point at which the difference between the total cost and total benefit is greatest. In marginal terms, the voter maximizes his returns when he can no longer gain more than he loses by adding another "unit" of information. If he invests in another bit of informational activity he will find his costs rising more rapidly than his benefits. If he proceeds beyond that point he would be gaining in total returns at a rapidly decreasing rate and would eventually have his total benefits equalled by his total expenditures. As in the marketplace, costs tend to rise more rapidly than benefits—making additional gains more and more costly. We should also note that total costs are higher than total benefits during the early stages of the information gathering since some investment is required before any returns will be forthcoming. The voter may be thought to have an information investment, acquired over 18 years, before he even begins to apply his information to the voting decision. . . .

Can I Influence Public Policy?

This question was rarely raised by youth prior to the Vietnam war although it has recently become something of a pre-occupation. The answer is complex but positive; voters can do something about policy. There is no guarantee, however, that each voter can either directly attain whatever he wants or prevent enactment of policies he disapproves of. Each voter will probably attain only a small portion of his preferred positions. Voters who wanted or want the United States to withdraw, unilaterally, from the Vietnam war have not had their first preference realized but they may have achieved a second or third preference in the graduated withdrawal of U.S. forces. While the rate of withdrawal may not have been satisfactory, forces were withdrawn by a President who may or may not have shared these policy preferences.

Why is it that the individual voter cannot directly influence policy as much as he would like? The reasons are fairly apparent. In a free market situation, the consumer can spend his resources almost any way he likes. A music lover can visit his favorite store and purchase a Beatles record. Another may choose a recording by the Rolling Stones, and a third may buy an oldie—a Louis Armstrong recording from the 1930s. Each record buyer can purchase the record of his choice, if his income permits, without insisting that others buy the same record. This is not the case in political systems and for very sound reasons.

Public choice in democracies is not a free market situation. It must entail some degree of coercion because only one policy can be pursued in a given area at any given time. Obviously, every voter cannot direct public policy to suit himself, just as the United States cannot simultaneously withdraw completely and increase the scale of the Vietnam war. It is equally impractical for a citizen to visit City Hall once a week and purchase $10 of police protection while another more fearful soul purchases $100 of the same service, and a paranoid demands $1,000 worth of services from the police. Individuals cannot purchase public services this way because government cannot provide discrete amounts to individual citizens. A public good, once created, is equally available to all citizens, whether they use it or not. While I am not forced to buy Beatles records, I am forced to help pay for public goods, programs, and activities I may have expressed myself as opposed to in elections and by other means. While it would be nice if individual citizens could have only those programs or policies they like, and only in the preferred amount, this is not possible in political systems including democracies. . . .

A voter becomes more realistic as he recognizes serious limitations on his capacity to influence the workings of the system. But when he does he is in a better position to pursue whatever ends he chooses. This voter should also recognize that not everyone exercises the same amount of influence on policy in the United States. This revelation may be disheartening, but it can act as spur to more successful participation. Knowledge of where the power is and where it is not enables the interested citizen to concentrate his efforts in the most fruitful places.

In addition to the necessity for coercion in political systems and thus the denial of free choice in selecting public policies, individual citizens are confronted with the fact that our system is huge (140 million of voting age) and extraordinarily complex. No system this large and intricate could possibly be operated like a local free market in which individual choice is maximized. Just as a division of labor is necessary in the free market, representatives are a necessity in the public policy arena. U.S. voters have more than 521,760 elected representatives, or one for every 230 adult citizens. Each of these politicians must find some way of giving voice to the diversity of opinion among his constituents. Accordingly, the individual cannot directly choose public policies. He can at best attempt to influence the votes of his representatives. The exceptions are occasional referenda in which the voter can directly shape policy. Referenda are usually on local and state issues, and even here the voter has to face impressive constraints on his choices; the alternatives are restricted and his choice is limited to expressing a preference for or against the proposals offered on the ballot. Most of the time, on the national and state levels, public policy is bargained out among elected officials, who are representatives of interest groups and powerful individuals. The voter is in the position of a member of an audience. He is able to encourage and discourage producers by his purchase of tickets and actors with his applause. The extent of direct individual influence over national policy formation is miniscule.

If greater influence were possible would it be worth the sacrifice entailed by its adoption? Greater participation may be desirable from some viewpoints, but it is necessarily more costly both for the participant and the entire system. It extends the time necessary to make collective decisions and increases the resources an individual must devote to the participation. Town meetings cannot be operated on a scale much larger than a few hundred citizens. Furthermore, even town meetings result in majority-rule decisions, and coercion continues in any issue in which unanimity does not prevail. Those who vote against the proposals must concede to the victors; those who vote against a tax must pay the tax along with those who vote for it.

We began this [discussion] optimistically contending that voting is normally worthwhile, but we have now conceded that the individual can do relatively little to directly attain the policies he prefers. So why vote? Just as the expenditure of a dollar in the market is a message to businessmen, the vote is a message to politicians, and although the message is ambiguous and brief, politicians know how to read it.

To expect that each individual can always have all that he wants, when he wants it, and in the form he wants, seems childish at best. Voters who suffer frustration because of lack of involvement should seek greater involvement by joining interest groups, becoming active in political parties, and perhaps running for public office, where their influence can be increased.

Other Means of Political Participation

While voting is clearly participation in politics, other means of participation are also available for those who do not fall into the category of the influential and powerful. During the last few years much has been written about "political participation" and participatory democracy. Interest in this type of political involvement has not been limited to the United States but has become a worldwide phenomenon. The next selection provides an introduction to the various kinds of political participation available to citizens and the objectives which may be achieved through such involvement.

TO BE OR NOT TO BE IN POLITICS

JAMES BURKHART / JAMES EISENSTEIN
THEODORE FLEMING / FRANK KENDRICK

Government by Everyman

Democracy is based on the proposition that man is worthy of citizenship and that his decisions concerning public questions are trustworthy. In the *Age of Reason,* Thomas Paine asserts: "Certain I am that when opinions are free, either in matters of government or religion, truth will finally and powerfully prevail." In his inaugural address on "The New Freedom," President Wilson—a former political science professor—acknowledged the belief: "I believe, as I believe in nothing else, in the average integrity and the average intelligence of the American people. . . . This great American people is at bottom just, virtuous and hopeful; the roots of its being are in the soil of what is lovely, pure and of good report." In other words, given sufficient information, the ordinary citizen will usually make reasonable decisions and act upon them.

Most advocates of democracy would probably feel that both Thomas Paine and President Wilson were overly idealistic about the infallibility of the common man. Nonetheless, these democratic supporters would most likely suggest that democracy is the recurrent suspicion that more than half the people are right more than half the time. They would also add that there are really three major ways of settling a public issue—by bargaining or compromise, by force, or by talking and then head counting.

Civic education courses (civics and citizenship) generally stress that enlightened political participation is a civic virtue and that those who

Reprinted from James Burkhart, James Eisenstein, Theodore Fleming, and Frank Kendrick, Strategies for Political Participation, pp. 10–18, by permission of the publisher. Copyright © 1972 by Winthrop Publishers, Inc.

engage in such activities are the most responsible citizens. In fact, part of the Anglo-American heritage is that the ideal citizen is politically concerned and devotes a great deal of his time and energy to public matters. America's entire political culture glorifies the concept of "government by and with the consent of the governed." The country's basic political values suggest that there is no better prerequisite for maintaining a free society than public vigilance and enlightened participation.

Reasons for Participation

. . . Political participation is an intricate activity, and an individual's motives for engaging in (or refraining from) the political process are diverse. These motives may range from self-interest, friendship and the desire for approval, personal response, the need to alleviate psychological tension, and the desire for influence to perhaps the motive most commonly mentioned—the quest for political power.

Patterns of Participation

Once bitten by the political bug, the individual may stay politically minded, but there is no guarantee that his activism will escalate or even endure, for the American political culture is characterized by an ebb and flow in interest and participation. . . .

Electoral politics is only one aspect of political participation. . . . Elections occur at scheduled times and are characterized by an episodic pattern of peaks and lows, depending on issues and candidates. But between elections there is another type of political activity that goes on constantly—"issue politics." Decisions are made and influence is applied by interest groups and reform groups all the time. Through organization, interested and energetic individuals can move an issue toward a policy solution by giving it visibility and circulaton. There is reason to believe that issue politics will become more important as more and more groups are organized to persuade mass numbers on particular issues or clusters of issues.

In the realm of issue politics, participation and interest also ebb and flow. In times of national crisis—the depression and the Vietnam war are outstanding examples—many people are stimulated into political activity. Events with a narrower geographic focus, such as local decisions to achieve racial balance in schools through extensive busing, may also lead to intense political activity.

However, everyone does not participate in politics to the same degree; specialization in virtually every area of modern life is reflected in the realm of politics. The very fact that political participation demands a tremendous amount of time is an obvious limiting factor. Few people are able to devote a substantial portion of their lives to politics. Many appear to be content with the role of half-interested spectator. Spectatorism is encouraged by the complexity and multiplicity of issues. The dilemma of the citizen is aggravated further by the nature of the issues with which he must contend. Modern politics seems to be plagued with more and more issues which invite only a blurred and ambiguous stance. The rush and push of modern life also detracts from the time, energy and attention which an individual can devote to political participation. Everyone is challenged on all sides by groups and activities that call for or demand his allegiances, and there is intense competition for the time one can spend on political activities.

The intensity of citizen participation and involvement at any one time, then, reflects the current mood of the country, the prevailing political climate, and the urgency of issues and problems. During the post-Civil War period in American history, for example, politics took second place to business and private interests. In the 1920's, both political parties appeared to treat the average voter as a vegetable and the political leaders of the era were analogous to alligators floating downstream without making a ripple to disturb the rising current of financial speculation and privatism. Obviously, critical issues and crisis situations intensify civic interest and political participation; thus, the elections which the individual perceives as important stir his interest and incite participation. Along the same line, when a voter feels that a particular candidate will respond meaningfully to pressing issues, and his own political involvement will prod the government to respond, he will be more likely to participate. In this connection, closely contested elections stimulate interest and participation. In the larger states which have competitive parties and an important vote, such as New York and California, voting is appreciably higher than it is in one-party areas. The striking conclusion is clear; citizens are more inclined to become interested and involved when relevant issues are contested in a realistic way.

The Importance of "Slack" in the System

Differences in participation both in elections and in issue politics suggest a basic characteristic of the political system that has important consequences. This characteristic is called "slack." "Slack" is a shorthand term which refers to the fact that at any given time, the actual number of people and resources actively engaged in the politics of an election or issue is far below the maximum possible. Even during periods when political activity is at its peak (as during the fall of Presidential election years), most people are only marginally involved in political activity, and some manage to remain completely uninvolved.

The concept of slack is so important to political participation that it is worth emphasizing. At any time, the number of people who are merely observers of the political scene may number about 50 percent, while activists may number less than 10 percent. As noted, the category of disinterested and apathetic citizens fluctuates with elections, issues and areas. But if one breaks down the hierarchy of political involvement, it appears that only one or two percent of the population may engage in such highly participatory activities as running for or holding public office or soliciting contributions for political activity.

Lester Milbrath, in his study *Political Participation,* has devised a hierarchy of political involvement. Although it does not include all the activities which students are likely to engage in, such as participating in mass demonstrations, it is a useful device.

HIERARCHY OF POLITICAL INVOLVEMENT [1]

1. Holding public and party office
2. Being a candidate for office
3. Soliciting political funds
4. Attending a caucus or a strategy meeting
5. Becoming an active member in a political party
6. Contributing time in a political campaign   Gladiatorial
7. Attending a political meeting or rally   Activities
8. Making a monetary contribution to a party or candidate
9. Contacting a public official or a political leader   Transitional
10. Wearing a button or putting a sticker on a car   Activities
11. Attempting to talk another into voting a certain way
12. Initiating a political discussion
13. Voting
14. Exposing oneself to political stimuli

    Spectator
    Activities

    Apathetics

In the top three categories of behavior, usually less than one percent of the eligible population participate. Categories 4–7 attract about four or

[1] Lester W. Milbrath, *Political Participation* (Chicago: Rand McNally & Company, 1965), pp. 18–19.

five percent; category 8 accounts for about ten percent; category 9, for about thirteen percent; category 10, for about fifteen percent; and category 11, for about twenty-five to thirty percent. Below these categories (12–14) the listed activities account for from forty to seventy percent of the eligible population.

This is, then, truly the picture of a slack political system which makes little relative use of all its available human resources.

The existence of slack does have significant consequences for those who do decide to participate, however. Because opportunities for political activity are seized by so few so infrequently, those who do become involved often find that the field is nearly free of competitors. Strong and well-established organizations take advantage of slack in the system to put pressure on the decision-making process at many points. Because they frequently encounter no opposing groups, they are able to enact their programs or "ambush" proposals that lack effective support from their opponents. In this way, slack presents great possibilities for influence.

But the existence of slack also poses some problems for political participants: One is that political activity by one group may stimulate other previously non-active opposing groups into activity. To a certain extent, organization and activity beget counter-organization and counter-activity. Another is that power may be so diffuse and fragmented in a slack system that it is difficult for anyone to make meaningful decisions producing change. . . .

Reasons for Participation

Balanced against these legitimate reasons for non-participation are a number of good reasons for participation. . . . Basically, they all more or less stem from the fact that there are a number of things each person wants to accomplish in life that can most effectively (at times, only) be pursued through political activity.

A student has some obvious disadvantages when it comes to participation—lack of experience and political sophistication, contacts with only a relatively narrow segment of society, little money—but a student also enjoys certain advantages. Usually he is not completely or irrevocably committed to a permanent job or career. He is not locked into the pressures, prejudices and struggle to make a living; thus he can find the time and resources to devote to politics. In short, young adulthood is an ideal time to act and to influence public policy for good causes, to work within the system for values and needed priorities.

Another positive factor is that the political environment students in the early 1970's are entering is beginning to show some changes that should encourage participation. The arena of political decision-making is enlarging. Public interest groups, protest groups and reform crusaders are jumping into the ring. An interesting development is that a number of reform groups (such as Common Cause) have passed their political initiation and are beginning to exert considerable influence upon the system. Citizens are more willing now to sign petitions, to testify before decision-making groups and, if need be, to picket for what they believe in. One estimate of the number of people seeking a share in political power and influence is as high as 15 to 20 percent of the population. This figure is in sharp contrast to the 5 percent estimate of a few years ago. . . .

The "Powerless" and Politics

Finally, we would like to focus the attention of our readers on a special case of the powerless, namely, those living in black ghettos. In this last selection of the chapter, Kenneth B. Clark discusses the special means by which blacks residing in ghettos have been able to make their voices heard and create a significant input into the political system. He emphasizes the many sacrifices blacks already make simply by living in the ghetto and the special efforts necessary to form groups that can assume the leadership and garner the necessary influence to change the outcome of political struggles.

THE POWER STRUCTURE OF THE GHETTO

KENNETH B. CLARK

Power must be understood to be used properly, if it is to avoid dilution into the appearance of power. Power, misunderstood or miscalculated, increases the dangers of its explosive dissipation or stagna-

From pp. 154–190, Dark Ghetto by Kenneth B. Clark. Copyright © 1965 by Kenneth B. Clark. Reprinted by permission of Harper & Row Publishers, Inc. and Victor Gollanz Ltd.

tion. It is essential to analyze the sources of power—the strengths and weaknesses—within America's dark ghettos if any realistic diagnosis and predictions about their future are to be possible.

The ghetto is, in a manner, self-perpetuating, and while it encourages some for attempting change, it rewards others for loyalty to things as they are. Inside the ghetto lie sources of energy that are ordinarily mobilized, overtly or covertly, to prevent change and to perpetuate and exploit the *status quo*. Outside the ghetto, too, are sources of energy that depend on the ghetto for their own security—all exploitation rests upon real or imagined advantages to the exploiters. Therefore, any social action to transform the ghetto must expect to face apathy and hostility from both Negroes and whites—for a ghetto can be a cocoon as well as a cage.

Social institutions—the church, the courts, the legislature, the executive regulatory agencies, the police and, in ultimate cases, the military—are intended generally to protect society-as-it-is, though at times, they themselves may—as the Supreme Court did in the 1954 school desegregation cases—be a powerful stimulus to change. Democratic government tends to be limited in its capacity to respond to the demands of minority or lower-status groups because it is necessarily dependent either upon majority support or upon those groups that already have economic, political, and social status and power. The successful politician seeks to find a balance between the demands of those who wish to change and the resistance of those who are determined to prevent it. American political history is the record of adjustment to the needs of those minorities most restless at any one time—and a postponement or dilution of the requests of those groups that are, at the time, relatively satisfied or quiescent. The strategy of such compromise responds to tension among competing forces and is inevitable in a democratic society. Ironically, the earlier minorities whose needs have been satisfied may themselves join to form a coalition against the rising demands of a newly articulate minority, as many labor unions have done in the past, in response to the claims of Negroes.

If Negroes are to use their new-found energy most effectively, it will be necessary for them to learn the ways of power and to avoid the delusion of pseudopower.

Political Power

The most obvious of the social sources of power is political, yet Negroes have failed so far to translate their vote into effective action in their own behalf. In the South, persecution has combined with apathy to keep Negroes from the polls, but registration drives and some federal protection have reversed the trend in recent years. In the North, Negroes vote, though usually in smaller proportion than whites. There is a circular pattern in political behavior, for ineffective use of the vote limits a group's political influence while its political powerlessness may in turn seem convincing evidence that voting is useless, leading to apathy. But votes alone do not necessarily imply actual political power, in the sense of control of the direction of social changes, for seldom are the issues of an election clear-cut enough for victory to imply a mandate for a particular program.

The effective exercise of power in the urban ghetto is crippled severely by the inexperience of the ghetto's own political leaders. Their inexperience and political unsophistication have a fundamental root—the psychology of the ghetto with its pervasive and total sense of helplessness. It is difficult, if not impossible, to behave as one with power when all one's experience has indicated that one has none. Because their house of political power is built on sand without a solid base of economic or social influence, ghetto politicians are likely to accept a limited jurisdiction and to seek immediate and concrete rewards. They often subject themselves to the control of others they believe to hold the primary power, and some are prepared to make petty deals and to toy with political corruption. But even in corruption the Negro is accorded second-class citizenship. Negro urban leaders, to illustrate, seldom have access to decisions on bids for multimillion-dollar construction projects. Those who are susceptible to temptation are restricted to marginal graft like the numbers racket. Negroes felt it an ironic confirmation of their low status that when the first Negro to be borough president of Manhattan lost his position it involved not a million-dollar conspiracy but a less than $5,000 apartment renovation. In political patronage, too, Negro politicians are restricted to the lower levels of reward. The hard facts generally tend to limit the outreach and the effectiveness of the ghetto politicians. Unable to compete successfully for power or patronage, they tend to compete among themselves for the available crumbs, and this struggle, in turn, makes them more vulnerable to manipulation by real political leadership—i.e., white leadership. When no one has much patronage or much power, rivalry for a minimal share keeps everyone divided and everyone important. . . .

With the exceptions of Congressmen William Dawson of Chicago and Adam Clayton Powell of New York, and J. Raymond Jones, no Negro political leader in America has ever moved from his constricted ghetto position into any really top post. Top posts have gone to others. For example, William Hastie, who was the first Negro judge of a federal circuit court, was appointed from his vantage point of experience as dean of Howard University Law School and as governor of the Virgin Islands. Thurgood Marshall, the second Negro to reach the United States Court of Appeals, moved there from his job as director of the NAACP Legal Defense and Educational Fund. Ralph Bunche accepted a position as undersecretary in the United Nations after a distinguished career with Howard University as professor of political science, with the Office of Strategic Services, and with the State Department. Carl Rowan became director of the United States Information Agency after a strong newspaper career in the "white press," followed by a brief but distinguished service in the State Department. Robert C. Weaver arrived at his post as director of the Federal Housing and Home Finance Agency after a career as economist and as an authority on state and local housing problems. Edward Brooke, the first Negro attorney general of a state, achieved this position by way of a successful legal career in Massachusetts and through his recognized effectiveness as a member of the Boston Finance Commission. He was appointed to this post in 1960 by a Republican governor. He was elected in 1962 and elected in 1964 despite an overwhelming national Democratic landslide. Franklin H. Williams, United States Ambassador serving on the Economic and Social Council of the United Nations, moved to this post from an apprenticeship on the staff of the NAACP, and was West Coast representative of that organization until he joined the Peace Corps under Sargent Shriver. Negroes who have made a name for themselves through competition in the white community in the professions and through the civil rights movement have therefore been far more likely to reach a place of power than have the Negro politicians themselves. Most Negro politicians have never been given a chance to operate outside of the ghetto sphere, in part because they have not focused their energies on civil rights or matters of general public concern but on representing Negro constituents within their districts—in the manner of politicians generally. Whereas this does not handicap a white politician unduly from advacement, it is part of the nature of the ghetto that the white power structure comes to see Negro political figures as reflections of the limitations of the ghetto itself, as men without potential for other larger jobs. Some top civil rights leaders, who have operated within the nonghetto power structure, e.g., in the courts, which are essentially white-dominated, have been compelled to meet the competitive standards of the community at large, which is white, and they have been able to wrest concessions from it and thereby to gain respect and further power.

Traditional Negro politicians would have preferred that Negroes appointed to federal judgeships, for example, be those who had moved gradually up the political ladder. But white officials have tended rather to appoint Negroes who have achieved stature by another route. Where the Negroes chosen were of stature, as with Hastie and Marshall, the politicians had to accept the appointments in good grace. Where the prospective appointees have not been of commanding stature, the Negro politicians have succeeded in blocking the promotions even at the cost of losing the post for a Negro altogether. Negro politicians have justified such pressure as a simple political expedient; if rewards go to those who have not served a political apprenticeship, Negroes will not have the patience to persist in the political effort necessary to build sound party structure.

It should be pointed out, moreover, that some Negroes express concern about the increasing tendency of government—federal, state, and local—to tap the limited pool of Negro talent available to the civil rights movement. There is some justification for the contention that if this continues it will weaken the civil rights movement itself. Some Negroes have even been cynical enough to ask whether this result is intended; and others, in turn, question the motivation of the civil rights leaders who do take such jobs, suggesting that this "proves" that they were only using the movement as a steppingstone to personal success. Such cynicism is consistent with one of the main characteristics of ghetto psychology—suspiciousness and doubt concerning the possibility that anyone, either white or Negro, can be motivated by other than self-serving interests. According to the laws of the ghetto, everyone has an angle. . . .

Experiments in Power

Negroes are sensitive to the pervasive pattern of powerlessness in the ghetto. They recognize that the real influence of Negroes in the nation's cities is woefully below what their numbers would suggest. They see that other groups, the Irish, the Italians, the Jews, have power—religious, economic, social—far beyond their own.

A few years ago, in an attempt to bring coherence and effectiveness to leadership in the New York ghetto community, a group of about fifteen Negroes formed themselves into an organization which they referred to simply as the Group. Some were at high-level positions in the municipal government; others were former judges, lawyers, directors of civil rights agencies; one was a college professor. The incident which united them was an attack they considered unjust upon one of them. His forced resignation from a government post had come on the heels of a similar onslaught on a Negro magistrate and on the Negro borough president of Manhattan. It seemed to these fifteen Negroes that here was a common pattern of exaggerated civic scrutiny of the behavior of

Negroes in public positions. More seemed to be demanded of them in their public and private lives than was demanded of whites. These stringent requirements seemed to reflect a desire on the part of white political power to avoid any sharing of real influence with Negroes.

The Group's goal was to combine individual power, such as it was, to protect Negroes exposed to examination because of their conspicuousness in top positions. Its strategy was for each to share information with the others, for each to do what he could to influence public understanding, and to form direct personal contacts with the primary sources of government. Each incident was to be dealt with separately. For example, members of the Group visited former Governor Lehman to try to persuade him that J. Raymond Jones deserved the post of head of the New York County Democratic Committee, Tammany Hall. . . . Their mission was in vain.

Members of the Group communicate with one another orally, never by written invitation. Its existence has been known to few Negroes and fewer whites. For the past four or five years it has met fairly regularly and, over brandy and cigars, discussed the persistent problems of the Harlem community. While the Group cannot claim credit for effective social change, it did have some success in terms of the Harlem press, bringing pressure for some retractions of statements it considered irresponsible. Those whom the Group tried to protect often did not know they were protected. When the issue at stake was clear-cut and concrete, success was more likely. One of its major achievements was a change in administration of an important city commission.

The Group's failure to influence the city administration's decision on J. Raymond Jones was due in large part to the fact that it could not promise that any threats made could be fulfilled. They knew Negroes would go on voting Democratic without regard to what happened to Jones, and both Lehman and Wagner knew it, too. The Group had no resources with which to cajole or threaten. The only power they had was what they believed to be the rightness of their cause. They believed, undoubtedly naively, that the combination of a just cause and a well-planned and appropriate strategy could influence public opinion and win for the Negro his rightful place in city affairs. There was an element of fantasy in this confidence.

The Group talked frankly about the psychological problems of ghetto leadership, including the personal ambition which allowed itself to be satisfied with mere fragments of power. The discussions were thoughtful, balanced, and dignified, and came to have value more for their own sake as the members shared their troubled feelings and concerns, cathartic in the sense of communion.

Yet, when a genuine crisis arose in which the integrity of the

Harlem Community seemed to be at stake, the Group found itself immobile and silent. The dimensions of the crisis were too formidable. Ironically, and perhaps appropriately, the Group did not even meet to discuss what could be done. It sought to explain its silence by pointing out that the individual whom they genuinely wished to protect had not asked for their help. Later, with real self-reproach, they chastised themselves for failing in the task they had been organized to fulfill. But the fact was that the Group did not possess the power it thought it had, and its guilt was unnecessary; responsibility can be demanded only for duties which one has the capacity to achieve. In law, no one can be convicted of a crime he has not the ability to commit or prevent.

Whatever the causes—naivete, personal vested interest, lack of real power—the Group was never able to face directly the fact of its own impotence. The evidence of helplessness intruded itself after the repeated experience that the Group could not obtain even limited goals. The Group sought, then, to expand its membership indirectly as chief agent in the formation of a larger group known as the Hundred Men, not as intimate or as confidential as the Group, but intended as a forum to talk over basic problems of the ghetto, and hopefully to resolve some of them. As the Hundred Men grew, the inherent weakness of the quiet sponsorship by the Group became even more apparent, for in the end it lost any control over the affairs of its offspring.

Why was not the Group more effective? The most obvious reason was that the majority of its members were themselves office holders. Each had something to protect and something to lose. Only two were totally independent, in the sense of freedom from reliance on elective or appointive office. No one in the Group had achieved the level of economic independence that would permit him to be publicly identified with the conflict at issue. Indeed, few persons with such freedom exist in the entire Harlem community. The psychology of the Negro of wealth, like that of the Negro poor, is in its own way a psychology of insecurity. The wealthy Negro is not sure that his wealth will bring power, though he sees that money often brings power in white society. He uses most of his psychic energy to protect his wealth; he is conservative and careful of his wealth and does not easily share it with the ghetto community at large.

The present generation of Negroes is the first to break through to that economic level on which philanthropy is possible; for a tradition of philanthropy seems to require at least two generations of fairly secure, nonspeculative wealth before civic responsibility can be assured. In the entire country there are probably no more than three or four Negro families who can support the claim of inherited wealth. Negroes have not had enough time or enough opportunity to accumulate family fortunes. Even Negroes who are "comfortably off" are not yet meaningfully involved in Wall Street, nor is any Negro well known for philanthropic leadership. The civil rights agencies, local and national, are not generally supported by large grants from individual Negroes but by large grants from whites and many smaller gifts from Negroes.

Basically, too, the ghetto pathology includes an unwillingness to make any personal sacrifice beyond those already required by the ghetto itself. *The ghetto fails to prepare one for voluntary sacrifices precisely because it demands so many voluntary ones.* Negroes who are successful financially usually escape from the ghetto, though a number continue to depend upon the ghetto economy for their own source of wealth— Negro physicians, undertakers, publishers. Most Negro wealth comes from businesses that white society did not wish to control or from services peculiarly personal—newspaper publishing of the segregated press; real estate and insurance, which grew out of Negro burial societies; and undertaking, which owes its Negro monopoly in the ghetto to the fact that white undertakers did not wish to handle Negro bodies. Whatever the source of wealth, those who attain it tend to divorce themselves from the community itself and refuse to assume generally any major responsibility for the community. . . .

Economics and Politics

We would like to close our introductory comments by attempting to draw the boundaries between politics and economics. Our discussion so far has made it evident that politics is closely related to man's other social pursuits and that a particularly intimate relationship exists between politics and economics. In many instances the dividing line between the political and economic orders is blurred; sometimes the two orders overlap each other, and in most cases they affect each other in varying degrees. To return to the example mentioned at the outset of this chapter—the agency authorized to regulate the price of milk—it is obvious that a political relationship exists between the dairy farmers and the agency. But this relationship is also economic, because the production and distribution of milk are affected by the decisions of the agency. The decision of a city government to reserve an area for recreational purposes is political because it affects the distribution of recreational facilities, making them available to the community as a whole instead of only to the few that might own land in the particular area. On the other hand, the decision is also economic, because it prevents the land from being tilled to produce food or from being mined to extract the wealth that lies below it. The activities of labor unions are also economic and political. They seek to obtain the best wages possible for their members through collective bargaining with the employers, and at the same time they are interested in influencing pending legislation to their advantage. Similar considerations apply also to many other economic interest groups.

From the foregoing examples it is evident that when we discuss politics and economics in a society, we may refer in many instances to the political and economic aspects of the same action. In Chapter 7 we will return to this subject in greater detail when we examine certain relationships between the political and economic orders from the end of the Middle Ages until the present.

We have observed that answering the question about politics has challenged political thinkers from ancient Greece to our times, and we have given examples of some of the attempts to define the nature of politics. Undoubtedly, politics was part of organized society prior to the time Aristotle wrote his famous book on the subject. It has been with us through successive periods of history and will hold a central place in the future of man. It exists in democratic societies as well as in totalitarianism regimes, in primitive governmental systems, present and past, as well as in the advanced industrial societies. It has pervaded the international scene throughout history. Politics has many faces. As Peter Merkl put it so aptly, "At its best, politics is a nobel quest for a good order and justice; at its worst, a selfish grab for power, glory, and riches." * In the following chapters some of the fundamental questions bearing on both the favorable and unfavorable sides of politics will be explored.

---

* Peter H. Merkl, *Political Continuity and Change* (New York: Harper & Row, 1967), p. 13.

AUTHORITY

2

POINT

The maintenance of authority.

If, then, the state of force continues, I shall have to take, in order to maintain the Republic and according to the Constitution, other paths than the immediate polling of the country. . . .

France is indeed threatened by dictatorship. Some want to force her to resign herself to a power that would impose itself in national despair, a power that would then obviously be mainly that of the conqueror, that is of totalitarian communism. Naturally, to begin, it would be colored with a deceptive appearance, by using the

COUNTERPOINT

The right to rebel.

. . . Certainly the student of the English civil wars, of the revolutions of France and of Russia, will note as not the least remarkable of their features, the patient efforts of the common people to await reform before they turned to violence. And in any society violence is unlikely if the conviction is widespread that the state is seriously attempting to fulfill its obligations. Violence comes when the facts persuade men to believe that the bonafides of their rulers is no longer to be trusted.*

---

* From *The State in Theory and Practice* by Harold J. Laski. Copyright 1935 by Harold J. Laski, renewed © 1963 by Frida Laski. Reprinted by permission of The Viking Press, Inc.

ambition and the hatred of shelved
politicians. After which, these people
would carry no more than their own
weight, which would not be great.

Well, no. The Republic will not abdi-
cate. The people will collect themselves. Progress, independence and
peace will prevail, along with liberty.

Long live the Republic!

Long live France! *

President DeGaulle's speech during a general strike in France, part of which
is reproduced above, demonstrates how governmental officials appeal to principles stressing the legal aspects of authority. He attacks his opponents by
stating that in a time of crisis they would use illegal force while he, as the
constitutionally elected president, would use emergency powers to prevent the
destruction of the French Republic. The counterpoint, on the other hand, considers the right if not the duty of the people to rebel if the government is not
responsive to their needs.

We observed in the preceding chapter that the exercise of authority
suggests the possession of power. *The Encyclopedia of the Social Sciences*
states that authority "is a manifestation of power and implies obedience on
the part of those subject to it." In modern states, authority generally means
legal power. "Legality" here implies the population's willing support of governmental power.

The complexity of the idea of "authority" may also be seen in the multitude of terms employed in attempts to explain it. A representative list of
recurrent words in these writings might include "support," "obedience," "coercion," "legitimacy," and "effectiveness." What is phenomenal about the
subject of authority is the fact that it has been discussed at length from the
time of the ancient Greeks until the present without the slightest indication
that it is an exhausted topic in the study of politics. Political theorists have
written volumes on the essence of authority in different kinds of political systems, whether totalitarian or democratic, stable or unstable, developed or
underdeveloped, and so forth.

---

* Charles DeGaulle, May 30, 1968.

Max Weber, a German sociologist who lived around the turn of the century, constructed a framework of analysis from which one could get many insights into the sources of authority. Weber distinguished three types of authority: traditional, institutionalized, and charismatic. The source of traditional authority is custom or belief in an elite of elders or the divine right of kings. The traditions of the society dictate who shall rule. Traditional authority is typical of preindustrial, preliterate, or primitive societies.

In contrast, institutionalized authority is peculiar to modern industrialized societies and develops when the population gains confidence in the governmental structure. A large and efficient civil service strengthens the governmental and political structure in that such a bureaucracy reinforces the channels of power. Government becomes a routine. For example, when President Kennedy was assassinated, the expectations of the American people were in full accord with the smooth transition of power within the political structure. Some observers outside the United States erroneously predicted a coup or major plot.

Weber's third source of authority, which he discusses in our first selection here, is "charisma," defined as the power of a leader bordering on the mystical, which enables him to elicit active support from the people. A charismatic leader may be found most often in a political system undergoing change. Authority founded upon charismatic leadership alone is difficult to maintain for an extended period. Weber offers the following description.

THE SOCIOLOGY OF CHARISMATIC AUTHORITY

MAX WEBER

The General Character of Charisma

Bureaucratic and patriarchal structures are antagonistic in many ways, yet they have in common a most important peculiarity: permanence. In this respect they are both institutions of daily routine. Patriarchal power especially is rooted in the provisioning of recurrent and normal needs of the workaday life. Patriarchal authority thus has its original locus in the economy, that is, in those branches of the economy that can be satisfied by means of normal routine. The patriarch is the

From From Max Weber: Essays in Sociology *edited and translated by H. H. Gerth and C. Wright Mills, pp. 245–48. Copyright 1946 by Oxford University Press, Inc. Reprinted by permission.*

"natural leader" of the daily routine. And in this respect, the bureaucratic structure is only the counter-image of patriarchalism transposed into rationality. As a permanent structure with a system of rational rules, bureaucracy is fashioned to meet calculable and recurrent needs by means of a normal routine.

The provisioning of all demands that go beyond those of everyday routine has had, in principle, an entirely heterogeneous, namely, a *charismatic*, foundation; the further back we look in history, the more we find this to be the case. This means that the "natural" leaders—in times of psychic, physical, economic, ethical, religious, political distress—have been neither office-holders nor incumbents of an "occupation" in the present sense of the word, that is, men who have acquired expert knowledge and who serve for remuneration. The natural leaders in distress have been holders of specific gifts of the body and spirit; and these gifts have been believed to be supernatural, not accessible to everybody. The concept of "charisma" is here used in a completely "value-neutral" sense.

The capacity of the Irish culture hero, Cuchulain, or of the Homeric Achilles for heroic frenzy is a manic seizure, just as is that of the Arabian berserk who bites his shield like a mad dog—biting around until he darts off in raving bloodthirstiness. For a long time it has been maintained that the seizure of the berserk is artificially produced through acute poisoning. In Byzantium, a number of "blond beasts," disposed to such seizures, were kept about, just as war elephants were formerly kept. Shamanist ecstasy is linked to constitutional epilepsy, the possession and the testing of which represents a charismatic qualification. Hence neither is "edifying" to our minds. . . . All of them have practiced their arts and ruled by virtue of this gift (charisma) and, where the idea of God has already been clearly conceived, by virtue of the divine mission lying therein. This holds for doctors and prophets, just as for judges and military leaders, or for leaders of big hunting expeditions.

It is to his credit that Rudolf Sohm brought out the sociological peculiarity of this category of domination-structure for a historically important special case, namely, the historical development of the authority of the early Christian church. Sohm performed this task with logical consistency, and hence, by necessity, he was one-sided from a purely historical point of view. In principle, however, the very same state of affairs recurs universally, although often it is most clearly developed in the field of religion.

In contrast to any kind of bureaucratic organization of offices, the charismatic structure knows nothing of a form or of an ordered procedure of appointment or dismissal. It knows no regulated "career," "advancement," "salary," or regulated and expert training of the holder of charisma or of his aides. It knows no agency of control or appeal, no local bailiwicks or exclusive functional jurisdictions; nor does it embrace permanent institutions like our bureaucratic "departments," which are independent of persons and of purely personal charisma.

Charisma knows only inner determination and inner restraint. The holder of charisma seizes the task that is adequate for him and demands obedience and a following by virtue of his mission. His success determines whether he finds them. His charismatic claim breaks down if his mission is not recognized by those to whom he feels he has been sent. If they recognize him, he is their master—so long as he knows how to maintain recognition through "proving" himself. But he does not derive his "right" from their will, in the manner of an election. Rather, the reverse holds: it is the *duty* of those to whom he addresses his mission to recognize him as their charismatically qualified leader.

In Chinese theory, the emperor's prerogatives are made dependent upon the recognition of the people. But this does not mean recognition of the sovereignty of the people any more than did the prophet's necessity of getting recognition from the believers in the early Christian community. The Chinese theory, rather, characterizes the charismatic nature of the *monarch's position,* which adheres to his *personal* qualification and to his *proved* worth.

Charisma can be, and of course regularly is, qualitatively particularized. This is an internal rather than an external affair, and results in the qualitative barrier of the charisma holder's mission and power. In meaning and in content the mission may be addressed to a group of men who are delimited locally, ethnically, socially, politically, occupationally, or in some other way. If the mission is thus addressed to a limited group of men, as is the rule, it finds its limits within their circle.

In its economic substructure, as in everything else, charismatic domination is the very opposite of bureaucratic domination. If bureaucratic domination depends upon regular income, and hence at least *a priori* on a money economy and money taxes, charisma lives in, though not off, this world. This has to be properly understood. Frequently charisma quite deliberately shuns the possession of money and of pecuniary income *per se,* as did Saint Francis and many of his like; but this is of course not the rule. Even a pirate genius may exercise a "charismatic" domination, in the value-neutral sense intended here. Charismatic political heroes seek booty and, above all, gold. But charisma, and this is decisive, always rejects as undignified any pecuniary gain that is methodical and rational. In general, charisma rejects all rational economic conduct.

The sharp contrast between charisma and any "patriarchal" structure that rests upon the ordered base of the "household" lies in this rejection of rational economic conduct. In its "pure" form, charisma is never a source of private gain for its holders in the sense of economic exploitation by making a deal. Nor is it a source of income in the form of pecuniary compensation, and just as little does it involve an orderly taxation for the material requirements of its mission. If the mission is one of peace, individual patrons provide the necessary means for charismatic structures; or those to whom the charisma is addressed provide honorific gifts, donations, or other voluntary contributions. In the case of charismatic warrior heroes, booty represents one of the ends as well as the material means of the mission. "Pure" charisma is contrary to all patriarchial domination (in the sense of the term used here). It is the opposite of all ordered economy. It is the very force that disregards economy. This also holds, indeed precisely, where the charismatic leader is after the acquisition of goods, as is the case with the charismatic warrior hero. Charisma can do this because by its very nature it is not an "institutional" and permanent structure, but rather, where its "pure" type is at work, it is the very opposite of the institutionally permanent.

In order to do justice to their mission, the holders of charisma, the master as well as his disciples and followers, must stand outside the ties of this world, outside of routine occupations, as well as outside the routine obligations of family life. The statutes of the Jesuit order preclude the acceptance of church offices; the members of orders are forbidden to own property or, according to the original rule of St. Francis, the order as such is forbidden to do so. The priest and the knight of an order have to live in celibacy, and numerous holders of a prophetic or artistic charisma are actually single. All this is indicative of the unavoidable separation from this world of those who partake of charisma. In these respects, the economic conditions of participation in charisma may have an (apparently) antagonistic appearance, depending upon the type of charisma—artistic or religious, for instance—and the way of life flowing from its meaning. Modern charismatic movements of artistic origin represent "independents without gainful employment" (in everyday language, rentiers). Normally such persons are the best qualified to follow a charismatic leader. This is just as logically consistent as was the medieval friar's vow of poverty, which demanded the very opposite.

Foundations and Instability of Charismatic Authority

By its nature, the existence of charismatic authority is specifically unstable. The holder may forego his charisma; he may feel "forsaken by his God," as Jesus did on the cross; he may prove to his followers that "virtue is gone out of him." It is then that his mission is extinguished, and hope waits and searches for a new holder of charisma. The charismatic holder is deserted by his following, however, (only) because pure charisma does not know any "legitimacy" other than that flowing from personal strength, that is, one which is constantly being proved. The charismatic hero does not deduce his authority from codes and statutes, as is the case with the jurisdiction of office; nor does he deduce his authority from traditional custom or feudal vows of faith, as is the case with patrimonial power.

The charismatic leader gains and maintains authority solely by proving his strength in life. If he wants to be a prophet, he must perform miracles; if he wants to be a war lord, he must perform heroic deeds. Above all, however, his divine mission must "prove" itself in that those who faithfully surrender to him must fare well. If they do not fare well, he is obviously not the master sent by the gods.

This very serious meaning of genuine charisma evidently stands in radical contrast to the convenient pretensions of present rulers to a "divine right of kings," with its reference to the "inscrutable" will of the Lord "to whom alone the monarch is responsible." The genuinely charismatic ruler is responsible precisely to those whom he rules. He is responsible for but one thing, that he personally and actually be the God-willed master.

During these last decades we have witnessed how the Chinese monarch impeaches himself before all the people because of his sins and insufficiencies if his administration does not succeed in warding off some distress from the governed, whether it is inundations or unsuccessful wars. Thus does a ruler whose power, even in vestiges and theoretically, is genuinely charismatic deport himself. And if even this penitence does not reconcile the deities, the charismatic emperor faces dispossession and death, which often enough is consummated as a propitiatory sacrifice.

Meng-tse's (Mencius') thesis that the people's voice is "God's voice" (according to him the *only* way in which God speaks!) has a very specific meaning: if the people cease to recognize the ruler, it is expressly stated that he simply becomes a private citizen; and if he then wishes to be more, he becomes a usurper deserving of punishment. The state of affairs that corresponds to these phrases, which sound highly revolutionary, recurs under primitive conditions without any such pathos. The charismatic character adheres to almost all primitive authorities with the exception of domestic power in the narrowest sense, and the chieftain is often enough simply deserted if success does not remain faithful to him.

The subjects may extend a more active or passive "recognition" to the personal mission of the charismatic master. His power rests upon this purely factual recognition and springs from faithful devotion. It is devotion to the extraordinary and unheard-of, to what is strange to all rule and tradition and which therefore is viewed as divine. It is a devotion born of distress and enthusiasm.

Genuine charismatic domination therefore knows of no abstract legal codes and statutes and of no "formal" way of adjudication. Its "objective" law emanates concretely from the highly personal experience of heavenly grace and from the god-like strength of the hero. Charismatic domination means a rejection of all ties to any external order in favor of the exclusive glorification of the genuine mentality of the prophet and hero. Hence, its attitude is revolutionary and trans-values everything; it makes a sovereign break with all traditional or rational norms: "It is written, but I say unto you."

The specifically charismatic form of settling disputes is by way of the prophet's revelation, by way of the oracle, or by way of "Solomonic" arbitration by a charismatically qualified sage. This arbitration is determined by means of strictly concrete and individual evaluations, which, however, claim absolute validity. Here lies the proper locus of "Kadi-justice" in the proverbial—not the historical—sense of the phrase. In its actual historical appearance the jurisdiction of the Islamic Kadi, is, of course, bound to sacred tradition and is often a highly formalistic interpretation.

Only where these intellectual tools fail does jurisdiction rise to an unfettered individual act valuing the particular case; but then it does indeed. Genuinely charismatic justice always acts in this manner. In its pure form it is the polar opposite of formal and traditional bonds, and it is just as free in the face of the sanctity of tradition as it is in the face of any rationalist deductions from abstract concepts.

This is not the place to discuss how the reference to the *aegum et bonum* in the Roman administration of justice and the original meaning of English "equity" are related to charismatic justice in general and to the theocratic Kadi-justice of Islamism in particular. Both the *aegum et bonum* and "equity" are partly the products of a strongly rationalized administration of justice and partly the product of abstract conceptions of natural law. In any case the *ex bona fide* contains a reference to the "mores" of business life and thus retains just as little of a genuine irrational justice as does, for instance, the German judge's "free discretion."

Any kind of ordeal as a means of evidence is, of course, a derivative of charismatic justice. But the ordeal displaces the personal authority of the holder of charisma by a mechanism of rules for formally ascertaining the divine will. This falls in the sphere of the "routinization" of charisma, with which we shall deal below.

Charismatic Kingship

In the evolution of political charisma, kingship represents a particularly important case in the historical development of the charismatic legitimization of institutions. The king is everywhere primarily a war lord, and kingship evolves from charismatic heroism.

In the form it displays in the history of civilized peoples, kingship is not the oldest evolutionary form of "political" domination. By "political" domination is meant a power that reaches beyond and which is, in principle, distinct from domestic authority. It is distinct because, in the first place, it is not devoted to leading the peaceful struggle of man with nature; it is, rather, devoted to leading in the violent conflict of one human community with another.

The predecessors of kingship were the holders of all those charismatic powers that guaranteed to remedy extraordinary external and internal distress, or guaranteed the success of extraordinary ventures. The chieftain of early history, the predecessor of kingship, is still a dual figure. On the one hand, he is the patriarchal head of the family or sib, and on the other, he is the charismatic leader of the hunt and war, the sorcerer, and the rainmaker, the medicine man—and thus the priest and the doctor—and finally, the arbiter. Often, yet not always, such charismatic functions are split into as many special holders of charisma. Rather frequently the chieftain of the hunt and of war stands beside the chieftain of peace, who has essentially economic functions. In contrast to the latter, the chieftain of war acquires his charisma by proving his heroism to a voluntary following in successful raids leading to victory and booty. Even the royal Assyrian inscriptions enumerate booties of the hunt and cedars from Lebanon—dragged along for building purposes—alongside figures on the slain enemies and the size of the walls of conquered cities, which are covered with skins peeled off the enemies.

The charismatic position (among primitives) is thus acquired without regard to position in the sibs or domestic communities and without any rules whatsoever. This dualism of charisma and everyday routine is very frequently found among the American Indians, for instance, among the Confederacy of the Iroquois, as well as in Africa and elsewhere.

Where war and the big game hunt are absent, the charismatic chieftain—the "war lord" as we wish to call him, in contrast to the chieftain of peace—is absent as well. In peacetime, especially if elemental calamities, particularly drought and diseases, are frequent, a charismatic sorcerer may have an essentially similar power in his hands. He is a priestly lord. The charisma of the war lord may or may not be unstable in nature, according to whether or not he proves himself and whether or not there is any need for a war lord. He becomes a permanent figure when warfare becomes a chronic state of affairs. It is a mere terminological question whether one wishes to let kingship, and with it the state, begin only when strangers are affiliated with and integrated into the community as subjects. For our purposes it will be expedient to continue delimiting the term "state" far more narrowly.

The existence of the war lord as a regular figure certainly does not depend upon a tribal rule over subjects of other tribes or upon individual slaves. His existence depends solely upon a chronic state of war and upon a comprehensive organization set for warfare. On the other hand, the development of kingship into a regular royal administration does emerge only at the stage when a following of royal professional warriors rules over the working or paying masses; at least, that is often the case. The forceful subjection of strange tribes, however, is not an absolutely indispensable link in this development. Internal class stratification may bring about the very same social differentiation: the charismatic following of warriors develops into a ruling caste. But in every case, princely power and those groups having interests vested in it—that is, the war lord's following—strive for legitimacy as soon as the rule has become stable. They crave for a characteristic which would define the charismatically qualified ruler.

Finally, especially in democratic societies, the basis of authority may be anchored in the consensus of the government. In his famous work *The Social Contract,* eighteenth-century philosopher Jean Jacques Rousseau states that the act of association by individual persons creates a moral and collective body in place of the individual personality of each contracting party in society. This body, in turn, receives from this act its unity, its common attitudes, its life, and its will. "This public person, so formed by the union of all other persons, . . . is called by its members *State* when passive, *Sovereign* when active, and *Power* when compared with others like it." Rousseau concludes that although through the social contract man "deprives himself of some advantages which he got from nature, he gains in return others so great, his faculties are so stimulated and developed, his ideas so extended, his feelings so ennobled and his whole soul so uplifted, that . . . he would be bound to bless continually the happy moment which took him from it for ever, and, instead of a stupid and unimaginative animal, made him an intelligent being and a man." *

The concept of democratic authority, for which Rousseau's ideas con-

---

* Further elaboration of Rousseau's theory is found on page 161 in Chapter 5.

stitute the line of departure, stipulates that in the event that government should begin to act in an arbitrary manner it becomes the duty of the citizen to withdraw legitimacy from the authority of the leaders.

Authority in the United States

In a stable political system like that of the United States, it is difficult to trace the precise roots of authority. The Constitution, traditions, institutions, and the consensus are but a few of the diverse elements to which theorists attribute authority. Ascertaining the bases of authority in the United States becomes such a problem that some writers speak of authority mainly in terms of "effectiveness." In our second reading, Seymour M. Lipset states: "Effectiveness means actual performance, the extent to which the system satisfies the basic functions of government as most of the population" sees those functions. When the Depression struck during a Republican Administration, the majority of voters saw that party as ineffective in handling the crisis. With a mandate from the people, the Franklin D. Roosevelt Administration exercised unprecedented powers in the search for solutions to economic dislocation. Action, or performance, was uppermost in the public mood during that period.

Another theme of authority, which is more fundamental than Lipset's functional view, is the dedication to legalism. The legacy of English Common Law, reinforced by a long history of respect for the Constitution and for law in general, makes authority and law in the United States almost indistinguishable.

LEGITIMACY AND EFFECTIVENESS

SEYMOUR MARTIN LIPSET

The stability of any given democracy depends not only on economic development but also upon the effectiveness and the legitimacy of its political system. Effectiveness means actual performance, the extent to which the system satisfies the basic functions of government as most of the population and such powerful groups within it as big business or the armed forces see them. Legitimacy involves the capacity of the system to engender and maintain the belief that the existing political institutions are the most appropriate ones for the society. The extent to which contemporary democratic political systems are legitimate depends in large measure upon the ways in which the key issues which have historically divided the society have been resolved.

While effectiveness is primarily instrumental, legitimacy is evaluative. Groups regard a political system as legitimate or illegitimate according to the way in which its values fit with theirs. Important segments of the German Army, civil service, and aristocratic classes rejected the Weimar Republic, not because it was ineffective, but because its symbolism and basic values negated their own. Legitimacy, in and of itself, may be associated with many forms of political organization, including oppressive ones. Feudal societies, before the advent of industrialism, undoubtedly enjoyed the basic loyalty of most of their members. Crises of legitimacy are primarily a recent historical phenomenon, following the rise of sharp cleavages among groups which are able, because of mass communication, to organize around different values than those previously considered to be the only acceptable ones.

A crisis of legitimacy is a crisis of change. Therefore, its roots must be sought in the character of change in modern society. Crises of legitimacy occur during a transition to a new social structure, if (1) the *status* of major conservative institutions is threatened during the period of structural change; (2) all the major groups in the society do not have access to the political system in the transitional period, or at least as soon as they develop political demands. After a new social structure is established, if the new system is unable to sustain the expectations of major groups (on the grounds of "effectiveness") for a long enough period to develop legitimacy upon the new basis, a new crisis may develop.

Tocqueville gives a graphic description of the first general type of loss of legitimacy, referring mainly to countries which moved from aristocratic monarchies to democratic republics: ". . . epochs sometimes occur in the life of a nation when the old customs of a people are changed, public morality is destroyed, religious belief shaken, and the spell of tradition broken . . ." The citizens then have "neither the instinctive patriotism of a monarchy nor the reflecting patriotism of a republic; . . . they have stopped between the two in the midst of confusion and distress." [1]

---

[1] Alexis de Tocqueville, *Democracy in America* (New York: Alfred A. Knopf, Vintage ed., 1945), I, 251–52.

If, however, the status of major conservative groups and symbols is not threatened during this transitional period, even though they lose most of their power, democracy seems to be much more secure. And thus we have the absurd fact that ten out of the twelve stable European and English-speaking democracies are monarchies. Great Britain, Sweden, Norway, Denmark, the Netherlands, Belgium, Luxembourg, Australia, Canada, and New Zealand are kingdoms, or dominions of a monarch, while the only republics which meet the conditions of stable democratic procedures are the United States and Switzerland, plus Uruguay in Latin America.

The preservation of the monarchy has apparently retained for these nations the loyalty of the aristocratic, traditionalist, and clerical sectors of the population which resented increased democratization and equalitarianism. And by accepting the lower strata and not resisting to the point where revolution might be necessary, the conservative orders won or retained the loyalty of the new "citizens." In countries where monarchy was overthrown by revolution, and orderly succession was broken, forces aligned with the throne have sometimes continued to refuse legitimacy to republican successors down to the fifth generation or more.

The one constitutional monarchy which became a fascist dictatorship, Italy, was, like the French Republic, considered illegitimate by major groups in the society. . . . Both the Italian and French democracies have had to operate for much of their histories without loyal support from important groups in their societies, on both the left and the right. Thus one main source of legitimacy lies in the continuity of important traditional integrative institutions during a transitional period in which new institutions are emerging.

The second general type of loss of legitimacy is related to the ways in which different societies handle the "entry into politics" crisis—the decision as to when new social groups shall obtain access to the political process. In the nineteenth century these new groups were primarily industrial workers; in the twentieth, colonial elites and peasant peoples. Whenever new groups become politically active (*e.g.,* when the workers first seek access to economic and political power through economic organization and the suffrage, when the *bourgeoisie* demand access to and participation in government, when colonial elites insist on control over their own system), easy access to the *legitimate* political institutions tends to win the loyalty of the new groups to the system, and they in turn can permit the old dominating strata to maintain their own status.

Political systems which deny new strata access to power except by revolution also inhibit the growth of legitimacy by introducing millennial hopes into the political arena. Groups which have to push their

way into the body politic by force are apt to overexaggerate the possibilities which political participation affords. Consequently, democratic
regimes born under such stress not only face the difficulty of being regarded as illegitimate by groups loyal to the *ancien régime* but may
also be rejected by those whose millennial hopes are not fulfilled by the
change. France, where right-wing clericalists have viewed the Republic
as illegitimate and sections of the lower strata have found their expectations far from satisfied, is an example. And today many of the newly
independent nations of Asia and Africa face the thorny problem of
winning the loyalties of the masses to democratic states which can do
little to meet the utopian objectives set by nationalist movements during the period of colonialism and the transitional struggle to independence.

In general, even when the political system is reasonably effective,
if at any time the status of major conservative groups is threatened, or
if access to politics is denied to emerging groups at crucial periods, the
system's legitimacy will remain in question. On the other hand, a breakdown of effectiveness, repeatedly or for a long period, will endanger
even a legitimate system's stability.

A major test of legitimacy is the extent to which given nations
have developed a common "secular political culture," mainly national
rituals and holidays. The United States has developed a common homo-
geneous culture in the veneration accorded the Founding Fathers, Abraham Lincoln, Theodore Roosevelt, and their principles. These common
elements, to which all American politicians appeal, are not present in
all democratic societies. In some European countries, the left and the
right have a different set of symbols and different historical heroes. . . .

. . .

The political experiences of different countries in the early 1930s
illustrate the effect of other combinations. In the late 1920s, neither
the German nor the Austrian republic was held legitimate by large and
powerful segments of its population. Nevertheless, both remained reasonably effective. . . . When the effectiveness of various governments
broke down in the 1930s, those societies which were high on the scale
of legitimacy remained democratic, while such countries as Germany,
Austria, and Spain lost their freedom, and France narrowly escaped a
similar fate. . . . The military defeat of 1940 underlined French democracy's low position on the scale of legitimacy. It was the sole defeated democracy which furnished large-scale support for a Quisling
regime.

. . . From a short-range point of view, a highly effective but
illegitimate system, such as a well-governed colony, is more unstable
than regimes which are relatively low in effectiveness and high in legiti-

macy. The social stability of a nation like Thailand, despite its periodic *coups d'état,* stands out in sharp contrast to the situation in neighboring former colonial nations. On the other hand, prolonged effectiveness over a number of generations may give legitimacy to a political system. In the modern world, such effectiveness means primarily constant economic development. Those nations which have adapted most successfully to the requirements of an industrial system have the fewest internal political strains, and have either preserved their traditional legitimacy or developed strong new symbols.

The social and economic structure which Latin America inherited from the Iberian peninsula prevented it from following the lead of the former English colonies, and its republics never developed the symbols and aura of legitimacy. In large measure, the survival of the new political democracies of Asia and Africa will depend on their ability to meet the needs of their populations over a prolonged period, which will probably mean their ability to cope with industrialization.

In Europe when writers like Rousseau were rejecting authority based upon hereditary monarchies, the United States became the laboratory for testing new ideas concerning the rights of man. Jerome Hall explains that not only did European writers admire the noble experiment in the New World, but that Americans came to view themselves as unique in their pursuit of freedom.

AUTHORITY IN ITS AMERICAN PHASE:
Its Originality, and Some Speculations

JEROME HALL

When Americans first learned through their studies of history and philosophy how real the limitation of authority is in every case, they

Reprinted from Jerome Hall in Authority, *ed. Carl J. Friedrich for the American Society of Political and Legal Philosophy (New York: Atherton Press, 1958), pp. 20–27, by permission of the author.*

conceived the further idea of setting up in a written constitution a system of limited powers that would make quite sure of the new authority for their union as a free people. The division of the powers of government would be the Americans' own special guarantee of personal liberty. Besides choosing their own government from time to time in elections, besides fostering a good education in principles, they hoped, by their deliberate artifice of distributing powers, to make some advance upon the melancholy history of human authority and hold forth a fresh hope to mankind with their great experiment in "free government."

But there is far more merit in the early American experiment than this mere device of government. A more careful examination of the Americans' own thinking about authority reveals a richer and more balanced view of it than has long been traditional in the subsequent American ethos. They actually started a theory of authority which may be more useful to us now than has yet been realized.

We should recall some well-known phrases of the debates in the Convention and the *Federalist*. "All authority is derived from the people." *From* the people, but where is it lodged? First, with honor and respect, in the Constitution itself, the fundamental law organizing the government. Then in the government: "The express authority of the people alone could give due validity of the government." [1] Through the Constitution the authority of the United States is distributed to the several parts of the federal government. Furthermore, in cases of conflicts of authority, a recourse to the people, the source of authority, was anticipated: "As the people are the only legitimate foundation of power, and it is from them that the Constitutional character is derived . . . to recur to the same original authority . . . wherever any one of the departments may commit encroachments on the chartered authorities of the others . . ." [2] Thus constitutional amendments needed to be ratified by the people through their states or through special conventions. The obvious features of the early American experiment are, then, that all authority is derived from the people and that it is delegated and distributed in accordance with the law which they have previously authorized in the manner prescribed.

The design of the Constitution of the United States was being drawn up in the light of experience with the previously established constitutions of the states. John Adams had been, for instance, the "principal engineer" of the Constitution of Massachusetts which had been adopted in June 1780 while he was absent in France. . . .

Why copy the English system division of powers, the critics asked,

---

[1] James Madison, *The Federalist*, XLIII.

[2] *The Federalist*, XLIX.

when America was a distinct nation with an individual life of its own conditioned by the many different factors which Montesquieu had taught men to take account of in their political arrangements and lawmaking? The American nation was not one in which the traditional class system of kings and lords and commoners was repeated. It was one nation, and why not conceive of it with power indivisible instead of divided powers which were only necessary where there were already established and traditional parties of interest? Why could it not be sovereign people functioning as a democracy? Why not unified central government without the oft-demonstrated fatal weakness of the federal form?

Adams and his fellow statesmen were taking a distinctively American "line" and were more or less conscious of it. They knew that they had an alternative between the British and the French conceptions of government. But their alternative theory had to be worked out through laborious argument and debate which on that occasion furnished as good an example of practical philosophy as there ever had been in western history.

The spirit rather than the letter of the British constitution persisted in the American plan of government. That spirit had sounded forth in the triumphant words of John Wildman in the Putney Army Debates of 1647: "Authority hath been broken into pieces." The Puritans and others meant to keep it so, and the British-Americans were like-minded. The detested memory of the government of a single divine-right authority lived long in their traditions, and their lawyers were well schooled in the history of the English revolution and the formation of its constitutional order. . . .

The objection which troubled Adams most in the criticisms of the American Constitution was one which derived from a conjunction of the traditional connotation of sovereignty with the national idea. Turgot, as Adams understood, was for collecting all authority "into one centre, the nation." But what can this mean "when the centre is to be the nation?" All it says is, "the nation will be the authority, and the authority the nation." But why should Adams cavil at that truism . . . are not the people "sovereign"? Yes, Adams concedes, "our people are undoubtedly sovereign," the meaning of which in the context might be more plainly seen if the order were "undoubtedly our people are sovereign," that is, if one insists on talking about sovereignty.[3] But Adams found it "difficult to comprehend" such a proposition as Turgot's that simply identified "the authority" with "the nation." He went on to make his own point that any "collection" of authority (no matter where

---

[3] *The Political Writings of John Adams*, pp. 123–24.

it be placed, in a center or distributed) must come from the voluntary agreement of individuals "to form themselves into a nation, people, community, or body politic, and to be governed." [4] Thus the authority must be conceived to be a constituted thing, set up for specific purposes of government. It is a resultant of a nation's will—the substantive result, to put it differently, of an action: "We the people authorise . . . ."

Adams was trying to avoid a simple identification of the authority of the people with the sovereignty of the people. One can declare that all authority derives from the people and still not be committed to the alien doctrine that the people themselves act as a sovereign, exercising authority as one body with undivided power, performing all the functions of government. The reasons for saying "alien" is that the smell of absoluteness clung to the notion of sovereignty which had been defined by Bodin, Grotius, and many others in that line, as the power to make laws "without the consent of those governed," independently of anybody on earth, either within or without the state, that is, in reality, unlimited power. To substitute the nation for a personal sovereign is not to change the meaning of such sovereign authority. Moreover, if the authority of the people is thought of as always inherent in the whole body politic, then the very significance of the original act of constituting an authority and delegating it is lost. All authority must be determinate and vested in a particular body of officers who are to perform certain duties of government and who are responsible to the nation whence they derive their power and authority. It is possible to think of such responsible government with limited powers without having recourse to the concept of sovereignty which has quite different connotations and implications.

In the days of constitution-making a distinction between authority and sovereignty was scarcely made. During the Constitutional Convention various men versed in politics and philosophy insisted on talking about sovereignty, which seems often to have confused the discussion rather than advanced matters. The resurrection of the sovereignty idea was inevitable when those who were jealous of the powers of the separate states sought to bolster their position with the claim to the independent sovereignty of the states. The skill with which Madison and others firmly but diplomatically worked around these diversions to the formation of a genuine union of the people of the United States while retaining a proper authority for the states is one of the exciting pieces not only of political history but of philosophical dialogue in actual affairs. But, in not confronting at that time the difference between authority as they were working with it and sovereignty, the founding fathers left it for the crisis of civil war, and even then no decision was made as to whether

---

[4] *The Political Writings of John Adams*, p. 124.

Americans thinking about government should develop and apply the concept of authority with which they had begun or should continue to cling to the notion of sovereignty whose "historic conception" was in a Europe of an earlier absolutist phase before freedom and democracy had much meaning. . . .

The people, according to the early American formula, are the "source of authority." Do they themselves not have as a people that which they can delegate to certain specific bodies of the government? Yes and no. Of course the authority is theirs that issues from them to the agents who are to exercise it according to the law. But only when it is actually issued and effective is it authority; what it is before that actual "emanation" is not properly called "authority." The nation or the people are the "source." The metaphor is significant: a source is like a spring running down a hillside, taking its courses according to the lay of the land. There is power in it, but the power is delivered only through the particular sluices into which it is channeled for purposes of doing work. Authority should thus always be thought of as power vested in a *determinate* agency, either in the law or in the various bodies that perform the functions of government. The people or nation are the great indeterminate reservoir of all the power that is so put to work. . . .

Acts to determine authority are required throughout the life and history of the nation. The Constitution provides for a redetermination of the fundamental law through the procedure of amendment, which involves a reference to the people and a requirement of substantial majority ratifying it. Within the activities of government there is redetermination, at frequent and stated intervals, of those especially who shall exercise executive and legislative power. The determinate authority, whether of the law or of the offices of government, is thus only relatively so—one can never be sure in important vital issues which one or whether any of our institutions "has authority." A redetermination of where the authority of the people lies and who is properly acting or speaking in their name is always likely to become a problem of the day. What this means is that "the people" is not merely a substitution for the "sovereign" of the older European tradition, and further that sovereignty in a democratic society is a legendary survival. The sovereignty of the states is an ancient myth resurrected for other than either legal or peace-making reasons. The doctrine "all authority derives from the people" carries with it the consequence, then, that the original authority is indeterminate, not absolutely fixed on anything, and that it is necessary in every generation, or whenever serious issues arise, to redetermine and redefine what the relevant authority is and in which body it is vested. Authority never settles anything really important, because when matters are very important, we have to settle the authority itself which is to function in the case.

Authority in its American phase, so viewed, abolishes not only divinely authorized royal lineage and perpetual rule but also any absolutely fixed rights and powers of the government. Constitutional, democratic authority requires that the working of such a flexible system of government with shifting of the order of authority within the system shall be carried on by due process of law and not arbitrarily or recklessly. Such a system calls for an incalculable amount of labor on the part of those engaged in the work of the statesman, and others in the work of the education of the nation. For in the end, whatever form authority may take depends upon the kind of knowledge that is the fruit of free discussion and upon the patience and good will that are necessary both to the holding of public discussions, in meetings or in the press or in conventions, and to seeing the decisions through. The nation is always in the making, and so is liberty, so is authority.

While the minds of many Americans love to dwell on the accomplishments of the nation, achieved by an unwavering attachment to the Constitution, other Americans charge that the ideals described by Jerome Hall in the previous selection have not been fulfilled. Donald McDonald reflects upon the disillusionment exhibited by a large number of young people. A loss of confidence in authority in the United States as seen in the youth revolution is traceable to the inability or unwillingness of successive administrations to solve the pressing problems of racial conflict, the war in Vietnam, poverty, and pollution.

In keeping with the theme of the book, before we proceed with the selection by Donald McDonald it might be well to note that resistance to authority or moral judgments about authority are not new to American political history. To illustrate this one can look at the following words of Henry David Thoreau, written in the mid-nineteenth century. His essay *Civil Disobedience* inspired such political leaders as Mahatma Gandhi and Dr. Martin Luther King in their programs of passive resistance:

> The mass of men serve the state thus, not as men mainly, but as machines, with their bodies. They are the standing army, and the militia, jailers, constables, *posse comitatus*, etc. In most cases there is no free exercise whatever of the judgment or of the moral sense; but they put themselves on a level with wood and earth and stones; and wooden men can perhaps be manufactured that will serve the purpose as well. Such command no more respect than men of straw or a lump of dirt. They have the same sort of worth only as horses and dogs. Yet such as these even are commonly esteemed good citizens. Others—as most legis-

lators, politicians, lawyers, ministers, and office holders—serve the state chiefly with their heads; and as they rarely make any moral distinctions, they are as likely to serve the devil, without *intending* it, as God. A very few—as heroes, patriots, martyrs, reformers in the great sense, and *men*—serve the state with their consciences also, and so necessarily resist it for the most part; and they are commonly treated as enemies by it.

YOUTH IN REVOLT:
What Kind of Revolution?

DONALD McDONALD [1]

A persistent question—on the minds of adults, if not young people— is whether there will be violent political revolution in the classic sense of a seizure of the political and governing power in the society and a rearrangement of the distribution of that power. When the question is asked that way, the answer must almost inevitably be no. Even if the young people were not disorganized, even if they were not splintered into liberals and radicals, crazies and destructivists, their seizure capabilities are almost nil. But their capacity for disruption through confrontation and through hit-and-run terrorism (actual and threatened) has already been demonstrated. However, disruption does not necessarily lead to seizure of political power, nor does it hold much promise of radicalizing and enlisting the sympathies of the massive middle class in the American society. Far from it. American industrial workers and their sons have shown that, if provoked, they will protect their jobs by any means from the threats posed by anti-war demonstrators; and they are joined by craft construction workers who are determined to keep blacks out of their unions.

If violent confrontation politics persist and intensify and if society becomes ungovernable and human life is in constant jeopardy, what seems most likely is a militarily imposed "order," a more or less continuing garrison existence under martial law. According to Irving Howe,

Reprinted by permission from July/August 1970 issue of The Center Magazine, *a publication of the Center for the Study of Democratic Institutions, Santa Barbara, California.*

---

[1] Mr. McDonald is Executive Editor of *The Center Magazine* of the Center for the Study of Democratic Institutions.

violent confrontation politics will only awaken sleeping dogs it would be well to let lie.

The political revolution question can be asked in a more realistic, but perhaps unanswerable, way: Is the youthful cultural revolution so deep, pervasive, and irresistible that it will, in time, work similarly deep, pervasive, and irresistible changes in the political and economic life of the American society? Even posing the question that way is not entirely satisfactory, since it implies that the cultural revolution can be thought of as purely cultural, with no political character and no ideological content. Young people do not come in such neat, exclusive categories. But the cultural character of their revolution; the ethical, moral, psychological, and aesthetic qualities that are summed up in the word "life-style," may in the end—if the society can hold itself together long enough—work profound and permanent change. Much will depend on the extent to which the activists will carry their political militancy and the way in which the adult community will respond to both the political militancy and the cultural innovations.

Admittedly there is little justification for thinking that the young people will exercise restraint or that their elders will exhibit understanding. There may be symbolic speech in the politics of confrontation and the counter-politics of repression. And such symbolism may be a necessary prelude to dialogue, but it is not dialogue. As this is written, the American college students, almost as one, are enraged by the Ohio National Guard's killing of four Kent State University students who had gathered on their own campus to protest President Nixon's spreading of the war into Cambodia. The killing followed by a few days Mr. Nixon's characterization of campus anti-war protesters as "bums."

Other adult responses to the young, though less lethal and dramatic, are no less adamant. The severity of marijuana laws, the writing of new constitutionally dubious conspiracy laws, the refusal of senior faculty members to let university students have a genuine voice in the way their educational program is conducted, the manner in which Chicago police were absolved for the brutality they visited on the young and the innocent bystanders on the streets during the 1968 Democratic Convention—all these adult reactions must seem to the young to constitute an insurmountable barrier between themselves and their elders.

One thinks of Oswald Spengler's description of younger and older cultures in *The Decline of the West:* "By the term 'historical pseudomorphosis' I propose to designate those cases in which an older alien lies so massively over the land that a young culture cannot get its breath and fails not only to achieve pure and specific expression-forms, but even to develop fully its own self-consciousness. All that wells up from the depths of the young soul is cast in the old molds, young feelings stiffen in senile practices, and instead of expanding its own creative power, it can only hate the distant power with a hate that grows to be monstrous."

But the young today are in fact achieving their own "pure and specific expression-forms," they are developing fully their "own self-consciousness." Autocratic society is dead (though a lot more heads will undoubtedly be bloodied before its death is universally recognized). Also, the young have already forced many reluctant college and university administrations and faculties to make reforms that these educators now acknowledge were long overdue. One is therefore entitled to entertain the hope that in the cultural revolution both the young and the old will find it possible to accommodate each other, and in the accommodation perhaps learn to trust each other and, in that trust, to make the nation's political behavior square with the youth-heightened moral vision, and its economic arrangements coincide with the official rhetoric about equality of opportunity.

Almost a hundred and fifty years ago, Alexis de Tocqueville wrote in *Democracy in America* something that is especially appropriate today as we seek not only for meaning but also for some hope from the contemporary scene:

"It is evident to all alike," de Tocqueville wrote, "that a great democratic revolution is going on among us, but all do not look at it in the same light. To some it appears to be novel but accidental, and, as such, they hope it may still be checked; to others it seems irresistible, because it is the most uniform, the most ancient, and the most permanent tendency that is to be found in history."

Authority and Revolution

Respect for the law is noticeably absent in politically unstable societies. The pattern for political change in such societies involves the instrument of force. In the United States, political leaders may earnestly seek to uphold the pronouncement that this is a society ruled by law, but in many countries there is no such tradition of law. Lipset explains, for example, that the Latin American republics "never developed the symbols and aura of legitimacy." Simon Bolivar, the leader of the Latin American wars for independence, once complained, "Constitutions are but scraps of paper." Recent upheavals in Cuba and the Dominican Republic illustrate the interaction of instability and the nature of power.

Toward the end of 1958, the Batista regime in Cuba collapsed, leaving a power vacuum soon to be filled by Fidel Castro's charismatic leadership.

One apparent facet of this political change was the emerging support from the population for a movement striving to become the legitimate authority of Cuba. This rise to power was accompanied by the decline of the existing government's effective control over the population. On the other hand, in the Dominican Republic during April 1965, a civil war resulted in a stalemate between two diverse factions with neither group strong enough to seize power.

In comparing the Cuban and Dominican situations, we need to inquire into the sources of authority available in each country at the time when the established governments collapsed. In Cuba, apart from the activities of various revolutionary groups, the major source of authority arose from the enormous charismatic qualities of Fidel Castro. In the Latin American political style of the *caudillo*, or strong leader, Castro was able to speak as the legitimate ruler of Cuba. Moreover, at least until January 1959, Castro had the enthusiastic support of the majority of the Cuban people.

There was no strong leadership in the Dominican Republic when the Reid Cabral government fell. Forces of the left and right battled to a standstill without much prospect that either faction would be capable of assuming power. An apathetic peasantry did not throw its weight to the side of either conflicting group in the capital city of Santo Domingo. Even after intervention from the United States, politics in the Dominican Republic has remained badly fragmented.

The repressive measures of Batista and Trujillo, the former dictators of Cuba and the Dominican Republic respectively, inspired reactions from politically active elements of the population, especially young people and intellectuals, to challenge the authority of those regimes. In each case, the loss of control in an unstable society reveals the fabric of authorty and illustrates how dictatorship relies upon the maximum application of power while expecting acquiescence rather than support from the majority of the people.

A pattern may be observed in pre-revolutionary societies. Crane Brinton in *Anatomy of Revolution* discusses some of the signs present in societies on the brink of revolution. You may reexamine your old notions about revolution after looking at Brinton's findings on collapsing regimes.

THE ANATOMY OF REVOLUTION

CRANE BRINTON

As good children of our age, we are bound to start any such study as this with the economic situation. All of us, no matter how little sympathy we may have with organized Communism, betray the extent of Marx's influence in the social studies—and of the influences that worked on Marx —by the naturalness with which we ask the question: "What had economic interests to do with it all?" Since Beard's study of our Constitution, many American scholars have indeed seemed to feel this is the only question they need ask.

Now it is incontestable that in all four of the societies we are studying, the years preceding the outbreak of revolution witnessed unusually serious economic, or at least financial, difficulties of a special kind. The first two Stuarts were in perpetual conflict with their parliaments over taxes. The years just before 1640 resounded with complaints about Ship Money, benevolences, tonnage and poundage, and other terms now strange to us, but once capable of making a hero of a very rich Buckinghamshire gentleman named John Hampden, who was financially quite able to pay much larger taxes than he did. Americans need not be reminded of the part trouble over taxation played in the years just before the shot fired at Concord defied all the laws of acoustics. "No taxation without representation" may be rejected by all up-to-date historians as in itself an adequate explanation of the beginnings of the American Revolution, but the fact remains that it was in the 1770's a slogan capable of exciting our fathers to action. In 1789 the French Estates-General, the calling of which precipitated the revolution, was made unavoidable by the bad financial state of the government. Official France in 1789 was financially in as unhappy a way as, until our own times, one would have believed it possible for a government to be. In Russia in 1917 financial collapse did not perhaps stand out so prominently because the Czarist regime had achieved an all-round collapse in all fields of governmental activity, from war to village administration. But three years of war had

Reprinted from the book The Anatomy of Revolution *by Crane Brinton.* © *1938, 1952 by Prentice-Hall, Inc. Published by Prentice-Hall, Inc., Englewood Cliffs. N.J.*

put such a strain on Russian finances that, even with the support of the Allies, high prices and scarcity were by 1917 the most obvious factors in the general tension.

Yet in all of these societies, it is the *government* that is in financial difficulties, not the societies themselves. To put the matter negatively, our revolutions did not occur in societies economically backward, or in societies undergoing widespread economic misery or depression. You will not find in these societies of the old regime anything like unusually widespread economic want. In a specific instance, of course, the standard against which want or depressions is measured must be the standard of living more or less acceptable to a given group at a given time. What satisfied an English peasant in 1640 would be misery and want for an English farm laborer in 1952. It is possible that certain groups in a society may be in unusual want even though statistically that abstraction "society as a whole" is enjoying an increasing—and almost equally abstract—"national income." Nevertheless, when national income is rapidly increasing, someone does get the benefit. . . .

Even in our imperfect statistics we can distinguish short-term cyclical variations, and it seems clear that in some respects, notably in the wheat harvest, 1788–89 was a bad year. It was, however, by no means a deep trough year, as 1932 was for this country. If businessmen in eighteenth-century France had kept charts and made graphs, the lines would have mounted with gratifying consistency through most of the period preceding the French Revolution. Now this prosperity was certainly most unevenly shared. The people who got the lion's share of it seem to have been the merchants, bankers, businessmen, lawyers, peasants who ran their own farms as businesses—the middle class, as we have come to call it. It was precisely these prosperous people who in the 1780's were loudest against the government, most reluctant to save it by paying taxes or lending it money.

Yet the notion persists that somehow or other the men who made the French Revolution must have suffered serious economic deprivation. A very distinguished contemporary scholar, C. E. Labrousse, has spent his life struggling with research into time-series of prices, [applying] economic indices, and the like during the second half of the eighteenth century in France, seeking to prove that there were sufficiently bad price squeezes on little and middling men so that they were spurred to revolution by actual want or at least hardship. Despite his hard work, his general thesis is not convincing. The men who made the French Revolution were getting higher and higher real income—so much that they wanted a great deal more. And above all, as we shall see, they wanted much that cannot be measured by the economist.

In America, of course, with an empty continent available for the distressed, general economic conditions in the eighteenth century show increasing wealth and population, with economic distress a purely relative matter. There can be no talk of starvation, of grinding poverty in the New England of the Stamp Act. Even the minor fluctuations of the business cycle fail to coincide with the revolution, and the early years of the 1770's were distinctly years of prosperity. There were economic stresses and strains in colonial America, as we shall soon see, but no class ground down with poverty.

Nor is it easy to argue that early Stuart England was less prosperous than late Tudor England had been. There is rather evidence that, especially in the years of personal government which preceded the Long Parliament, England was notably prosperous. Ramsay Muir writes that "England had never known a more steady or more widely diffused prosperity and the burden of taxation was less than in any other country. The coming revolution was certainly not due to economic distress."

Even in the Russia of 1917, apart from the shocking breakdown of the machinery of government under war strain, the productive capacity of society as a whole was certainly greater than at any other time in Russian history; and to take again the long view, the economic graphs had all been mounting for Russia as a whole in the late nineteenth and early twentieth centuries, and the progress in trade and production since the abortive revolution of 1905 had been notable. Hardly any non-Marxist historian nowadays questions the fact that the Russia of the first three Dumas (1906–12) was on its way upward as a Western society.

Our revolutions, then, clearly were not born in societies economically retrograde; on the contrary, they took place in societies economically progressive. This does not, of course, mean that no groups within these societies cherished grievances mainly economic in character. Two main foci for economic motives of discontent seem to stand out. First, and much the less important, is the actual misery of certain groups in a given society. No doubt in all our societies, even in America, there was a submarginal group of poor people whose release from certain forms of restraint is a very important feature of the revolution itself. But in studying the preliminary signs of revolution, these people are not very important. French republican historians have long insisted on the importance of the bad harvest of 1788, the cold winter of 1788–89, and the consequent sufferings of the poor. Bread was relatively dear in that spring when the Estates-General first assembled. There was apparently a tightening up of business conditions in America in 1774–75, but certainly nothing like widespread distress or unemployment. The local sufferings of Boston, considerable under the Port Bill, were really a part of the revolution itself, and not a sign. The winter of 1916–17 was certainly a bad one in Russia, with food rationing in all the cities.

The important thing to note, however, is that French and Russian history are filled with famines, plagues, bad harvests, sometimes local, sometimes national in sweep, many of which were accompanied by sporadic rioting, but in each case only one by revolution. In neither the English nor the American Revolution do we find even this degree of localized want or famine. Clearly, then, the economic distress of the underprivileged, though it may well accompany a revolutionary situation, is not one of the symptoms we need dwell upon. This the subtler Marxists themselves recognize, and Trotsky has written, "In reality, the mere existence of privations is not enough to cause an insurrection; if it were, the masses would always be in revolt."

Of much greater importance is the existence among a group, or groups, of a feeling that prevailing conditions limit or hinder their economic activity. We are especially aware of this element in our American Revolution, and Professor A. M. Schlesinger, Sr., has shown how the prosperous merchants, their immediate interests damaged by the new imperial policy of the British government, led an agitation against the legislation of 1764 and 1765 and helped stir up a discontent among the less well-to-do which these merchants later found a bit embarrassing. No doubt, too, that many of the firm spots in the very uneven and wavering policy of the British government—the Stamp Act and subsequent disorders, the announced intention of enforcing the Navigation Act, and so on—did have momentary ill effects on business, did throw men out of work. The currency question was of course mismanaged in a day when common sense did not very effectively supplement ignorance of economic processes. The colonies were always lacking in specie, and business enterprise suffered from this lack. Paper money, to which recourse was inevitable, was also an inevitable source of further quarrels between governors and governed.

The working of economic motives to revolt among possessing classes normally inclined to support existing institutions is especially clear among the aristocrats of tidewater Virginia. Largely dependent on a single crop (tobacco), used to a high standard of living, increasingly indebted to London bankers, many of the planters hoped to recoup their fortunes in the western lands they regarded as clearly belonging to Virginia. George Washington's own involvements in western land speculations make one of the favorite topics of the debunkers. By the Quebec Act of 1774, however, the British government took the trans-Allegheny lands north of the Ohio from Virginia and other claimant colonies, and incorporated them with Canada. This act gave a grievance to others besides the planter-speculator. The closing of this frontier was also an offense to a class perhaps normally more inclined to revolt—the restless woodsmen and fur traders, and the only slightly less restless small pioneer farmers who had already occupied the Appalachian valleys, and were ready to pour over into the Kentucky and Ohio country. The Quebec Act in itself does not, of course, explain the American Revolution; but taken with a long series of other acts, the Stamp Act, the Navigation act, the Molasses Act, it accounts for the feeling so evident among active and ambitious groups in America that British rule was an unnecessary and incalculable restraint, an obstacle to their full success in life.

In France the years preceding 1789 are marked by a series of measures which antagonized different groups. With striking awkwardness, the government offered with one hand what it withdrew with the other. Tax-reform efforts, never completely carried through, offended privileged groups without pleasing the underprivileged. Turgot's attempted introduction of laissez-faire offended all the vested interests of the old guilds; his failure to make his reforms stick offended the intellectuals and the progressives generally. . . .

Thus we see that certain economic grievances—usually not in the form of economic distress, but rather a feeling on the part of some of the chief enterprising groups that their opportunities for getting on in this world are unduly limited by political arrangements—would seem to be one of the symptoms of revolution. These feelings must, of course, be raised to an effective social pitch by propaganda, pressure-group action, public meetings, and preferably a few good dramatic riots, like the Boston Tea Party. As we shall see, these grievances, however close they are to the pocketbook, must be made respectable, must touch the soul. What is really but a restraint on a rising and already successful group or on several such groups, must appear as rank injustice toward everyone in the society. Men may revolt partly or even mainly because they are hindered, or, to use Dr. George Pettee's expressive word, *cramped*, in their economic activities; but to the world—and, save for a very few hypocrites, also to themselves—they must appear *wronged*. "Cramp" must undergo moral transfiguration before men will revolt. Revolutions cannot do without the word "justice" and the sentiments it arouses.

All this, however, is rather less than what the Marxists seem to mean when they talk about the revolutions of the seventeenth, eighteenth, and nineteenth centuries as deliberately the work of a class-conscious bourgeoisie. Not having the benefit of the writings of Marx to go by, nor indeed those of the still little-known Adam Smith, even eighteenth-century revolutionists and discontented spirits used a very non-economic vocabulary. . . .

To sum up so far, we look at economic life in these societies in the years preceding revolution, we note first, that they have been on the whole prosperous; second, that their governments are chronically short of money—shorter, that is, than most governments usually are; third, that certain groups feel that governmental policies are against their particular economic interests; fourth, that, except in Russia, class economic interests are not openly advanced in propaganda as a motive for attempting to overturn existing political and social arrangements. It is interesting to note here that R. B. Merriman, in a study of six seventeenth-century revolutions in England, France, the Netherlands, Spain, Portugal, and Naples, finds that they all had in common a financial origin, all began as protests against taxation.

If we now turn from the stresses and strains of economic life to the actual workings of the machinery of government, we find a much clearer situation. Here, again, we must not posit perfection as a normal condition. Government here on earth is at best a rough-and-ready thing, and the governed will always find something to grumble about, from favoritism in distributing low-number automobile license plates to post-office pen points. But there are obviously degrees of governmental inefficiency, and degrees of patience on the part of the governed. In our four societies the governments seem to have been relatively inefficient, and the governed relatively impatient.

Indeed, the near bankruptcy of a government in a prosperous society might be regarded as good *a priori* evidence of its inefficiency, at least in the old days when governments undertook few social or "socialized" services. Totalitarian methods in Germany and Russia suggest that perhaps from now on mere financial bankruptcy need never trouble a government, since the facts of its finances cannot be known. France in 1789 is a striking example of a society the government of which simply no longer works well. For generations French kings and their ministers had fought the particularistic tendencies of the provinces to get out of the control of Paris by devising a whole series of agencies of centralization, which may be said in a sense to run from the *missi dominici* of Charlemagne to the *intendants* of Richelieu and Louis XIV. Almost as if they had been Anglo-Saxons, however, they destroyed very little of the old in the process, so that France in 1789 was like an attic stuffed full of all kinds of old furniture—including some fine new chairs of Turgot's that just wouldn't fit in the living room. We need not go too deeply into the details of the situation, which can perhaps be summed up graphically by saying that in the sense in which you could make a map of the United States showing all our administrative areas—townships, counties, states—you could not possibly make *one* map of the administrative areas of old France. Even the confusion added to an administrative map of the United States by the various, and relatively new, federal commissions, bureaus, agencies, administrations, does not begin to equal that of France in 1789. . . .

All this means that in eighteenth-century France it was very hard to get action from the government, which is one of the most important forms of Dr. Pettee's "cramp." There is told about Louis XV one of those revealing anecdotes the actual historical truth of which is unimportant, since they reflect contemporary opinion of a concrete condition. Traveling in the provinces, his majesty saw that a town hall or some such building in which he was to be received had a leaky roof. "Ah, if I were only a minister, I'd have that fixed," he remarked. A government of which such a tale could be told was perhaps despotic, but most certainly inefficient. In general, it would seem the inefficiency is more readily recognized by those who suffer from it than is the despotism.

The incompetence of the English government under the first two Stuarts is much less clear, but one can safely say that the central government was not as well run, especially under James I, as it had been under Elizabeth. What is most striking in the English situation is the total inadequacy to modern government of a tax system based on the modest needs of a feudal central government. . . .

In America the failure of the machinery was a double one. First, the central colonial administration in Westminster had been allowed to grow in the hit-or-miss fashion Anglophiles have long regarded as the height of political wisdom. In this crisis, however, muddling through clearly was not enough. The attempted reform in colonial administration after the Seven Years' War only made matters worse, as did Turgot's attempted reforms in France, since it was carried out in a series of advances and retreats, cajolings and menaces, blowings-hot and blowings-cold. Second, within most of the colonies the machinery of government had never been properly adjusted to the frontier. The newer western regions of many colonies complained that representation, courts, administrative areas, were rigged in favor of the older seaboard settlements.

The breakdown of Czarist administration is now so much a commonplace that one is tempted to suspect that it has been a bit exaggerated. Looking at the decades preceding 1917—for in all these countries, we have been considering the background of the revolutions and not their actual outbreaks—it seems possible to maintain that the government of Russia in peacetime, at least, was perhaps a bit more of a going concern than the other governments we have been studying. From Catherine the Great to Stolypin a great deal of actual improvement can be seen in Russian government. But one thing is clear from the hundred years preceding 1914, Russia could not organize herself for war, and failure in war had, especially in 1905, brought with it a partial collapse of the machinery of internal administration. We must be very careful here to stick to facts and to avoid judgments which have so insinuated themselves into our awareness of Russia that we regard them as facts.

For our purposes, it is sufficient to note that the Russian *governmental* breakdown, clear in 1917 or even 1916, was by no means clear, say, in 1912.

Finally, one of the most evident uniformities we can record is the effort made in each of our societies to reform the machinery of government. Nothing can be more erroneous than the picture of the old regime as an unregenerate tyranny, sweeping to its end in a climax of despotic indifference to the clamor of its abused subjects. Charles I was working to "modernize" his government, to introduce into England some of the efficient methods of the French. Strafford was in some ways but an unlucky Richelieu, George III and his ministers were trying very hard to pull together the scattered organs of British colonial government. Indeed, it was this attempt at reform, this desire to work out a new colonial "system," that gave the revolutionary movement in America a start. In both France and Russia, there had been a series of attempted reforms, associated with names like Turgot, Malesherbes, Necker, Witte, and Stolypin. It is true that these reforms were incomplete, that they were repealed or nullified by sabotage on the part of the privileged. But they are on record, an essential part of the process that issued on revolution in these countries.

Authority in the Soviet Union

The formal governmental structure in the Soviet Union is a subject of much controversy among observers in the West. Why do the Soviet leaders give lip service to the Constitution of 1936? Why are elections held? Central to the understanding of authority in the Soviet Union is the recognition of the role of the legal façade in that country.

Power in the Soviet Union belongs to the Communist Party. However, the institutions of government, which are parallel at every level with an agency of the Party, serve many functions. The people in the Soviet Union are allowed to participate in the governmental process through such devices as elections, legislative chambers, and people's courts. Admittedly, whatever power these agencies may possess is counteracted by the Party. Nonetheless, there is established an atmosphere of mass participation as a means to win support of the regime from the people. This ostensible inclusion of the people in the political process has a substantial impact upon a population which has never experienced anything but despotism. In these circumstances, the governmental institutions may serve to fulfill Lenin's scheme of having a "transmission belt" by means of which the Party elite keeps in constant communication with the people.

Another source of authority is Marxist-Leninist theory. Soviet leaders look upon this theory as a scientific formula for molding the perfect society. While the masses of the people may not comprehend the full implications of the ideology, they are impressed by scientific advances made by Russia since the Revolution. From the reading by R. Judson Mitchell, one can see that although progress through science may well be one of the chief props for popular acceptance of the regime, social modernization, which accompanies technological advances, has placed strains upon totalitarian politics.

MANAGERIAL POLITICS AND AUTHORITY UNDER MATURING SOVIET TOTALITARIANISM

R. JUDSON MITCHELL

The new Soviet leadership faced four major general problems in 1964: the decline of Soviet great power prestige, resulting in large part from Premier Nikita Khrushchev's adventurist foreign policy, notably his Cuban missile gamble; the fragmentation of the world Communist system and the hostility of China; the difficulties in Soviet economic development and the effects of the East European economic crisis of the early 1960's; and the challenge of maintaining party control in a maturing totalitarian system—control that appeared somewhat threatened both by the effects of the experimentation of the Khrushchev years and by the increasing functional complexity of the Soviet Union's developing social system.

The pattern of response to these major problems by the post-Khrushchev leadership can be broadly characterized as neo-Stalinist. The restoration without fanfare of Stalin's statue outside the Kremlin wall symbolizes the approach of the current Soviet rulers: a low-key totalitarianism that leaves no doubt concerning the realities of power but avoids confrontation whenever possible. There has been a remarkable consistency in this pragmatic politics of consolidation since 1964 and, despite evidence of internal struggle among the leaders, a virtually unbroken facade of harmony and collective leadership, in striking contrast to both the Stalin and Khrushchev eras. Where violent confrontation has occurred, both internally and externally, the outcomes have

R. Judson Mitchell, "Party and Society in the Soviet Union," Current History (October, 1972), 170–74. Reprinted with permission of the author and publisher. © 1972, Current History Inc.

tended to confirm the impression of rationally controlled power-seeking. During 1971–1972, however, certain strains within the Soviet system raise questions concerning the continuing viability of the cautious managerial approach that is characteristic of the current Soviet leadership.

Escalation of the campaign against novelist Aleksandr Solzhenitsyn indicates that dissent is a growing problem for the leadership. Solzhenitsyn was attacked by *Literaturnaya Gazeta* (January, February, and April, 1972) for the publication of his novel *August 1914* by a West German publisher. In the January article, an attempt was made to discredit the Solzhenitsyn family on grounds of its anti-revolutionary social origins; the second and third articles concentrated upon claimed historical inaccuracies in Solzhenitsyn's novel and his alleged pro-German, anti-Russian bias. The April article defended the gains made by Byelorussians under the Communist regime and pointed out the war losses sustained by the Byelorussians at the hands of the Germans, whom Solzhenitsyn was claimed to favor. The appeal to nationalism in these articles is not surprising in view of the increasingly close connection between nationalities problems and dissent related to civil liberties that has become apparent within the past year. This connection can be observed in the continuing tension between the regime and Soviet Jews and in unrest in the Ukraine and Lithuania.

Expulsion of Dissidents

The Committee for State Security (KGB) has recently forced Jewish (and in some cases non-Jewish) dissidents to emigrate to Israel in lieu of indefinite imprisonment. Because of discrimination within the Soviet Union, emigration of Soviet Jews to Israel has greatly increased within the past two years. The KGB has used this emigration as a cover for the expulsion of political dissidents, many of whom have no real connection with Zionism or with Israel. The most notable of these cases has been that of Yosif Brodsky, a Leningrad poet and a leader in the movement for the expansion of civil liberties. Brodsky, who spent a year in a labor colony above the Arctic Circle in the 1960's for publication in the underground press *(samizdat)*, was forced to emigrate in June, 1972.

The Ukraine has long been a source of trouble for the Kremlin; Ukrainian nationalism has apparently not diminished very much after 50 years of repression. Recently, many prominent members of the Ukrainian intelligentsia have become closely identified with the civil liberties movement. The Moscow response has been a predictable crackdown on dissidents. In November, 1970, the historian Valentin Moroz was sentenced to nine years' imprisonment and five years in exile. In mid-January, 1972, a wave of arrests of some 40 dissidents in Moscow, Leningrad, Kiev, and elsewhere included such prominent Ukrainian writers as Vyacheslav Choronovil, author of the *Choronovil Papers,* which recounted the illegalities of earlier arrests and trials of Ukrainian dissidents and had been published in the West, and the literary critic Ivan Svitlichny. The house of Ivan Dzhuba, another prominent literary critic, was searched; in March, Dzhuba was expelled from the Writers Union of the Ukraine. Waves of repression have occurred periodically in the Ukraine since 1965. It thus appears that elimination of the obvious manifestations of political dissent with nationalist overtones in the Ukraine is a continuing important goal for the current leadership. While the regime has certainly not stamped out opposition in the Ukraine, the movement for civil liberties there has been at least temporarily checked by the virtually complete removal of the dissidents' leadership.

Two days of rioting by several thousand youths in the Lithuanian city of Kaunas in mid-May, 1972, pointed to a link between nationalism and the drive for civil liberties in the Baltic area. The rioting was set off by the self-immolation of a 20-year-old Lithuanian Catholic, Roman Kalanta, who apparently committed suicide to protest discrimination against Lithuanian Catholics. Soldiers had to be called in to assist police in suppressing the riot by the young Lithuanians who shouted "Freedom for Lithuania" as they clashed with the security forces. The situation in Lithuania had been simmering since late March, when some 17,000 Lithuanian Catholics signed a petition to the United Nations complaining about discrimination and denial of religious freedom.

Reports in the Soviet press containing criticisms of party organizational work in Georgia demonstrate that the top party leadership is also dissatisfied with the continuing strength of Georgian nationalism and the maintenance of a high degree of cultural autonomy by the Georgians; party officials in that republic have been sharply criticized for failure properly to inculcate party members and citizens with a "Marxist-Leninist world-view" and the spirit of "proletarian internationalism."

These developments are rather embarrassing to the leadership in view of repeated claims that the Soviet Union has solved its nationalities problem and that the regime enjoys almost universal consensual support. While the proportion of Soviet citizens directly involved in political dissent remains, of course, small, the problem is growing and can no longer be lightly dismissed by the leadership. The general roundup of dissidents in the Moscow area before President Richard Nixon's May, 1972, visit shows that the leadership is highly sensitive to the threat of negative effects upon the regime's international image posed by overt expressions of discontent. The arrest of historian Pyotr Yakir in late June by the KGB makes it clear that the Kremlin is determined to silence dissent, whatever the cost to its image. Yakir, the most outspoken of Moscow's dissidents, had long enjoyed an unusual degree of protection because his father was General Iona Yakir, who was executed in Stalin's purge of the Red Army and posthumously rehabilitated by Khrushchev. The obvious evocation of Stalinism involved in a move against someone like Yakir no longer deters the leadership.

The Party and Coercive Forces in the System

The drive against dissent would appear to give the police a greater functional role in the system than has been the case at any time since 1953. This raises the question of a possible resurgence of police power outside regular institutional channels as in the time of Lavrenti Beria. Since 1953, this power has been checked by a division of police functions among governmental structures in addition to the elimination of certain aspects of the police apparatus. The leading role of the KGB, led by Yury V. Andropov, an alternate member of the Politburo, in the campaign against dissent, may well appear to many in the Soviet system as the harbinger of a return to an undisguised police state. An action by the Collegium of the Ministry of Internal Affairs (MVD) in the winter of 1971–1972 suggests that certain elements in the system are aware of the dangers in any expansion of KGB power and are prepared to move against it. The Collegium put forward a proposal for a central all-Union authority for the volunteer militia, which numbers nearly seven million members.

There is clearly a competitive situation between Andropov's KGB and the MVD, directed by Nikolai A. Shchelokov; this proposal originating with the MVD is no doubt partially aimed at providing an additional check against the rise of KGB power. From the standpoint of the general policy of the top leadership, such a centralization offers the additional advantage of maximum control of the masses at minimal cost, in terms of both material resources and public relations. The proposal was strongly endorsed by *Izvestia,* indicating support from the governmental apparatus. What is envisioned is apparently a diffusion of power among four nationally centralized security forces: the KGB, the MVD, the volunteer militia and the Border Guards.

The expansion of externally oriented coercive forces also raises questions concerning the relationship of these forces to the party. The increasing emphasis upon the Warsaw Treaty Organization called for by the Brezhnev Doctrine, the buildup of Soviet naval forces in the Mediterranean and elsewhere, the achievement of nuclear parity with the United States, and the massive deployment of forces against China have all tended to increase the internal influence of the military establishment. The Defense Minister, Marshal Andrei A. Grechko, is the most powerful figure in that position since Marshal G. K. Zhukov in the mid-1950's. However, Grechko's influence appears to be confined to defense and foreign policy. There has not been a military member of the Politburo since Zhukov.

On the other hand, one indication of the increasing importance of coercive forces within the system is the fact that 13.4 percent of new full members of the party's Central Committee elected in 1971 were drawn from military and police ranks, as compared to 8.5 percent of the old members; percentages of military and police representation among full members of the Central Committee elected in 1956 and 1966 were 7.5 and 8.2, respectively. While this increase is impressive and reflects the influence of the coercive structures in the political system as a whole, the effect of this representation upon the internal functioning of the party appears minimal.

The party has apparently largely realized the objective set after the death of Stalin of reestablishing its predominant position in Soviet society and keeping other social structures firmly under its control. The main outlines of the political process in this maturing totalitarian system now appears as follows: institutionalized bargaining between the party and other structures created by the revolutionary transformation of society; a relationship between the party and the masses, featuring an attempt to build consensus, supplemented by coercion where necessary; and the mobilization of social resources to achieve the regime's goals in great power politics and in economic development. . . .

Party Organization and Leadership

Certain aspects of Lenin's original model of party organization have been strongly emphasized in both the rhetoric and the practice of the current leadership: centralization of authority, a professional elite, rigorous grounding in theory, and concentration upon a political, as opposed to a strictly economic, struggle. There has also been strong emphasis upon the party as bearing a multi-functional responsibility in Soviet society, with the consequent requirement for high levels of efficiency throughout the party organization.

The tendency toward an even more pronounced elitist role for the party than heretofore is indicated by the slowing down of increments in party membership. Increases in total membership, full and candidate, averaged about six percent annually between 1962 and 1966. Between 1966 and 1970, the average annual increase was 3.8 percent. The tendency to render the CPSU more of a quantitatively measurable elite will be accentuated by the purge of party ranks through means of the exchange of membership cards, to be carried out in 1973 and 1974. This exchange of party cards, approved by the 24th Party Congress in 1971, is designed to weed out "inactive and unreliable" party members. Plans for the exchange were completed in June, 1972, by Ivan V. Kapitonov, the member of the party secretariat in charge of cadres, who will direct the purge.

Not only has there been a general slowdown and stabilization in party membership; there has also developed a remarkable stability in the upper echelons of the party. This is reflected strikingly in the composition of the Central Committee. A record number, 139 of the 175 1961 full members, were retained at the 23d Congress in 1966, when total full membership was expanded to 195; 153 of the 235 full members elected at the 24th Congress of 1971 were incumbents.

The Politburo also displays a high degree of stability. The 11 full Politburo members elected in 1966 were all retained at the 24th Congress of 1971, when four new full members were added. Of the 26 persons who held rank as full or candidate members of the Politburo or members of the Secretariat between 1966 and 1969, 25 were still in this top ruling circle in the summer of 1972.

This stability at the tops lends superficial credence to Kremlin claims concerning the reality of collective leadership. However, it is clear that a power struggle continues, reflected in changes within the government and party during the past year. These changes indicate that Brezhnev is more fully in control than ever before. First, Gennadi Voronov, a full member of the Politburo, was replaced as Premier of the Russian Republic last year by Mikhail Solomentsev, Party Secretary for Heavy Industry. Then, in May, 1972, Pyotr Shelest, Party Secretary for the Ukraine since 1963 and a full member of the Politburo, was replaced by Vladimir Scherbitsky, a Brezhnev protégé and perhaps the First Secretary's strongest supporter among the full members of the Politburo. Scherbitsky was one of four new full members added to the Politburo at the 24th Party Congress in 1971. All of the others, V. V. Grishin, D. A. Kunaev, and F. D. Kulakov, have also been closely identified with Brezhnev in the past.

The jockeying for power at the top of the party is connected with positions on major issues. Some members of the Politburo, including Premier Aleksei Kosygin and President Nikolai Podgorny, are believed consistently to take positions somewhat more liberal than those of First

Secretary Leonid Brezhnev. At the other extreme are the hard-liners who consider Brezhnev's centrist positions too liberal. Shelest, clearly identified with the right wing, is known to have opposed both the new orientation toward consumer goods and the policy of accommodation with the United States. This, no doubt, was a factor in his ouster but there are indications that Shelest's failure to curb dissent effectively in the Ukraine also contributed heavily to his downfall.

Brezhnev has also moved to secure his influence in certain areas where his control was previously reported to be uncertain, notably in Kazakhstan. The signal honors and unusual praise in the press accorded to D. A. Kunaev, full Politburo member and First Secretary of the Kazakhstan party, on the occasion of his sixtieth birthday last winter, is probably reflective of a clear orientation by Kunaev toward Brezhnev's camp.

There has been speculaion concerning a probable shakeup in the Politburo. In a reshuffle, Solomentsev is almost certain to move up to full Politburo membership. Such a change would further solidify Brezhnev's power; however, there are still checks upon the First Secretary's complete domination of the party. In addition to Kosygin and Podgorny, Politburo members who retain a large measure of independence from Brezhnev include Andrei Kirilenko and Mikhail Suslov. Alexander Shelepin has long been recognized as an opponent of Brezhnev, but this influence has been steadily declining for several years. The exclusion of Shelepin's close associate, V. Y. Semitchastny, from the new Central Committee in 1971 completed the virtual elimination of the "Komsomol" group that had strongly supported the trade union leader. Notably, Shelepin's name appeared last among the old members in Brezhnev's announcement concerning the new Politburo at the 24th Party Congress in 1971. The two members immediately ahead of Shelepin on the list, Shelest and Voronov, have since lost their jobs.

Average age of the Politburo is now almost 62: Brezhnev is 66, Kosygin, 68, and Podgorny, 69. Real innovation is unlikely from this aging leadership, whether or not Brezhnev further consolidates his power. Conservative policies are likely to continue, featuring stern repression of dissent and caution both in economic development at home and the expansion of national power abroad. However, the continuing modernization of Soviet society is likely to provide increasingly severe tests for such policies. The record of the post-Khrushchev years indicates that in any crisis posed by the essential conflict between totalitarian politics and social modernization, the party leadership will turn further to the right.

THE MANY SHADES OF DICTATORSHIP

3

POINT

Dictatorship based upon the unity of the masses.

A state of the Soviet type [is] an example of direct power wielded by the organised and armed workers, an example of the dictatorship of workers and peasants. The role of the Soviets, the significance of such a dictatorship, is that they apply organised force against the counterrevolution, safeguard the gains of the revolution for the benefit of the majority and with the support of the majority. There can be no dual power in a state. . . . and there can be no return to the monarchy. The army and the people must merge into one—therein lies the triumph of liberty! *

COUNTERPOINT

Dictatorship based upon personal leadership.

I am at the head of my people not only by a decree of destiny. I am there because, without knowing it perhaps, I prepared myself for it as though I had known that someday this responsibility and privilege would be my lot. . . . †

. . . I committed myself to a higher ideal and to loyalty without reservation to this soldier and visionary friend, loyalty which I profess and will continue to profess, observing it at the cost of the greatest sacrifices.‡

* V. I. Lenin, *Collected Works*, Vol. 24.

† Juan Perón quoted in Tad Szulc, *Twilight of the Tyrants* (New York: Holt, Rinehart & Winston, Inc., 1959), p. 129.

‡ A statement of loyalty by a follower of Perón, quoted in Joseph R. Barager, ed., *Why Perón Came to Power* (New York: Alfred A. Knopf, 1968), p. 179.

The point and counterpoint show two ways commonly employed to justify dictatorship. In Lenin's writing we see a strong attachment to ideology and the will of the masses. Generally, leaders in communist states are convinced that Marxist-Leninist formulas for revolution provide a logical path for success. The counterpoint is representative of personalistic dictatorship in which an individual is thought to possess extraordinary visions concerning the leadership of people. Juan Perón is a charismatic figure who has managed to retain a fanatical following in Argentina despite the fact that he was ousted from power in 1955. Recently when Perón returned to Argentina from political exile in Spain at the invitation of the Argentine government, he received a rousing welcome from his admirers and was successful in influencing the outcome of the 1973 elections in that country. The distinctions between ideological and personalistic dictatorship will be discussed in more detail later in this chapter.

In Chapter 1 we referred to Aristotle's *Politics* in which he distinguished between "right" and "perverted" constitutions. Corresponding to "perverted" constitutions are three perversions of government typical of his era: tyranny, oligarchy, and "democracy." These perverted forms of government are alike in that each serves the interest of a particular group in society and rejects the common good. Tyranny is a monarchy which pursues the selfish goals of the monarch and seeks to repress the people. Similarly, oligarchy operates to preserve the privileged position of the wealthy class without regard for the common interest. In Aristotle's observations of autocratic rule of the needy, which he calls "democracy" but equates with mob rule, one can see many traits to be found in modern demagogic regimes. This form, according to Aristotle, has a leadership that tries to identify itself with the aspirations of the masses but overlooks the interest of the state.

Throughout history various kinds of dictatorship have appeared. Alfred Cobban, a leading author on the subject, sets forth in the reading on Caesarism the characteristics of a Roman type of autocratic rule which had certain refinements not to be found in the forms of dictatorship in ancient Greece as seen by Aristotle. It appears then that in different ages and diverse cultures unique dictatorships have arisen. This assumption will be followed in our treatment of the topic of dictatorship.

Roman Dictatorships

Militarism and imperialism are closely related to an ascending dictatorship. This is shown by Alfred Cobban to be true of Caesarism as an example of Roman autocratic rule. The strains of expanding the empire, along with emerging economic problems, demanded some kind of strong leadership. For

Julius Caesar the absolute power of the Senate had to be broken for the good of the Roman Empire. His political maneuvering involved the waging of wars and the winning of the support of the soldiers as well as of the common people. The term "Caesarism" has been applied to modern dictatorships because of the way in which some leaders have achieved complete power. Although there are significant differences between Caesar and modern dictators, certain twentieth-century demagogues have resembled him in strategy. Benito Mussolini and Juan Perón, for example, won the enthusiastic endorsement of substantial numbers of the people while keeping the leadership of the army in check but gathering support from the rank and file.

Cobban tells us that Roman leaders were constantly aware of the importance of legitimacy and were able to sanction their regimes through various means. Dedication to an established body of law and appeal to religion seem to have been the most effective devices for legitimation. It is interesting to note that some dictatorial regimes in modern times have come to office legitimately. But, as in the case of Hitler, the constitution became a vehicle for the assumption of extraordinary powers of government. As you read the following selection by Cobban, consider how Caesar's techniques for attaining complete power in Rome may be similar to means used by some modern dictators.

THE RISE OF CAESARISM

ALFRED COBBAN

Since the Greek word tyranny, though more appropriate, did not express quite the meaning modern advocates of tyrannical government wished to convey, it was from a Roman institution that the term dictatorship was borrowed. The Roman dictatorship was an honourable and universally respected constitutional device of the Republic for meeting a crisis during a war. In common with dictatorship as the word is used today it implied that supreme power was placed in the hands of one man. But the Roman dictator was constitutionally appointed, held office only for a limited term, and when he laid down his power was judged for his deeds while he had exercised it.

Reprinted from Alfred Cobban, Dictatorship: Its History and Theory *(London: Jonathan Cape Ltd., 1939), pp. 325–33, by permission of Jonathan Cape Ltd. and Mrs. Muriel Eckert.*

Signs of dictatorship in the modern sense do not appear in the Roman republic until after the end of the Punic wars, when Rome was already discovering the difficulty of combining republican government with Empire. They are associated, as earlier in the Greek cities, with the appearance of economic troubles. The freemen were declining in number because of the wars; for the same reason a large slave population had grown up, whose cheap labour was undermining the standard of life of the citizens. The yeomen farmers, overburdened with debt, were forced to sell their lands to members of the Senatorial and Equestrian orders, who were building up . . . extensive estates worked by slave labour. In the city of Rome itself a large and impoverished urban population was developing. Faced with the dual task of governing extensive conquests and solving a complex economic problem the old system of government broke down.

The proposals of the Gracchi represent the first attempt to cope with these problems. Fog, in the words of the *Cambridge Ancient History,* "enshrouds the history of the Gracchan age." But evidently both Tiberius and Caius Gracchus were endeavouring to reform some of the worst abuses in the state, and were relying to some extent on the support of the populace of Rome in their struggle with the conservative Senatorial party. The measures they wished to force through seem to have been moderate and reasonable enough, but to overcome the resistance of the Senate they had to aim at making themselves permanent tribunes of the plebs; that is, they had to violate the constitution and obtain personal power. Caius Gracchus even went so far as to form a bodyguard of his supporters. But the Senators were too experienced and too well entrenched in power to yield; Tiberius and Caius Gracchus were each in turn attacked and killed by their opponents. Neither was a dictator, nor even aimed at a dictatorship, but their history indicates that a situation out of which dictatorship might arise already existed in Rome.

A long step was taken towards dictatorship in the modern sense of the word during the next generation; it is summed up in the careers of the two great generals, Marius and Sulla, who although they led opposite factions reflect the same political tendency in the state. The political struggle which had begun in the time of the Gracchi was now becoming clarified. It was one between those who desired more efficient and less corrupt government, and who were at the same time not uninfluenced by a desire to share in the perquisites of Empire themselves, and the clique of Senatorial families, claiming a monopoly of the consulship, and an hereditary right to loot the Empire; for the biggest prizes that went with Senatorial rule were the corrupt provincial governorships. In the struggle the new men, trying to break into the Senatorial monopoly, called in the assistance of more popular elements in the state, but they must not for that reason be regarded as democrats.

However, Marius, a new man, who by his military ability had climbed into the consulship, which he held for five successive years (104–100 B.C.), reduced the property qualification for membership of the legions and enlisted large numbers of *proletarii* in them. It has plausibly been argued that this was the most decisive step in the whole history of the declining republic. The citizens who had filled the ranks of the legions in the earlier days of the republic, and who, when peace was declared, anxious to return to their farms and businesses, had insisted on demobilization, no longer served the state in war. The proletarians who now flocked behind the standards were prepared, so long as they received pay and booty, to remain permanently under arms. They became a standing army whose chief loyalty was to their general, and this was the force that henceforth could be flung into the struggle, and that was eventually to dominate the political system of Rome.

The existence of this standing army was in itself an invitation to would-be tyrants; added to the rivalry between the Senatorial class and the new men, and the evident insufficiency of the republican system of administration, it made the tendency towards dictatorship irresistible. Not only did the party hostile to the Senate put up as a potential dictator a far more extreme politician than either of the Gracchi, in the person of Marius, but the need for strong personal leadership was felt even by the Senate, which in self-defence accepted first Sulla as its champion, and then Pompey, although neither of these was in a position to be an effective dictator. Their function was to bolster up existing institutions, not to refashion the state: a real dictator could only come from the anti-Senatorial side.

He appeared when Julius Caesar rose to power as the representative of the Marian party. By alternating politics in Rome with war in the provinces, Caesar built up an army devoted to himself in the field and a large body of political supporters in the capital. The Senate had no better recourse against him than to call on a counter-dictator, Pompey. The defeat and death of Pompey settled the issue and the Senate accepted its master, heaped offices on Caesar, made him dictator for life, gave him . . . a seat in the Senate between the two consuls, and the right of expressing his opinion there first—perhaps to give the Senators warning as to the opinion they themselves should express. . . . He . . . was even voted a statue and the title of demigod.

Caesar was truly a dictator, and not in the old Roman sense. A dictator in some sense or other Rome certainly needed: only an absolute ruler could put down the misrule of the Senatorial cliques. Moreover, Caesar was far from being a mere tyrannical general. As well as military power, political authority in Rome had been equally necessary to him, and he had built it up skillfully from the nucleus provided by the remnants of the Marian party. In early days he had acted as prosecutor against two corrupt provincial governors—not so much from a love of the old republican virtue, as because the prosecutions enabled him to put himself forward as an opponent of Senatorial corruption, while their failure would show that no remedy was to be expected from Senatorial juries. He made a reputation for himself as the "general refuge of men in trouble," and even while he was absent from the capital provided games and public holidays to please the "mongrel mob" which had taken the place of the *populus Romanus,* borrowing money on a huge scale to finance these activities.

Once in power Caesar showed himself a genuine administrative reformer and began to introduce changes on a grand scale; he planned great public works—roads through Italy and buildings in Rome; marshes were to be drained, new cities founded for the legionaries, libraries established, a new digest of the law planned, and, with all this, a degree of financial stability was restored in the republic.

On the other hand, we must not neglect the steps he took to complete the degradation of the Senate, packing it with new men, including even sons of freedmen and provincials, levelling downwards as well as upwards, and encouraging members of the upper classes to disgrace themselves. But the aristocracy had not yet lost all sense of shame, nor, in spite of their corruptions, had the memory of their ancient traditions entirely deserted them. Intellectually, and in executive ability, in the task of peace as well as in those of war, and even in practical political morality, Caesar stood head and shoulders above the whole Senatorial class. He represented efficient personal government against the inefficient and corrupt anarchy which was the only result of Senatorial rule. Yet in spite of all this he had made a mistake in despising his opponents, just as he had made a mistake in thinking that he could either win them over by a somewhat contemptuous patronage or else, who knows, rule the Empire without them. For the Senators still possessed the administrative tradition that was needed for the task of government, and they were still too imbued with the republican spirit to accept permanently Caesar's open dictatorship. In 49 B.C. he crossed the Rubicon, and in effect staked out his claim as dictator. After five years of civil strife he overcame all opposing forces: he triumphed in 45 B.C., in 44 became dictator for life, and in the same year fell beneath the daggers of Senatorial conspirators in the Forum at Rome.

The Empire plunged into a second, and even more violent and prolonged civil war, which ended in the triumph of Octavian, the heir to Caesar. Lacking, perhaps, the genius and the personal fascination of

Julius, he was a more cautious, and in the end a more successful states-man. He claimed no dictatorial powers, but merely concentrated the normal republican offices in his own person; taking for himself the tribunician powers, he refrained from being made a tribune. Dictator, King or Emperor were not titles he envied, the most he would allow to be called was *princeps*—first citizen of the republic. The highest office he reserved for himself was that of high priest, *pontifex maximus*—not un-aware that though the Roman state religion was a mockery to the smart society of Rome, it was acquiring significance in the provinces, and conscious that the old Roman *pietas* was still needed if a government was to be respected as well as obeyed. Wherever the religion of Rome spread, the name, and in the end the worship of Augustus spread with it. Not that he relied altogether on spiritual forces: by keeping the appointment of the proconsuls of the frontier provinces in his own hands, Augustus preserved his control of the armies, while the govern-ment of the peaceful inner provinces was left as a sop to the vanity and a bribe to the pockets of the Senate.

In effect Augustus was all that Caesar had been, and more, but his tyranny was a concealed one; it preserved the republican decencies; it showed that profound respect for existing forms which was part of the Roman genius for government. Where Julius had degraded the Senate, Augustus restored to it the dignity it had lost, purged it of the lowborn or barbarian elements, assisted the Senators with loans to maintain their status, and in appearance shared his power with them fairly. The truth, of course, was that the Senators were little better than puppets in the hands of the Princeps: they were of use to him, but he was their master. And whereas Julius had died under the daggers of a score of assassins, Augustus lived to an old age, revered and obeyed, the unquestioned master of the Roman world, passed on his authority peacefully to his successor, and laid down a structure of Empire that was to last with modifications for some four or five hundred years—the one dictator in the whole of our records to found a government which so far as human history goes can be called permanent. . . .

Special Types of Despotism

In a book entitled *Oriental Despotisms*, Karl A. Wittfogel, a contemporary his-torian, examines in detail what he calls "hydraulic societies" in which there existed a framework of total power. In these societies the governments con-structed irrigation systems to yield the maximum in agricultural production. The pace of life in such a community allowed very little freedom for the individual.

The extensive control over the population exercised by the foreman class prompted Wittfogel to conclude that few political systems in history have been as oppressive as the oriental despotisms.

Again, analyzing dictatorship historically, one must note the tyrannies existing in the Italian city-states. Niccolo Machiavelli, writing in the sixteenth century, describes the statecraft of that age in Italy. He devotes most of his attention to the formulation of theories as to how a prince maintains power and builds a great state. For him, greatness of a state consists of wealth, power, and empire; while he recognizes the virtues of a republican form of government, his unceasing admiration for the shrewd dictator has led critics to condemn him as an advocate of evil.

What is the quality in a ruler most respected by Machiavelli? Above all else, a ruler should be cunning. The prince should try to appear to be religious and merciful if this will help his political image. Immoral acts of deceit or cruelty are permissible or desirable when such acts are done in the interest of the nation. The test of a good ruler is his resourcefulness, even if at times he resorts to immoral practices. Machiavelli's work is viewed by some readers as the epitome of the dictum that "might makes right." Others say that Machiavelli was an astute political theorist who looked at political phenomena with objectivity.

Jacobinism

In the late eighteenth century, French revolutionary political leaders such as Robespierre defended dictatorial rule by appealing to the national interest or to what the famed French philosopher Rousseau called the "General Will." Robespierre was a leader of the Jacobins, a political club founded in 1789 which actively supported the Reign of Terror and the radical changes demanded in the wake of the French Revolution. The Jacobins sought to control France through terror, propaganda, and spectacular ceremonies. Robespierre and other Jacobin leaders claimed to have special insights into the "General Will," and therefore justified their monopoly of power in order to govern without obstruction from other groups and parties.

Jacobinism was a new form of dictatorship in that it introduced an official ideology consisting of the idea of the "General Will" and slogans, symbols, and ceremonies which were aimed at instilling loyalty in the masses. Modern totalitarian dictatorship of the twentieth century was to refine these methods by employing such technological advances as mass communications.

Totalitarian Dictatorship

No dictatorship in history has approached the level of control exercised by modern totalitarian dictatorships, the best examples of which are the Soviet

Union under Stalin and Germany under Hitler. Under totalitarian dictatorship a society is transformed to such a degree that every aspect of the individual's life is touched by the regime. Hannah Arendt, a contemporary political theorist, refers to this atmosphere as the atomization of the population, a process which isolates individuals by means of the methodical use of terror as well as the application of other instruments of control.*

In 1953, Professor Carl J. Friedrich first presented a list of general characteristics of totalitarian dictatorship to a group of eminent social scientists who were meeting to discuss the topic of totalitarianism. Later Professors Friedrich and Zbigniew K. Brzezinski co-authored a book in which they discussed in detail these characteritiscs: an official ideology, a single party, the use of terror, monopoly of communications, monopoly of weapons, and central control and direction of the economy.† It is useful to take a closer look at these six traits of totalitarianism by discussing them in relation to twentieth-century dictatorships.

Marxist-Leninist doctrine is the best illustration of a totalitarian ideology. Soviet leaders, as official interpreters of ideology, draw guides for action from the theories of Marx and Lenin. Every move by the regime may be explained in terms of the principles of Marxism-Leninism. The leaders see the ideology as systematic and scientific, a gospel offering answers to all problems confronting them. Since the ideology is taken to be the law of history and the path to utopia, there is no room for deviation or heresy. The Communist Party apparatus is the guardian of the ideology.

The Communist Party in the Soviet Union is a monolithic structure composed of a small percentage of the population fervently dedicated to the ideology. The Party parallels the governmental institutions at all levels and enters every part of society. By reaching into society, the Party keeps the top leaders in touch with the people. In order to maintain the infallibility of its directives to the people, the Party machine rarely admits a mistake in policy. If a major policy change occurs due to a miscalculation, there may be a shakeup or purge of party ranks with accompanying accusations—such as charges of counterrevolutionary activities and treason—against individuals. This is the nature of the monolithic party in its pursuit of fulfilling Marxist-Leninist dogma.

While the ideology of National Socialism lacked the coherence of Marxism-Leninism, it exhibited a penchant for symbols and equaled the Soviet regime in the systematic use of terror. Hannah Arendt explains "total terror" as a unique tool of modern totalitarian dictatorship which carefully isolates

---

* See Hannah Arendt, The Origins of Totalitarianism (New York: Harcourt Brace Jovanovich, Inc., 1960).

† Carl J. Friedrich and Zbigniew K. Brzezinski, Totalitarian Dictatorship and Autocracy (Cambridge, Mass.: Harvard University Press, 1956).

men and makes them feel superfluous. Total terror destroys any living space of freedom" by pressing individuals "within its iron band." * The Nazi terror organizations executed their orders with bureaucratic efficiency so that even such grave evils as mass liquidation became part of routine fulfillment of the precepts of the ideology.

Monopoly of weapons usually involves the politicizing of the armed forces. The Bolsheviks set out to form Party cells within the army and to introduce a commissar system whereby the military was periodically checked by political agents. All officers were required to join the Party as a precaution against disloyalty. The Nazis instituted a similar pattern of control over the German armed forces by means of the Gestapo.

A fifth characteristic of totalitarian dictatorship advanced by Friedrich and Brzezinski is the monopoly of communications. Here we could look at a regime which fell short of being classified as "totalitarian" but which operated effectively in the domination of communications—namely, the Perón government of Argentina. Under Perón, teachers had to devote part of their class time to instructing the children on the merits of Perónismo. Newspapers and magazines which in any way voiced opposition to the government's policies were closed down. The Argentine radio stations were forced to broadcast the regime's propaganda. George Blanksten, writing in 1953, said that "all media of communication of information and ideas—whether by the schools, the press, the radio, or the theatre—have been chained in the 'new Argentina' to the service of Perón." †

Last on the list of traits of totalitarianism is the central control and direction of the economy. The extent of control ranges from government ownership of industries, as under the Soviet government, to tight regulation of private enterprises, as under the Nazis or the Italian Fascists. Consumer preference is minimized while the whole economy is geared to the regime's specific plans.

Hannah Arendt in the next selection examines the unique character of the application of terror in a totalitarian system.

---

* Arendt, The Origins of Totalitarianism, pp. 460–79.

† George I. Blanksten, Perón's Argentina (Chicago: University of Chicago Press, 1953), p. 219.

IDEOLOGY AND TERROR:
A Novel Form of Government

HANNAH ARENDT

. . . [T]otalitarianism differs essentially from other forms of political oppression known to us as despotism, tyranny and dictatorship.
Wherever it rose to power, it developed entirely new political institutions and destroyed all social, legal and political traditions of the country. No matter what the specifically national tradition or the particular
spiritual source of its ideology, totalitarian government always transformed classes into masses, supplanted the party system, not by one-party
dictatorships, but by a mass movement, shifted the center of power from
the army to the police, and established a foreign policy openly directed
toward world domination. Present totalitarian governments have developed from one-party systems; whenever these became truly totalitarian,
they started to operate according to a system of values so radically different from all others, that none of our traditional legal, moral, or common sense utilitarian categories could any longer help us to come to
terms with, or judge, or predict their course of action.

If it is true that the elements of totalitarianism can be found by
retracing the history and analyzing the political implications of what we
usually call the crisis of our century, then the conclusion is unavoidable
that this crisis is no mere threat from the outside, no mere result of
some aggressive foreign policy of either Germany or Russia, and that
it will no more disappear with the death of Stalin than it disappeared
with the fall of Nazi Germany. It may even be that the true predicaments
of our time will assume their authentic form—though not necessarily the
cruelest—only when totalitarianism has become a thing of the past.

It is in the line of such reflections to raise the question whether
totalitarian government, born of this crisis and at the same time its
clearest and only unequivocal symptom, is merely a makeshift arrangement, which borrows its methods of intimidation, its means of orga-

nization and its instruments of violence from the well-known political arsenal of tyranny, despotism and dictatorships, and owes its existence only to the deplorable, but perhaps accidental failure of the traditional political forces—liberal or conservative, national or socialist, republican or monarchist, authoritarian or democratic. Or whether, on the contrary, there is such a thing as the *nature* of totalitarian government, whether it has its own essence and can be compared with and defined like other forms of government such as Western thought has known and recognized since the times of ancient philosophy. If this is true, then the entirely new and unprecedented forms of totalitarian organization and course of action must rest on one of the few basic experiences which men can have whenever they live together, and are concerned with public affairs. If there is a basic experience which finds its political expression in totalitarian domination, then, in view of the novelty of the totalitarian form of government, this must be an experience which, for whatever reason, has never before served as the foundation of a body politic and whose general mood—although it may be familiar in every other re-spect—never before has pervaded, and directed the handling of, public affairs. . . .

It is the monstrous, yet seemingly unanswerable claim of totali-tarian rule that, far from being "lawless," it goes to the sources of authority from which positive laws received their ultimate legitimation, that far from being arbitrary it is more obedient to these suprahuman forces than any government ever was before, and that far from wielding its power in the interest of one man, it is quite prepared to sacrifice everybody's vital immediate interests to the execution of what it assumes to be the law of History or the law of Nature. Its defiance of positive laws claims to be a higher form of legitimacy which, since it is inspired by the sources themselves, can do away with petty legality. Totalitarian lawfulness pretends to have found a way to establish the rule of justice on earth— something which the legality of positive law admittedly could never attain. . . .

At this point the fundamental difference between the totalitarian and all other concepts of law comes to light. Totalitarian policy does not replace one set of laws with another, does not establish its own *consensus iuris*, does not create, by one revolution, a new form of legal-ity. Its defiance of all, even its own positive laws implies that it believes it can do without any *consensus iuris* whatever, and still not resign itself to the tyrannical state of lawlessness, arbitrariness and fear. It can do without the *consensus iuris* because it promises to release the fulfillment of law from all action and will of man; and it promises justice on earth because it claims to make mankind itself the embodiment of the law. . . .

In the interpretation of totalitarianism, all laws have become laws of movement. When the Nazis talked about the law of nature or when the Bolsheviks talk about the law of history, neither nature nor history is any longer the stabilizing source of authority for the actions of mortal men; they are movements in themselves. Underlying the Nazis' belief in race laws as the expression of the law of nature in man, is Darwin's idea of man as the product of a natural development which does not necessarily stop with the present species of human beings, just as under the Bolshevik's belief in class-struggle as the expression of the law of history lies Marx's notion of society as the product of a gigantic historical movement which races according to its own law of motion to the end of historical times when it will abolish itself. . . .

. . . In the body politic of totalitarian government, this place of positive laws is taken by total terror, which is designed to translate into reality the law of movement of history or nature. Just as positive laws, though they define transgressions, are independent of them—the absence of crimes in any society does not render laws superfluous but, on the contrary, signifies their most perfect rule—so terror in totalitarian government has ceased to be a mere means for the suppression of opposition, though it is also used for such purposes. Terror becomes total when it becomes independent of all opposition; it rules supreme when nobody any longer stands in its way. If lawfulness is the essense of non-tyrannical government and lawlessness is the essence of tyranny, then terror is the essence of totalitarian domination. . . .

By pressing men against each other, total terror destroys the space between them; compared to the condition within its iron band, even the desert of tyranny, insofar as it is still some kind of space, appears like a guarantee of freedom. Totalitarian government does not just curtail liberties or abolish essential freedoms; nor does it, at least to our limited knowledge, succeed in eradicating the love for freedom from the hearts of man. It destroys the one essential prerequisite of all freedom which is simply the capacity of motion which cannot exist without space. . . .

In a perfect totalitarian government, where all men have become One Man, where all action aims at the acceleration of the movement of nature or history, where every single act is the execution of a death sentence which Nature or History has already pronounced, that is, under conditions where terror can be completely relied upon to keep the movement in constant motion, no principle of action separate from its essence would be needed at all. . . .

The inhabitants of a totalitarian country are thrown into and caught in the process of nature or history for the sake of accelerating its movement; as such, they can only be executioners or victims of its inherent law. The process may decide that those who today eliminate races and individuals or the members of dying classes and decadent peoples are tomorrow those who must be sacrificed. What totalitarian rule needs to guide the behavior of its subjects is a preparation to fit each of them equally well for the role of executioner and the role of victim. This two-sided preparation, the substitute for a principle of action, is the ideology.

Ideologies—isms which to the satisfaction of their adherents can explain everything and every occurrence by deducing it from a single premise—are a very recent phenomenon and, for many decades, played a negligible role in political life. Only with the wisdom of hindsight can we discover in them certain elements which have made them so disturbingly useful for totalitarian rule. Not before Hitler and Stalin were the great political potentialities of the ideologies discovered. . . .

An ideology is quite literally what its name indicates: It is the logic of an idea. Its subject matter is history, to which the "idea" is applied; the result of this application is not a body of statements about something that *is*, but the unfolding of a process which is in constant change. The ideology treats the course of events as though it followed the same "law" as the logical exposition of its "idea." Ideologies pretend to know the mysteries of the whole historical process—the secrets of the past, the intricacies of the present, the uncertainties of the future—because of the logic inherent in their respective ideas. . . .

First, in their claim to total explanation, ideologies have the tendency to explain not what is, but what becomes, what is born and passes away. They are in all cases concerned solely with the element of motion, that is, with history in the customary sense of the word. Ideologies are always oriented toward history, even when, as in the case of racism, they seemingly proceed from the premise of nature; here, nature serves merely to explain historical matters and reduce them to matters of nature. The claim to total explanation promises to explain all historical happenings, the total explanation of the past, the total knowledge of the present, and the reliable prediction of the future. Secondly, in this capacity ideological thinking becomes independent of all experience from which it cannot learn anything new even if it is a question of something that has just come to pass. Hence ideological thinking becomes emancipated from the reality that we perceive with our five senses, and insists on a truer reality concealed behind all perceptible things, dominating them from this place of concealment and requiring a sixth sense that enables us to become aware of it. . . .

Thirdly, since the ideologies have no power to transform reality, they achieve this emancipation of thought from experience through certain methods of demonstration. Ideological thinking orders facts into an absolutely logical procedure which starts from an axiomatically accepted premise, deducing everything else from it; that is, it proceeds with a consistency that exists nowhere in the realm of reality. . . .

The device both totalitarian rulers used to transform their respective ideologies into weapons with which each of their subjects could force himself into step with the terror movement was deceptively simple and inconspicuous: they took them dead seriously, took pride the one in his supreme gift for "ice cold reasoning" (Hitler) and the other in the "mercilessness of his dialectics," and proceeded to drive ideological implications into extremes of logical consistency which, to the onlooker, looked preposterously "primitive" and absurd: a "dying class" consisted of people condemned to death; races that are "unfit to live" were to be exterminated. Whoever agreed that there are such things as "dying classes" and did not draw the consequence of killing their members, or that the right to live had something to do with race and did not draw the consequence of killing "unfit races," was plainly either stupid or a coward. This stringent logicality as a guide to action permeates the whole structure of totalitarian movements and governments. It is exclusively the work of Hitler and Stalin who, although they did not add a single new thought to the ideas and propaganda slogans of their movements, for this reason alone must be considered ideologists of the greatest importance. . . .

Totalitarian rulers rely on the compulsion with which we can compel ourselves, for the limited mobilization of people which even they still need; this inner compulsion is the tyranny of logicality against which nothing stands but the great capacity of men to start something new. The tyranny of logicality begins with the mind's submission to logic as a never-ending process, on which man relies in order to engender his thoughts. By this submission, he surrenders his inner freedom as he surrenders his freedom of movement when be bows down to an outward tyranny. Freedom as an inner capacity of man is identical with the capacity to begin, just as freedom as a political reality is identical with a space of movement between men. Over the beginning, no logic, no cogent deduction can have any power, because its chain presupposes, in the form of a premise, the beginning. As terror is needed lest with the birth of each new human being a new beginning arise and raise its voice in the world, so the self-coercive force of logicality is mobilized lest anybody ever start thinking—which as the freest and purest of all human activities is the very opposite of the compulsory process of deduction. Totalitarian government can be safe only to the extent that it can mobilize man's own will power in order to force him into that gigantic movement of History or Nature which supposedly uses mankind as its material and knows neither birth nor death.

The compulsion of total terror on one side, which, with its iron band, presses masses of isolated men together *and* supports them in a world which has become a wilderness for them, and the self-coercive force of logical deduction on the other, which prepares each individual in his lonely isolation against all others, correspond to each other and need each other in order to set the terror-ruled movement into motion and keep it moving. Just as terror, even in its pre-total, merely tyrannical form ruins all relationships between men, so the self-compulsion of ideological thinking ruins all relationships with reality. . . .

What prepares men for totalitarian domination in the non-totalitarian world is the fact that loneliness, once a borderline experience usually suffered in certain marginal social conditions like old age, has become an everyday experience of the evergrowing masses of our century. The merciless process into which totalitarianism drives and organizes the masses looks like a suicidal escape from this reality. The "ice-cold reasoning" and the "mighty tentacle" of dialectics which "seizes you as in a vise" appears like a last support in a world where nobody is reliable and nothing can be relied upon. It is the inner coercion whose only content is the strict avoidance of contradictions that seems to confirm a man's identity outside all relationships with others. It fits him into the iron band of terror even when he is alone, and totalitarian domination tries never to leave him alone except in the extreme situation of solitary confinement. By destroying all space between men and pressing men against each other, even the productive potentialities of isolation are annihilated; by teaching and glorifying the logical reasoning of loneliness where man knows that he will be utterly lost if ever he lets go of the first premise from which the whole process is being started, even the slim chances that loneliness may be transformed into soliutde and logic into thought are obliterated. If this practice is compared with that of tyranny, it seems as if a way had been found to set the desert itself in motion, to let loose a sand storm that could cover all parts of the inhabited earth.

The conditions under which we exist today in the field of politics are indeed threatened by these devastating sand storms. Their danger is not that they might establish a permanent world. Totalitarian domination, like tyranny, bears the germs of its own destruction. Just as fear and the impotence from which fear springs are antipolitical principles and throw men into a situation contrary to political action, so loneliness and the logical-ideological deducing the worst that comes from it represent an antisocial situation and harbor a principle destructive for all human living-together. Nevertheless, organized loneliness is considerably more dangerous than the unorganized impotence of all those who are ruled by the tyrannical and arbitrary will of a single man. Its danger is that it threatens to ravage the world as we know it—a world which everywhere seems to have come to an end—before a new beginning rising from this end has had time to assert itself.

Apart from such considerations—which as predictions are of little avail and less consolation—there remains the fact that the crisis of our time and its central experience have brought forth an entirely new form of government which as a potentiality and an ever-present danger is only too likely to stay with us from now on, just as other forms of government which came about at different historical moments and rested on different fundamental experiences have stayed with mankind regardless of temporary defeats—monarchies, and republics, tyrannies, dictatorships and despotism.

But there remains also the truth that every end in history necessarily contains a new beginning: this beginning is the promise, the only "message" which the end can ever produce. Beginning, before it becomes a historical event, is the supreme capacity of man; politically, it is identical with man's freedom. *Initium ut esset homo creatus est*—"that a beginning be made man was created" said Augustine. This beginning is guaranteed by each new birth; it is indeed every man.

Nonideological Dictatorships

Dictatorships in Latin America have often been described by writers as growing out of a tradition of strong leadership known as *caudillismo*. The political culture of Latin America is conducive to the development of dictatorial rule. George Hallgarten, a researcher of dictatorship, contends that Latin American dictatorship is a classical type. According to Hallgarten, a classical dictator is a talented individual not of the upper class who feels humiliated socially and uses the "revolutionary masses as tools for taking revenge on the upper stratum and for overpowering it." *

Classical dictatorships fall short of reaching the degree of control exercised by totalitarian dictatorships. Noticeably absent in the classical dictatorship is a well-developed ideology even to the point that the classical dictator may install himself as the protector of the status quo and form alliances with the upper-class groups whom he attacks in demagogic speeches. Many Latin American dictators have certainly prospered by serving the interests of foreign investors and other conservative political forces.

---

* George W. F. Hallgarten, *Why Dictators? The Causes and Forms of Tyrannical Rule Since 600 B.C.* (New York: Macmillan, 1954), pp. 333–44.

G. M. Gilbert, a contemporary psychologist, emphasizes the psychological aspects of dictatorship and points out that the rise of dictatorships may be due in part to a cultural lag which prevents the society's acceptance of democratic institutions. Hallgarten concurs with Gilbert that strong men or dictators are intriguing subjects for psychological study. There may be certain psychocultural elements motivating the individual to assume power as a dictator. The strong man needs the masses to break the power monopoly held by the upper classes in the same fashion as explained previously under "Caesarism." The psychological and cultural roots of dictatorship are examined by G. M. Gilbert in the final essay.

THE EMERGENT PATTERN OF DICTATORSHIP—
A PSYCHOCULTURAL VIEW

G. M. GILBERT

Since wars begin in the minds of men, it is in the minds of men that the defenses of peace must be constructed.

—*Constitution, UNESCO*

In modern history, man's quest for collective security through self-government has been characterized by an increasing revolt against submission to the autocratic rule of royal dynasties. These revolutionary reactions to royal despotism have taken two significant and opposite directions in Western civilization: representative democracy and ideological totalitarianism. World War II has generally been regarded as a climax in the continuing struggle between these two incompatible systems in the government of men. In a larger sense, it was acute phase of the conflict between constructive and destructive potentialities in man's behavior— a conflict in which no nation or system of government may be presumed to have a monopoly on the good or the evil. Nevertheless, the extremes to which a fanatic dictatorship can go in organized aggression was dem-

Reprinted from G. M. *Gilbert,* The Psychology of Dictatorship—Based on an Examination of the Leaders of Nazi Germany. *Copyright 1950, The Ronald Press Company, New York.*

onstrated by Nazi Germany as perhaps never before in human history.

The question may well be raised whether the psychological examination of leading personalities in that dictatorship can provide any significant insights into social conflicts of such magnitude and deep historical roots. It would admittedly be unrealistic to overestimate the importance of the psychodynamics of leading personalities in producing these major social upheavals, as against the socioeconomic, political, and historical forces at work. Nevertheless, we must recognize that such forces do not exist as pure abstractions, but become manifest only through the behavior of human beings; that throughout history social movements of far-reaching consequences have been decisively influenced by leaders, and that the behavior of such leaders is necessarily motivated to some extent by psychological tensions rooted in their individual character development. We must futhermore recognize the fact that the personalities of political leaders, like all human beings, are largely the products of their cultural mores and social tensions, and that they become leaders only if they effectively express the aspirations (or frustrations) of significant segments of their contemporary society. The study of political leadership thus provides a fertile field for interrelating psychodynamics with the broader social processes involved in these historic conflicts.

. . .

The Authoritarian Cultural Lag

The Western revolt against royal despotism first came to a head at the end of the eighteenth century. This social upheaval was marked by the outbreak of major republican revolutions in Europe and the New World, and the revolutionary dictatorships which followed in their wake. The link between dictatorship and democracy has been generally overlooked in the assumed incompatibility of these two systems of government. Yet that link does exist from a psychocultural viewpoint, and is of the utmost significance for our study.

The Napoleonic rule which followed within a decade after the French Revolution is generally conceded to be the prototype of modern dictatorships. It was the forerunner not only historically, but psychologically as well, for it demonstrated a principal function of dictatorship as a psychocultural emergent: *a reversion to authoritarian rule after a too drastic attempt to impose democracy on an authoritarian culture.* Napoleon's assumption of the role of dictator and then emperor, with the wholehearted support of significant segments of postrevolutionary French society, illustrates a fact that has been true of virtually every dictatorship since then: the inability of an authoritarian culture to absorb too much self-government too suddenly without reverting, at least temporary, to some form of paternalistic-authoritarian rule. From the first French Republic to the German Weimar Republic, it has been proved again and again that, while the outward forms of democracy may be achieved overnight by revolution, the psychological changes necessary to sustain it cannot.

On the contrary, there is invariably a cultural lag (in which we emphasize the psychocultural aspect, rather than the technological) that leaves both the masses and the leaders of entrenched institutions psychologically predisposed to support any reversion to their accustomed way of life. This involves not merely the obvious material motivation of the "vested interests," which have been abundantly treated elsewhere, but the socioeconomic and psychological insecurity of the common people that follows in the wake of any drastic social change. It is a psychological truism that man abhors the insecurity of lost meanings as much as nature abhors a vacuum. In the confusion of revolutionary social change, the security of familiar patterns of behavior and a reliable frame of reference for social meanings and values are not readily abandoned, unless the social change immediately provides its own adequate rewards and substitutes. Since social upheaval invariably accentuates psychological and socioeconomic insecurity, and the acculturation process in personality development is not readily reversed, there is apt to be a persistence of the older patterns of behavior for at least a generation or two after the revolution.

Great statesmen have had insight into this cultural lag long before social psychology developed its sophisticated terminology. Thomas Jefferson, evaluating the prospects for the ultimate success of democracy in his generation of republican revolutions, wrote to Adams in 1823:

> The generation which commences a revolution rarely completes it. Habituated from infancy to passive submission of body and mind to their kings and priests,. they are not qualified when called on to think for themselves; and in their inexperience, their ignorance and bigotry make them instruments often, in the hands of the Bonapartes and Iturbides, to defeat their own rights and purposes. This is the present situation in Europe and Spanish America. But it is not desperate. . . . As a younger and more instructed [generation] comes on, the sentiment becomes more intuitive . . . some subsequent one of the ever renewed attempts will ultimately succeed.

Jefferson's insight and faith were vindicated by the ultimate triumph of democracy in France and in some of the other European and Latin American countries. But it was not surprising that the France and Latin America of Jefferson's time should have reverted to authoritarian rule after going through revolutions to throw off the yoke of royal tyranny. The masses could not be educated overnight to understand democracy and to adopt it as a way of life, nor could truly democratic leadership suddenly spring from their midst after centuries of autocratic rule had firmly established an authoritarian frame of reference for their thinking and behavior.

It is our thesis that authoritarian leadership, like any other, reflects the nature of the culture in which it emerges. This is expressed, first of all, in the social values developed among the potential leaders of the given culture. Case histories of Napoleon and other dictators (whose biographies provide us with some clues) would necessarily reveal the authoritarian influences in their upbringing and the cultural channeling of their aggressions. The cultural lag is also expressed in the nature of the support available for any revolutionary or counterrevolutionary movement. Not even a power-driven dictator can seize and hold supreme power in the modern state by sheer personal dominance, as if it were a boy's gang or a seal's harem. His success depends principally on the support he is able to muster from other powerful and influential leaders and the institutions they represent. Historians have pointed out that even Napoleon could not have seized and maintained his power except for the support of other powerful militarists, certain politicians, financiers, etc. The emergence of a dictatorship requires an expression of the cultural lag in terms of the support of influential leaders whose purposes are thought to be served by reversion to autocratic rule.

It must not be assumed, however, that the dictator is merely the passive tool of cultural forces. On the contrary, we must recognize that social interaction implies a two-way process, in which cultural mores help to determine the nature of political leadership, and the latter in turn influences the development of the cultural pattern. It would be fruitless, in the absence of first-hand observations, to speculate on the psychodynamics of Napoleon's drive for power and the way in which it affected the course of European history. But there would presumably be ample room for the investigation of personality differences and individually motivated aggressions among dictators and their supporters. Certainly there has been as much variation in the personalities of dictators as there has been in the personalities of kings—from benevolent despots to destructive maniacs; and the history of their reigns has varied accordingly.

Yet it was precisely to eliminate that element of caprice from government that men were beginning to rebel against rule by the "divine right of kings." In the case of the successful republican revolutions, the purpose was achieved. But even where the rebellion resulted in dictatorship, the original purpose must not be lost sight of. Napoleon came to power, not merely as a reversion to the despotic-paternalistic emperor-figure, but as a strong symbol of peace and security, sanctioned by the will of the people. This may appear ironic, if not slightly incredible in retrospect, but there too Napoleon was the prototype of the modern dictator. For Napoleon, as historians point out, was supported by men of power and influence and was welcomed by the people, not so much to tyrannize them or to wage aggressive wars as to put an end to the chaos and insecurity of life in the postrevolutionary republic.

The struggle for security, which is an underlying motive of all social behavior, was necessarily a predominant motive for all these revolutionary changes. With the expansion of the ethnic identificaton group from the primitive tribe to the modern state, the socially identified security of the individual has been correspondingly extended. The aggressive nationalism that has characterized many dictatorships must be regarded as an enlarged manifestation of that continuing quest for security through group solidarity. As we have already intimated, dictatorship provided an easy solution in cultures that had always conceived of personal and group security in an ethnocentric-authoritarian frame of reference. But there was a conflict of value judgments in this revolutionary period following the Enlightenment. On the one hand, men realized that there was greater security for the group and freedom for the individual if they asserted their right to self-government. On the other hand, the man on horseback was, and continued to be, the recognized symbol of law and order, strength and security for the nation. The heroic myth persisted even after men had rebelled against the mailed fist of royal despotism. To reconcile the apparently incompatible, Napoleon and his supporters had merely to resort to a device that dictators have repeatedly resorted to since—the "free plebiscite" with formal deference to constitutional government. Even a constitution presented no serious obstacle to dictatorship, since many of its provisions could be suspended in a "national emergency" where the security of the nation was threatened; and such emergencies, as Napoleon knew only too well, could always be provided by propaganda. Nevertheless, the people were enabled through these devices to maintan the illusion of government by popular mandate, while merely substituting a new form of despotism for the accustomed one.

Dictatorship thus emerged in an era of democratic revolution as a retrogressive phenomenon in man's quest for security through self-government, representing a compromise between his revolt against old symbols of suppressive authority and his inability to structure his purposes without them.

What was true of the Napoleonic era applied to the revolutionary period following World War I. The war had brought to a head the growing revolt against the remaining symbols of suppressive authority in Continental Europe, while the cultural lag perpetuated the quest for new authority. But now this quest took a new form: the political ideology. It was not any longer the "man on horseback" but the man with the ideological panacea who now represented authority for security. Heroic mythology was beginning to give way to political demagoguery in the modern version of dictatorship. . . .

The revolutionary movements that came into being at the turn of the century expressed and appealed to the need for security by offering a variety of politico-economic ideologies. Essentially, this was a perverted recognition of the growth of social science since the nineteenth century. Unfortunately, in view of the cultural lag, it was still a case of a little insight being a dangerous thing. . . .

The clash of ideologies came to a head in the period of social disorganization at the end of World War I. War, defeat, and social chaos had created new demands for social and political reform. Ethnic tensions had been strained by war-born hostilities and postwar "settlements." The breakdown of old institutions and the economic chaos were creating increasing mass frustration. The meaning and justification of old values, authorities, and institutions were being questioned by others. The literature and arts of dissent were flourishing as a symptom of social unrest. Revolutionary movements gathered momentum while political parties multiplied. . . .

In several countries the struggle started with attempts to establish representative government and liberal social reforms as antidotes to suppression and politico-economic privilege. The war was scarcely over when the Communist revolutionists under Lenin overthrew the Czarst regime in Russia and established a socialist republic. Revolts shattered the remains of the Hohenzollern dynasty in Germany, and the Weimar Republic came into being under Allied auspices. A fascist movement under Mussolini with a pseudo-radical reform program established a constitutional "corporate state" in Italy. Some years later a liberal republic was established in Spain. But in every one of these countries (and several others that need not concern us here), it was dictatorship, rather than free representative government or truly liberal social reform that eventually emerged.

Of the numerous factors that may have contributed to this reversion to totalitarian government in these countries, the authoritarian cultural lag would appear to be at least one fundamental common denominator. As in postrevolutionary France, more than a century earlier, the attempts to impose the forms of representative government were defeated in part by the inability of these cultures to absorb too much self-government too suddenly, especially in the social chaos and insecurity that followed the overthrow of the old institutions. The long tradition of submission to despotism which had prevailed for centuries in Germany, Russia, Spain, and Italy had left too strong a trace of authoritarian thinking and ego-involvement among the people and their potential leaders to be readily abandoned in favor of the democratic-socialistic millennium. . . .

Thus the emergence of successful dictatorship would seem to be determined in large part by the interaction of (a) *social unrest* carried over from the revolt against royal despotism; (b) an *authoritarian cultural lag,* with its persistent quest for security through strong leadership and political demagoguery; (c) a *favorable constellation of leadership* and the group interests they represent, providing the authoritative formula and its material implementation; (d) *crucial events,* sometimes of minor intrinsic significance, which favor the establishment and continuance of the dictator in power.

Ultrarevolutionary Dictatorships

In concluding this discussion on dictatorship, we might make note of George Hallgarten's application of the phrase "ultra-revolutionary dictatorship" to the Maoist movement in China.* Professional ultrarevolutionary leaders such as Mao Tse-Tung mobilize the lowest classes in order to overturn the established power structure. In the "revolution from the bottom" the leaders are determined not to revert to accommodation with the old ruling class. "People's democracy" is the label given to the dictatorships governing in the interest of the oppressed classes.

The ultrarevolutionary period in the Soviet Union ended with Lenin and Stalin, but in China the "ultra-revolution" rages continued into the seventies with Mao's periodic appeal to the revolutionary spirit as demonstrated by the so-called "cultural revolution" and the Red Guard movement. Some of the Communist ideologists refer to this process of turmoil as the "permanent revolution." Once the revolutionary fervor subsides, the movement will fail. Similarly, Mao wonders about the fate of his movement when he passes from the scene.

---

* Hallgarten, *Why Dictators?*

FREEDOM
AND
EQUALITY

4

POINT

*Secrecy in government is funda-
mentally anti-democratic and unacceptable.*

Mr. Justice Douglas, with whom Mr.
Justice Black joins, concurring . . .

The dominant purpose of the First
Amendment was to prohibit the widespread practice of governmental suppression of embarrassing information.
It is common knowledge that the First
Amendment was adopted against the
widespread use . . . of the common
law of seditious libel to punish the dis-
semination of material that . . . is
embarrassing to the powers-that-be.
. . . The present cases will, I think,
go down in history as the most dramatic illustration of that principle. A
debate of large proportions goes on

COUNTERPOINT

*There are no liberties of the indi-
vidual that must be respected by
the government.*

Not until the nationalistic political
[Nazi] philosophy had become dominant could the liberalistic idea of
basic rights be really overcome. The
concept of personal liberties of the
individual as opposed to the authority
of the state had to disappear. . . .
There are no personal liberties of the
individual which fall outside of the
realm of the state and which must
be respected by the state. . . .
There can no longer be any question
of a private sphere, free of state influence, which is sacred and untouch-
able before the political unity. The
constitution of the nationalistic Reich
is therefore not based upon a system

118

in the Nation over our posture in Vietnam. That debate antedated the disclosure of the contents of the present documents. The latter are highly relevant to the debate in progress.

Secrecy in government is fundamentally anti-democratic, perpetuating bureaucratic errors. Open debate and discussion of public issues are vital to our national health. On public questions there should be "open and robust debate." . . .*

of inborn and inalienable rights of the individual. . . . †

The point on the left above emphasizes that democratic freedoms must have an informed electorate to exist, that the people of a country must have a good idea of what is going on if there are to be real personal liberties. The Nazi German official theory on the right above, on the other hand, stresses that the authority of the government cannot be questioned by the individual citizen.

Personal freedom and equality are often spoken of together as if they were aspects of the same thing or as if they were synonyms. The truth of the matter is, however, that these two ideas involve conflicting elements. In several ways it can be argued that where you have the most freedom, there is the least equality. Along this same line of reasoning, in view of the unequal distribution of talents, strength, intellect, and ambition, it can be said that the greater the equality, the less freedom. In discussing democracy two thousand years ago, the ancient Greeks also spoke of a balance between freedom and equality and the need for finding some kind of compromise through legal measures, and today we still try to strike a medium between the two.

Personal Liberty

Personal liberty means more than just the right to be free from various types of governmental action. The right to privacy, for example, embraces

---

* From a Supreme Court decision, New York Times Co. v. U.S., 403 U.S. 713 (1971).

† From Ernst R. Huber, Constitutional Law of the Greater German Reich, 1939. Reprinted from a report by the Division of European Affairs, U.S. Department of State, entitled National Socialism (Washington, D.C.: Government Printing Office, 1943).

freedom to be let alone by government and by other persons as well. Like other rights, however, it is not absolute and is narrowed by the demands of other personal liberties which are enjoyed by other citizens. The "equal protection of the laws" guarantee in the Constitution requires government to step in to ensure that public money is spent fairly with regard to everyone; and this sometimes impinges on an individual's privacy. The right to privacy is limited by the other constitutional rights including freedom of speech and press. In one sense this means that all persons in a free society have the right to know what public officials and celebrities have done, are doing, and plan to do.

The right of access to information is part of the rights to free speech and press. These rights have been expanded in recent years by the United States Supreme Court. Another way to describe freedoms of speech and press is to call them freedom of expression. Although we can express our thoughts and opinions in ever increasing ways today—by speeches, books, newspapers, radio, television, motion pictures, and plays—the basic principles of free expression were well stated over three centuries ago in England in the historical example that follows. This selection is written in the language of early English.

Historical Example

John Milton in *Areopagitica:*

> . . . books are not temptations, nor vanities; but usefull drugs and materialls wherewith to temper and compose effective and strong medicines, which man's life cannot want. [That is, the kind of strong medicines that man cannot do without.] The rest, as children and childish men, who have not the art to qualifie and prepare these working mineralls, well may be exhorted to forebear, . . . That this order of licencing conduces nothing to the end for which it was framed; and hath almost prevented me. . . . See the ingenuity of Truth, who when she gets a free and willing hand, opens herself faster, then the pace of method and discourse can overtake her.

John Milton was an outstanding champion of freedom of expression who published his monumental work, the *Areopagitica,* in 1644. He was in opposition to a new law of Parliament that required all books to be licensed by an official censor before publication. The objective of this act was to silence political opposition and to bring about religious uniformity. Milton and other men of independent outlook saw in the act a revival of the tyranny of the Stuart kings. For several years prior to the act, printing had been practically free of government control, and numerous pamphlets had been published representing every shade of political and religious opinion. Milton saw this diversity of writing as a wholesome sign of the free exchange of ideas stimulating intellectual creativity and progress. He argued that it was necessary to read books of every sort to attain knowledge in a world where good and evil grew up together and interconnected. He also pointed out that it was impossible to make men virtuous by imposing external prohibitions. Because degrading influences were to be found everywhere, the attempt to "purify" published writings was seen by Milton as an exercise in futility. The only way to combat corrupting factors was to encourage man's internal discipline and his intellect.

In our quoted excerpt, Milton attacks the law as a deterrent to intellectual activity and the pursuit of truth. He also points out that books are like powerful drugs out of which strong medicines may be compounded and from which children and fools should be protected. However, according to Milton, general censorship was not the answer. A modern parallel to this premise is the United States Supreme Court's reasoning that literature and motion pictures should not be prohibited on the grounds that they are not suitable for children. Finally, Milton points out the improbability of obtaining truly learned and judicious minds to serve as censors under the act. The result would be, he asserted, licensers who are ignorant—a most unhappy prospect for an enlightened society.

A contradiction to the growth of freedom of access to information is the right to be let alone in many areas of our lives. One of the newest problem areas concerning freedom for the ordinary citizens is invasion of privacy. The growing ability of government and other powerful organizations to collect information—by ever more sophisticated and effective electronic devices—and to organize the information and use it for long periods—by means of computers and data banks—makes everyone's life much more subject to inspection than ever before in the history of mankind. Professor of Law Arthur R. Miller poses a warning about surveillance activities in his "The Assault on Privacy."

THE ASSAULT ON PRIVACY:
How Far Must Surveillance Go?

ARTHUR R. MILLER

Have you applied for a credit card or life insurance, filed a tax return, traveled by airplane, rented a car, or stayed at a member of a national hotel chain recently?

Do you receive any governmental benefits, such as Social Security or welfare payments?

Are you a member of the American Civil Liberties Union, the Women's Strike for Peace or the NAACP?

Have you attended an antiwar meeting or demonstrated for increased benefits for the poor?

Since the answer to at least one of these questions undoubtedly is "yes," then a dossier on you exists in somebody's data bank.

Most Americans are unaware of the extent to which governmental agencies and private companies are using computers and microfilm to collect, store, and exchange sensitive information about the activities of private citizens. These efforts typically go unnoticed because they are well intentioned and easily justified.

The law enforcement establishment claims file-building is necessary to fight organized crime and restore "law and order." The F.B.I., C.I.A. and the Army rationalize their surveillance efforts in terms of combating subversion or quelling campus disruptions and riots in our cities.

As to the information activities of credit grantors and insurance companies, which include considerable snooping into an individual's private life, it simply is good business to know as much as possible about a man before you lend him money or insure his life. Unfortunately, the public seems oblivious to the negative implications of spiraling data gathering.

Potentially the most dangerous application of the new look in information collection is the Army's surveillance and storage of information

Professor Miller teaches law at the University of Michigan. His book The Assault on Privacy—Computers, Data Banks, and Dossiers *will be published later this year. From* "The Surveillance Society: Just How Far Can It Go?" *by Arthur R. Miller, Los Angeles* Times, *September 6, 1970, by permission of the author.*

on the lawful *political* activity of a wide range of groups and the preparation of "incident" reports and dossiers on individual citizens. This data bank apparently is a by-product of the military's role in the civil disorders of the mid-1960's.

Although information collection is essential to many of the Army's duties, the development of investigatory files on people seeking lawful social and political objectives bears little relationship to the military's functions during periods of social unrest—especially when many of those being scrutinized are extremely unlikely to be involved in a riot. Yet the mere knowledge that dossiers are being created on those who are politically active could deter people from exercising their constitutional rights of free speech and assembly.

Surveillance by Indirection

After a flurry of publicity about the Army's activities, the institution of a lawsuit by the American Civil Liberties Union, and sharply worded letters from several congressmen, the Army announced that it was abandoning its data bank. A close analysis of the military directives, however, leaves one in doubt as to what has actually been changed. The Army will continue to collect and distribute substantial quantities of data, albeit more discreetly.

Moreover, (1) the existing data will not actually be destroyed—it will be turned over to the Internal Security Division of the Justice Department, (2) an entirely separate computer-aided data bank on civilian disturbances has been discovered at the Counter-intelligence Analysis Division at the Pentagon, and (3) work is continuing on a computerized master index of all investigation subjects, which will enable the quick assembling of an individual's files held by various federal agencies.

The situation is made more ominous by the existence of an unregulated Secret Service computer containing dossiers on supposed "activists," "malcontents," and potential presidential assassins, as well as a data bank maintained by the Justice Department's civil disturbance group.

The development of a number of other information systems in the law enforcement arena magnifies the threat to personal privacy. The F.B.I.'s constantly expanding National Crime Information Center [N.C.I.C.] (prominently featured on the television series "The F.B.I.") provides state and city police forces with immediate access to computerized files on a vast array of people.

N.C.I.C. is the keynote of an emerging information network that will tie together the nation's law enforcement information centers. By the end of 1969 the F.B.I.'s center reportedly was already exchanging data with state and local police agencies in every state except Alaska.

State and local law enforcement surveillance systems also are becoming increasingly sophisticated—several with the aid of funding from the federal government. New York already has the essential features of a network built around a single computer center designed to store information for state and local agencies and permit them to retrieve data through terminals placed throughout the state.

An Ohio system allows 38 agencies to share its computerized information and is connected both to N.C.I.C. and the Ohio State Highway Patrol computer center; plans are under way to tie it to systems in Kentucky and Indiana.

Scotland Yard is developing an information system that will be available to constables throughout the British Isles. Similar data banks are being developed in other nations and by international organizations such as Interpol. Satellite or cable transmission will enable these centers to exchange data with N.C.I.C., which can then forward it to state and local systems.

The same quest for efficiency and expediency that is leading to information integration among different units of government is encouraging the collection of increasingly sensitive personal data and the development of even more comprehensive networks.

The U.S. Office of Education is supporting a migrant worker children data bank, the Department of Housing and Urban Development is sponsoring computerized municipal information systems and building files on housing loan applicants (with particular attention to those who are ineligible), and President Nixon's welfare reform proposal (the Family Assistance Act) will give HEW authority to exchange individualized data with state welfare agencies. It would be foolish to ignore the ease with which each of these data stores could be made a part of the law enforcement and surveillance information flow.

At present there are no effective restraints on these activities and no one is monitoring the mushrooming systems to insure that individuals are protected against their misuse. Indeed, a survey by one congressional subcommittee revealed many instances of agency demands for information that are not even authorized by Congress. Thus, it comes as no surprise that the Army's surveillance efforts have never been authorized by the nation's lawmakers.

What is more, muscle flexing is a common government technique for furthering its data-gathering efforts. Information collectors often deceive people by intimating that the law requires a response to questionnaires that in fact are voluntary, or they use coercive practices to extract information from citizens.

Nor is the business community immune from these activities. For example, in an effort to trace the movement of American funds abroad—particularly to Swiss banks, draft evaders and the Viet Cong—the F.B.I. is watching many domestic banking and credit transactions. Financial institutions rarely object to these intrusions on their files, in part because a large number of bank and corporate security officers are former F.B.I. and law enforcement agents.

The FBI and the Business Community

Furthermore, since the F.B.I. has jurisdiction over bank fraud cases, the banks find it to their advantage to "cooperate" with the government —especially since they may want an informational favor from the government tomorrow. Small wonder that the F.B.I. was able to examine over 25,000 credit bureau files last year without bothering to secure subpoenas.

The government's hyperactivity in collecting information is not offset by its exercise of restraint in using it. On one occasion the F.B.I. publicly released 1,200 pages of transcripts of electronically recorded conversations among alleged Mafia figures in which numerous prominent Americans were talked about, often disparagingly.

Even conceding the desirability of informing the public of the threat that organized crime poses to our society, need it be done by encouraging the daily press to publish unsworn conversations procured surreptitiously by governmental bugging? In a similar vein, why shouldn't citizens have doubts about entrusting personal information to the government when they learn that supposedly confidential tax returns are readily available to presidential assistants and are cavalierly given to state and local taxing agencies?

The computerized data banks of the future most assuredly will be a magnet for snoopers, muckraking newsmen, and political operatives. Tomorrow's dossier may well contain public record data gathered from many sources and intermingled with subjective intelligence reports, information given by the data subject or other people with the understanding that it would remain confidential, and informaton transferred from numerous computer systems.

It is unrealistic to assume that the managers or proprietors of these systems—whether governmental or private—will take it upon themselves to protect us against misuse of the data in their care.

Surprisingly, only a few voices have been raised to protest the potential ill effects of this rising tide of information collection. Perhaps the most forceful has been that of Sen. Sam J. Ervin Jr. (D-NC), who has repeatedly taken to the Senate floor to argue that "the very existence of government files on how people exercise First Amendment rights, how they think, speak, assemble and act in lawful pursuits, is a form of official psychological coercion to keep silent and to refrain from acting."

Although the senator is effectively serving as the nation's conscience in matters relating to personal privacy, he cannot fight the march toward 1984 alone. Unless the public sheds its complacency, we will soon find ourselves at the mercy of the data-philes and the computerniks.

The long-range solution, if we are to preserve any control over our own information profile and prevent the abusive manipulation of data banks and dossiers, is effective legislation outlining what is legitimate information collection and prescribing the proper uses to which personal information may be put. We all want society to benefit from the computer and modern information science, but that can be achieved only if we strike a rational balance between technocracy and democracy.

While some proponents of freedom call for curtailing government involvement in the economic and social spheres, others consider it a moral obligation of government to take positive action for assuring the well-being of the citizen. To Harold Laski, professor at the London School of Economics until his death in 1950, freedom is not merely the negative concept of absence of government restraints, but a positive notion of creating an atmosphere for individual self-fulfillment. According to his line of reasoning, to call a resident of a ghetto in a city in the United States "a free man" is deceitful. If the individual lacks an education, is poor and in bad health, and sees no hope for a change in his situation, does he enjoy freedom? This view of freedom is often termed "freedom from want or fear." In our next reading, Laski discusses positive government actions to secure what he sees as fundamental individual rights and freedoms.

LIBERTY AND EQUALITY

HAROLD J. LASKI

By liberty I mean the eager maintenance of that atmosphere in which men have the opportunity to be their best selves. Liberty, therefore, is a product of rights. A State built upon the conditions essential

Reprinted from Harold J. Laski, Grammar of Politics *(London: George Allen and Unwin Ltd., 1937), pp. 142–49, by permission of the publisher.*

to the full development of our faculties will confer freedom upon its citizens. It will release their individuality. It will enable them to contribute their peculiar and intimate experience to the common stock. It will offer security that the decisions of the government are built upon the widest knowledge open to its members. It will prevent that frustration of creative impulse which destroys the special character of men. Without rights there cannot be liberty, because, without rights, men are the subjects of law unrelated to the needs of personality.

Liberty, therefore, is a positive thing. It does not merely mean absence of restraint. Regulation, obviously enough, is the consequence of gregariousness; for we cannot live together without common rules. What is important is that the rules made should embody an experience I can follow and, in general, accept. I shall not feel that my liberty is endangered when I am refused permission to commit murder. My creative impulses do not suffer frustration when I am bidden to drive on a given side of the road. I am not even deprived of freedom when the law ordains that I must educate my children. Historic experience has evolved for us rules of convenience which promote right living. To compel obedience to them is not to make a man unfree. Wherever there are avenues of conduct which must be prohibited in the common interest, their removal from the sphere of unrestrained action need not constitute an invasion of liberty.

That is not, of course, to argue that every such prohibition is justified merely because it is made by an authority legally competent to issue it. Governments may in fact invade liberty even while they claim to be acting in the common interest. The exclusion of Nonconformists from full political privilege was an invasion of liberty. The restriction of the franchise to the owners of property was an invasion of liberty. . . . I must be able to feel that my will has access to avenues through which it can impress itself upon the holders of power. If I have the sense that the orders issued are beyond my scrutiny or criticism, I shall be, in a vital sense, unfree.

Liberty, therefore, is not merely obedience to a rule. My self is too distinct from other selves to accept a given order as good unless I feel that my will is embodied in its substance. I shall, of course, be compelled to endure irksome restraints. I must fill up income-tax returns; I must light the lamps upon my own motor-car at a set time. But no normal person will regard restrictions of this kind as so unrelated to his will as to constitute coercion of it. Where restraint becomes an invasion of liberty is where the given prohibition acts so as to destroy that harmony of impulses which comes when a man knows that he is doing something it is worthwhile to do. Restraint is felt as evil when it frustrates the life of spiritual enrichment. What each of us desires in life is room for our personal initiative in the things that add to our moral stature. What is destructive of our freedom is a system of prohibitions which limits the initiative there implied. And it is imporant that the initiative be a continuous one. The minds of citizens must be active minds. They must be given the habit of thought. They must be given the avenues through which thought can act. They must be accustomed to the exercise of will and conscience if they are to be alert to the duties implied in their function as citizens. Liberty consists in nothing so much as the encouragement of the will based on the instructed conscience of humble men.

In such a background, we cannot accept Mill's famous attempt to define the limits of State interference. All conduct is social conduct in the sense that whatever I do has results upon me as a member of society. There are certain freedoms I must have in order to be more than an inert recipient of orders; there is an atmosphere about those freedoms of quick vigilance without which they cannot be maintained. Liberty thus involves in its nature restraints, because the separate freedoms I use are not freedoms to destroy the freedoms of those with whom I live. My freedoms are avenues of choice through which I may, as I deem fit, construct for myself my own course of conduct. And the freedoms I must possess to enjoy a general liberty are those which, in their sum, will constitute the path through which my best self is capable of attainment. That is not to say it will be attained. It is to say only that I alone can make that best self, and that without those freedoms I have not the means of manufacture at my disposal.

Freedoms are therefore opportunities which history has shown to be essential to the development of personality. And freedoms are inseparable from rights because, otherwise, their realisation is hedged about with an uncertainty which destroys their quality. If, for example, my utterance of opinion is followed by persecution, I shall, in general, cease to express my mind. I shall cease, in fact, to be a citizen; and the state for me ceases to have meaning. For if I cannot embody my experience in its will, it ceases, sooner or later, to assume that I have a will at all. Nothing, therefore, is so likely to maintain a condition of liberty as the knowledge that the invasion of rights will result in protest, and, if need be, resistance. Liberty is nothing if it is not the organised and conscious power to resist in the last resort. The implied threat of contingent anarchy is a safeguard against the abuse of government.

I have set liberty here in the context of opportunity, and, in its turn, opportunity in the context of the State. That is the only atmosphere in which it admits of organisation. We can create channels; we cannot force men to take advantage of those channels. We can, further, create channels only in limited number. A man may feel that all that he cares for in life depends upon success in love; we can remove the barriers of caste or race or religion which, in the past, have barred his access to that love. But we cannot guarantee to him that his plea will be successful. The avenues which organisation can create are always limited by the fact that the most intimate realisation of oneself is personal and built upon isolations which evade social control.

Yet the social control is important. If in the last resort, the State cannot make me happy, certainly it can, if it so will, compel unhappiness. It can invade my private life in wanton fashion. It can degrade me as a political unit in a fashion which distinguishes me from other citizens. It can protect an economic order which "implicates," in William James' phrase, unfreedom. None of these things is, of course, a genuinely separate category; at most the distinction is one of convenience. For liberty is a definite whole, because the life I lead is a totality in which I strive to realise a whole personality as harmonious. Yet each of these aspects is sufficiently clear to warrant a separate word.

But it must first be urged that in this context State-action is action by government. It means the maintenance of rules which affect my liberty. Those rules will be issued by persons, and, normally, those persons will be the government. Theories which seek to differentiate between State and government almost always ignore the substance of the administrative act. Rights withheld mean rights which the holders of power withhold. To say that in a democratic theory the mass of citizens are the holders of power is to miss the vital fact that the people, in the pressure of daily affairs, cannot exercise that power in detail in States of the modern size. They may have influence and opinion; but these are not the power of government. It is the cumulative force of administrative acts which are the heart of the modern State. The principles behind these acts are, of course, of prime importance. But principles may be invalidated by the method of their application; and it is governments which have the actual administration of them.

Liberty, therefore, is never real unless the government can be called to account; and it should always be called to account when it invades rights. It will always invade them unless its organization prevents it from being weighted in some special interest. The three aspects of liberty I have noted are always relative to this situation. By private liberty, for example, I mean the opportunity to exercise freedom of choice in those areas of life where the results of my effort mainly affect me in that isolation by which, at least ultimately, I am always surrounded. Religion is a good instance of this aspect. I am not truly free to decide without hindrance upon my creed unless there is not merely no penalty on any form of religious faith, but, also, no advantage of a political kind attached to one form rather than another. . . .

. . . In the complex modern State invasions of private liberty may be more subtle. Private liberty may be denied when the poor citizen is unable to secure adequate legal protection in the Courts of Justice. A divorce law, for example, which gives the rich access to its facilities but, broadly, makes them difficult, if not impossible, for the poor, invades their private freedom. So does the demand for excessive bail; so, too, when the poor prisoner, with inadequate counsel, confronts the legal ability at the command of government. Private liberty is thus that aspect of which the substance is mainly personal to a man's self. It is the opportunity to be fully himself in the private relations of life. It is the chance practically to avail himself of the safeguards evolved for the maintenance of those relations.

Political liberty means the power to be active in affairs of State. It means that I can let my mind play freely about the substance of public business. I must be able without hindrance to add my special experience to the general sum of experience. I must find no barriers that are not general barriers in the way of access to positions of authority. I must be able to announce my opinion and to concert with others in the announcement of opinion. For political liberty to be real, two conditions are essential. I must be educated to the point where I can express what I want in a way that is intelligible to others. Anyone who has seen the dumb inarticulateness of the poor will realise the urgency of education in this regard. Nothing is more striking than the way in which our educational systems train the children of rich or well-born men to habits of authority while the children of the poor are trained to habits of deference. Such a division of attitude can never produce political freedom, because a class trained to govern will exert its power because it is conscious of it, while a class trained to deference will not fulfil its wants because it does not know how to formulate its demands. Combination in the period of experience will, of course, as with trade unions, do something to restore the balance; but it will never fully compensate for the defect of early training. For the inculcation of deferential habits will never produce a free people. It is only when men have learned that they themselves make and work institutions that they can learn to adjust them to their needs.

The second condition of political liberty is the provision of an honest and straightforward supply of news. Those who are to decide must have truthful material upon which to decide. Their judgment must not be thwarted by the presentation of a biased case. We have learned, especially of late years, that this is no easy matter. A statesman cannot seldom be made what the press chooses to make him. A policy may be represented as entirely good or bad by the skillful omission of relevant facts. Our civilisation has stimulated the creation of agencies which live deliberately on the falsification of news. It would, indeed, not be very wide of the mark to argue that much of what had been achieved by the art of education in the nineteenth century had been frustrated by the art of propaganda in the twentieth. The problem is made more complex than in the past by the area over which our judgment must pass. We have no leisure to survey that area with comprehensive accuracy. We must, very largely, take our facts on trust. But if the facts are deliberately perverted, our judgment will be unrelated to the truth. A people without reliable news is, sooner or later, a people without the basis of freedom. For to exercise one's judgment in a miasma of distortion is, ultimately, to go disastrously astray.

By economic liberty I mean security and the opportunity to find reasonable significance in the earning of one's daily bread. I must, that is, be free from the constant fear of unemployment and insufficiency which, perhaps more than any other inadequacies, sap the whole strength of personality. I must be safeguarded against the wants of tomorrow. I must know that I can build a home, and make that home a means of self-expression. I must be able to make my personality flow through my effort as a producer of services, and find in that effort the capacity of enrichment. For, otherwise, I become a stunted and shrunken being in that aspect of myself which lends colour and texture to all that I am. Either I must, in this sense, be free, or I become one of those half-souls who are found in the slums and prisons as the casualties of civilisation. Nor is this all. I must be more than the recipient of orders which I must obey unthinkingly because my labour is only a commodity bought and sold in the market, like coal and boots and chairs. Without these freedoms, or, at least, an access to them, men are hardly less truly slaves than when they were exposed for purchase and sale.

Economic liberty, therefore, implies democracy in industry. That means two things. It means that industrial government is subject to the system of rights which obtain for men as citizens, and it means that industrial direction must be of a character that makes it the rule of laws made by co-operation and not by compulsion. Obivously, the character of those laws must depend upon the needs of production. Those needs leave less room for spontaneity than is true either of private or of political liberty. A man is entitled to be original about his politics or his religion; he is not entitled to be original when he is working with others, say, in a nitro-glycerine factory. But he is entitled to co-operate in the setting of the standards by which he is judged industrially and in the application of those standards. Otherwise, he lives at the behest of other men. His initiative becomes not the free expression of his own individuality, but a routine made from without and enforced upon him by fear of starvation. A system built upon fear is always fatal to the release of the creative faculties, and it is therefore incompatible with liberty.

The basis for much of our present law on the subject of equality, Section I of the Fourteenth Amendment to the United States Constitution, proposed by Congress in 1868, is the next selection.

AMENDMENT XIV (1868)

THE CONSTITUTION OF THE UNITED STATES

Section 1. All persons born or naturalized in the United States, and subject to the jurisdictions thereof, are citizens of the United States and of the State wherein they reside. No State shall make or enforce any law which shall abridge the privileges or immunities of citizens of the United States; nor shall any States deprive any person of life, liberty, or property, without due process of law; nor deny to any person with its jurisdiction the equal protection of the laws.

The "equal protection of the laws" clause has been the foundation for the bulk of civil rights cases of recent decades. The Supreme Court case of *Brown v. Topeka Board of Education* (1954) is quoted as the next reading. This landmark decision is an example of the official reasoning of our national government with regard to the meaning of equality before the law in contemporary America. In 1896, the Supreme Court decision of *Plessy v. Ferguson* had established the "separate but equal" doctrine. This meant that equal protection of the laws was given by governmental authorities if equal facilities, such as schools, public waiting rooms, seats on public conveyances, and public recreation facilities, were provided for blacks even though these facilities were separated from those provided for whites. This decision legalized racial segregation, commonly called "Jim Crow" laws, in a number of states from 1896 to 1954. The *Brown* v. *Topeka Board of Education* decision overruled the Plessy case by stating that separate facilities are "inherently unequal."

BROWN v. BOARD OF EDUCATION OF TOPEKA

UNITED STATES SUPREME COURT

Mr. Chief Justice Warren delivered the opinion of the Court.

These cases come to us from the States of Kansas, South Carolina, Virginia, and Delaware. They are premised on different facts and different local conditions, but a common legal question justifies their consideration together in this consolidated opinion.

In each of the cases, minors of the Negro race, through their legal representatives, seek the aid of the courts in obtaining admission to the public schools of their community on a non-segregated basis. In each instance, they had been denied admission to schools attended by white children under laws requiring or permitting segregation according to race. This segregation was alleged to deprive the plaintiffs of the equal protection of the laws under the Fourteenth Amendment. In each of the cases other than the Delaware case, a three-judge federal district court denied relief to the plaintiffs on the so-called "separate but equal" doctrine announced by this Court in *Plessy* v. *Ferguson,* 163 U. S. 537. Under that doctrine, equality of treatment is accorded when the races are provided substantially equal facilities, even though these facilities be separate. In the Delaware case, the Supreme Court of Delaware adhered to that doctrine, but ordered that the plaintiffs be admitted to the white schools because of their superiority to the Negro schools.

The plaintiffs contend that segregated public schools are not "equal" and cannot be made "equal," and that hence they are deprived of the equal protection of the laws. Because of the obvious importance of the question presented, the Court took jurisdiction. Argument was heard in the 1952 Term, and reargument was heard this Term on certain questions propounded by the Court.

. . . In the first cases in this Court construing the Fourteenth Amendment, decided shortly after its adoption, the Court interpreted

347 U.S. 483, 74 S. Ct. 686, 98 L. Ed. 873 (1954).

it as proscribing all state-imposed discriminations against the Negro race. The doctrine of "separate but equal" did not make its appearance in this Court until 1896 in the case of *Plessy* v. *Ferguson,* supra, involving not education but transportation. American courts have since labored with the doctrine for over half a century. . . . In more recent cases, all on the graduate level, inequality was found in that specific benefits enjoyed by white students were denied to Negro students of the same educational qualifications. . . . In none of these cases was it necessary to reexamine the doctrine to grant relief to the Negro plaintiff. And in *Sweatt* v. *Painter,* supra, the Court expressly reserved decision on the question whether *Plessy* v. *Ferguson* should be held inapplicable to public education.

In the instant cases, that question is directly presented. Here, unlike *Sweatt* v. *Painter,* there are findings below that the Negro and white schools involved have been equalized, or are being equalized, with respect to buildings, curricula, qualifications and salaries of teachers, and other "tangible" factors. Our decision, therefore, cannot turn on merely a comparison of these tangible factors in the Negro and white schools involved in each of the cases. We must look instead to the effect of segregation itself on public education.

In approaching this problem, we cannot turn the clock back to 1868 when the Amendment was adopted, or even to 1896 when *Plessy* v. *Ferguson* was written. We must consider public education in the light of its full development and its present place in American life throughout the Nation. Only in this way can it be determined if segregation in public schools deprives these plaintiffs of the equal protection of the laws.

Today, education is perhaps the most important function of state and local governments. Compulsory school attendance laws and the great expenditures for education both demonstrate our recognition of the importance of education to our democratic society. It is required in the performance of our most basic public responsibility, even service in the armed forces. It is the very foundation of good citizenship. Today it is a principal instrument in awakening the child to cultural values, in preparing him for later professional training, and in helping him to adjust normally to his environment. In these days, it is doubtful that any child may reasonably be expected to succeed in life if he is denied the opportunity of an education. Such an opportunity, where the state has undertaken to provide it, is a right which must be made available to all on equal terms.

We come then to the question presented: Does segregation of children in public schools solely on the basis of race, even though the physical facilities and other "tangible" factors may be equal, deprive the children of the minority group of equal education opportunities? We believe that it does.

In *Sweatt* v. *Painter,* supra, in finding that a segregated law school for Negroes could not provide them equal educational opportunities, this Court relied in large part on "those qualities which are incapable of objective measurement but which make for greatness in a law school." In *McLaurin* v. *Oklahoma State Regents,* supra, the Court, in requiring that a Negro admitted to a white graduate school be treated like all other students, again resorted to intangible considerations: ". . . his ability to study, to engage in discussions and exchange views with other students, and, in general, to learn his profession." Such considerations apply with added force to children in grade and high schools. To separate them from others of similar age and qualifications solely because of their race generates a feeling of inferiority as to their status in the community that may affect their hearts and minds in a way unlikely ever to be undone. The effect of this separation on their educational opportunities was well stated by a finding in the Kansas case by a court which nevertheless felt compelled to rule against the Negro plaintiffs:

> Segregation of white and colored children in public schools has a detrimental effect upon the colored children. The impact is greater when it has the sanction of the law; for the policy of separating the races is usually interpreted as denoting the inferiority of the Negro group. A sense of inferiority affects the motivation of a child to learn. Segregation with the sanction of law, therefore, has a tendency to retard the educational and mental development of Negro children and to deprive them of some of the benefits they would receive in a racially integrated school system.

Whatever may have been the extent of psychological knowledge at the time of *Plessy* v. *Ferguson,* this finding is amply supported by modern authority. Any language in *Plessy* v. *Ferguson* contrary to this finding is rejected.

We conclude that in the field of public education the doctrine of "separate but equal" has no place. Separate educational facilities are inherently unequal. Therefore, we hold that the plaintiffs and others similarly situated for whom the actions have been brought are, by reason of the segregation complained of, deprived of the equal protection of the laws guaranteed by the Fourteenth Amendment. This disposition makes unnecessary any discussion whether such segregation also violates the Due Process Clause of the Fourteenth Amendment.

The next selection of the chapter is from the Supreme Court decision of *Miranda v. Arizona* (1966) and is an example of judicial interpretation of several other parts of our Bill of Rights. The decision makes it clear that there is an underlying right to a fair trial included in the guarantees found in the Fifth and Fourteenth Amendments. The Fifth Amendment also includes the right to remain silent (the right not to be compelled to be a witness against oneself). Finally, the Sixth Amendment guarantees the right to have the assistance of counsel in all criminal prosecutions. The Court is attempting to make a reality of the American motto "Equal justice under the law." A defense attorney is considered a necessity rather than a luxury in the reasoning of this case. The judicial language concludes with these words: "Were we to limit these constitutional rights to those who can retain an attorney, our decision today would be of little significance."

MIRANDA v. ARIZONA

UNITED STATES SUPREME COURT

Mr. Chief Justice Warren delivered the opinion of the Court.

The cases before us raise questions which go to the roots of our concepts of American criminal jurisprudence: the restraints society must observe consistent with the Federal Constitution in prosecuting individuals for crime. More specifically, we deal with the admissibility of statements obtained from an individual who is subjected to custodial police interrogation and the necessity for procedures which assure that the individual is accorded his privilege under the Fifth Amendment to the Constitution not to be compelled to incriminate himself.

We dealt with certain phases of this problem recently in *Escobedo v. Illinois*, 378 U. S. 478 (1964). There, as in the four cases before us, law enforcement officials took the defendant into custody and interrogated him in a police station for the purpose of obtaining a confession.

384 U.S. 436, 86 S. Ct. 1602, 16 L. Ed. 2d 694 (1966).

The police did not effectively advise him of his right to remain silent or of his right to consult with his attorney. Rather, they confronted him with an alleged accomplice who accused him of having perpetuated a murder. When the defendant denied the accusation and said "I didn't shoot Manuel, you did it," they handcuffed him and took him to an interrogation room. There, while handcuffed and standing, he was questioned for four hours until he confessed. During this interrogation, the police denied his request to speak to his attorney, and they prevented his retained attorney, who had come to the police station, from consulting with him. At his trial, the State, over his objection, introduced the confession against him. We held that the statements thus made were constitutionally inadmissible.

This case has been the subject of judicial interpretation and spirited legal debate since it was decided two years ago. Both state and federal courts, in assessing its implications, have arrived at varying conclusions. A wealth of scholarly material has been written tracing its ramifications and underpinnings. Police and prosecutor have speculated on its range and desirability.[1] We granted certiorari in these cases, 382 U.S. 924, 925, 937, in order further to explore some facets of the problems thus exposed, of applying the privilege against self-incrimination to incustody interrogation, and to give concrete constitutional guidelines for law enforcement agencies and courts to follow.

---

[1] For example, the Los Angeles Police Chief stated that "If the police are required . . . to . . . establish that the defendant was apprised of his constitutional guarantees of silence and legal counsel prior to the uttering of any admission or confession, and that he intelligently waived these guarantees . . . a whole Pandora's box is opened as to under what circumstances . . . can a defendant intelligently waive these rights. . . . Allegations that modern criminal investigation can compensate for the lack of a confession or admission in every criminal case is totally absurd!" Parker, 40 L. A. Bar Bull. 603, 607, 642 (1965). His prosecutorial counterpart, District Attorney Younger, stated that "[I]t begins to appear that many of these seemingly restrictive decisions are going to contribute directly to a more effective, efficient and professional level of law enforcement." L. A. Times, Oct. 2, 1965, p. 1. The former Police Commissioner of New York, Michael J. Murphy, stated of *Escobedo:* "What the Court is doing is akin to requiring one boxer to fight by Marquis of Queensbury rules while permitting the other to butt, gouge and bite." N. Y. Times, May 14, 1965, p. 39. The former United States Attorney for the District of Columbia, David C. Acheson, who is presently Special Assistant to the Secretary of the Treasury (for Enforcement), and directly in charge of the Secret Service and the Bureau of Narcotics, observed that "Prosecution procedure has, at most, only the most remote causal connection with crime. Changes in court decisions and prosecution procedures would have about the same effect on the crime rate as an aspirin would have on a tumor of the brain." Quoted in Herman, *supra,* n. 2, at 500, n. 270. Other views on the subject in general are collected in Weisberg, Police Interrogation of Arrested Persons: A Skeptical View, 52 J. Crim. L., C. & P. S. 21 (1961).

We start here, as we did in *Escobedo,* with the premise that our holding is not an innovation in our jurisprudence, but is an application of principles long recognized and applied in other settings. We have undertaken a thorough re-examination of the *Escobedo* decision and the principles it announced, and we reaffirm it. That case was but an explication of basic rights that are enshrined in our Constitution—that "No person . . . shall be compelled in any criminal case to be a witness against himself," and that "the accused shall . . . have the Assistance of Counsel"—rights which were put in jeopardy in that case through official overbearing. These precious rights were fixed in our Constitution only after centuries of persecution and struggle. And in the words of Chief Justice Marshall, they were secured "for ages to come, and . . . designed to approach immortality as nearly as human institutions can approach it," *Cohens* v. *Virginia,* 6 Wheat. 264, 387 (1821). . . .

. . .

Because of the nature of the problem and because of its recurrent significance in numerous cases, we have to this point discussed the relationship of the Fifth Amendment privilege to police interrogation without specific concentration on the facts of the cases before us. We turn now to these facts to consider the application to these cases of the constitutional principles discussed above. In each instance, we have concluded that statements were obtained from the defendant under circumstances that did not meet constitutional standards for protection of the privilege.

No. 759. *Miranda* v. *Arizona*

On March 13, 1963, petitioner, Ernesto Miranda, was arrested at his home and taken in custody to a Phoenix police station. He was there identified by the complaining witness. The police then took him to "Interrogation Room No. 2" of the detective bureau. There he was questioned by two police officers. The officers admitted at trial that Miranda was not advised that he had a right to have an attorney present.[2] Two hours later, the officers emerged from the interrogation room with a written confession signed by Miranda. At the top of the statement

---

[2] Miranda was also convicted in a separate trial on an unrelated robbery charge not presented here for review. A statement introduced at that trial was obtained from Miranda during the same interrogation which resulted in the confession involved here. At the robbery trial, one officer testified that during the interrogation he did not tell Miranda that anything he said would be held against him or that he could consult with an attorney. The other officer stated that they had both told Miranda that anything he said would be used against him and that he was not required by law to tell them anything.

was a typed paragraph stating that the confession was made voluntarily, without threats or promises of immunity and "with full knowledge of my legal rights, understanding any statement I make may be used against me." [3]

At his trial before a jury, the written confession was admitted into evidence over the objection of defense counsel, and the officers testified to the prior oral confession made by Miranda during the interrogation. Miranda was found guilty of kidnapping and rape. He was sentenced to 20 to 30 years' imprisonment on each count, the sentences to run concurrently. On appeal, the Supreme Court of Arizona held that Miranda's constitutional rights were not violated in obtaining the confession and affirmed the conviction. 98 Ariz. 18, 401 P. 2d 721. In reaching its decision, the court emphasized heavily the fact that Miranda did not specifically request counsel.

We reverse. From the testimony of the officers and by the admission of respondent, it is clear that Miranda was not in any way apprised of his right to consult with an attorney and to have one present during the interrogation, nor was his right not to be compelled to incriminate himself effectively protected in any other manner. Without these warnings the statements were inadmissible. The mere fact that he signed a statement which contained a typed-in clause stating that he had "full knowledge" of his "legal rights" does not approach the knowing and intelligent waiver required to relinquish constitutional rights. . . .

Therefore, in accordance with the foregoing, the judgment of the Supreme Court of Arizona is reversed.

After the Miranda case was decided in 1966 a heavy burden rested upon the government to demonstrate that a defendant's confession was voluntary and that he knowingly and intelligently waived his privilege to remain silent and right to counsel. Otherwise his confession was inadmissible in court.

In 1968, however, the Congress responded to claims that police procedure was too severely restricted by considerably reducing the impact of *Miranda*. By enacting the Omnibus Crime Control and Safe Streets Act, quoted in part below, evidence against an accused person was made more readily admissible in court. The law made voluntariness much more a matter for the trial judge to determine. TITLE II OF THE OMNIBUS CRIME CONTROL AND SAFE STREETS ACT OF 1968—ADMISSIBILITY OF CONFESSIONS amends

---

[3] One of the officers testified that he read this paragraph to Miranda. Apparently, however, he did not do so until after Miranda had confessed orally.

Chapter 223, title 18, United States Code, by adding the following new section:

> § 3501. *Admissibility of confessions*
> (a) In any criminal prosecution brought by the United States or by the District of Columbia, a confession, as defined in subsection (e) hereof, shall be admissible in evidence if it is voluntarily given. Before such confession is received in evidence the trial judge shall, out of the presence of the jury, determine any issue as to voluntariness. If the trial judge determines that the confession was voluntarily made it shall be admitted in evidence and the trial judge shall permit the jury to hear relevant evidence on the issue of voluntariness and shall instruct the jury to give such weight to the confession as the jury feels it deserves under all the circumstances.

At the beginning of this chapter it was noted that freedom and equality can be seen as two conflicting elements, that where you have the most freedom you have the least equality. Our last selection on this subject is a penetrating analysis by Professor John H. Schaar that questions the validity of the widely announced notion of equality of opportunity in our society.

EQUALITY OF OPPORTUNITY AND BEYOND

JOHN H. SCHAAR

The first thing to notice is that the usual formulation of the doctrine—equality of opportunity for all to develop their capacities—is rather misleading, for the fact always is that not all talents can be developed equally in any given society. Out of the great variety of human resources available to it, a given society will admire and reward some abilities more than others. Every society has a set of values, and these are arranged in a more or less tidy hierarchy. These systems of evaluation vary from society to society: Soldierly qualities and virtues were highly admired and rewarded in Sparta, while poets languished. Hence, to be accurate, the equality of opportunity formula must be revised to read: equality

John H. Schaar, "Equality of Opportunity and Beyond," in Equality: Nomos IX, edited by J. Roland Pennock and John Chapman (New York: Lieber-Atherton, Inc., 1967), pp. 230–33, 243–44. Reprinted by permission of the publishers, Lieber-Atherton, Inc. Copyright © 1967 by Atherton Press. All Rights Reserved.

of opportunity for all to develop those talents which are highly valued by a given people at a given time.

When put in this way, it becomes clear that commitment to the formula implies prior acceptance of an already established social-moral order. Thus, the doctrine is, indirectly, very conservative. It enlists support for the established pattern of values. It also encourages change and growth, to be sure, but mainly along the lines of tendency already apparent and approved in a given society. The doctrine is "progressive" only in the special sense that it encourages and hastens progress within a going pattern of institutions, activities, and values. It does not advance alternatives to the existing pattern. Perhaps we have here an example of those policies that Dwight D. Eisenhower and the theorists of the Republican Party characterized as the method of "dynamic conservatism."

If this argument is correct, then the present-day "radicals" who demand the fullest extension of the equal-opportunity principle to all groups within the society, and especially to Negroes and the lower classes, are really more conservative than the "conservatives" who oppose them. No policy formula is better designed to fortify the dominant institutions, values, and ends of the American social order than the formula of equality of opportunity, for it offers *everyone* a fair and equal chance to find a place within that order. In principle, it excludes no man from the system if his abilities can be put to use within the system. We have here another example of the repeated tendency of American radicals to buttress the existing framework of order even while they think they are undermining it, another example of the inability of those who see themselves as radical critics of the established system to fashion a rhetoric and to formulate ends and values that offer a genuine alternative to the system. Time after time, never more loyally than at the present, America's radicals have been her best conservatives.

Before one subscribes to the equality-of-opportunity formula, then, he should be certain that the dominant values, institutions, and goals of his society are the ones he really wants. The tone and content of much of our recent serious literature and social thought—thought that escapes the confines of the conservative-radical framework—warn that we are well on the way toward building a culture our best men will not honor. The facile formula of equal opportunity quickens that trend. It opens more and more opportunities for more and more people to contribute more and more energies toward the realization of a mass, bureaucratic, technological, privatized, materialistic, bored, and thrill-seeking, consumption-oriented society—a society of well-fed, congenial, and sybaritic monkeys surrounded by gadgets and pleasure-toys.

Secondly, it is clear that the equal-opportunity policy will increase the inequalities among men. In previous ages, when opportunities were restricted to those of the right birth and station, it is highly probable, given the fact that nature seems to delight in distributing many traits in the pattern of a normal distribution, and given the phenomenon of regression toward the mean, that many of those who enjoyed abundant opportunities to develop their talents actually lacked the native ability to benefit from their advantages. It is reasonable to suppose that many members of ascribed elites, while appearing far superior to the ruck, really were not that superior in actual attainment. Under the regime of equal opportunity, however, only those who genuinely are superior in the desired attributes will enjoy rich opportunities to develop their qualities. This would produce, within a few generations, a social system where the members of the elites really were immensely superior in ability and attainment to the masses. We should then have a condition where the natural and social aristocracies would be identical—a meritocracy, as Michael Young has called it.[1]

Furthermore, the more closely a society approaches meritocracy, the wider grows the gap in ability and achievement between the highest and the lowest social orders. This will happen because in so many fields there are such huge quantities of things to be learned before one can become certified as competent that only the keenest talents, refined and enlarged by years of devoted study and work, can make the grade.[2] We call our age scientific, and describe it further as characterized by a knowledge explosion. What these labels mean from the perspective of equalitarianism is that a handful of men possess a tremendous fund of scientific knowledge, while the rest of us are about as innocent of science as we have always been. So the gap widens: The disparity between the scientific knowledge of an Einstein and the scientific knowledge of the ordinary man of our day is greater than the disparity between a Newton and the ordinary man of his day.

Another force helps widen the gap. Ours is an age of huge, complex, and powerful organizations. Those who occupy positions of command in these structures wield enormous power over their underlings, who, in the main, have become so accustomed to their servitude that they hardly feel it for what it is. The least efficient of the liberal-social welfare states

---

[1] Michael Young, *The Rise of Meritocracy* (London: Thomas and Hudson, 1958). Young's book imaginatively explores the conditions under which Jefferson's lovely dream of rule by the natural aristocracy turns into a nightmare of banality and outrage. The main condition, of course, is the dedication of virtually all creative energies to the goal of material abundance.

[2] Success is a function of both inborn talent and the urge to do well, and it is often impossible to tell which is the more important in a particular case. It is certain that the urge to do well can be stimulated by social institutions. How else can we account for Athens or Florence, or the United States?

of our day, for example, enjoys a degree of easy control over the ordinary lives of its subjects far beyond the wildest ambitions of the traditional "absolute" rulers. As the commanding positions in these giant organizations come to be occupied increasingly by men who have been generously endowed by nature and, under the equal-opportunity principle, highly favored by society, the power gap between the well- and the poorly-endowed widens. The doctrine of equality of opportunity, which in its origins was a rather nervous attempt to forestall moral criticisms of a competitive and inequalitarian society while retaining the fiction of moral equality, now ironically magnifies the natural differences among men by policies based on an ostensibly equalitarian rationale. The doctrine of equal opportunity, social policies and institutions based on it, and advances in knowledge all conspire with nature to produce more and more inequality.

This opens a larger theme. We untiringly tell ourselves that the principle of equality of opportunity is a generous one. It makes no distinctions of worth among men on any of the factitious grounds, such as race, religion, or nationality, that are equally offered for such distinctions. Nor does it set artificial limits on the individual. On the contrary, it so arranges social conditions that each individual can go as high as his natural abilities will permit. Surely, nothing could be fairer or more generous.

The generosity dissolves under analysis. The doctrine of equal opportunity, followed seriously, removes the question of how men should be treated from the realm of human responsibility and returns it to "nature." What is so generous about telling a man he can go as far as his talents will take him when his talents are meager? Imagine a foot-race of one mile in which ten men compete, with the rules being the same for all. Three of the competitors are forty years old, five are overweight, one has weak ankles, and the tenth is Roger Bannister. What sense does it make to say that all ten have an equal opportunity to win the race? The outcome is predetermined by nature, and nine of the competitors will call it a mockery when they are told that all have the same opportunity to win.

The cruelty of the jest, incidentally, is intensified with each increase in our ability to measure traits and talents at an early age. Someday our measuring instruments may be so keen that we will be able to predict, with high accuracy, how well a child of six or eight will do in the social race. Efficiency would dictate that we use these tools to separate the superior from the inferior, assigning the proper kinds and quantites of growth resources, such as education, to each group. . . .

The equality-of-opportunity principle, as formulated above, also implies the equal right of each member to share in the political life of the community to the fullest extent of his interest and ability. But this is the point at which the principle, no matter how carefully formulated, easily leads one away from a democratic view. The equal-opportunity principle as employed today in, for example, discussions of representation and voting rights, really does nothing more than fortify the prevailing conception of political action as just another of the various steps individuals and groups take to secure and advance their own interests and advantages. In this view, politics is but another aspect of the struggle for competitive advantage, and men need political power in order to protect and advance their private powers. This conception of politics is drawn from the economic sphere, and never rises above the ethical and psychological possibilities of that sphere.

When it is understood that the principle of equal opportunity is in our time an expression of the competitive, capitalistic spirit, and not of the democratic spirit, then the boundaries of its applicability begin to emerge. To the extent that competition is inescapable, or socially useful, all competitors should have the same advantages, and this the equal-opportunity principle guarantees. In any competitive situation, some will do better than others, and it seems just that those who do well should be rewarded more generously than those who do poorly. This too the principle guarantees.

The basic question, however, is not whether competition should be praised or condemned, but where and under what conditions competition is a desirable principle of action and judgment and where and under what conditions it is not. Some kinds of competition actually draw men more closely together whereas others produce antagonism and isolation. The problem is to distinguish between these kinds, encouraging the former and discouraging the latter. Peace is but a euphemism for slavery unless men's competitive energies are given adequate outlet. Most people probably have some need for both inward and outward striving. Perhaps the struggles against other people and the struggles within the self can be brought to some kind of balance in each individual and the society as a whole. Ideally, we might strive toward a truly pluralistic society in which nearly everybody could find a specialty he could do fairly well and where he would enjoy friendly competition with others. Judged by this imaginative possibility, our present social order is a mean thing. It is a kind of institutionalized war game, or sporting contest, in which the prizes are far too limited in kind, the referees and time-keepers far too numerous, and the number of reluctant and ill-adjusted players far too high. We need a social order that permits a much greater variety of games. Such a social order could, I think, be based on an effort to find a place for the greatest possible range of natural abilities among men. The variety of available natural abilities is enormous and worth much more exploration than any of the currently dominant conceptions of social order are willing to undertake. In the United States today, the fundamental justification of the equal-opportunity principle is that it is an efficient means for achieving an indefinite expansion of wealth and power. Many men are unsuited by nature for that competition, so that nature herself comes to seem unjust. But many of the injustices we regard nature as having perpetrated on individuals are actually no more than artifacts of the narrow view we take of nature's possibilities and a consequent distortion of the methods and ideals by which we attempt to transcend nature. For example, in defining intelligence as what I.Q. tests measure, we constrict the meanings of intelligence, for there are many modes of intelligence that the tests do not capture—nature is more protean than man's conception of her. Furthermore, having defined intelligence in a certain way, we then proceed to reward the people who have just that kind of intelligence and encourage them to use it in the pursuit of knowledge, which they are likely to do by building computers, which in turn give only certain kinds of knowledge. Thus our constricted definition of nature is confirmed by the methods we use to study nature. In this special sense, there might still be something to say for the eighteenth-century idea that society should imitate nature.

We must learn to ask questions like these about the method of competition and the principle of equal opportunity. The task is to define their proper spheres of action, not to treat them as blocks to be totally accepted or rejected. . . .

From the preceding selections we can reach a number of conclusions. In the first place the belief in democratic societies that personal freedoms and rights are basic necessities for a good life is contradicted by those (like the Nazis) who believe that the good of the state is the most important thing and that there should not be any private sphere free of state control.

We have also seen that personal liberties are not absolute and that one man's freedom is sometimes restricted by another right of some other men. One of the newest threats to freedom is the power of government and other groups to invade our privacy on a scale never dreamed of in earlier years.

Finally, we can observe that equality before the law means that the government must act positively in several ways to ensure that all of us have a relatively equal chance to develop our talents and our capabilities. In this regard, also, we must keep in mind that an enduring question remains—a question about which talents should be encouraged in an enlightened society.

DEMOCRACY, JUSTICE, AND RIGHTS

5

POINT

The essence of democracy is that political power resides in the people.

. . . that government of the people, by the people, for the people shall not perish from the earth.*

COUNTERPOINT

There can be tyrannical actions by the majority of the people.

. . . measures are too often decided, not according to the rules of justice and the rights of the minor party, but by the superior force of an interested and overbearing majority.†

These two remarks by towering figures of American history illustrate one of the enduring questions of politics: how to protect the rights or viewpoints of the minority when the majority has the power to force its wishes on everyone.

The following selection by Henry B. Mayo discusses the basic feature of

---

* Address at Gettysburg, November 19, 1863, Abraham Lincoln.

† The Federalist No. 10, James Madison, from *The New York Packet,* November 23, 1787.

a working democracy: popular control over the government. Professor Mayo details certain procedures and beliefs that must be present in a society before control by the majority of the people can be said to exist.

THE THEORY OF DEMOCRACY OUTLINED

HENRY B. MAYO

The original democratic system of Athens could be described in one phrase as "rule by the people," if "people" was construed narrowly to mean adult male citizens, comprising a small proportion of the total persons in a small state. This definitive operating principle, traced out into secondary principles and institutions, made it easy for Athenians—and for us—to distinguish the democracy from other ancient political systems. Such a principle was both accurately descriptive and quite workable, given the scale of operations. But the principle is neither descriptive of nor feasible in any modern state. It makes sense to say that one person rules, or that a few persons do, no matter how large the state; but it makes almost no sense to say that the people rule in any modern state, in any ordinary sense of the word "rule." (In this sense "rule" means to make directly the binding political decisions—or the major ones, including the decision as to what is major—and to receive the obedience. . . .

The only exception to this is the occasional use of "direct democratic devices" such as the referendum.

Democracy, then, as a political system must have identifiable features other than the people's actually "governing," to distinguish it from other methods of making public policies. The problem is to separate the accidental features from the characteristic. Some political features, such as whether the government is federal or unitary, presidential or parliamentary, unicameral or bicameral, republican or monarchical, are by general agreement accidental variations from a common type. So, too, is the kind of economic system with which the political system is associated—although this is more debatable. These and other features are

From An Introduction to Democratic Theory *by Henry B. Mayo (New York: Oxford University Press, 1960), pp. 58–70. Copyright © 1960 by Oxford University Press, Inc. Reprinted by permission.*

not necessarily related, either in logic or practice, with features of the political system ordinarily listed as democratic. Since one cannot analyze all of a system, except perhaps in a treatise on comparative democratic systems, we seek here only the differentiating features or principles of organization typical of all democracies and not typical of any other systems.

What, then, in any contemporary state corresponds to the "rule by the people" in the Athenian system? We are inevitably driven to conclude, I think, that such a corresponding factor lies in the effectiveness of the popular control over the rulers or decision-makers. In short, a political system is democratic to the extent that the decision-makers are under effective popular control. (One should perhaps add: to the extent to which decisions are *influenced* by the people, but this is a more amorphous concept, for which allowance will be made later.)

Plainly however, this, although in the spirit of the Athenian democracy, is a much vaguer test to apply than the Athenian. To distinguish ancient democracy from other types of the Greek *polis* was easy, and there could scarcely be dispute about it. But when the test is the extent of effective popular control, then the existence of democracy in any system is obviously a matter of degree. At one extreme will be the absolute ruler—a Hitler, a Stalin, a Perón—who, however despotic, must sometimes take popular sentiment into account (but who will endeavor, through education, censorship, propaganda, and other means, to engineer the popular sentiment which he wishes), and whose elections and plebiscites, if they are held at all, are carefully "rigged." At the other will be an elected government anxious to be re-elected, and an opposition anxious to become the government, both of them therefore sensitive to public opinion, with a wide range of political freedoms through which continuing influence as well as periodic control can be exercised.

Popular control of policy-makers is then the basic feature or principle, and political systems can be classified as more or less democratic according to a number of criteria associated with popular control and designed to make it effective; only if a particular system meets the tests of a substantial number of these criteria do we, by common consent, agree to call it democratic. But although the existence of democracy then becomes a matter of degree, the distinction is valid enough as we shall see, and the criteria will enable us to say in what respects and to what extent a system is democratic.

It must now be our purpose to try to make this somewhat vague language more precise. Accordingly I shall first sketch what I take to be a consistent and coherent theory of democracy in the forms of the minimum number of distinguishing principles. At the same time, the outline will be reasonably close to contemporary usage, and is recognizably approximated by a number of existing democracies. . . .

Distinguishing Principles of a Democratic System

Influence over decision-makers and hence over public policies may be exercised in many ways, even in a non-democratic system. The policies of an absolute ruler or of an oligarchy, for instance, may be affected by palace intrigue and court favorites, or by careful calculation of what the subjects will stand in the way of taxes and the like; it is possible to conceive of a benevolent autocrat who will in fact keep his ear to the ground and often graciously accede to public demands. But popular influence, although necessary, is not enough even if institutionalized to make a political system democratic.

1. *Popular control of policy-makers*, however, is a democratic stigmatum, and this is our first and most general principle. The one institutional embodiment of the principle universally regarded as indispensable in modern democracies is that of choosing the policy-makers (representatives) at elections held at more or less regular intervals. This is as close as we usually get—which is not very close—to imitating the making and control of decisions in the Athenian *ecclesia*.

Other methods of choosing and authorizing representatives—e.g., by lot or heredity—have died out, except for remnants of the lot such as are left in the choice of a jury. Even the Soviet type of "democracy" pays tribute to the method of electing representatives, although their practice of it is quite different from that in other kinds of democracies. In this as in other respects, the Soviet Union has borrowed some of the forms and language of democracy and stripped them of their spirit and meaning.

Three riders must be added to our general principle at the outset in order to avoid misunderstanding:

(a) On the whole, no democratic system operates on the principle that voters directly decide public policies at elections. The control over policy is much more indirect—through the representatives. This will be made clear later . . . but if we accept provisionally that voters choose representatives at elections and do not normally decide policies, then the usual criticism aimed at modern democracies on grounds of the incompetence of voters to judge policies is wide of the mark, however true it may have been of Athens where the citizens did decide directly.

(b) The popular influence upon policies, as distinct from control over policy-makers, goes on all the time and may take many institution-alized and legitimate forms. The extent of such influence, however, can-not be reduced to any public test which can be incorporated at the present time into a general theory. The reason is that popular influence and consultation take such an infinity of forms—of which interest or pressure groups are perhaps the best known—that hardly any general principle can as yet be enunciated. What gives popular influence its sanction is that it can affect the chances of a representative at election time, or, more accurately, the representative's estimate of his chances.

(c) Popular control by means of modern elections has only a faint resemblance to the old principle that, in some sense, authority stems from the people, and to old practices such as an elective monarchy. The assumption or belief that authority *should* derive from the people—some-times called the doctrine of popular sovereignty—does of course underlie the practice of popular elections, but our immediate concern is with the translation of the assumption into an operating principle or institutional practice.

2. The second principle of democracy is that of *political equality,* which in turn is institutionalized as the equality of all adult citizens in voting.

It makes little difference whether we think of this principle as co-ordinate with the first or derivative—a widening of the meaning of "pop-ular." Political equality is a principle common to Athenian and modern democracies. There is, of course, more to citizenship than voting, and hence other ways in which political equality or inequality can prevail, but it is not debatable today that in any democracy the principle of equality of voting is taken for granted.

Although the general principle may be cast in the Athenian form, the modern expression of it is quite different. For one thing, equality of voting is not, as in Athens, an equal share directly over the decisions; the share in the decisions is indirect—only the share in the control of the decision-makers is direct. For another, political equality today covers a wider range of citizens and voters than the Athenian, and in this respect we should call modern democracies more democratic than Athens.

Political equality is complex, like all general principles, and may be broken down into several elements, consisting at least of the follow-ing:

(a) Every adult should have the vote—the familiar device of the universal adult suffrage. Popular control defines the "people" as all adult citizens, although there are of course minor differences in the definitions of an "adult."

(b) One person should have one vote—that is, there should be no plural voting.

(c) Each vote should count equally—that is, votes are not weighted in any way.

In terms of representation, the belief in equal voting is expressed in the old slogan of "representation by population" or in Bentham's formula regarding happiness, that "everybody is to count for one, nobody for more than one." In terms of control over policy-makers, it is expressed by saying that every vote should have an equal share in that control.

(d) If every vote is to count equally, the corollary follows that the number of representatives elected should be directly proportional to the number of votes cast for them. If we assume, for simplicity of argument, a two-party system, then the number of representatives elected from each party will be cast for that party. Thus, in a two-party system, if party A gets 60 percent of the popular vote it will get 60 percent of the seats, and party B will get 40 per cent. Any other result would not be counting each vote equally.[1] It is just at this point, however, as we shall see, that the practice of many democracies diverges from this aspect of political equality, and often does so for very good reasons.

A little reflection will show that equality of voting, even if followed to the letter, is not enough of itself to distinguish a democratic system from an elected dictatorship. The belief and indeed the practice of equal voting are both official in the Soviet Union. Equality of voting, with its corollary, may thus be regarded as a necessary, but not a sufficient, principle of democracy. Is there, then, anything else about political equality and the franchise to distinguish a democratic political system? The answer must lie in the fact that voting alone does not ensure the reality of popular control; the mechanism may be manipulated to prevent such control.

3. The third principle may be stated either in terms of the *effectiveness of the popular control* or in terms of *political freedoms*.

Again, it makes little difference whether we regard "effectiveness" as part of the first principle (popular control) or as specifying the conditions of effective control. Can one set of decision-makers be turned out of office at elections and another set installed? Is there a free choice among alternatives, whether independent candidates or parties? That is, is the voting merely ritual, or does it effectively (freely) control the decision-makers?

This again is a very general statement of what prevails in a democracy. To make the general standard specific enough to test in practice, we must once more break it into components.

---

[1] Note that the reference is in terms of actual votes, not in terms of eligible adults—a point to which fuller reference is made later.

(a) To say that the voting must be effective is to say that there must be a free choice, without coercion or intimidation of the voters. This in turn drives us back upon the secrecy of the ballot, whether we draw the conclusion from reflecting on human nature—that we live in an imperfect world of imperfect people—or from reflecting upon the historical experience of many countries with open voting. Yet the condition of the secret ballot alone is not enough to ensure free choice, since even a Soviet election may provide the voter with privacy in the voting booth.

(b) In order that voting may be effective, it must, then, be free in another sense, i.e., at least two candidates for each position must be able to come forward if they wish. This minimum in itself is also not enough, because it could be cleverly imitated even in the Soviet Union by the simple device of putting forward more official candidates than seats to be filled.

An effective choice for the voter entails freedom for candidates to stand for election outside of the single party, not deterred by legal obstacles. . . . At this point we come close to the most characteristic feature of a modern democracy: the meaningful choice or control when candidates are free to run for office, when they and their supporters are free to press their claims publicly, to put forward alternative policies, to criticize the present decision-makers and other candidates; in short, when there is . . . a competitive bidding for votes.

The effectiveness of popular control thus entails a range of political freedoms. Among them are certainly the freedoms of speech, assembly, and organization, as well as the freedom to run for office. These widespread political liberties were characteristic of the Athenian form of democracy, and are likewise typical of all historical versions, though lacking in the Soviet system.

These formal rules or conditions or devices of effective choice—secret ballot, freedom to run for office, and freedom to speak, assemble, and organize for political purposes—are procedural political freedoms, necessary if there is to be any meaningful choice at the polls, if the voters are to control the decision-makers at election times and through them indirectly to sanction the decisions. Or they may be looked upon as the rules which insure free competition for office, men being what they are and the world being what it is.

Among those political freedoms, that of organization leads almost inevitably . . . to the formation of political parties, with different sets of candidates and sometimes with different outlooks and policy alternatives. The pure theory, of itself, will hardly tell us whether or not political parties will make their appearance in a democracy. They are not, so to speak, logically entailed as part of popular control, of effective choice in free and equal voting, and they do not always appear at local levels of government. Experience and history, however, give an enormous weight of evidence to show that political parties invariably do appear, despite the early, and mostly non-democratic, objection to "factions."

The existence and extent of these political liberties, as manifested above all in political opposition, is perhaps the most crucial test of the extent of democracy within a country. They are often summed up in the single concept of "freedom to oppose." The touchstone of a democratic system is political freedoms, opposition, and parties. Not one of the indispensable freedoms, nor the open and legitimate opposition which is always the consequence of freedoms, is present, for example, in the Soviet Union, despite the noble language of liberty embalmed in the Soviet constitution of 1936. For that reason we are fully justified in saying there is no effective choice or popular control of the decision-makers in the Soviet Union.

The result of political activity taking place within these rules— equality of voting and political liberties—is to enable the effective choice of representatives to take place, i.e., to ensure the popular control of decision-makers at election time, and to keep the channels open to legitimate influence at all times. From the viewpoint of the individual voter, the vote is the formal means by which he takes his share in political power. It scarcely needs pointing out that other implications also follow, for instance that the outvoted citizens accept the verdict of the polls with fortitude if not with gladness.

Although equality of voting within the context of political freedoms is a basic part of a democratic system, it is not all. Another essential part, already implicit, is that the policy decisions are made by the elected representatives, since only these are susceptible to popular control. The policies are not made, for instance, by others behind the scenes—as Marxists allege—nor by any non-elected body, such as a hereditary upper house. Insofar as they are made elsewhere, to that extent we say democracy is lacking. (To say this, however, is not to ignore the political reality of executive or Cabinet leadership.)

It is plain that we cannot expect the representatives to be unanimous, any more than we can expect the electorate to be so. Political systems are devised *because* there is conflict and disagreement. There must, then, be a principle or rule according to which decisions are made among the representatives themselves.

4. The fourth principle is that *when the representatives are divided, the decision of the majority prevails.*

This is, in fact, the nearly universal rule for decision-making in all legislatures. Let us be clear how it links with the previous principles. Equality of voting, in a context of political freedoms, turns up representatives who are authorized to make the policies for the time being.

This may be loosely called "consent of the governed" in the sense that there is a choice and one set of representatives rather than another is chosen. But "consent" is a slippery term, and it is better to think of election results as authorizing the successful candidates to make decisions, or in other words, as investing the government and its policies with legitimacy.

The common assumption is that with an electoral system based on equality of voting a majority of the representatives have been chosen by a majority of the voters, and hence the majority rule in the legislature yields decisions as legitimate "as if" they had been made directly by a majority of the voters, and indeed by a majority of all the adult citizens. That is why this fourth principle is sometimes called "majority rule." In fact, however, if governments depended for their legitimacy on this strict relation of votes to representatives, half the democratic governments of the world could at times claim no rightful authority from the "people." . . .

The principle of decision-making by a majority of representatives is much disputed, and is examined *in extenso* later . . . particularly the justification for the majority principle. The case *against* may be put in a nutshell: that it is both necessary and feasible to maintain legal limits upon a majority of the decision-makers (and hence by implication upon a majority of the citizens), and by so doing we may achieve the best of all possible systems: a "wise" minority veto of "unwise" majority decisions. Democracy would then be identical with ideal government, and the historic search for a government with power to rule wisely, but powerless to do wrong, would be over. To state the case is almost enough to refute it.

From this method of policy-making there follow certain implications, which may be called the rules of the game for representatives.

First, the majority of the representatives makes the policy decisions within the framework of the political freedoms mentioned earlier. These freedoms are taken as given, as part of the formal principles or essential conditions of democracy. Whatever else the majority may do—and it may mete very ill treatment through some of its decisions—it does not shut up the opposition, the critics, the dissenters, whether these are within or without the legislature. Opponents may be coerced into obedience to law, but not abolished or silenced or shorn of their political liberties: this is the one inhibition upon the majority decisions so long as a democracy exists. When the political liberties and the legitimate opposition are gone, so, too, is democracy.

Second, the minority of representatives and their supporters among the public obey even though under protest, while working either to alter the policy to which they object or to dislodge the government and if possible to become a majority—by all peaceful political means, but only by these. No doubt it is often difficult to obey a law which is heartily disliked, but for the moment it is enough to state the formal rule.

Third, when the opposition in its turn has grown into a majority and attains office, the play begins all over again with different actors in the role of government and opposition. The minority also agrees before- hand that they, too, will extend the same political freedoms and follow the same rules of the game should they arrive in the seats of office. The problem which arises here is that created by the existence of a minority party which uses the political freedoms in order to abolish democracy. . . .

Many social conditions are, of course, necessary if the majority principle is to work well, but those formal conditions just stated are the minimum rules of the game for majorities and minorities in the legisla- ture if democracy is to work *at all.* Moreover, in any functioning democ- racy, regardless of the niceties of the electoral system, the rules apply in those common cases where the majority of representatives happens to be elected by the minority of voters. No identity of voters and repre- sentatives need be assumed as long as the unwritten constitution does not require it, although there is, I think, an obligation to reduce the likelihood of wide discrepancies by eliminating abuses from the electoral system and thus closely approximating the principle of political equal- ity. . . .

A working definition may be constructed from the above: a demo- cratic political system is one in which public policies are made, on a majority basis, by representatives subject to effective popular control at periodic elections which are conducted on the principle of political equality and under conditions of political freedom.

Limited Government

Chapter 4 brought out the point that various personal rights have a limiting effect on one another. The concept of limits on each person's liberty for the good of all must always be discussed within the subject of personal freedom. The age-old problem of trying to reconcile freedom to do as you please on the one hand and restraint to protect the weaker members of society on the other has been discussed from the beginnings of civilization. It has been de- scribed as the right to swing your arms until you get close to the face of your neighbor. Various legal doctrines in English and Roman law permit each person to use his own property freely until he starts infringing upon the next person's right to use his.

Another problem concerning limitation for the good of all concerns limits on the government itself. The problem may be posed as a question: How far should organized society (government) be permitted to impose restraints on each one for the good of all (as seen by the majority)? One of the earliest explanations of the origin of governments, as well as an argument in favor of limited government, is the social contract theory. Under this doctrine all history is regarded as being divided into two periods, the state of nature and the period of civil society. Life in the state of nature had become increasingly dangerous, and men felt a natural inclination to join into an organized society. The social order itself, however, is based on conventions or contractual agreements. John Locke, an English political philosopher of the late seventeenth century, was one of the first to consider government as flowing from a contract between the sovereign and the people. Using this explanation for the establishment of government, he logically postulated the limits of government. Our next selection reproduces Locke's pertinent section of the *Two Treatises of Government*. It was written in 1690.

It should be noted that Thomas Jefferson borrowed heavily from John Locke's ideas in writing the Declaration of Independence in 1776. The leaders of the American Revolution used many ideas borrowed from the past on which to base their position. In the long struggles against the unbridled power of kings the champions of democratic rights argued and fought for limitations on the power of government in general.

OF THE EXTENT OF THE LEGISLATIVE POWER

JOHN LOCKE

The great end of men's entering into society being the enjoyment of their properties in peace and safety, and the great instrument and means of that being the laws established in that society, the first and fundamental positive law of all commonwealths is the establishing of the legislative power; as the first and fundamental natural law which is

Reprinted from John Locke, Two Treatises of Government, *ed. Thomas I. Cook (New York: Hafner Publishing Co., Inc., 1947), pp. 188–94, by permission of the publisher.*

to govern even the legislative itself is the preservation of the society and, as far as will consist with the public good, of every person in it. This legislative is not only the supreme power of the commonwealth, but sacred and unalterable in the hands where the community have once placed it; nor can any edict of anybody else, in what form soever conceived or by what power soever backed, have the force and obligation of a law which has not its sanction from that legislative which the public has chosen and appointed; for without this the law could not have that which is absolutely necessary to its being a law: the consent of the society over whom nobody can have a power to make laws, but by their own consent and by authority received from them. And therefore all the obedience, which by the most solemn ties any one can be obliged to pay, ultimately terminates in this supreme power and is directed by those laws which it enacts; nor can any oaths to any foreign power whatsoever, or any domestic subordinate power, discharge any member of the society from his obedience to the legislative acting pursuant to their trust, nor oblige him to any obedience contrary to the laws so enacted, or farther than they do allow; it being ridiculous to imagine one can be tied ultimately to obey any power in the society which is not supreme.

Though the legislative, whether placed on one or more, whether it be always in being, or only by intervals, though it be the supreme power in every commonwealth; yet:

First, It is not, nor can possibly be, absolutely arbitrary over the lives and fortunes of the people; for it being but the joint power of every member of the society given up to that person or assembly which is legislator, it can be no more than those persons had in a state of nature before they entered into society and gave up to the community; for nobody can transfer to another more power than he has in himself, and nobody has an absolute arbitrary power over himself, or over any other, to destroy his own life, or take away the life or property of another. A man, as has been proved, cannot subject himself to the arbitrary power of another; and having in the state of nature no arbitrary power over the life, liberty, or possession of another, but only so much as the law of nature gave him for the preservation of himself and the rest of mankind, this is all he doth or can give up to the commonwealth, and by it to the legislative power, so that the legislative can have no more than this. Their power, in the utmost bounds of it, is limited to the public good of the society. It is a power that hath no other end but preservation, and therefore can never have a right to destroy, enslave, or designedly to impoverish the subjects. The obligations of the law of nature cease not in society but only in many cases are drawn closer and have by human laws known penalties annexed to them to enforce their observation. Thus the law of nature stands as an eternal rule to all men, legislators as well as others. The rules that they make for other men's actions must, as well as their own and other men's actions, be conformable to the law of nature—*i.e.*, to the will of God, of which that is a declaration—and the fundamental law of nature being the preservation of mankind, no human sanction can be good or valid against it.

Secondly, The legislative or supreme authority cannot assume to itself a power to rule by extemporary, arbitrary decrees, but is bound to dispense justice and to decide the rights of the subject by promulgated, standing laws, and known authorized judges. For the law of nature being unwritten, and so nowhere to be found but in the minds of men, they who through passion or interest shall miscite or misapply it, cannot so easily be convinced of their mistake where there is no established judge; and so it serves not, as it ought, to determine the rights and fence the properties of those that live under it, especially where every one is judge, interpreter, and executioner of it, too, and that in his own case; and he that has right on his side, having ordinarily but his own single strength, hath not force enough to defend himself from injuries, or to punish delinquents. To avoid these inconveniences which disorder men's properties in the state of nature, men unite into societies that they may have the united strength of the whole society to secure and defend their properties, and may have standing rules to bound it by which every one may know what is his. To this end it is that men give up all their natural power to the society which they enter into, and the community put the legislative power into such hands as they think fit with this trust, that they shall be governed by declared laws, or else their peace, quiet, and property will still be at the same uncertainty as it was in the state of nature.

Absolute arbitrary power, or governing without settled standing laws, can neither of them consist with the ends of society and government which men would not quit the freedom of the state of nature for, and tie themselves up under, were it not to preserve their lives, liberties, and fortunes, and by stated rules of right and property to secure their peace and quiet. It cannot be supposed that they should intend, had they a power so to do, to give to any one or more an absolute arbitrary power over their persons and estates and put a force into the magistrate's hand to execute his unlimited will arbitrarily upon them. This were to put themselves into a worse condition than the state of nature wherein they had a liberty to defend their right against the injuries of others and were upon equal terms of force to maintain it, whether invaded by a single man or many in combination. . . . And, therefore, whatever form the commonwealth is under, the ruling power ought to govern by declared and received laws and not by extemporary dictates and undetermined resolutions; for then mankind will be in a far worse condition than in the state of nature if they shall have armed one or a few men with the joint power of a multitude, to force them to obey at pleasure the exorbitant and unlimited decrees of their sudden thoughts or unrestrained and, till that moment, unknown wills, without having any measures set down which may guide and justify their actions. For all the power the government has, being only for the good of the society, as it ought not to be arbitrary and at pleasure, so it ought to be exercised by established and promulgated laws; that both the people may know their duty and be safe and secure within the limits of the law; and the rulers too kept within their bounds, and not be tempted by the power they have in their hands to employ it to such purposes and by such measures as they would not have known, and own not willingly.

Thirdly, The supreme power cannot take from any man part of his property without his own consent; for the preservation of property being the end of government and that for which men enter into society, it necessarily supposes and requires that the people should have property, without which they must be supposed to lose that, by entering into society, which was the end for which they entered into it—too gross an absurdity for any man to own. Men, therefore, in society having property, they have such right to the goods which by the law of the community are theirs, that nobody hath a right to take their substance or any part of it from them without their own consent; without this, they have no property at all, for I have truly no property in that which another can by right take from me when he pleases, against my consent. Hence it is a mistake to think that the supreme or legislative power of any commonwealth can do what it will, and dispose of the estates of the subject arbitrarily, or take any part of them at pleasure. This is not much to be feared in governments where the legislative consists, wholly or in part, in assemblies which are variable, whose members, upon the dissolution of the assembly, are subjects under the common laws of their country, equally with the rest. But in governments where the legislative is in one lasting assembly, always in being, or in one man, as in absolute monarchies, there is danger still that they will think themselves to have a distinct interest from the rest of the community, and so will be apt to increase their own riches and power by taking what they think fit from the people; for a man's property is not at all secure, though there be good and equitable laws to set the bounds of it between him and his fellow subjects, if he who commands those subjects have power to take from any private man what part he pleases of his property and use and dispose of it as he thinks good.

But government, into whatsoever hands it is put, being, as I have before shown, entrusted with this condition, and for this end, that men might have and secure their properties, the prince, or senate, however it may have power to make laws for the regulating of property between the subjects one amongst another, yet can never have a power to take to themselves the whole or any part of the subject's property without their own consent; for this would be in effect to leave them no property at all. . . .

It is true, governments cannot be supported without great charge, and it is fit every one who enjoys his share of the protection should pay out of his estate his proportion for the maintenance of it. But still it must be with his own consent—*i.e.*, the consent of the majority, giving it either by themselves or their representatives chosen by them. For if any one shall claim a power to lay and levy taxes on the people, by his own authority and without such consent of the people, he thereby invades the fundamental law of property and subverts the end of government; for what property have I in that which another may by right take, when he pleases, to himself?

Fourthly, The legislative cannot transfer the power of making laws to any other hands; for it being but a delegated power from the people, they who have it cannot pass it over to others. The people alone can appoint the form of the commonwealth, which is by constituting the legislative and appointing in whose hands that shall be. And when the people have said, we will submit to rules and be governed by laws made by such men, and in such forms, nobody else can say other men shall make laws for them; nor can the people be bound by any laws but such as are enacted by those whom they have chosen and authorized to make laws for them. The power of the legislative, being derived from the people by a positive voluntary grant and institution, can be no other than what that positive grant conveyed, which being only to make laws, and not to make legislators, the legislative can have no power to transfer their authority of making laws and place it in other hands.

These are the bounds which the trust that is put in them by the society and the law of God and nature have set to the legislative power of every commonwealth, in all forms of government:

First, They are to govern by promulgated established laws, not to be varied in particular cases, but to have one rule for rich and poor, for the favourite at court and the countryman at plough.

Secondly, These laws also ought to be designed for no other end ultimately but the good of the people.

Thirdly, They must not raise taxes on the property of the people without the consent of the people, given by themselves or their deputies. And this properly concerns only such governments where the legislative is always in being, or at least where the people have not reserved any part of the legislative to deputies to be from time to time chosen by themselves.

Fourthly, The legislative neither must nor can transfer the power of making laws to anybody else, or place it anywhere but where the people have.

Another version of the social contract theory was expounded by a famous French philosopher, Jean Jacques Rousseau, in 1762. Rousseau's ideas, incorporated into a book entitled *The Social Contract,* were to have a considerable impact upon the leaders of the French Revolution a generation later. The theory of a contract between the government and the people was used as a support for popular liberties, a device for upholding individual rights against the government. According to Rousseau, popular consent to a government required a constitutional means of expression if it was to be more than just lip service. He indicated that active agreement, periodically reasserted, was the proper means of expression. Thus, public participation in lawmaking was a necessary ingredient of popular consent. Rousseau's theory was designed for a city-state much like his native Geneva. He was unable to believe that large-scale, representative democracy as practiced in the United States Congress could operate effectively.

The social contract theory grew into the concept of a written constitution guaranteeing certain individual rights against the government. The national leaders who met at Philadelphia to write our Constitution in 1787 believed in democratic government as embodied in the social contract doctrine, especially as presented by Locke. Today our vastly increased knowledge in the areas of history, anthropology, and archeology does not support the concept of men in a state of nature entering into a formal contract to establish civil government. Nevertheless, the theory that government is obligated to perform within certain bounds and the whole setting of constitutional conventions have a considerable flavor of contractual arrangements.

Elements of Justice

Another aspect of limitations on officials to be dealt with in this chapter is due process of law, probably the most fundamental and far-reaching element in the Anglo-American tradition of personal liberty. In accordance with the belief in limits placed on government, the Magna Charta signed by King John in 1215 provided that he would not take any action against his subjects except by "the law of the land." Our founding fathers put this theory into more familiar language in the Fifth Amendment in 1791, later copied in the Fourteenth Amendment in 1868, to the effect that life, liberty, or property shall not be taken from a person by the national or state governments without due process of law. The generally accepted purpose of due process is procedural, which means that the way or method used by officials in governing must be fair and familiar.* In the Joint Anti-Fascist Refugee Committee case, also included as a reading, Justice Felix Frankfurter made the following very expressive point:

> . . . "due process," unlike some legal rules, is not a technical conception with a fixed content unrelated to time, place and circumstances. Expressing as it does in its ultimate analysis respect enforced by law for that feeling of just treatment which has been evolved through centuries of Anglo-American constitutional history and civilization, "due process" cannot be imprisoned within the treacherous limits of any formula. Representing a profound attitude of fairness between man and man, more particularly between the individual and government, "due process" is compounded of history, reason, the past course of decisions, and stout confidence in the strength of the democratic faith which we profess.

Just as the rules of equity developed in England to supplement the common law and were designed to ensure fair dealings between individual citizens, due process has become a similar set of rules used in judicial review of actions by all branches of the government. Executive, administrative, legislative, and judicial policies which arbitrarily restrict individual rights may be struck down in this manner.

In the Joint Anti-Fascist Refugee Committee case the Supreme Court examined the problem of the fair hearing and found that the Attorney General and the Department of Justice had not provided necessary procedural safeguards to the associations labeled as subversive. The court majority set aside the administrative action as being invalid because it was made "without notice, without disclosure of any reason justifying it, without opportunity to meet the undisclosed evidence or suspicion on which designation may have been based, and without opportunity to establish affirmatively that the aims and acts of the organization are innocent."

In a Supreme Court case decided within the past decade and a half the concept of administrative due process was summed up in the following langauge: "Certain principles have remained relatively immutable in our jurisprudence. One of these is that where governmental action seriously injures an individual, and the reasonableness of the action depends on fact findings, the evidence used to prove the Government's case must be disclosed to the individual so that he has an opportunity to show that it is untrue." †

---

* In the late nineteenth and early twentieth centuries, the Supreme Court of the United States embarked on a course of striking down laws, especially state laws, because of disapproval of the substance of or object of these laws rather than the procedure used. This is frequently referred to as substantive due process, a notion largely abandoned by the Court since 1937.

† Green v. McElroy, 360 U.S. 474 (1959).

In several countries there are special agencies established to provide just treatment to the citizen in dealings with administrative officials. The French and Germans have a separate system of administrative courts which are very inexpensive and zealous in safeguarding the private citizen from arbitrary governmental action. Many common-law countries (and several American states) have adopted the Scandinavian office of *Ombudsman,* who is something of a public defender in administrative matters. The *Ombudsman,* on request or on his own initiative, inquires into allegations of administrative unfairness. He may publicize his findings and bring public opinion into operation if the administrator at fault does not correct the improper action.

JOINT ANTI-FASCIST REFUGEE COMMITTEE CASE

UNITED STATES SUPREME COURT

Actions for declaratory and injunctive relief by the Joint Anti-Fascist Refugee Committee, and by the National Council of American-Soviet Friendship, Inc., and others, and by the International Workers Order, Inc., and another, against Tom C. Clark, Attorney General of the United States, and others, J. Howard McGrath was substituted as the Attorney General. . . .

In each of these cases the same issue is raised. . . . That issue is whether, in the face of the facts alleged in the complaint and therefore admitted by the motion to dismiss, the Attorney General of the United States has authority to include the complaining organization in a list of organizations designated by him as Communist and furnished by him to the Loyalty Review Board of the United States Civil Service Commission. He claims to derive authority to do this from the following provisions of Executive Order No. 9835 issued by the President, March 21, 1947.

The Loyalty Review Board shall currently be furnished by the Department of Justice the name of each foreign or domestic organiza-

Joint Anti-Fascist Refugee Committee v. McGrath, Atty. Gen. of the United States, et al., National Council of American-Soviet Friendship, Inc., et al. v. McGrath, Atty. Gen. of the United States, et al., International Workers Order, Inc., et al. v. McGrath, Atty. Gen. of the United States, et al., 341 U.S. 123, 71 S. Ct. 624 (1951), Nos. 8, 7, 71. Argued Oct. 11, 1950. Decided April 30, 1951.

tion, association, movement, group or combination of persons which the Attorney General, after appropriate investigation and determination, designates as totalitarian, fascist, communist or subversive. . . .

The respective complaints describe the complaining organizations as engaged in charitable or civic activities or in the business of fraternal insurance. . . .

For the reasons hereinafter stated, we conclude that, *if the allegations of the complaints are taken as true* (as they must be on the motions to dismiss), the Executive Order does not authorize the Attorney General to furnish the Loyalty Review Board with a list containing such a designation as he gave to each of these organizations without other justification. . . .

. . .

No. 8. *The Refugee Committee Case.*

The complainant is the Joint Anti-Fascist Refugee Committee, an unincorporated association in the City and State of New York. It is the petitioner here. The defendants in the original action were the Attorney General, Tom C. Clark, and the members of the Loyalty Review Board. J. Howard McGrath has been substituted as the Attorney General and he and the members of that Board are the respondents here.

The following statement, based on the allegations of the complaint, summarizes the situation before us: The complainant is "a charitable organization engaged in relief work" which carried on its relief activities from 1942 to 1946 under a license from the President's War Relief Control Board. Thereafter, it voluntarily submitted its program, budgets and audits for inspection by the Advisory Committee on Voluntary Foreign Aid of the United States Government. Since its inception, it has, through voluntary contributions, raised and disbursed funds for the benefit of anti-Fascist refugees who assisted the Government of Spain against its overthrow by force and violence. . . .

It has disbursed $1,011,448 in cash, and $217,903 in kind, for the relief of anti-Fascist refugees and their families. This relief has included money, food, shelter, educational facilities, medical treatment and supplies, and clothing to recipients in 11 countries including the United States. The acts of the Attorney General and the Loyalty Review Board, purporting to be taken by them under authority of the Executive Order, have seriously and irreparably impaired, and will continue to so impair, the reputation of the organization and the moral support and good will of the American people necessary for the continuance of its charitable activities. Upon information and belief, these acts have caused many contributors, especially present and prospective civil servants, to reduce or discontinue their contributions to the organization; members and participants in its activities have been "vilified and subjected to public shame, disgrace, ridicule and obloquy . . ." thereby inflicting upon it economic injury and discouraging participation in its activities; it has been hampered in securing meeting places; and many people have refused to take part in its fund-raising activities.

. . .

Nothing we have said purports to adjudicate the truth of petitioners' allegations that they are not in fact communistic. We have assumed that the designations made by the Attorney General are arbitrary because we are compelled to make that assumption by his motions to dismiss the complaints. Whether the complaining organizations are in fact communistic or whether the Attorney General possesses information from which he could reasonably find them to be so must await determination by the District Court upon remand.

Reversed and remanded.

Mr. Justice BLACK, concurring.

Without notice or hearing and under color of the President's Executive Order No. 9835, the Attorney General found petitioners guilty of harboring treasonable opinions and designs, officially branded them as Communists, and promulgated his findings and conclusions for particular use as evidence against government employees suspected of disloyalty. In the present climate of public opinion it appears certain that the Attorney General's much publicized findings, regardless of their truth or falsity, are the practical equivalents of confiscation and death sentences for any blacklisted organization not possessing extraordinary financial, political or religious prestige and influence. The Government not only defends the power of the Attorney General to pronounce such deadly edicts but also argues that individuals or groups so condemned have no standing to seek redress in the courts, even though a fair judicial hearing might conclusively demonstrate their loyalty. My basic reasons for rejecting these and other contentions of the Government are in summary the following: I agree with Mr. Justice BURTON that petitioners have standing to sue for the reason among others that they have a right to conduct their admittedly legitimate political, charitable and business operations free from unjustified governmental defamation. Otherwise, executive officers could act lawlessly with impunity. . . .

Expansion of Rights

Still another aspect of this chapter dealing with "Democracy, Justice, and Rights" concerns the expansion of rights in our society today. There appears to be developing a new set of personal rights in the case of persons entitled to social benefits like old-age assistance, aid to dependent children, the disabled, and so on.

In recent years the courts have increasingly spoken out against legislative handling of welfare or assistance statutes resulting in violation of constitutional guarantees. It has become increasingly clear that denying a benefit can deprive a citizen of his liberties as effectively as imposing some criminal punishment upon him. The greater awareness of personal rights has also been evident in judicial review of administrative actions. For example, judges have found a violation of the First Amendment right of free exercise of religion in the refusal of an application for unemployment benefits on the ground that the applicant objected to Saturday work due to religious beliefs [Sherbert v. Verner, 374 US 398 (1963)]. Courts have also eliminated administrative conditions designed to prevent tenants in public housing facilities from expressing political views [Holt v. Richmond Redevelopment and Housing Authority, 266 F. Supp. 397 (1966)].

Welfare programs ordinarily employ the "means test" in order to establish eligibility. This is defined as proving that a person is without income or property in order to get assistance. This is the "charity" principle, and enforcement is typically turned over to bureaucrats and social workers. In order to establish "need," social workers are authorized to make intensive investigation of an applicant's finances, including the property of his close relatives. Under the means test the needy applicant must prove that he is in the poverty category in order to meet the legal requirements. In so doing the applicant not only invites periodic investigation by social workers, but also may receive a social stigma as well.

Other social programs, however, are based on a foundation very different from the charity principle. These provide benefits which are almost beyond the manipulation of administrative officials. Non-charity programs include veterans' benefits, social security retirement payments, and unemployment compensation. They have clearly defined eligibility requirements which sharply reduce the discretion of administrators. In general any applicant for these benefits who follows the administrative rules may obtain eligibility by meeting the requirements. The dividing line between charity and non-charity programs is some version of the means test as the basis for eligibility.

One way to reduce the degrading aspects of need-based or charity assistance is to broaden it to include more affluent classes. In this way the poor and the affluent could share the same benefits. When this happens, administrative high-handedness is likely to be diminished because middle-class recipients are less passive toward administrators.* Such programs would be

---

* L. M. Friedman, "Social Welfare Legislation: An Introduction," *Stanford Law Review*, Vol. 21, January 1969, p. 226.

expensive, but they would not require large numbers of social worker investigators to establish eligibility.

In our next reading, the Supreme Court case of *Shapiro* v. *Thompson* (1969), the Court struck down waiting period or residence requirements set up by Connecticut, Pennsylvania, and the District of Columbia (Congress itself) for applicants under the family assistance program. Rulings of this kind may be seen as additional steps in the creation of new rights for the needy in our society.

SHAPIRO v. THOMPSON

UNITED STATES SUPREME COURT

The Connecticut Welfare Department invoked Connecticut state law to deny the application of Vivian Marie Thompson for assistance under the program for Aid to Families with Dependent Children. She was a 19-year-old unwed mother of one child and pregnant with her second child when she changed her residence in June 1966 from Dorchester, Massachusetts, to Hartford, Connecticut, to live with her mother. . . . Because of her pregnancy, she was unable to work or enter a work training program. Her application for assistance . . . was denied . . . solely on the ground that . . . she had not lived in the State for a year before her application was filed.

Similar cases from the District of Columbia and Pennsylvania were consolidated for trial. Judgment in the trial court was in favor of the applicants, and the welfare authorities appealed to the Supreme Court.

Mr. Justice Brennan delivered the opinion of the Court . . .

There is no dispute that the effect of the waiting-period requirement in each case is to create two classes of needy resident families indistinguishable from each other except that one is composed of residents who have resided a year or more, and the second of residents who have resided less than a year, in the jurisdiction. On the basis of this sole difference the first class is granted and the second class is denied welfare aid upon which may depend the ability of the families to obtain the very means to subsist—food, shelter, and other necessities of life. In each

394 U.S. 618, 89 S. Ct. 1322 (1969).

case the District Court found that appellees met the test for residence in their jurisdictions, as well as all other eligibility requirements except the requirement of residence for a full year prior to their applications. . . .

Primarily, appellants justify the waiting-period requirement as a protective device to preserve the fiscal integrity of state public assistance programs. It is asserted that people who require welfare assistance during their first year of residence in a State are likely to become continuing burdens on state welfare programs. Therefore, the argument runs if such people can be deterred from entering the jurisdiction by denying them welfare benefits during the first year, state programs to assist long-time residents will not be impaired by a substantial influx of indigent newcomers.

There is weighty evidence that exclusion from the jurisdiction of the poor who need or may need relief was the specific objective of these provisions. . . .

We do not doubt that the one-year waiting period device is well-suited to discourage the influx of poor families in need of assistance. An indigent who desires to migrate, resettle, find a new job, and start a new life will doubtless hesitate if he knows that he must risk making the move without the possibility of falling back on state welfare assistance during his first year of residence, when his need may be most acute. But the purpose of inhibiting migration by needy persons into the State is constitutionally impermissible.

This Court long ago recognized that the nature of our Federal Union and our constitutional concepts of personal liberty unite to require that all citizens be free to travel throughout the length and breadth of our land uninhibited by statutes, rules, or regulations which unreasonably burden or restrict this movement. . . .

Thus the purpose of deterring the immigration of indigents cannot serve as justification for the classification created by the one-year waiting period, since that purpose is constitutionally impermissible. If a law has "no other purpose . . . than to chill the assertion of constitutional rights by penalizing those who choose to exercise them, then it [is] patently unconstitutional.". . .

More fundamentally, a State may no more try to fence out those indigents who seek higher welfare benefits than it may try to fence out indigents generally. Implicit in any such distinction is the notion that indigents who enter a State with the hope of securing higher welfare benefits are somehow less deserving than indigents who do not take this consideration into account. But we do not perceive why a mother who is seeking to make a new life for herself and her children should be regarded as less deserving because she considers, among other factors, the level of a State's public assistance. Surely such a mother is no less deserving than a mother who moves into a particular State in order to take advantage of its better educational facilities.

Appellants argue further that the challenged classification may be sustained as an attempt to distinguish between new and old residents on the basis of the contribution they have made to the community through the payment of taxes. We have difficulty seeing how long-term residents who qualify for welfare are making a greater present contribution to the State in taxes than indigent residents who have recently arrived. If the argument is based on contributions made in the past by the long-term residents, there is some question, as a factual matter, whether this argument is applicable in Pennsylvania where the record suggests that some 40% of those denied public assistance because of the waiting period had lengthy prior residence in the State. But we need not rest on the particular facts of these cases. Appellants' reasoning would logically permit the State to bar new residents from schools, parks, and libraries, or deprive them of police and fire protection. Indeed it would permit the State to apportion all benefits and services according to the past tax contributions of its citizens. The Equal Protection Clause prohibits such an apportionment of state services.

[9–12] We recognize that a State has a valid interest in preserving the fiscal integrity of its programs. It may legitimately attempt to limit its expenditures, whether for public assistance, public education, or any other program. But a State may not accomplish such a purpose by invidious distinctions between classes of its citizens. It could not, for example, reduce expenditures for education by barring indigent children from its schools. Similarly, in the cases before us, appellants must do more than show that denying welfare benefits to new residents saves money. The saving of welfare costs cannot justify an otherwise invidious classification. . . .

We conclude therefore that appellants in these cases do not use and have no need to use the one-year requirement for the governmental purposes suggested. Thus, even under traditional equal protection tests a classification of welfare applicants according to whether they have lived in the State for one year would seem irrational and unconstitutional. But, of course, the traditional criteria do not apply in these cases. Since the classification here touches on the fundamental right of interstate movement, its constitutionality must be judged by the stricter standard of whether it promotes a *compelling* state interest. Under this standard, the waiting-period requirement clearly violates the Equal Protection Clause. . . .

The waiting-period requirement in the District of Columbia Code involved in No. 33 is also unconstitutional even though it was adopted by Congress as an exercise of federal power. In terms of federal power, the discrimination created by the one-year requirement violates the Due

Process Clause of the Fifth Amendment. "[W]hile the Fifth Amendment contains no equal protection clause it does forbid discrimination that is 'so unjustifiable as to be violative of due process.' ". . . For the reasons we have stated in invalidating the Pennsylvania and Connecticut provisions, the District of Columbia provision is also invalid—the Due Process Clause of the Fifth Amendment prohibits Congress from denying public assistance to poor persons otherwise eligible solely on the ground that they have not been residents of the District of Columbia for one year at the time their applications are filed.

Accordingly, the judgments in Nos. 9, 33, and 34 are Affirmed.

Our next selection is the famous "Letter from Birmingham Jail—April 16, 1963," by Dr. Martin Luther King, Jr. Many of the achievements in the area of legal equality of black people are attributable to leaders whose philosophy is epitomized here. It should be noted that today, after having obtained significant gains in civil rights, many black spokesmen believe that a new phase of development has been reached—that of political implementation of the organized minority's voting and other legal powers.

LETTER FROM BIRMINGHAM JAIL—
April 16, 1963

MARTIN LUTHER KING, JR.[1]

My dear Fellow Clergymen,

While confined here in the Birmingham City Jail, I came across your recent statement calling our present activities "unwise and un-

Martin Luther King, Jr., "Letter from Birmingham Jail—April 16, 1963," from Why We Can't Wait *(New York: Harper & Row, Publishers, Inc., 1963), pp. 77–100. Copyright © 1963 by Martin Luther King, Jr. Reprinted by permission of Harper & Row, Publishers, Inc., and Joan Daves.*

[1] The late Dr. Martin Luther King was the founder of the Southern Christian Leadership Conference and the winner of the Nobel Peace Prize for 1964. He was assassinated in 1968.

timely." Seldom, if ever, do I pause to answer criticism of my work and ideas. If I sought to answer all of the criticisms that cross my desk, my secretaries would be engaged in little else in the course of the day, and I would have no time for constructive work. But since I feel that you are men of genuine goodwill and your criticisms are sincerely set forth, I would like to answer your statement in what I hope will be patient and reasonable terms.

I think I should give the reason for my being in Birmingham, since you have been influenced by the argument of "outsiders coming in." I have the honor of serving as president of the Southern Christian Leadership Conference, an organization operating in every Southern state, with headquarters in Atlanta, Georgia. We have some eighty-five affiliate organizations all across the South—one being the Alabama Christian Movement for Human Rights. Whenever necessary and possible we share staff, educational and financial resources with our affiliates. Several months ago our local affiliate here in Birmingham invited us to be on call to engage in a nonviolent direct action program if such were deemed necessary. We readily consented and when the hour came we lived up to our promises. So I am here, along with several members of my staff, because we were invited here. I am here because I have basic organizational ties here.

Beyond this, I am in Birmingham because injustice is here. Just as the eighth century prophets left their little villages and carried their "thus saith the Lord" far beyond the boundaries of their home towns; and just as the Apostle Paul left his little village of Tarsus and carried the gospel of Jesus Christ to practically every hamlet and city of the Graeco-Roman world, I too am compelled to carry the gospel of freedom beyond my particular home town. Like Paul, I must constantly respond to the Macedonian call for aid.

Moreover, I am cognizant of the interrelatedness of all communities and states. I cannot sit idly by in Atlanta and not be concerned about what happens in Birmingham. Injustice anywhere is a threat to justice everywhere. We are caught in an inescapable network of mutuality, tied in a single garment of destiny. Whatever affects one directly affects all indirectly. Never again can we afford to live with the narrow, provincial "outside agitator" idea. Anyone who lives inside the United States can never be considered an outsider anywhere in this country.

You deplore the demonstrations that are presently taking place in Birmingham. But I am sorry that your statement did not express a similar concern for the conditions that brought the demonstrations into being. I am sure that each of you would want to go beyond the superficial social analyst who looks merely at effects, and does not grapple with underlying causes. I would not hesitate to say that it is unfortunate that so-called demonstrations are taking place in Birmingham at this time, but I would say in more emphatic terms that it is even more unfortunate that the white power structure of this city left the Negro community with no other alternative.

In any nonviolent campaign there are four basic steps: 1) Collection of the facts to determine whether injustices are alive. 2) Negotiation. 3) Self-purification and 4) Direct Action. We have gone through all of these steps in Birmingham. There can be no gainsaying of the fact that racial injustice engulfs this community.

Birmingham is probably the most thoroughly segregated city in the United States. Its ugly record of police brutality is known in every section of this country. Its injust treatment of Negroes in the courts is a notorious reality. There have been more unsolved bombings of Negro homes and churches in Birmingham than any city in this nation. These are the hard, brutal and unbelievable facts. On the basis of these conditions Negro leaders sought to negotiate with the city fathers. But the political leaders consistently refused to engage in good faith negotiation.

Then came the opportunity last September to talk with some of the leaders of the economic community. In these negotiating sessions certain promises were made by the merchants—such as the promise to remove the humiliating racial signs from the stores. On the basis of these promises Rev. Shuttlesworth and the leaders of the Alabama Christian Movement for Human Rights agreed to call a moratorium on any type of demonstrations. As the weeks and months unfolded we realized that we were the victims of a broken promise. The signs remained. Like so many experiences of the past we were confronted with blasted hopes, and the dark shadow of a deep disappointment settled upon us. So we had no alternative except that of preparing for direct action, whereby we would present our very bodies as a means of laying our case before the conscience of the local and national community. We were not unmindful of the difficulties involved. So we decided to go through a process of self-purification. We started having workshops on nonviolence and repeatedly asked ourselves the questions, "Are you able to accept blows without retaliating?" "Are you able to endure the ordeals of jail?" We decided to set our direct action program around the Easter season, realizing that with the exception of Christmas, this was the largest shopping period of the year. Knowing that a strong economic withdrawal program would be the by-product of direct action, we felt that this was the best time to bring pressure on the merchants for the needed changes. Then it occurred to us that the March election was ahead and so we speedily decided to postpone action until after election day. When we discovered that Mr. Connor was in the run-off, we decided again to postpone action so that the demonstrations could not be used to cloud the issues. At this time we agreed to begin our nonviolent witness the day after the run-off.

This reveals that we did not move irresponsibly into direct action. We too wanted to see Mr. Connor defeated; so we went through postponement after postponement to aid in this community need. After this we felt that direct action could be delayed no longer.

You may well ask, "Why direct action? Why sit-ins, marches, etc.? Isn't negotiation a better path?" You are exactly right in your call for negotiation. Indeed, this is the purpose of direct action. Nonviolent direct action seeks to create such a crisis and establish such creative tension that a community that has constantly refused to negotiate is forced to confront the issue. It seeks so to dramatize the issue that it can no longer be ignored. I just referred to the creation of tension as a part of the work of the nonviolent resister. This may sound rather shocking. But I must confess that I am not afraid of the word tension. I have earnestly worked and preached against violent tension, but there is a type of constructive nonviolent tension that is necessary for growth. Just as Socrates felt that it was necessary to create a tension in the mind so that individuals could rise from the bondage of myths and half-truths to the unfettered realm of creative analysis and objective appraisal, we must see the need of having nonviolent gadflies to create the kind of tension in society that will help men to rise from the dark depths of prejudice and racism to the majestic heights of understanding and brotherhood. So the purpose of the direct action is to create a situation so crisis-packed that it will inevitably open the door to negotiation. We, therefore, concur with you in your call for negotiation. Too long has our beloved Southland been bogged down in the tragic attempt to live in monologue rather than dialogue.

One of the basic points in your statement is that our acts are untimely. Some have asked, "Why didn't you give the new administration time to act?" The only answer that I can give to this inquiry is that the new administration must be prodded about as much as the outgoing one before it acts. We will be sadly mistaken if we feel that the election of Mr. Boutwell will bring the millennium to Birmingham. While Mr. Boutwell is much more articulate and gentle than Mr. Connor, they are both segragationists, dedicated to the task of maintaining the status quo. The hope I see in Mr. Boutwell is that he will be reasonable enough to see the futility of massive resistance to desegregation. But he will not see this without pressure from the devotees of civil rights. My friends, I must say to you that we have not made a single gain in civil rights without determined legal and nonviolent pressure. History is the long and tragic story of the fact that privileged groups seldom give up their privileges voluntarily. Individuals may see the moral light and voluntarily give up their unjust posture; but as Reinhold Niebuhr has reminded us, groups are more immoral than individuals.

We know through painful experience that freedom is never voluntarily given by the oppressor; it must be demanded by the oppressed. Frankly, I have never yet engaged in a direct action movement that was "well timed," according to the timetable of those who have not suffered unduly from the disease of segregation. For years now I have heard the words "Wait!" It rings in the ear of every Negro with a piercing familiarity. This "Wait" has almost always meant "Never." It has been a tranquilizing thalidomide, relieving the emotional stress for a moment, only to give birth to an ill-formed infant of frustration. We must come to see with the distinguished jurist of yesterday that "justice too long delayed is justice denied." We have waited for more than three hundred and forty years for our constitutional and God-given rights. The nations of Asia and Africa are moving with jet-like speed toward the goal of political independence, and we still creep at horse and buggy pace toward the gaining of a cup of coffee at a lunch counter. I guess it is easy for those who have never felt the stinging darts of segregation to say, "Wait." But when you have seen vicious mobs lynch your mothers and fathers at will and drown your sisters and brothers at whim; when you have seen hate-filled policemen curse, kick, brutalize and even kill your black brothers and sisters with impunity; when you see the vast majority of your twenty million Negro brothers smothering in an air-tight cage of poverty in the midst of an affluent society; when you suddenly find your tongue twisted and your speech stammering as you seek to explain to your six-year-old daughter why she can't go to the public amusement park that has just been advertised on television, and see tears welling up in her little eyes when she is told that Funtown is closed to colored children, and see the depressing clouds of inferiority begin to form in her little mental sky, and see her begin to distort her little personality by unconsciously developing a bitterness toward white people; when you have to concoct an answer for a five-year-old son asking in agonizing pathos: "Daddy, why do white people treat colored people so mean?"; when you take a cross country drive and find it necessary to sleep night after night in the uncomfortable corners of your automobile because no motel will accept you; when you are humiliated day in and day out by nagging signs reading "white" and "colored"; when your first name becomes "nigger" and your middle name becomes "boy" (however old you are) and your last name becomes "John," and when your wife and mother are never given the respected title "Mrs."; when you are harried by day and haunted at night by the fact that you are a Negro, living constantly at tip-toe stance never quite knowing what to expect next, and plagued with inner fears and outer resentments; when you are forever fighting a degenerating sense of "nobodiness"; then you will understand why we find it difficult to wait. There comes a time when the cup of endurance runs over, and men are no longer willing to be plunged into an abyss of injustice where they experience the blackness of corroding despair. I hope, sirs, you can understand our legitimate and unavoidable impatience.

You express a great deal of anxiety over our willingness to break laws. This is certainly a legitimate concern. Since we so diligently urge people to obey the Supreme Court's decision of 1954 outlawing segregation in the public schools, it is rather strange and paradoxical to find us consciously breaking laws. One may well ask, "How can you advocate breaking some laws and obeying others?" The answer is found in the fact that there are two types of laws: There are *just* and there are *unjust* laws. I would agree with Saint Augustine that "An unjust law is no law at all."

Now what is the difference between the two? How does one determine when a law is just or unjust? A just law is a man-made code that squares with the moral law or the law of God. An unjust law is a code that is out of harmony with the moral law. To put it in the terms of Saint Thomas Aquinas, an unjust law is a human law that is not rooted in eternal and natural law. Any law that uplifts human personality is just. Any law that degrades human personality is unjust. All segregation statutes are unjust because segregation distorts the soul and damages the personality. It gives the segregator a false sense of superiority, and the segregated a false sense of inferiority. To use the words of Martin Buber, the great Jewish philosopher, segregation substitutes an "I-it" relationship for the "I-thou" relationship, and ends up relegating persons to the status of things. So segregation is not only politically, economically and sociologically unsound, but it is morally wrong and sinful. Paul Tillich has said that sin is separation. Isn't segregation an existential expression of man's tragic separation, an expression of his awful estrangement, his terrible sinfulness? So I can urge men to disobey segregation ordinances because they are morally wrong.

Let us turn to a more concrete example of just and unjust laws. An unjust law is a code that a majority inflicts on a minority that is not binding on itself. This is difference made legal. On the other hand a just law is a code that a majority compels a minority to follow that it is willing to follow itself. This is sameness made legal.

Let me give another explanation. An unjust law is a code inflicted upon a minority which that minority had no part in enacting or creating because they did not have the unhampered right to vote. Who can say that the legislature of Alabama which set up the segregation laws was democratically elected? Throughout the state of Alabama all types of conniving methods are used to prevent Negroes from becoming registered voters and there are some counties without a single Negro registered to vote despite the fact that the Negro constitutes a majority of the population. Can any law set up in such a state be considered democratically structured?

These are just a few examples of unjust and just laws. There are some instances when a law is just on its face and unjust in its application. For instance, I was arrested Friday on a charge of parading without a permit. Now there is nothing wrong with an ordinance which requires a permit for a parade, but when the ordinance is used to preserve segregation and to deny citizens the First Amendment privilege of peaceful assembly and peaceful protest, then it becomes unjust.

I hope you can see the distinction I am trying to point out. In no sense do I advocate evading or defying the law as the rabid segregationist would do. This would lead to anarchy. One who breaks an unjust law must do it *openly, lovingly* (not hatefully as the white mothers did in New Orleans when they were seen on television screaming "nigger, nigger, nigger"), and with a willingness to accept the penalty. I submit that an individual who breaks a law that conscience tells him is unjust, and willingly accepts the penalty by staying in jail to arouse the conscience of the community over its injustice, is in reality expressing the very highest respect for law.

Of course, there is nothing new about this kind of civil disobedience. It was seen sublimely in the refusal of Shadrach, Meshach and Abednego to obey the laws of Nebuchadnezzar because a higher moral law was involved. It was practiced superbly by the early Christians who were willing to face hungry lions and the excruciating pain of chopping blocks, before submitting to certain unjust laws of the Roman empire. To a degree academic freedom is a reality today because Socrates practiced civil disobedience.

We can never forget that everything Hitler did in Germany was "legal" and everything the Hungarian freedom fighters did in Hungary was "illegal." It was "illegal" to aid and comfort a Jew in Hitler's Germany. But I am sure that if I had lived in Germany during that time I would have aided and comforted my Jewish brothers even though it was illegal. If I lived in a Communist country today where certain principles dear to the Christian faith are suppressed, I believe I would openly advocate disobeying these anti-religious laws. I must make two honest confessions to you, my Christian and Jewish brothers. First, I must confess that over the last few years I have been gravely disappointed with the white moderate. I have almost reached the regrettable conclusion that the Negro's great stumbling block in the stride toward freedom is not the White Citizen's Council-er or the Ku Klux Klanner, but the white moderate who is more devoted to "order" than to justice; who prefers a negative peace which is the absence of tension to a positive peace which is the presence of justice; who constantly says, "I agree with you in the goal you seek, but I can't agree with your methods of direct action"; who paternalistically feels that he can set the timetable for another man's freedom; who lives by the myth of time and who constantly advises the Negro to wait until a "more convenient season." Shallow understanding from people of goodwill is more frustrating than absolute misunderstanding from people of ill will. Lukewarm acceptance is much more bewildering than outright rejection.

I had hoped that the white moderate would understand that law and order exist for the purpose of establishing justice, and that when they fail to do this they become dangerously structured dams that block the flow of social progress. I had hoped that the white moderate would understand that the present tension of the South is merely a necessary phase of the transition from an obnoxious negative peace, where the Negro passively accepted his unjust plight, to a substance-filled positive peace, where all men will respect the dignity and worth of human personality. Actually, we who engage in nonviolent direct action are not the creators of tension. We merely bring to the surface the hidden tension that is already alive. We bring it out in the open where it can be seen and dealt with. Like a boil that can never be cured as long as it is covered up but must be opened with all its pus-flowing ugliness to the natural medicines of air and light, injustice must likewise be exposed, with all of the tension its exposing creates, to the light of human conscience and the air of national opinion before it can be cured.

In your statement you asserted that our actions, even though peaceful, must be condemned because they precipitate violence. But can this assertion be logically made? Isn't this like condemning the robbed man because his possession of money precipitated the evil act of robbery? Isn't this like condemning Socrates because his unswerving commitment to truth and his philosophical delvings precipitated the misguided popular mind to make him drink the hemlock? Isn't this like condemning Jesus because His unique God-Consciousness and never-ceasing devotion to His will precipitated the evil act of crucifixion? We must come to see, as federal courts have consistently affirmed, that it is immoral to urge an individual to withdraw his efforts to gain his basic constitutional rights because the quest precipitates violence. Society must protect the robbed and punish the robber.

I had also hoped that the white moderate would reject the myth of time. I received a letter this morning from a white brother in Texas which said: "All Christians know that the colored people will receive equal rights eventually, but it is possible that you are in too great of a religious hurry. It has taken Christianity almost 2000 years to accomplish what it has. The teachings of Christ take time to come to earth." All that is said here grows out of a tragic misconception of time. It is the strangely irrational notion that there is something in the very flow of time that will inevitably cure all ills. Actually time is neutral. It can be used either destructively or constructively. I am coming to feel that the people of ill will have used time much more effectively than the people of goodwill. We will have to repent in this generation not merely for the vitriolic words and actions of the bad people, but for the appalling silence of the good people. We must come to see that human progress never rolls in on wheels of inevitability. It comes through the tireless efforts and persistent work of men willing to be co-workers with God, and without this hard work time itself becomes an ally of the forces of social stagnation. We must use time creatively, and forever realize that the time is always ripe to do right. Now is the time to make real the promise of democracy, and transform our pending national elegy into a creative psalm of brotherhood. Now is the time to lift our national policy from the quicksand of racial injustice to the solid rock of human dignity.

You spoke of our activity in Birmingham as extreme. At first I was rather disappointed that fellow clergymen would see my nonviolent efforts as those of the extremist. I started thinking about the fact that I stand in the middle of two opposing forces in the Negro community. One is a force of complacency made up of Negroes who, as a result of long years of oppression, have been so completely drained of self-respect and a sense of "somebodiness" that they have adjusted to segregation, and, of a few Negroes in the middle class who, because of a degree of academic and economic security, and because at points they profit by segregation, have unconsciously become insensitive to the problems of the masses. The other force is one of bitterness and hatred, and comes perilously close to advocating violence. It is expressed in the various black nationalist groups that are springing up over the nation, the largest and best known being Elijah Muhammad's Muslim movement. This movement is nourished by the contemporary frustration over the continued existence of racial discrimination. It is made up of people who have lost faith in America, who have absolutely repudiated Christianity, and who have concluded that the white man is an incurable "devil." I have tried to stand between these two forces, saying that we need not follow the "do-nothingism" of the complacent or the hatred and despair of the black nationalist. There is the more excellent way of love and nonviolent protest. I'm grateful to God that, through the Negro church, the dimension of nonviolence entered our struggle. If this philosophy had not emerged, I am convinced that by now many streets of the South would be flowing with floods of blood. And I am further convinced that if our white brothers dismiss as "rabble rousers" and "outside agitators" those of us who are working through the channels of nonviolent direct action and refuse to support our nonviolent efforts, millions of Negroes, out of frustration and despair, will seek solace and security in black nationalist ideologies, a development that will lead inevitably to a frightening racial nightmare.

Oppressed people cannot remain oppressed forever. The urge for freedom will eventually come. This is what happened to the American Negro. Something within has reminded him of his birthright of freedom; something without has reminded him that he can gain it. Consciously and unconsciously, he has been swept in by what the Germans call the *Zeitgeist,* and with his black brothers of Africa, and his brown and yellow brothers of Asia, South America and the Caribbean, he is moving with a sense of cosmic urgency toward the promised land of racial justice. Recognizing this vital urge that has engulfed the Negro community, one should readily understand public demonstrations. The Negro has many pent-up resentments and latent frustrations. He has to get them out. So let him march sometime; let him have his prayer pilgrimages to the city hall; understand why he must have sit-ins and freedom rides. If his repressed emotions do not come out in these nonviolent ways, they will come out in ominous expressions of violence. This is not a threat; it is a fact of history. So I have not said to my people "get rid of your discontent." But I have tried to say that this normal and healthy discontent can be channelized through the creative outlet of nonviolent direct action. Now this approach is being dismissed as extremist. I must admit that I was initially disappointed in being so categorized.

But as I continued to think about the matter I gradually gained a bit of satisfaction from being considered an extremist. Was not Jesus an extremist in love—"Love your enemies, bless them that curse you, pray for them that despitefully use you." Was not Amos an extremist for justice—"Let justice roll down like waters and righteousness like a mighty stream." Was not Paul an extremist for the gospel of Jesus Christ—"I bear in my body the marks of the Lord Jesus." Was not Martin Luther an extremist—"Here I stand; I can do none other so help me God." Was not John Bunyan an extremist—"I will stay in jail to the end of my days before I make a butchery of my conscience." Was not Abraham Lincoln an extremist—"This nation cannot survive half slave and half free." Was not Thomas Jefferson an extremist—"We hold these truths to be self-evident, that all men are created equal." So the question is not whether we will be extremist but what kind of extremist will we be. Will we be extremists for hate or will we be extremists for love? Will we be extremists for the preservation of injustice—or will we be extremists for the cause of justice? In that dramatic scene on Calvary's hill, three men were crucified. We must not forget that all three were crucified for the same crime—the crime of extremism. Two were extremists for immorality, and thusly fell below their environment. The other, Jesus Christ, was an extremist for love, truth and goodness, and thereby rose above his environment. So, after all, maybe the South, the nation and the world are in dire need of creative extremists.

I had hoped that the white moderate would see this. Maybe I was too optimistic. Maybe I expected too much. I guess I should have realized that few members of a race that has oppressed another race can understand or appreciate the deep groans and passionate yearnings of those that have been oppressed and still fewer have the vision to see that injustice must be rooted out by strong, persistent and determined action. I am thankful, however, that some of our white brothers have grasped the meaning of this social revolution and committed themselves to it. They are still all too small in quantity, but they are big in quality. Some like Ralph McGill, Lillian Smith, Harry Goden and James Dabbs have written about our struggle in eloquent, prophetic and understanding terms. Others have marched with us down nameless streets of the South. They have languished in filthy roach-infested jails, suffering the abuse and brutality of angry policemen who see them as "dirty nigger lovers." They, unlike so many of their moderate brothers and sisters, have recognized the urgency of the moment and sensed the need for powerful "action" antidotes to combat the disease of segregation.

Let me rush on to mention my other disappointment. I have been so greatly disappointed with the white church and its leadership. Of course, there are some notable exceptions. I am not unmindful of the fact that each of you has taken some significant stands on this issue. I commend you, Rev. Stallings, for your Christian stand on this past Sunday, in welcoming Negroes to your worship service on a non-segregated basis. I commend the Catholic leaders of this state for integrating Springhill College several years ago.

But despite these notable exceptions I must honestly reiterate that I have been disappointed with the church. I do not say that as one of the negative critics who can always find something wrong with the church. I say it as a minister of the gospel, who loves the church; who was nurtured in its bosom; who has been sustained by its spiritual blessings and who will remain true to it as long as the cord of life shall lengthen.

I had the strange feeling when I was suddenly catapulted into the leadership of the bus protest in Montgomery several years ago that we would have the support of the white church. I felt that the white ministers, priests and rabbis of the South would be some of our strongest allies. Instead, some have been outright opponents, refusing to understand the freedom movement and misrepresenting its leaders; all too many others have been more cautious than courageous and have remained silent behind the anesthetizing security of the stained-glass windows.

In spite of my shattered dreams of the past, I came to Birmingham with the hope that the white religious leadership of this community would see the justice of our cause, and with deep moral concern, serve as the channel through which our just grievances would get to the power structure. I had hoped that each of you would understand. But again I have been disappointed. I have heard numerous religious leaders of the South call upon their worshippers to comply with a desegregation decision because it is the *law,* but I have longed to hear white ministers say, "Follow this decree because integration is morally *right* and the Negro is your brother." In the midst of blatant injustices inflicted upon the Negro, I have watched white churches stand on the sideline and merely mouth pious irrelevancies and sanctimonious trivialities. In the midst of a mighty struggle to rid our nation of racial and economic injustice, I have heard so many ministers say, "Those are social issues with which the gospel has no real concern," and I have watched so many churches commit themselves to a completely other-worldly religion which made a strange distinction between body and soul, the sacred and the secular.

So here we are moving toward the exit of the twentieth century with a religious community largely adjusted to the status quo, standing as a tail-light behind other community agencies rather than a headlight leading men to higher levels of justice.

I have traveled the length and breadth of Alabama, Mississippi and all the other southern states. On sweltering summer days and crisp autumn mornings I have looked at her beautiful churches with their lofty spires pointing heavenward. I have beheld the impressive outlay of her massive religious education buildings. Over and over again I have found myself asking: "What kind of people worship here? Who is their God? Where were their voices when the lips of Governor Barnett dripped with words of interposition and nullification? Where were they when Governor Wallace gave the clarion call for defiance and hatred? Where were their voices of support when tired, bruised and weary Negro men and women decided to rise from the dark dungeons of complacency to the bright hills of creative protest?"

Yes, these questions are still in my mind. In deep disappointment, I have wept over the laxity of the church. But be assured that my tears have been tears of love. There can be no deep disappointment where there is not deep love. Yes, I love the church; I love her sacred walls. How could I do otherwise? I am in the rather unique position of being the son, the grandson and the great-grandson of preachers. Yes, I see the church as the body of Christ. But, oh! How we have blemished and scarred that body through social neglect and fear of being nonconformists.

There was a time when the church was very powerful. It was during that period when the early Christians rejoiced when they were deemed worthy to suffer for what they believed. In those days the church was not merely a thermometer that recorded the ideas and principles of popular opinion; it was a thermostat that transformed the mores of society. Wherever the early Christians entered a town the power structure got disturbed and immediately sought to convict them for being "disturbers of the peace" and "outside agitators." But they went on with the conviction that they were "a colony of heaven," and had to obey God rather than man. They were small in number but big in commitment. They were too God-intoxicated to be "astronomically intimated." They brought an end to such ancient evils as infanticide and gladiatorial contest.

Things are different now. The contemporary church is often a weak, ineffectual voice with an uncertain sound. It is so often the arch supporter of the status quo. Far from being disturbed by the presence of the church, the power structure of the average community is consoled by the church's silent and often vocal sanction of things as they are.

But the judgment of God is upon the church as never before. If the church of today does not recapture the sacrificial spirit of the early church, it will lose its authentic ring, forfeit the loyalty of millions, and be dismissed as an irrelevant social club with no meaning for the twentieth century. I am meeting young people every day whose disappointment with the church has risen to outright disgust.

Maybe again, I have been too optimistic. Is organized religion too inextricably bound to the status quo to save our nation and the world? Maybe I must turn my faith to the inner spiritual church, the church within the church, as the true *ecclesia* and the hope of the world. But again I am thankful to God that some noble souls from the ranks of organized religion have broken loose from the paralyzing chains of conformity and joined us as active partners in the struggle for freedom. They have left their secure congregations and walked the streets of Albany, Georgia, with us. They have gone through the highways of the South on tortuous rides for freedom. Yes, they have gone to jail with us. Some have been kicked out of their churches, and lost support of their bishops and fellow ministers. But they have gone with the faith that right defeated is stronger than evil triumphant. These men have been the leaven in the lump of the race. Their witness has been the spiritual salt that has preserved the true meaning of the Gospel in these troubled times. They have carved a tunnel of hope through the dark mountain of disappointment.

I hope the church as a whole will meet the challenge of this decisive hour. But even if the church does not come to the aid of justice, I have no despair about the future. I have no fear about the outcome of our struggle in Birmingham, even if our motives are presently misunderstood. We will reach the goal of freedom in Birmingham and all over the nation, because the goal of America is freedom. Abused and scorned though we may be, our destiny is tied up with the destiny of America. Before the pilgrims landed at Plymouth we were here. Before the pen of Jefferson etched across the pages of history the majestic words of the Declaration of Independence, we were here. For more than two centuries our foreparents labored in this country without wages; they made cotton king; and they built the homes of their masters in the midst of brutal injustice and shameful humiliation—and yet out of a bottomless vitality they continued to thrive and develop. If the inexpressible cruelties of slavery could not stop us, the opposition we now face will surely fail. We will win our freedom because the sacred heritage of our nation and the eternal will of God are embodied in our echoing demands.

I must close now. But before closing I am impelled to mention one other point in your statement that troubled me profoundly. You warmly commended the Birmingham police force for keeping "order" and "preventing violence." I don't believe you would have so warmly commended the police force if you had seen its angry violent dogs literally biting six unarmed, nonviolent Negroes. I don't believe you would so quickly commend the policemen if you would observe their ugly and inhuman treatment of Negroes here in the city jail; if you would watch them push and curse old Negro women and young Negro girls; if you would see them slap and kick old Negro men and young boys; if you will observe them, as they did on two occasions, refuse to give us food because we wanted to sing our grace together. I'm sorry that I can't join you in your praise for the police department.

It is true that they have been rather disciplined in their public handling of the demonstrators. In this sense they have been rather publicly "nonviolent." But for what purpose? To preserve the evil system of segregation. Over the last few years I have consistently preached that nonviolence demands that the means we use must be as pure as the ends we seek. So I have tried to make it clear that it is wrong to use immoral means to attain moral ends. But now I must affirm that it is just as wrong, or even more so, to use moral means to preserve immoral ends.

Maybe Mr. Connor and his policemen have been rather publicly non-violent, as Chief Pritchett was in Albany, Georgia, but they have used the moral means of nonviolence to maintain the immoral end of flagrant racial injustice. T. S. Eliot has said that there is no greater treason than to do the right deed for the wrong reason.

I wish you had commended the Negro sit-inners and demonstrators of Birmingham for their sublime courage, their willingness to suffer and their amazing discipline in the midst of the most inhuman provocation. One day the South will recognize its real heroes. They will be the James Merediths, courageously and with a majestic sense of purpose facing jeering and hostile mobs and the agonizing loneliness that characterizes the life of the pioneer. They will be old, oppressed, battered Negro women, symbolized in a seventy-two year old woman of Montgomery, Alabama, who rose up with a sense of dignity and with her people decided not to ride the segregated buses, and responded to one who inquired about her tiredness with ungrammatical profundity: "My feet is tired, but my soul is rested." They will be the young high school and college students, young ministers of the Gospel and a host of their elders courageously and nonviolently sitting-in at lunch counters and willingly going to jail for conscience's sake. One day the South will know that when these disinherited children of God sat down at lunch counters they were in reality standing up for the best in the American dream and the most sacred values in our Judeo-Christian heritage, and thusly, carrying our whole nation back to those great wells of democracy which were dug deep by the founding fathers in the formulation of the Constitution and the Declaration of Independence.

Never before have I written a letter this long (or should I say a book?). I'm afraid that it is much too long to take your precious time. I can assure you that it would have been much shorter if I had been writing from a comfortable desk, but what else is there to do when you are alone for days in the dull monotony of a narrow jail cell other than write long letters, think strange thoughts, and pray long prayers?

If I have said anything in this letter that is an overstatement of the truth and is indicative of an unreasonable impatience, I beg you to forgive me. If I have said anything in this letter that is an understatement of the truth and is indicative of my having a patience that makes me patient with anything less than brotherhood, I beg God to forgive me.

I hope this letter finds you strong in the faith. I also hope that circumstances will soon make it possible for me to meet each of you, not as an integrationist or a civil-rights leader, but as a fellow clergyman and a Christian brother. Let us all hope that the dark clouds of racial prejudice will soon pass away and the deep fog of misunderstanding will be lifted from our fear-drenched communities and in some not too distant tomorrow the radiant stars of love and brotherhood will shine over our great nation with all of their scintillating beauty.

Yours for the cause of Peace and Brotherhood,

Martin Luther King, Jr.

Our last selection, by Karl Mannheim, was written in 1945 when the practices of Nazi Germany were fresh in people's minds. His thoughts, however, are still appropriate today. Many of his references to Fascism are dealt with in detail in our Chapter 3 on dictatorships. Professor Mannheim presents the thesis that the modern technological society with its ever greater degree of organization can still increase our individual freedoms. He states that centralized social planning is necessary to our modern, complex way of life, but that many people argue that this will end in a totalitarian arrangement. Rejecting this argument, his contention is that advanced technology and behavioral knowledge, like advances in knowledge of the past, can lead to greater economic affluence, individual liberty, and democratic institutions if we act with courage and wisdom. He calls for a militant democracy designed to encourage diversity.*

DIAGNOSIS OF OUR TIME

KARL MANNHEIM

I. The Significance of the New Social Techniques

Let us take the attitude of a doctor who tries to give a scientific diagnosis of the illness from which we all suffer. There is no doubt that

Reprinted from Karl Mannheim, Diagnosis of Our Time: Wartime Essays of a Sociologist *(New York: Humanities Press, Inc.); (London: Routledge & Kegan Paul Ltd.), by permission of the publishers.*

---

* The 1972 Nobel Prize winners for economics made the point, however, that there can never be a theoretically perfect democracy. Professors John R. Hicks of Oxford and Kenneth J. Arrow of Harvard used mathematical models to show that there cannot be a perfect form of government (Associated Press release, October 26, 1972).

our society has been taken ill. What is the disease, and what could be its cure? If I had to summarize the situation in a single sentence I would say: "We are living in an age of transition from laissez-faire [1] to a planned society. The planned society that will come may take one of two shapes: it will be ruled either by a minority in terms of a dictatorship or by a new form of government which, in spite of its increased power, will still be democratically controlled."

If that diagnosis be true, we are all in the same boat—Germany, Russia, Italy, as well as Britain, France and U.S.A. Although in very many respects still different, we are all moving in the same direction towards a kind of planned society, and the question is whether it will be a good sort of planning or a bad one; for planning with dictatorship or on the basis of democratic control will emerge. But a diagnosis is not a prophecy. The value of a diagnosis does not mainly consist in the forecast as such, but in the reasons one is able to give for one's statements. The value of a diagnosis consists in the acuteness of the analysis of the factors which seem to determine the course of events. The main changes we are witnessing today can ultimately be traced to the fact that we are living in a Mass Society. Government of the masses cannot be carried on without a series of inventions and improvements in the field of economic, political and social techniques. By "Social Techniques" [2] I understand the sum of those methods which aim at influencing human be-

---

[1] In this [selection], the terms "laissez-faire" and "Liberalism" are used as ideal types, i.e., the term does not exactly designate reality as it is or ever was, but it deliberately emphasizes certain features which are relevant for the purpose of the presentation and for the valuations prevailing in the latter. Without focussing on such ideal types for developing clear-cut antimonies, it would be impossible to make one's points in a political discussion.

On the other hand, justice to the source from which we draw so much of our sustenance is restored, if we remind the reader that Liberalism, neither in its philosophy nor in its practice, ever completely corresponded to what could be called pure laissez-faire, that is to say the belief that self-adjustment both in the economic field and in the other spheres of social activity spontaneously leads to an equilibrium. Especially classical English Liberalism never demanded the complete absence of controls.

Nevertheless, after these reservations have been made it is still true that the laissez-faire ideology hoped for something like spontaneous self-adjustment, and in its exaggerated form it was partly responsible for the disintegration of communal controls in the later phases of capitalist Democracy in the course of which not equilibrium but crises and monopolies developed.

[2] Cf. my *Man and Society in an Age of Reconstruction: Studies in Modern Social Structure* (3rd ed., London, 1942), especially part v. This [selection] is a brief restatement and further development of that book, where the reader can find a more detailed treatment of many of the problems presented here. Furthermore, the author is working on a book, "Essentials of Democratic Planning," which will deal in a more systematic manner with the different aspects of planning.

haviour and which, when in the hands of the Government, act as an especially powerful means of social control.

Now the main point about these improved social techniques is not only that they are highly efficient, but that this very same efficiency fosters minority rule. To begin with, a new military technique allows a much greater concentration of power in the hands of the few than did the technique of any previous period: Whereas the armies of the eighteenth and nineteenth centuries were equipped with rifles and guns, our armies work with bombs, aeroplanes, gas and mechanized units. A man with a rifle threatens only a few people, but a man with a bomb can threaten a thousand. That means that in our age the change in military technique contributes a great deal to the chances of a minority rule.

The same concentration has occurred in the field of government and administration. Telephone, telegraph, wireless, railways, motor-cars and, last but not least, the scientific management of any large-scale organization—all these facilitate centralized government and control. Similar concentration can also be observed in the means of forming public opinion. The mechanized mass production of ideas through press and wireless works in this direction. Add to this the possibility of controlling schools and the whole range of education from a single centre, and you will realize that the recent change from democratic government to totalitarian systems is due here also not so much to the changing ideas of men as to changes in social technique.

The new science of Human Behaviour brings into the service of the Government a knowledge of the human mind which can either be exploited in the direction of greater efficiency or made into an instrument playing on mass emotions. The development of the social services, especially of social work, allows the exertion of an influence which penetrates into our private lives. Thus, there is a possibility of subjecting to public control psychological processes which formerly were considered as purely personal.

The reason why I lay such emphasis on these social techniques is that they limit the direction in which modern society can develop at all. The nature of these social techniques is even more fundamental to society than the economic structure or the social stratification of a given order. By their aid one can hamper or remould the working of the economic system, destroy social classes and set others in their place.

I call them techniques because, like all techniques, they are neither good nor bad in themselves. Everything depends on the use that is made of them by the human will. The most important thing about these modern techniques is that they tend to foster centralization and, therefore, minority rule and dictatorship. Where you have bombs, aeroplanes and a mechanized army at your disposal, telephone, telegraph and wireless as means of communication, large-scale industrial technique and a hierarchic bureaucratic machinery to produce and distribute commodities and manage human affairs, the main decisions can be taken from key positions. The gradual establishment of key positions in modern society has made planning not only possible but inevitable. Processes and events are no longer the outcome of natural interplay between small self-contained units. No longer do individuals and their small enterprises arrive at an equilibrium through competition and mutual adjustment. In the various branches of social and economic life there are huge combines, complex social units, which are too rigid to reorganize themselves on their own account and so must be governed from the centre.

The greater efficiency, in many respects, of the totalitarian states is not merely due, as people usually think, to the more efficient and more blatant propaganda, but also to their instant realization that mass society cannot be governed by techniques of the homespun order, which were suited to an age of craftsmanship. The terror of their efficiency consists in the fact that by co-ordinating all these means they enslave the greater part of the population and superimpose creeds, beliefs and behaviour which do not correspond to the real nature of the citizen.

In this description of the concentration of social techniques I consciously refer to changes which characterize the very structure of modern society. That means, if the main reason for what happened in Germany, Italy, Russia and the other totalitarian countries is to be sought in the changed nature of social techniques, it is only a question of time and opportunity when some group in the so far democratic countries will make use of them. In this connection a catastrophe like war, rapid depression, great inflation, growing unemployment, which make extraordinary measures necessary (i.e., concentration of the maximum power in the hands of some Government), is bound to precipitate this process. Even before the outbreak of the war the present tension brought about by the existing totalitarian states forced the democratic countries to take measures very often similar to those which came into force in the totalitarian countries through revolution. It goes without saying that the tendencies towards concentration must greatly increase in a war when conscription and the co-ordination of food and other supplies becomes necessary.

After this brief description of the social techniques you might rightly say: "What a gloomy prospect. Is there a remedy for this? Are we simply the victims of a process which is blind but stronger than all of us?" No diagnosis is complete unless it seeks for a kind of therapy. It is only worth studying the nature of society as it is, if we are able to hint at those steps which, taken in time, could make society into what it should be. Fortunately, a further attempt at a diagnosis reveals to us some aspects of the situation which not only free us from the feeling of frustration but definitely call upon us to act.

II. The Third Way: A Militant Democracy

What I have so far described are social techniques. Like all techniques, they are neither good nor bad in themselves. Everything depends on the use that is made of them by human will and intelligence. If they are left to themselves and develop unguarded they lead to dictatorship. If they are made to serve a good purpose and are continually checked, if they do not master men but are mastered by men, they are among the most magnificent achievements of mankind. But we shall be able to turn the flow of events and avert the fate of Germany, Italy and Russia only if we are vigilant and use our knowledge and judgment for the better. The principle of laissez-faire will not help us any further, we shall have to face the forthcoming events at the level of conscious thought in terms of concrete knowledge of society. Such an analysis will have to start with some preliminary clarifications which might help us in defining our policy.

First of all—not all planning is evil. We shall have to make a distinction between planning for conformity and planning for freedom and variety. In both cases co-ordination plays a great rôle, co-ordination of the means of social techniques such as education, propaganda, administration, etc.; but there is a difference between co-ordination in the spirit of monotony and co-ordination in the spirit of variety. The conductor of an orchestra co-ordinates the different instruments and it rests with him to direct this co-ordination to the achievement of monotony or of variety. The goose-step co-ordination of the dictators is the most primitive misinterpretation of the meaning of co-ordination. Real co-ordination in the social sphere means only a greater economy and a more purposeful use of the social techniques at our disposal. The more we think about the best forms of planning, the more we might arrive at the decision that in the most important spheres of life one should deliberately refrain from interference, and that the scope for spontaneity should rather be kept free than distorted by superfluous management. You might plan the time-table of a boarding school and come to the decision that at certain hours the pupils should be left entirely free—it is still planning if you are the master of the whole situation and decide that with certain fields of life one should not interfere. This sort of deliberate refraining from interference by a planner will radically differ from the purposeless non-interference by the laissez-faire society. Although it seems obvious that planning should not necessarily mean goose-step co-ordination, it was the bureaucratic and militaristic spirit of the totalitarian states which distorted the meaning of planning in that way.

There is a simple reason why in the long run great society cannot survive if it only fosters conformity. The French sociologist Durkheim first pointed out in *The Division of Labour in Society* [3] that only very simple societies like those of primitive peoples can work on the basis of homogeneity and conformity. The more complex the social division of labour becomes, the more it demands the differentiation of types. The integration and unity of great society is not achieved through uniform behavior but through the mutual complementing of functions. In a highly industrialized society people keep together because the farmer needs the industrial worker, the scientist, the educationist, and vice versa. Besides this vocational differentiation, individual differentiation is needed for the sake of inventions and efficient control of the new developments. All this only corroborates our statement that the bureaucratic and military ideal of planning must be replaced by the new ideal of the planning for freedom.

Another necessary clarification is that planning need not be based upon dictatorship. Co-ordination and planning can be done on the basis of democratic advice. There is nothing to prevent parliamentary machinery from carrying out the necessary control in planned society.

But it is not only the abstract principle of democracy which must be saved as well as recast in a new form. The increasing demand for social justice has to be met if we wish to guarantee the working of the new social order. The working of the present economic system, if left to itself, tends in the shortest possible time to increase the differences in income and wealth between the various classes to such an extent that this itself is bound to create dissatisfaction and continuous social tension. But as the working of democracy is essentially based upon democratic consent, the principle of social justice is not only a question of ethics but also a precondition of the functioning of the democratic system itself. The claim for greater justice does not necessarily mean a mechanical concept of equality. Reasonable differences in income and in the accumulation of wealth to create the necessary stimulus to achievement might be maintained as long as they do not interfere with the main trends in planning and do not grow to such an extent as to prevent co-operation between the different classes.

This move towards greater justice has the advantage that it can be achieved by the existing means of reform—through taxation, control

---

[3] E. Durkheim, *On the Division of Labour in Society* (trans. by G. Simpson: New York, 1933).

of investment, through public works and the radical extension of social services; it does not call for revolutionary interference, which would lead at once to dictatorship. The transformation brought about through reform instead of revolution also has the advantage that it can reckon with the help of former leading democratic groups. If a new system starts with the destruction of the older leading groups in society, it destroys all the traditional values of European culture as well. Ruthless attacks on the Liberal and Conservative intelligentsia and the persecution of the Churches are designed to annihilate the last remnants of Christianity and humanism and to frustrate all efforts to bring peace to the world. If the new society is to last, and if it is to be worthy of the efforts humanity has made so far, the new leadership must be blended with the old. Together they can help to rejuvenate the valuable elements in tradition, continuing them in the spirit of creative evolution.

But it is obvious that a new social order cannot be brought about simply by a more skillful and human handling of the new social techniques—it needs the guidance by the spirit, which is more than a system of decision on technical issues. The system of laissez-faire Liberalism could leave the final decisions to chance, to the miracle of the self-equilibrating forces of economic and social life. The age of Liberalism, therefore, was characterized by a pluralism of aims and values and a neutral attitude towards the main issues of life.

Laissez-faire Liberalism mistook neutrality for tolerance. Yet, neither democratic tolerance nor scientific objectivity means that we should refrain from taking a stand for what we believe to be true or that we should avoid the discussion of the final values and objectives in life. The meaning of tolerance is that everybody should have a fair chance to present his case, but not that nobody should ardently believe in his cause. This attitude of neutrality in our modern democracy went so far that we ceased to believe, out of mere fairness, in our own objectives; we no longer thought that peaceful adjustment is desirable, that freedom has to be saved and democratic control has to be maintained.

Our democracy has to become militant if it is to survive. Of course, there is a fundamental difference between the fighting spirit of the dictators on the one hand, who aim at imposing a total system of values and a strait-jacket social organization upon their citizens, and a militant democracy on the other, which becomes militant only in the defence of the agreed right procedure of social change and those basic virtues and values—such as brotherly love, mutual help, decency, social justice, freedom, respect for the person, etc.—which are the basis of the peaceful functioning of a social order. The new militant democracy will therefore develop a new attitude to values. It will differ from the relativist laissez-faire of the previous age, as it will have the courage to agree on some basic values which are acceptable to everybody who shares the traditions of Western civilization.

The challenge of the Nazi system more than anything else made us aware of the fact that the democracies have a set of basic values in common, which are inherited from classical antiquity, and even more from Christianity, and that it is not difficult to state them and to agree on them. But militant democracy will accept from Liberalism the belief that in a highly differentiated modern society—apart from those basic values on which democratic agreement will be necessary—it is better to leave the more complicated values open to creed, individual choice or free experimentation. The synthesis of these two principles will be reflected in our educational system in so far as the agreed basic virtues will be brought home to the child with all the educational methods at our disposal. But the more complex issues will be left open to save us from the evil effects of fanaticism.

The main problems of our time can be expressed in the following questions. Is there a possibility of planning which is based upon co-ordination and yet leaves scope for freedom? Can the new form of planning deliberately refrain from interfering except in cases where free adjustment has led not to harmony but to conflict and chaos? Is there a form of planning which moves in the direction of social justice, gradually eliminating the increasing disproportion in income and wealth in the various strata of the nation? Is there a possibility of transforming our neutral democracy into a militant one? Can we transform our attitudes to valuations so that democratic agreement on certain basic issues becomes possible, while the more complex issues are left to individual choice?

III. The Strategic Situation

Our diagnosis would be incomplete if we examined the possibilities in the abstract only. Any sociological or political therapy must devote special attention to the concrete situation in which we find ourselves. What is then the strategic situation? There are a number of forces which seem to be moving automatically in the direction which I have indicated above. First, there is a growing disappointment with laissez-faire methods. It is gradually being realized that they have been destructive, not only in the economic field where they produced the trade cycle and devastating mass unemployment, but that they are partly responsible for the lack of preparedness in the liberal and democratic states. The principle of letting things slide cannot compete with the efficiency of co-ordination—it is too slow, is based too much upon improvization and encourages all the waste inherent in departmentalization. . . . [T]here are grave doubts concerning Communism, even in the minds of those to whom—as a doctrine—it first meant the panacea for all the evils of Capitalism. Not only are they forced to ponder upon the chances of Communism if it were to be introduced by revolutionary methods into the Western countries with their differentiated social structure, but they cannot close their eyes to certain changes which took place in the time between Lenin and Stalin. The more they have to admit that what has happened was an inevitable compromise with realities, the more they have to take into account the presence of these realities also elsewhere. What these realities teach us is, briefly, that Communism works, that it is efficient and has great achievements to its credit as far as the state of the masses goes. The miscalculation begins with the fact that neither Dictatorship nor the State seems to wither away. Marx and Lenin believed that dictatorship was only a transient stage, which would disappear after the establishment of a new society. To-day we know that this was a typical nineteenth-century delusion. When Marx conceived this idea, one could point to the fate of absolutism which everywhere was slowly giving way to democracy. But this process, in the light of our analysis, was due to the fact that in the nineteenth century social techniques were still very inefficient and those in power had to compromise with the forces working from below. In a modern totalitarian state once the whole apparatus is appropriated by a single party and its bureaucracy, there is little chance that they will give it up of their own accord.

Thus there is at least a chance that out of the general fear and disillusionment a more reformist attitude may develop. . . . The unbridled criticism of the form of freedom and democracy which has existed in the past decades must therefore cease. Even if we agree that freedom and democracy are necessarily incomplete as long as social opportunities are hampered by economic inequality, it is irresponsible not to realize what a great achievement they represent and that through them we can enlarge the scope of social progress. . . .

The depressing experiences of the past . . . years have taught us that a dictatorship can govern against the will of even a large majority of the population. The reason is that the techniques of revolution lag far behind the techniques of government. Barricades, the symbols of revolution, are relics of an age when they were built up against cavalry. This means that there is a high premium on evolutionary methods. . . .

In my opinion, a new social order can be developed and the dictatorial tendencies of modern social techniques can be checked if our generation has the courage, imagination and will to master them and guide them in the right direction. This must be done immediately, while the techniques are still flexible and have not been monopolized by any single group. It rests with us to avoid the mistakes of former democracies, which, owing to their ignorance of these main trends, could not prevent the rise of dictatorship, and it is the historical mission of this country on the basis of her long-standing tradition of democracy, liberty and spontaneous reform to create a society which will work in the spirit of the new ideal: "Planning for Freedom."

GOVERNMENT
AND
THE ECONOMIC ORDER

6

POINT

COUNTERPOINT

The supremacy of free market economy.

Governmental restraint on the economy.

The market economy is a social system of the division of labor under the private ownership of the means of production. Everybody acts on his own behalf; but everybody's actions aim at the satisfaction of other people's needs as well as the satisfaction of his own. Everybody in acting serves his fellow citizens. Everybody, on the other hand, is served by his fellow citizens. . . . No government and no civil law can guarantee to bring about freedom otherwise than by supporting and defending

The great problem of future economic development in America will be how to influence its directions so that it may serve the cause of human freedom and dignity. This problem is . . . becoming even more acute because the individual is rapidly losing his personality under the combined impact of the nature of modern work, the bigness of the economic unit, and the worldwide preoccupation with economic development.[*]

*Werner Levi, "Economic Development and Human Values" in *Problems of United States Economic Development, Volume II* (New York: Committee on Economic Development, May 1958), p. 243. Reprinted by permission.

the fundamental institutions of the market economy.*

Neither the government nor society at large rely any more exclusively upon the mechanics of the market to keep the game going. Both deem it the duty of the government to see to it that it does. . . . The rules of the game . . . seek to prevent any sector of the economy from gaining absolute power *vis à vis* other sectors of the economy, competitors, or the individuals as such by controlling and limiting its power. . . . [through] . . . legislation controlling and limiting the strong and supporting the weak. . . .†

The statement on the left, the point, is a relatively modern description of laissez-faire capitalism, a notion under which the economy and society operate best and most efficiently without governmental intervention. The counterpoint stresses the need for the protection of human values and for the restraint of excesses of powerful economic units through intervention of the government. The degree of influence that government should exert over the economic order has been debated by philosophers and economic theorists at length, especially during the last two centuries, and in fact the governmental intervention in the economy has varied greatly in different countries from the Middle Ages to modern times.

When the feudal system of the Middle Ages faded away, the merchant welcomed the power of kings and princes over increasingly large territorial units because it provided protection for his shipments and supplies. At the same time, the creation of state-wide markets brought competition to the cities and eroded the authority of merchants' and manufacturers' guilds to control prices and the distribution of goods on the local level. The need for additional taxes and the prospects that the emerging economic system might yield the

---

* Ludwig von Mises, *Human Action: A Treatise on Economics* (New Haven, Conn: Yale University Press, 1949), p. 258.

† Hans Morgenthau in *Problems of United States Economic Development, Volume I* (New York: Committee on Economic Development, January 1958), p. 282. Reprinted by permission.

necessary revenues prompted the rulers of the states evolving at the end of the Middle Ages to turn their attention to the economic order.

The governments began to intervene actively in the economy by protecting industry and agriculture through tariffs and bounties, by building merchant fleets and navies for the opening of new markets around the world, and by stimulating the manufacture of goods for export in order to bring gold and silver into the country. State intervention of this kind, which aimed at the accumulation of wealth, has been labeled mercantilism. Our first selection, by Henri Pirenne, a Belgian professor of history, describes briefly some of the activities that characterized the evolution from the feudal system to the mercantilist order in Western Europe. We should note that mercantilism has not only historical significance. Some of the concepts embodied in mercantilism are applied today by some industrially advanced nations such as Japan and by a number of developing countries seeking to improve their economic posture.

MERCANTILISM

HENRI PIRENNE

. . . The conception of the State which began to emerge as their [the kings' and princes'] power increased, led them to consider themselves as protectors of the "common good." The same fourteenth century which saw urban particularism at its height, also saw the advent of the royal power in the sphere of economic history. Hitherto it had intervened there only indirectly, or rather in pursuance of its judicial, financial and military prerogatives. Though in its capacity as guardian of the public peace it had protected merchants, laid tolls upon commerce, and in case of war placed embargoes on enemy ships and promulgated stoppages of trade, it had left the economic activities of its subjects to themselves. Only the towns made laws and regulations for them. But the competence of the towns was limited by their municipal boundaries, and their particularism caused them to be continually in opposition to each other and made it manifestly impossible for them to take measures to secure the general good, at the possible expense of their individual interests. The princes

Reprinted from Henri Pirenne, Economic and Social History of Medieval Europe *(New York: Harcourt Brace Jovanovich, Inc., 1937, and London: Routledge & Kegan Paul Ltd., 1936), pp. 216–19, by permission of the publishers.*

alone were capable of conceiving a territorial economy, which would comprise and control the urban economies. At the close of the Middle Ages men were, of course, still far from a decided movement, or a conscious policy, directed towards this end. As a rule only intermittent tendencies are to be observed, but they are such as to make it evident that, wherever it had the power, the State was moving in the direction of mercantilism. Obviously the word can only be used within strict limitations, but, alien as the conception of a national economy still was to the governments of the late fourteenth and early fifteenth centuries, it is plain from their conduct that they desired to protect the industry and commerce of their subjects against foreign competition, and even, here and there, to introduce new forms of activity into their countries. In this they were inspired by the example of the towns, and their policy was really no more than the urban policy writ large. It still retained the chief characteristic of that policy, to wit, its protectionism. It was the beginning of a process which in the long run was destined to throw aside medieval internationalism, and to imbue the relations of states with each other with a particularism every whit as exclusive as that of the towns had been for centuries.

The first signs of this evolution showed themselves in England, the country which enjoyed a more powerful and united government than any other. In the first half of the fourteenth century Edward II tried to prohibit the import of foreign cloth, except such as was destined for the use of nobility. In 1331 Edward III invited Flemish weavers to settle in England. Most significant of all, an Act was passed in 1381 reserving the trade of the country for English ships, an early forerunner of Cromwell's Navigation Act, which it was of course impossible to carry out. The movement became still more active in the fifteenth century. In 1455 the import of silken goods was forbidden in order to protect the native manufacture; in 1463 foreigners were forbidden to export wool; and in 1464 the prohibition of Continental cloth foreshadowed the resolutely protectionist and mercantilist policy of Henry VII (1485–1509), the first modern King of England, which had now become a country in which industry was gaining steadily upon agriculture.

These measures naturally provoked reprisals in the Low Countries, whose most important manufacture suffered from them. Philip the Good, Duke of Burgundy (1419–67), who had united the different territories under his rule, replied by prohibiting the entry of English cloth. . . . He set to work to promote the rising mercantile marine of Holland and to encourage it in a competition with the Teutonic Hanse, which was to be completely successful in the following century. Not only did he encourage the Dutch carrying trade and fishing industry . . . but he assisted the rise of the port of Antwerp, which . . . was to become, a century later, the greatest commercial entrepot in the world.

France was ruined by the Hundred Years' War, and it was not until Louis XI came to the throne that measures were taken to bring about its economic revival. The energy and ability with which he pursued his policy are well known. He . . . tried to acclimatise the silkworm in the kingdom and to introduce the mining industry in Dauphine, and even thought of organising a kind of exhibition at the French embassy in London. . . .

The political anarchy which reigned in Germany prevented it, in the absence of central government, from imitating its western neighbours. . . . Italy, torn between princes and republics all struggling for supremacy, continued to fall into independent economic areas, two at least of which, Venice and Genoa, were, by reason of their establishments on the Levant, great economic powers. Indeed, the supremacy of Italy in banking and luxury industries was still so marked that it was successfully maintained over the rest of Europe, in spite of her political disunion, until the discovery of new routes to the Indies turned the main current of navigation and commerce from the Mediterranean to the Atlantic.

The immediate consequences of mercantilism were the growth of commercial institutions and a rise in the importance of banking and credit. As the commercial classes became more prominent and assumed greater significance for the achievement of governmental objectives, they moved closer to the sources of political power. Their representation increased in Parliament, as in England, and their influence expanded in the royal courts on the Continent. A new elite, oriented toward economic activity and progress, began to emerge, slowly taking over political power that for centuries had been based on the holding of land.

Laissez-Faire Capitalism

Although there can be no doubt that mercantilism gave great impetus to the economic aspect of society, the intervention of the state in the economy came under increasing attack. In the forefront of this attack was Adam Smith, a Scottish professor of philosophy who lived from 1723 to 1790. In his book, *The Wealth of Nations*, he extolled the division of labor and the unfettered law of supply and demand as the keys to a successful, modern industrial society. If the market were left free, the economic self-interest of thousands of consumers and hundreds of producers would unconsciously direct the system toward ends that are best for the economic welfare of the whole society. The system, whose driving force was competition, would be continually expanding in such a way that capital surpluses would accumulate, which in turn would be reinvested to tap an ever expanding market. Smith opposed any kind of monopoly because it was incompatible with competition. He also believed that every man, as long as he did not violate the law, should be left completely free to pursue his own interest in his own way. The activities of the state should be restricted to three legitimate functions: the protection of society from violence and invasion, the administration of justice, and the establishment and maintenance of public institutions such as the postal service and educational facilities.

In the second, third, and fourth selections of this chapter we have reproduced passages of The Wealth of Nations that expand the preceding ideas. Smith has become famous as the foremost advocate of laissez faire, usually taken to mean noninterference by the government in the operation of a capitalist economy.

THE PRICE OF COMMODITIES

ADAM SMITH

. . . The market price of every particular commodity is regulated by the proportion between the quantity which is actually brought to market, and the demand of those who are willing to pay the natural price of the commodity, or the whole value of the rent, labour, and profit, which must be paid in order to bring it thither. Such people may be called the effectual demanders, and their demand the effectual demand; since it may be sufficient to effectuate the bringing of the commodity to market. It is different from the absolute demand. A very poor man may be said in some sense to have a demand for a coach and six; he might

From the book The Wealth of Nations *by Adam Smith. Everyman's Library Edition. Published by J. M. Dent & Sons Ltd. (London) and E. P. Dutton & Co., Inc. (New York) and used with their permission.*

like to have it; but his demand is not an effectual demand, as the commodity can never be brought to market in order to satisfy it.

When the quantity of any commodity which is brought to market falls short of the effectual demand, all those who are willing to pay the whole value of the rent, wages, and profit, which must be paid in order to bring it thither, cannot be supplied with the quantity which they want. Rather than want it altogether, some of them will be willing to give more. A competition will immediately begin among them, and the market price will rise more or less above the natural price, according as either the greatness of the deficiency, or the wealth and wanton luxury of the competitors, happen to animate more or less the eagerness of the competition. Among competitors of equal wealth and luxury the same deficiency will generally occasion a more or less eager competition, according as the acquisition of the commodity happens to be of more or less importance to them. Hence the exorbitant price of the necessaries of life during the blockade of town or in a famine.

When the quantity brought to market exceeds the effectual demand, it cannot be all sold to those who are willing to pay the whole value of the rent, wages, and profit, which must be paid in order to bring it thither. Some part must be sold to those who are willing to pay less, and the low price which they give for it must reduce the price of the whole. The market price will sink more or less below the natural price, according as the greatness of the excess increases more or less the competition of the sellers, or according as it happens to be more or less important to them to get immediately rid of the commodity. The same excess in the importation of perishable, will occasion a much greater competition than in that of durable commodities; in the importation of oranges, for example, than in that of old iron.

When the quantity brought to market is just sufficient to supply the effectual demand, and no more, the market price naturally comes to be either exactly, or as nearly as can be judged of, the same with the natural price. The whole quantity upon hand can be disposed of for this price, and cannot be disposed of for more. The competition of the different dealers obliges them all to accept of this price, but does not oblige them to accept of less.

The quantity of every commodity brought to market naturally suits itself to the effectual demand. It is the interest of all those who employ their land, labour, or stock, in bringing any commodity to market, that the quantity never should exceed the effectual demand; and it is the interest of all other people that it never should fall short of that demand.

If at any time is exceeds the effectual demand, some of the component parts of its price must be paid below their natural rate. If it is rent, the interest of the landlords will immediately prompt them to withdraw a part of their land; and if it is wages or profit, the interest of the labourers in the one case, and of their employers in the other, will prompt them to withdraw a part of their labour or stock from this employment. The quantity brought to market will soon be no more than sufficient to supply the effectual demand. All the different parts of its price will rise to their natural rate, and the whole price to its natural price.

If, on the contrary, the quantity brought to market should at any time fall short of the effectual demand, some of the component parts of its price must rise above their natural rate. If it is rent, the interest of all other landlords will naturally prompt them to prepare more land for the raising of this commodity; if it is wages or profit, the interest of all other labourers and dealers will soon prompt them to employ more labour and stock in preparing and bringing it to market. The quantity brought thither will soon be sufficient to supply the effectual demand. All the different parts of its price will soon sink to their natural rate, and the whole price to its natural price.

The natural price, therefore, is, as it were, the central price, to which the prices of all commodities are continually gravitating. Different accidents may sometimes keep them suspended a good deal above it, and sometimes force them down even somewhat below it. But whatever may be the obstacles which hinder them from settling in this centre of repose and continuance, they are constantly tending towards it.

The whole quantity of industry annually employed in order to bring any commodity to market naturally suits itself in this manner to the effectual demand. It naturally aims at bringing always that precise quantity thither which may be sufficient to supply, and no more than supply, that demand. . . .

PRINCIPLE OF DIVISION OF LABOUR

ADAM SMITH

This division of labour, from which so many advantages are derived, is not originally the effect of any human wisdom, which foresees and

From the book The Wealth of Nations *by Adam Smith. Everyman's Library Edition. Published by J. M. Dent & Sons Ltd. (London) and E. P. Dutton & Co., Inc. (New York) and used with their permission.*

intends that general opulence to which it gives occasion. It is the necessary, though very slow and gradual consequence of a certain propensity in human nature which has in view no such extensive utility; the propensity to truck, barter, and exchange one thing for another.

Whether this propensity be one of those original principles in human nature of which no further account can be given; or whether, as seems more probable, it be the necessary consequence of the faculties of reason and speech, it belongs not to our present subject to inquire. It is common to all men, and to be found in no other race of animals, which seem to know neither this nor any other species of contracts.

. . . In almost every other race of animals each individual, when it is grown up to maturity, is entirely independent, and in its natural state has occasion for the assistance of no other living creature. But man has almost constant occasion for the help of his brethren, and it is in vain for him to expect it from their benevolence only. He will be more likely to prevail if he can interest their self-love in his favour, and show them that it is for their own advantage to do for him what he requires of them. Whoever offers to another a bargain of any kind, proposes to do this. Give me that which I want, and you shall have this which you want, is the meaning of every such offer; and it is in this manner that we obtain from one another the far greater part of those good offices which we stand in need of. It is not from the benevolence of the butcher, the brewer, or the baker that we expect our dinner, but from their regard to their own interest. We address ourselves, not to their humanity but to their self-love, and never talk to them of our own necessities but of their advantages. . . .

As it is by treaty, by barter, and by purchase that we obtain from one another the greater part of those mutual good offices which we stand in need of, so it is this same trucking disposition which originally gives occasion to the division of labour. In a tribe of hunters or shepherds a particular person makes bows and arrows, for example, with more readiness and dexterity than any other. He frequently exchanges them for cattle or for venison with his companions; and he finds at last that he can in this manner get more cattle and venison than if he himself went to the field to catch them. From a regard to his own interest, therefore, the making of bows and arrows grows to be his chief business, and he becomes a sort of armourer. Another excels in making the frames and covers of their little huts or movable houses. He is accustomed to be of use in this way to his neighbours, who reward him in the same manner with cattle and with venison, till at last he finds it his interest to dedicate himself entirely to this employment, and to become a sort of house-carpenter. In the same manner a third becomes a smith or a brazier, a fourth a tanner or dresser of hides or skins, the principal part of the clothing of savages. And thus the certainty of being able to exchange all that surplus part of the produce of his own labour, which is over and above his own consumption, for such parts of the produce of other men's labour as he may have occasion for, encourages every man to apply himself to a particular occupation, and to cultivate and bring to perfection whatever talent or genius he may possess for that particular species of business. . . .

OF THE FUNDS OR SOURCES OF REVENUE WHICH MAY PECULIARLY BELONG TO THE SOVEREIGN OR COMMONWEALTH

ADAM SMITH

The funds or sources of revenue which may peculiarly belong to the sovereign or commonwealth must consist either in stock or in land.

The sovereign, like any other owner of stock, may derive a revenue from it, either by employing it himself, or by lending it. His revenue is in the one case profit, in the other interest. . . .

Small republics have sometimes derived a considerable revenue from the profit of mercantile projects. The republic of Hamburg is said to do from the profits of a public wine cellar and apothecary's shop. The state cannot be very great of which the sovereign has leisure to carry on the trade of a wine merchant or apothecary. The profit of a public bank has been a source of revenue to more considerable states. It has been so not only to Hamburg, but to Venice and Amsterdam. A revenue of this kind has even by some people been thought not below the attention of so great an empire as that of Great Britain. Reckoning the ordinary dividend of the Bank of England at five and a half per cent, and its capital at ten millions seven hundred and eighty thousand pounds, the net annual profit, after paying the expense of management, must amount, is it said, to five hundred and ninety-two thousand nine hundred pounds. Government, it is pretended, could borrow this capital at three per cent interest, and by taking the management of the bank into its own hands, might make a clear profit of two hundred and sixty-

From the book The Wealth of Nations *by Adam Smith. Everyman's Library Edition. Published by J. M. Dent & Sons Ltd. (London) and E. P. Dutton & Co., Inc. (New York) and used with their permission.*

nine thousand five hundred pounds a year. The orderly, vigilant, and parsimonious administration of such aristocracies as those of Venice and Amsterdam is extremely proper, it appears from experience, for the management of a mercantile project of this kind. But whether such a government as that of England—which, whatever may be its virtues, has never been famous for good economy; which in time of peace, has generally conducted itself with the slothful and negligent profusion that is perhaps natural to monarchies; and in time of war has constantly acted with all the thoughtless extravagance that democracies are apt to fall into—could be safely trusted with the management of such a project, must at least be a good deal more doubtful.

It is important to note that Smith was not opposed to every conceivable act of government in the sphere. He recognized that the economic system had to serve society, a situation which might require minimum governmental regulations. It was another British writer, Herbert Spencer, who, a few decades later, extended the concept of laissez faire to its extreme by linking it to the harsh doctrine of the "survival of the fittest," made famous by Charles Darwin, the proponent of the theory that man is the product of biological evolution. In economic terms this meant that the laws of supply and demand were elevated to the highest principles of society with which the government was not to interfere under any circumstances.

The operation of laissez-faire capitalism in the wake of the industrial revolution produced a number of unfortunate effects for the workers in the factories, especially in Europe. Working hours were extremely long, the working conditions in many factories unbelievably poor, and extensive use of child labor was often the order of the day. The wages were frequently so low that the workers were hardly able to eke out a mere subsistence. Many small merchants suffered in the merciless economic struggle which tended to destroy the weaker while adding to the strength of the already powerful and prosperous. As a consequence, broad movements of resentment and unrest arose against the strains and dislocations that the philosophy of laissez-faire capitalism wrought in the social and economic fabric. These movements spawned a new economic-political philosophy, socialism, which voiced strong protests not only against the deplorable conditions of life caused by unrestrained capitalism, but also against the lingering trappings of aristocratic society in Europe that were slow to disappear. Among the protestors none was more extreme, determined, and intellectually glittering than Karl Marx, who, in 1848, with his friend Friedrich Engels, indicted contemporary society in the Communist Manifesto. Pertinent parts of the Manifesto are our next reading selection.

MANIFESTO OF THE COMMUNIST PARTY

KARL MARX / FRIEDRICH ENGELS

A spectre is haunting Europe—the spectre of Communism. All the powers of old Europe have entered into a holy alliance to exorcise this spectre; Pope and Czar, Metternich and Guizot, French Radicals and German police-spies.

Where is the party in opposition that has not been decried as communistic by its opponents in power? Where the Opposition that has not hurled back the branding reproach of Communism, against the more advanced opposition parties, as well as against its reactionary adversaries?

Two things result from this fact.

I. Communism is already acknowledged by all European Powers to be itself a Power.

II. It is high time that Communists should openly, in the face of the whole world, publish their views, their aims, their tendencies, and meet this nursery tale of the Spectre of Communism with a Manifesto of the party itself.

To this end, Communists of various nationalities have assembled in London, and sketched the following manifesto, to be published in the English, French, German, Italian, Flemish and Danish languages.

Bourgeois and Proletarians

The history of all hitherto existing society is the history of class struggles.

Freeman and slave, patrician and plebeian, lord and serf, guild-master and journeyman, in a word, oppressor and oppressed, stood in constant opposition to one another, carried on an uninterrupted, now hidden, now open fight, a fight that each time ended, either in a revolutionary re-constitution of society at large, or in the common ruin of the contending classes.

Reprinted from Karl Marx and Friedrich Engels, Manifesto of the Communist Party, *authorized English translation: edited and annotated by Friedrich Engels (Chicago: Charles H. Kerr and Company, 1874), pp. 11–15, 22–23, and 30–42.*

In the earlier epochs of history, we find almost everywhere a complicated arrangement of society into various orders, a manifold graduation of social rank. In ancient Rome we have patricians, knights, plebeians, slaves; in the Middle Ages, feudal lords, vassals, guild-masters, journeymen, apprentices, serfs; in almost all of these classes, again, subordinate gradations.

The modern bourgeois society that has sprouted from the ruins of feudal society, has not done away with class antagonisms. It has but established new classes, new conditions of oppression, new forms of struggle in place of the old ones.

Our epoch, the epoch of the bourgeoisie, possesses, however, this distinctive feature; it has simplified the class antagonisms. Society as a whole is more and more splitting up into two great hostile camps, into two great classes directly facing each other: Bourgeoisie and Proletariat.

From the serfs of the middle ages sprang the chartered burghers of the earliest towns. From these burgesses the first elements of the bourgeoisie were developed.

The discovery of America, the rounding of the Cape, opened up fresh ground for the rising bourgeoisie. The East-Indian and Chinese markets, the colonization of America, trade with the colonies, the increase in the means of exchange and in commodities generally, gave to commerce, to navigation, to industry, an impulse never before known, and thereby, to the revolutionary element in the tottering feudal society, a rapid development.

The feudal system of industry, under which industrial production was monopolized by close guilds, now no longer sufficed for the growing wants of the new markets. The manufacturing system took its place. The guild-masters were pushed on one side of the manufacturing middle-class; division of labor between the different corporate guilds vanished in the face of division of labor in each single workshop.

Meantime the markets kept ever growing, the demand, ever rising. Even manufacture no longer sufficed. Thereupon, steam and machinery revolutionized industrial production. The place of manufacture was taken by the giant, Modern Industry, the place of the industrial middle-class, by industrial millionaires, the leaders of whole industrial armies, the modern bourgeois.

Modern industry has established the world-market, for which the discovery of America paved the way. This market has given an immense development to commerce, to navigation, to communication by land. This development has, in its turn, reacted on the extension of industry; and in proportion as industry, commerce, navigation, railways extended, in the same proportion the bourgeoisie developed, increased its capital, and pushed into the background every class handed down from the Middle Ages.

We see, therefore, how the modern bourgeoisie is itself the product of a long course of development, of a series of revolutions in the modes of production and of exchange.

Each step in the development of the bourgeoisie was accompanied by a corresponding political advance of that class. An oppressed class under the sway of the feudal nobility, an armed and selfgoverning association in the medieval commune, here independent urban republic (as in Italy and German), there taxable "third estate" of the monarchy (as in France), afterwards, in the period of manufacture proper, serving either the semi-feudal or the absolute monarchy as a counterpoise against the nobility, and, in fact, corner stone of the great monarchies in general, the bourgeoisie has at last, since the establishment of Modern Industry and of the world-market, conquered for itself, in the modern representative State, exclusive political sway. The executive of the modern State is but a committee for managing the common affairs of the whole bourgeoisie.

The bourgeoisie, historically, has played a most revolutionary part.

The bourgeoisie, wherever it has got the upper hand, has put an end to all feudal, patriarchal, idyllic . relations. It has pitilessly torn asunder the motley feudal ties that bound man to his "natural superiors," and has left remaining no other nexus between man and man than naked self-interest, than callous "cash payment." It has drowned the most heavenly ecstacies of religious fervor, of chivalrous enthusiasm, of philistine sentimentalism, in the icy water of egotistical calculation. It has resolved personal worth into exchange value, and in place of the numberless indefeasible chartered freedoms, has set up that single, unconscionable freedom—Free Trade. In one word, for exploitation, veiled by religious and political illusions, it has substituted naked, shameless, direct, brutal exploitation.

. . .

Modern industry has converted the little workshop of the patriarchal master into the great factory of the industrial capitalist. Masses of laborers, crowded into the factory, are organized like soldiers. As privates of the industrial army they are placed under the command of a perfect hierarchy of officers and sergeants. Not only are they the slaves of the bourgeois class, and of the bourgeois State, they are daily and hourly enslaved by the machine, by the over-looker, and, above all, by the individual borgeois manufacturer himself. The more openly this despotism proclaims gain to be its end and aim, the more petty, the more hateful and the more embittering it is.

The less the skill and exertion or strength implied in manual labor, in other words, the more modern industry becomes developed, the more is the labor of men superseded by that of women. Differences of age and sex have no longer any distinctive social validity for the working class. All are instruments of labor, more or less expensive to use, according to their age and sex.

No sooner is the exploitation of the laborer by the manufacturer, so far at an end, that he receives his wages in cash, than he is set upon by the other portions of the bourgeoisie, the landlord, the shopkeeper, the pawnbroker, etc.

The lower strata of the middle class—the small tradespeople, shop-keepers, and retired tradesmen generally, the handicraftsmen and peas-ants—all these sink gradually into the proletariat, partly because their diminutive capital does not suffice for the scale on which Modern Indus-try is carried on, and is swamped in the competition with the large cap-italists, partly because their specialized skill is rendered worthless by new methods of production. Thus the proletariat is recruited from all classes of the population.

.   .   .

Proletarians and Communists

In what relation do the Communists stand to the proletarians as a whole?

The Communists do not form a separate party opposed to other working-class parties.

They have no interests separate and apart from those of the prole-tariat as a whole.

They do not set up any sectarian principles of their own, by which to shape and mould the proletarian movement.

The Communists are distinguished from the other working class parties by this only: 1. In the national struggles of the proletarians of the different countries, they point out and bring to the front the com-mon interests of the entire proletariat independently of all nationality. 2. In the various stages of development which the struggle of the working class against the bourgeoisie has to pass through, they always and every-where represent the interests of the movement as a whole.

The Communists, therefore, are on the one hand, practically, the most advanced and resolute section of the working class parties of every country, that section which pushes forward all others; on the other hand, theoretically, they have over the great mass of the proletariat the ad-vantages of clearly understanding the line of march, the conditions, and the ultimate general results of the proletarian movement.

The immediate aim of the Communists is the same as that of all the other proletarian parties; formation of the proletariat into a class, overthrow of the bourgeois supremacy, conquest of political power by the proletariat.

The theoretical conclusions of the Communists are in no way based on ideas or principles that have been invented, or discovered, by this or that would-be universal reformer.

They merely express, in general terms, actual relations springing from an existing class struggle, from a historical movement going on under our very eyes. The abolition of existing property relations is not at all a distinctive feature of Communism. . . .

The distinguishing feature of Communism is not the abolition of property generally, but the abolition of bourgeois property. But modern bourgeois private property is the final and most complete expression of the system of producing and appropriating products, that is based on class antagonism, on the exploitation of the many by the few.

In this sense, the theory of the Communists may be summed up in the single sentence: Abolition of private property.

We Communists have been reproached with the desire of abolishing the right of personally acquiring property as the fruit of a man's own labor, which property is alleged to be the ground work of all personal freedom, activity and independence.

Hard-won, self-acquired, self-earned property! Do you mean the property of the petty artisan and of the small peasant, a form of property that preceded the bourgeois form? There is no need to abolish that; the development of industry has to a great extent already destroyed it, and is still destroying it daily.

Or do you mean modern bourgeois private property?

But does wage-labor create any property for the laborer? Not a bit. It creates capital, i.e., that kind of property which exploits wage-labor, and which cannot increase except upon condition of getting a new supply of wage-labor for fresh exploitation. Property, in its present form, is based on the antagonism of capital and wage-labor. Let us examine both sides of this antagonism.

To be a capitalist, is to have not only a purely personal, but a social status in production. Capital is a collective product, and only by the united action of many members, nay, in the last resort, only by the united action of all members of society, can it be set in motion.

Capital is therefore not a personal, it is a social power.

When, therefore, capital is converted into common property, into the property of all members of society, personal property is not thereby transformed into social property. It is only the social character of the property that is changed. It loses its class-character.

Let us now take wage-labor.

The average price of wage-labor is the minimum wage, i.e., that quantum of the means of subsistence, which is absolutely requisite to keep the laborer in bare existence as a laborer. What, therefore, the wage-laborer appropriates by means of his labor, merely suffices to prolong and reproduce a bare existence. We by no means intend to abolish this personal appropriation of the products of labor, an appropriation that is made for the maintenance and reproduction of human life, and that leaves no surplus wherewith to command the labor of others. All that we want to do away with is the miserable character of this appropriation, under which the laborer lives merely to increase capital, and is allowed to live only in so far as the interest of the ruling class requires it. . . .

And the abolition of this state of things is called by the bourgeois, abolition of individuality and freedom! And rightly so. The abolition of bourgeois individuality, bourgeois independence, and bourgeois freedom is undoubtedly aimed at.

By freedom is meant, under the present bourgeois conditions of production, free trade, free selling and buying.

But if selling and buying disappears, free selling and buying disappears also. This talk about free selling and buying, and all the other "brave words" of our bourgeoisie about freedom in general, have a meaning, if any, only in contrast with restricted selling and buying, with the fettered traders of the Middle Ages, but have no meaning when opposed to the Communistic abolition of buying and selling, of the bourgeois conditions of production, and of the bourgeoisie itself.

You are horrified at our intending to do away with private property. But in your existing society, private property is already done away with for nine-tenths of the population; its existence for the few is solely due to its non-existence in the hands of those nine-tenths. You reproach us, therefore, with intending to do away with a form of property, the necessary condition for whose existence is, the non-existence of any property for the immense majority of society.

In one word, you reproach us with intending to do away with your property. Precisely so; that is just what we intend.

From the moment when labor can no longer be converted into capital, money, or rent, into a social power capable of being monopolized, i.e., from the moment when individual property can no longer be transformed into bourgeois property, into capital, from that moment, you say, individuality vanishes.

You must, therefore, confess that by "individual" you mean no other person than the bourgeois, than the middle-class owner of property. This person must, indeed, be swept out of the way, and made impossible.

Communism deprives no man of the power to appropriate the

products of society: all that it does is to deprive him of the power to subjugate the labor of others by means of such appropriation.

It has been objected, that upon the abolition of private property all work will cease, and universal laziness will overtake us.

According to this, bourgeois society ought long ago to have gone to the dogs through sheer idleness; for those of its members who work, acquire nothing, and those who acquire anything, do not work. . . .

. . . Just as, to the bourgeois, the disappearance of class property is the disappearance of production itself, so the disappearance of class culture is to him identical with the disappearance of all culture.

That culture, the loss of which he laments, is, for the enormous majority, a mere training to act as a machine.

But don't wrangle with us so long as you apply, to our intended abolition of bourgeois property, the standard of your bourgeois notions of freedom, culture, law, etc. Your very ideas are but the outgrowth of the conditions of your bourgeois production and bourgeois property, just as your jurisprudence is but the will of your class made into a law for all, a will, whose essential character and direction are determined by the economic conditions of existence of your class.

The selfish misconception that induces you to transform into eternal laws of nature and of reason, the social forms springing from your present mode of production and form of property—historical relations that rise and disappear in the progress of production—this misconception you share with every ruling class that has preceded you. What you see clearly in the case of ancient property, what you admit in the case of feudal property, you are of course forbidden to admit in the case of your own bourgeois form of property.

Abolition of the family! Even the most radical flare up at this infamous proposal of the Communists.

On what foundation is the present family, the bourgeois family, based? On capital, on private gain. In its completely developed form this family exists only among the bourgeoisie. But this state of things finds its complement in the practical absence of the family among the proletarians, and in public prostitution.

The bourgeois family will vanish as a matter of course when its complement vanishes, and both will vanish with the vanishing of capital.

Do you charge us with wanting to stop the exploitation of children by their parents? To this crime we plead guilty.

But, you will say, we destroy the most hallowed of relations, when we replace home education by social.

And your education! Is not that also social, and determined by the social conditions under which you educate, by the intervention, direct or indirect, of society by means of schools, etc.? The Communists have not invented the intervention of society in education; they do but seek to alter the character of that intervention, and to rescue education from the influence of the ruling class.

The bourgeois clap-trap about the family and education, about the hallowed co-relation of parent and child, becomes all the more disgusting, the more, by the action of Modern Industry, all family ties among the proletarians are torn asunder, and their children transformed into simple articles of commerce and instruments of labor.

But you Communists would introduce community of women, screams the whole bourgeoisie in chorus.

The bourgeois sees in his wife a mere instrument of production. He hears that the instruments of production are to be exploited in common, and, naturally, can come to no other conclusion, than that the lot of being common to all will likewise fall to the women.

He has not even a suspicion that the real point aimed at is to do away with the status of women as mere instruments of production.

For the rest, nothing is more ridiculous than the virtuous indignation of our bourgeois at the community of women which, they pretend, is to be openly and officially established by the Communists. The Communists have no need to introduce community of women; it has existed almost from time immemorial.

Our bourgeois, not content with having the wives and daughters of their proletarians at their disposal, not to speak of common prostitutes, take the greatest pleasure in seducing each others' wives. . . .

The Communists are further reproached with desiring to abolish countries and nationalities.

The working men have no country. We cannot take from them what they have not got. Since the proletariat must first of all acquire political supremacy, must rise to be the leading class of the nation, must constitute itself the nation, it is, so far, itself national, though not in the bourgeois sense of the word. . . .

In proportion as the exploitation of one individual by another is put an end to, the exploitation of one nation by another will also be put an end to. In proportion as the antagonism between classes within the nation vanishes, the hostility of one nation to another will come to an end.

The charges against Communism made from a religious, a philosophical, and generally, from an ideological standpoint, are not deserving of serious examination.

Does it require deep intuition to comprehend that man's ideas, views, and conceptions, in one word, man's consciousness, changes with every change in the conditions of his material existence, in his social relations and in his social life? . . .

When people speak of ideas that revolutionize society, they do but express the fact, that within the old society, the elements of a new one have been created, and that the dissolution of the old ideas keeps even pace with the dissolution of the old conditions of existence.

When the ancient world was in its last throes, the ancient religions were overcome by Christianity. When Christian ideas succumbed in the 18th century to rationalist ideas, feudal society fought its death-battle with the then revolutionary bourgeoisie. The ideas of religious liberty and freedom of conscience, merely gave expression to the sway of free competition within the domain of knowledge.

But whatever form they may have taken, one fact is common to all past ages, viz., the exploitation of one part of society by the other. No wonder, then, that the social consciousness of past ages, despite all the multiplicity and variety it displays, moves within certain common forms, or general ideas, which cannot completely vanish except with the total disappearance of class antagonisms.

The Communist revolution is the most radical rupture with traditional property-relations; no wonder that its development involves the most radical rupture with traditional ideas.

But let us have done with the bourgeois objections to Communism.

We have seen above, that the first step in the revolution by the working class, is to raise the proletariat to the position of ruling class, to win the battle of democracy.

The proletariat will use its political supremacy, to wrest, by degrees, all capital from the bourgeoisie, to centralize all instruments of production in the hands of the State, i.e., of the proletariat organized as the ruling class; and to increase the total of productive forces as rapidly as possible.

Of course, in the beginning, this cannot be effected except by means of despotic inroads on the rights of property, and on the conditions of bourgeois production; but means of measures, therefore, which appear economically insufficient and untenable, but which in the course of the movement, outstrip themselves, necessitate further inroads upon the old social order, and are unavoidable as a means of entirely revolutionizing the mode of production.

These measures will of course be different in different countries.

Nevertheless in the most advanced countries the following will be pretty generally applicable:

1. Abolition of property in land and application of all rents of land to public purposes.

2. A heavy progressive or graduated income tax.

3. Abolition of all rights of inheritance.

4. Confiscation of the property of all emigrants and rebels.

5. Centralization of credit in the hands of the state, by means of a national bank with State capital and an exclusive monopoly.

6. Centralization of the means of communication and transport in the hands of the State.

7. Extension of factories and instruments of production owned by the state; the bringing into cultivation of waste lands, and improvement of the soil generally in accordance with a common plan.

8. Equal liability of all to labor. Establishment of industrial armies, especially for agriculture.

9. Combination of agriculture with manufacturing industries; gradual abolition of the distinction between town and country, by a more equable distribution of population over the country.

10. Free education for all children in public schools. Abolition of children's factory labor in its present form. Combination of education with industrial production, etc., etc.

When, in the course of development, class distinctions have disappeared, and all production has been concentrated in the hands of a vast association of the whole nation, the public power will lose its political character. Political power, properly so called, is merely the organized power of one class for oppressing another. If the proletariat during its contest with the bourgeoisie is compelled, by the force of circumstances, to organize itself as a class, if, by circumstances, to organize itself as a class, if, by means of a revolution, it makes itself the ruling class, and, as such sweeps away by force the old conditions of production, then it will, along with these conditions, have swept away the conditions for the existence of class antagonisms, and of classes generally, and will thereby have abolished its own supremacy as a class.

In place of the old bourgeois society, with its classes and class antagonisms, we shall have an association, in which the free development of each is the condition for the free development of all.

Marxists and Others

We must understand that the Communist Manifesto is a revolutionary pamphlet containing a mixture of penetrating insights into society, half-truths, and powerful propaganda. But Marx was more than an apostle of revolution. In his monumental work *Das Kapital,* or *Capital,* and other writings, he devised economic and historical theories which, although faulty, have left their imprint on mankind and continue to be followed in the communist one-third of the world. Although the theories of Marx have been modified by Lenin, Stalin, Mao

Tse-Tung, and others, and are applied in accordance with different interpretations, they are still aclaimed as infallible by the communists of the world and by many socialists.

While it would exceed the framework of this commentary to discuss in detail the theories of Marx, a few observations highlighting his concepts will assist the reader in better understanding the Manifesto. According to Marx, history was directed by changes that occurred in the forces of production, each of which required a particular set of social relations to be operative—i.e., ownership or nonownership of the means of production. Feudal farming arrangements, for example, were the result of a specific set of social relations inasmuch as land was cultivated by nonowners for the owners in return for personal and economic security. Small-scale manufacturers required another set of relations, namely, the individually owned factory and workers subject to the orders of a capitalist employer. The latter social relations had become the basis for the formation of classes—the "exploiting" and the "exploited"—because under the pressure of competition the capitalist was anxious to keep the wages of workers as low as possible and their working hours at maximum length. The resulting antagonism between the capitalist class, the *bourgoisie*, as Marx often calls it, and the workers, the *proletariat*, was to culminate in a revolutionary overthrow of the capitalist system, the abolition of private property, and the establishment of a classless society. The state, which had been the instrument of the capitalist class to keep the workers under its control, would wither away because in the resulting harmony of society the state as an instrument of coercion would not be necessary any longer. However, Marx thought that a transitional period for the state might be needed during which the dictatorship of the proletariat would transfer all instruments of production and capital from the bourgoisie to the state, resulting in the end of all exploitation.

While Marx stressed the revolutionary aspects of the socialist protest movement, others in Britain, France, and Germany placed their faith in the evolutionary element of the Marxist doctrines. These individuals were frequently called "revisionists" because they were accused of revising Marx's original doctrine. Some, such as Ferdinand Lassalle in Germany, demanded universal and direct suffrage to give the workers control of the government to eliminate the oppressive conditions of European life in the nineteenth century and achieve equality and a share of the fruits of the economy. French socialists hoped to reorganize society in the form of worker-run industries. Others again emphasized trade unionism and cooperative enterprises as the means for obtaining socialist objectives. Finally, there was the approach of the Fabian Society in England which, imbued with great idealism, sought to transform Great Britain into a socialist society in a pragmatic step-by-step manner and through democratic constitutional means, combining humane concern for the worker with at times the puritan desire to improve him. The Fabian Society, founded in 1883 and still in existence today, has counted among its member-ship a number of intellectually and politically very prominent Britons, including George Bernard Shaw, Sidney Webb, H. G. Wells, J. Ramsey MacDonald, Harold J. Laski, and G. D. H. Cole. The basic philosophy of the Society was enunciated in 1888 in the Fabian Essays, edited by G. B. Shaw.

In 1952 a book entitled *New Fabian Essays* was published which in eight essays discussed the evolution from the early principles of Fabianism to new concepts needed to meet the problems confronting the contemporary members of society. In particular, these essays advocated a new approach to "post-capitalist economics" analyzing what had happened to Western capitalism in contrast to what Marx said would happen and they redefined the nature of "progress" in a world which was not automatically progressing toward social democracy. These new essays also examined methods of bringing the private sector of industry under democratic control, stressed economic equalization, and emphasized the role which education had to play in the foundation of any socialist society.

The Pendulum Swings Back

Some of the nineteenth-century liberal thinkers in Great Britain, such as John Stuart Mill and Thomas Hill Green, also voiced concern about the ex-cesses of laissez-faire capitalism. Green considered poverty as one of the greatest obstacles to the freedom of the individual, and he held it to be one of the functions of the state to remove those obstacles. His concept of freedom was not the strict nonintervention of the state in the affairs of its citizens, but rather the assistance of the state to permit the citizen to develop fully his potential for individual freedom and responsibility. He laid the groundwork for the concept of Freedom from Fear and Want to which we have referred already in Chapter 4. For this reason he favored considerable intervention and regulation by the state to overcome poverty and ignorance; his arguments laid the intellectual foundations for today's modern social welfare state, and it is interesting to note that these arguments include concern with a clean and wholesome environment, concerns which have again come to the forefront of the political stage at the present time. The next selection contains brief excerpts from Green's *Lectures on the Principles of Political Obligation,* presenting some of his pertinent thoughts.

THE RIGHT OF THE STATE TO PROMOTE MORALITY

THOMAS HILL GREEN

. . . [T]he freedom of contract ought probably to be more restricted in certain directions than is at present the case. The freedom to do as they like on the part of one set of men may involve the ultimate disqualification of many others, or of a succeeding generation, for the exercise of rights. This applies most obviously to such kinds of contract or traffic as affect the health and housing of the people, the growth of population relatively to the means of subsistence, and the accumulation or distribution of landed property. In the hurry of removing those restraints on free dealing between man and man, which have arisen partly perhaps from some confused idea of maintaining morality, but much more from the power of class-interests, we have been apt to take too narrow a view of the range of persons—not one generation merely, but succeeding generations —whose freedom ought to be taken into account, and of the conditions necessary to their freedom ("freedom" here meaning their qualification for the exercise of rights). Hence the massing of population without regard to conditions of health; unrestrained traffic in deleterious commodities; unlimited upgrowth of the class of hired labourers in particular industries which circumstances have suddenly stimulated, without any provision against the danger of an impoverished proletariat in following generations. Meanwhile, under pretence of allowing freedom of bequest and settlement, a system has grown up which prevents the landlords of each generation from being free either in the government of their families or in the disposal of their land, and aggravates the tendency to crowd into towns, as well as the difficulties of providing healthy house-room, by keeping land in a few hands. It would be out of place here to consider in detail the remedies for these evils, or to discuss the question how far it is well to trust to the initiative of the state or of individuals in dealing with them. It is enough to point out the directions in which the state may remove obstacles to the realization of the

Reprinted from Thomas Hill Green, Lectures on the Principles of Political Obligation *in* Works of Thomas Hill Green, *ed. R. L. Nettleship, Vol. II (London: Longmans, Green, and Co., 1900), pp. 515–16.*

capacity for beneficial exercise of rights, without defeating its own object by vitiating the spontaneous character of that capacity.

THE RIGHT OF THE STATE IN REGARD TO PROPERTY

THOMAS HILL GREEN

. . . It is too long a business here to attempt an account of the process by which the organisation of rights in the state has superseded that of the clan, and at the same time the restriction of the powers of appropriation implied in the latter has been removed. It is important to observe, however, that this process has by no means contributed un-mixedly to the end to which, from the moral point of view, it should have contributed. That end is at once the emancipation of the individual from all restrictions upon the free moral life, and his provision with means for it. But the actual result of the development of rights of property in Europe, as part of its general political development, has so far been a state of things in which all indeed *may* have property, but great numbers in fact cannot have it in that sense in which alone it is of value, viz. as a permanent apparatus for carrying out a plan of life, for expressing ideas of what is beautiful, or giving effect to benevolent wishes. In the eye of the law they have rights of appropriation, but in fact they have not the chance of providing means for a free moral life, of developing and giving reality or expression to a good will, an interest in social well-being. A man who possesses nothing but his powers of labour and who has to sell these to a capitalist for bare daily mainte-nance, might as well, in respect of the ethical purposes which the posses-sion of property should serve, be denied rights of property altogether. Is the existence of so many men in this position, and the apparent liability of many more to be brought to it by a general fall of wages, if increase of population goes along with decrease in the productiveness of the earth, a necessary result of the emancipation of the individual and the free play given to powers of appropriation? or is it an evil incident, which may yet be remedied, of that historical process by which the de-velopment of the rights of property has been brought about, but in which

Reprinted from Green, Lectures on the Principles of Political Obligation, *pp. 525-34.*

the agents have for the most part had no moral objects in view at all?

Let us first be clear about the points in which the conditions of property, as it actually exists, are at variance with property according to its idea or as it should be. The rationale of property, as we have seen, is that everyone should be secured by society in the power of getting and keeping the means of realising a will, which in possibility is a will directed to social good. Whether any one's will is actualy and positively so directed, does not affect his claim to the power. This power should be secured to the individual irrespectively of the use which he actually makes of it, so long as he does not use it in a way that interferes with the exercise of like power by another, on the ground that its uncontrolled exercise is the condition of attainment by man of that free morality which is his highest good. . . . The rationale of property, in short, requires that everyone who will conform to the positive condition of possessing it, viz. labour, and the negative condition, viz. respect for it as possessed by others, should, so far as social arrangements can make him so, be a possessor of property himself, and of such property as will at least enable him to develop a sense of responsibility, as distinct from mere property in the immediate necessaries of life.

. . . It is difficult to summarise the influences to which is due the fact that in all the chief seats of population in Europe the labour market is constantly thronged with men who are too badly reared and fed to be efficient labourers; who for this reason, and from the competition for employment with each other, have to sell their labour very cheap; who have thus seldom the means to save, and whose standard of living and social expectation is so low that, if they have the opportunity of saving, they do not use it, and keep bringing children into the world at a rate which perpetuates the evil. It is certain, however, that these influences have no necessary connection with the maintenance of the right of the individual property and consequent unlimited accumulation of capital, though they no doubt are connected with that regime of force and conquest by which existing governments have been established—governments which do not indeed create the rights of individual property, any more than other rights, but which serve to maintain them. It must always be borne in mind that the appropriation of land by individuals has in most countries—probably in all where it approaches completeness —has been originally effected, not by the expenditure of labour or the results of labour on the land, but by force. The original landlords have been conquerors.

This has affected the condition of the industrial classes in at least two ways: (1) When the application of accumulated capital to any work in the way of mining or manufacture has created a demand for labour, the supply has been forthcoming from men whose ancestors, if not themselves, were trained in habits of serfdom; men whose life has been one of virtually forced labour, relieved by church-charities or the poor law (which in part took the place of these charities); who were thus in no condition to contract freely for the sale of their labour, and had nothing of that sense of family-responsibility which might have made them insist on having the chance of saving. Landless countrymen, whose ancestors were serfs, are the parents of the proletariat of great towns. (2) Rights have been allowed to landlords, incompatible with the true principle on which rights of property rest, and tending to interfere with the development of the proprietorial capacity in others. The right to freedom in unlimited acquisition of wealth, by means of labour and by means of the saving and successful application of the results of labour, does not imply the right of anyone to do as he likes with those gifts of nature, without which there would be nothing to spend labour upon. The earth is just as much an original natural material necessary to productive industry, as are air, light, and water, but while the latter from the nature of the case cannot be appropriated the earth can be and has been. The only justification for this appropriation, as for any other, is that it contributes on the whole to social well-being; that the earth as appropriated by individuals under certain conditions becomes more serviceable to society as a whole, including those who are not proprietors of the soil, than if it were held in common. The justification disappears if these conditions are not observed; and from government having been chiefly in the hands of appropriators of the soil, they have not been duly observed. Landlords have been allowed to "do what they would with their own," as if land were merely like so much capital, admitting of indefinite extension. The capital gained by one is not taken from another, but one man cannot acquire more land without others having less; and though a growing reduction in the number of landlords is not necessarily a social evil, if it is compensated by the acquisition of other wealth on the part of those extruded from the soil, it is only not an evil if the landlord is prevented from so using his land as to make it unserviceable to the wants of men (e.g. by turning fertile land into a forest), and from taking liberties with it incompatible with the conditions of general freedom and health; e.g. by clearing out a village and leaving the people to pick up houseroom as they can elsewhere (a practice common under the old poor-law, when the distinction between closed and open villages grew up), or, on the other hand, by building houses in unhealthy places or of unhealthy structure, by stopping up means of communication, or forbidding the erection of dissenting chapels. In fact the restraints which the public interest requires to be placed on the use of land if individual property in it is to be allowed at all, have been pretty much ignored, while on the other hand, that full development of its resources, which individual ownership would naturally favour, has been interfered with by laws or customs which, in securing estates to certain families, have taken away the interest, and tied the hands, of the nominal owner—the tenant for life—in making the most of his property.

Thus the whole history of the ownership of land in Europe has been of a kind to lead to the agglomeration of a proletariat, neither holding nor seeking property, wherever a sudden demand has arisen for labour in mines or manufactures. This at any rate was the case down to the epoch of the French Revolution; and this, which brought to other countries deliverance from feudalism left England, where feudalism had previously passed into unrestrained landlordism, almost untouched. And while those influences of feudalism and landlordism which tend to throw a shiftless population upon the centres of industry have been left unchecked, nothing till quite lately was done to give such a population a chance of bettering itself, when it had been brought together. Their health, housing, and schooling were unprovided for. They were left to be freely victimised by deleterious employments, foul air, and consequent craving for deleterious drinks. When we consider all this, we shall see the unfairness of laying on capitalism or the free development of individual wealth the blame which is really due to the arbitrary and violent manner in which rights over land have been acquired and exercised, and to the failure of the state to fulfill those functions which under a system of unlimited private ownership are necessary to maintain the conditions of a free life. . . .

A new wave of monopolies that emerged in America as the result of unrestrained economic power and threatened to dominate the business world also gave rise to demands by the people for governmental action. Clearly, the operation of the free market based on the forces of supply and demand was impaired by the overwhelming power of monopolies which sought to control the market and regulate the distribution of goods and services by shutting out free competition. Heeding the popular demands, Congress passed antitrust laws and set up commissions to regulate railroads and public utilities. Widespread repugnance for the frequently very poor conditions under which workers had to labor prompted other legislation designed to protect the health and safety of the workers, prevent the abuse of child labor, and regulate wages and hours for certain categories of workers.

Another factor arousing concern about the operation of laissez-faire capitalism was the tendency of the economic system to move in cycles between booms and depressions. Although this movement was viewed at first as self-correction of a free and growing economy, an increasing number of economists began to change their interpretation of this aspect of the economy during the early 1930s, the years of the Great Depression. It was John Maynard Keynes, an eminent British economist, who pointed out that the balancing and regulating mechanisms of a free market could in fact achieve equilibrium at so low a level that a large part of the labor force would be unemployed permanently. For this reason, the self-regulating market could halt an economic boom and turn the economy down into stagnation. Keynes suggested that the government step in and adjust or counteract the market regulators according to certain principles which would keep the economy at a high level of employment.

Although many economists disputed Keynes' contentions—and a few still do so—most of the modern countries of the world have now accepted many of the measures Keynes proposed. In the United States, the Keynesian notions are reflected to some degree in the public works programs of the 1930s, the social security programs including unemployment compensation, the minimum wage and maximum hour laws, the collective bargaining legislation, and the banking reserve requirements. The Council of Economic Advisors, a small group of prominent economists operating on the Presidential level, may also be seen as implementing the Keynesian conceptual framework. The Council makes frequent analyses of the American economy, and on the basis of these analyses the federal government—by far the largest buyer, employer, borrower, and investor on the American scene—adjusts its economic activities to counter and correct the swings of the economy. Changes in taxation and interest rates also fall within the context of these activities.

The theories of John Maynard Keynes are difficult for the average layman to grasp. However, John K. Galbraith, in his book *American Capitalism*, explains the main features of Keynes' theories and their influence on American economic thinking in a lucid manner; for this reason, excerpts from his book have been selected as the eighth reading of this chapter.

AMERICAN CAPITALISM

JOHN KENNETH GALBRAITH

. . . The competitive model of a capitalist economy allowed . . . for rhythmic increases and decreases in prices and production and even for occasional bouts of unemployment. It did not contemplate the possibility of a catastrophic and enduring depression. Economists, and through them politicians, businessmen and the public, were insulated from the need to think of such a tragedy by the benign theorem that the act of production provided the purchasing power for all that was produced at approximate full employment.

In 1930 a *really* serious depression was not part of the experience of the current generation of Americans. In late 1920 and early 1921 there was a sharp fall in prices and incomes, and, in somewhat lesser degree, in employment. But the recovery was prompt. Moreover, the whole episode was inextricably associated with the war and its aftermath and could be blamed on what economists are pleased to call exogenous forces. Except by farmers, who continued to feel themselves at a disadvantage, it was almost universally dismissed as the inevitable reaction to the wartime inflation in prices and profits. For an earlier slump of comparable importance it was necessary to go back to the preceding century.

One can only suppose that in 1929 the fates undertook, after great deliberation, to shake the confidence of the people of the United States in their economy. Nothing could have been more ingeniously or more elaborately designed to achieve this result. There was the shock effect— the sudden dramatic collapse in stock-market values with which the lives and fortunes of thousands of innocents, who only then became aware of their innocence, had become entwined. This was followed by the inexorable decline in output, values and employment which, in a little more than two years, cut the value of national production almost in half

Reprinted from John Kenneth Galbraith, American Capitalism *(Boston: Houghton Mifflin Company, 1956, and London: Hamish Hamilton Ltd.), pp. 63–83. Copyright © 1952 by John Kenneth Galbraith. Reprinted by permission of Houghton Mifflin Company and Hamish Hamilton Ltd.*

and left twelve million workers—ten and a half million more than in 1929—without jobs and mostly without reliable means of support. Those who still had jobs lived in the penetrating fear that their turn would be next. Meanwhile hundreds of thousands of well-to-do citizens either made a sudden and irretrievable descent into poverty or dwelt in the cold fear that they soon would. It would have added to the security of the country if businessmen and bankers had escaped the debacle. But their well-publicized plight suggested, all too plainly, that they too had no formula for contending with capitalism when the latter was on shipwreck tack. The broken banker was as commonplace a figure in the news as the unemployed worker, and a much less reassuring one. The economy was the impartial destroyer of all.

When there was nothing else to hope for, it could still be hoped that the depression would be temporary. A rhythm of good times and bad was the minimum promise of the competitive model. To this shaky standard the defenders of the system repaired in droves. Then, the most malicious act of all, the depression was made to last ten years. The very notion that depressions in the United States were self-correcting—that there were corners that would be turned—became a national jest. As if to sharpen the point, a modest recovery prior to the summer of 1937, which however had left between seven and eight million still unemployed, was followed by a slump in production that was even sharper than the one following 1929. The Great Depression of the thirties never came to an end. It merely disappeared in the great mobilization of the forties. For a whole generation it became the normal aspect of peacetime life in the United States—the thing to be both feared and expected. . . .

The depression not only contributed deeply to the insecurity with which Americans viewed their economy. It also had an important bearing on economic behavior. In the years following World War II the fear of a recurrence of depression was without question a dominant factor in the calculations of a large proportion of all businessmen. The convention, so scrupulously observed by the business community, which bans the public expression of fear of economic collapse lest to express fear be to invite the fact, concealed much of this alarm. Nonetheless, when *Fortune* magazine in 1946 asked some 15,000 leading business executives in confidence whether they expected an "extended major depression with large-scale unemployment in the next ten years—a phrasing that was not designed to minimize the scope of the contemplated disaster—fifty-eight per cent of those replying said they did. Of the remainder only twenty-eight per cent said they did not. In these same years labor was preoccupied with measures to maintain the level of employment and farmers with support prices that would provide shelter in a slump. Even the radicals had long ceased to talk about the inequality or exploitation under capitalism or its "inherent contradictions." They stressed only the utter unreliability of its performance.

These attitudes have since changed. With prosperity and the passage of time the fear of depression has been somewhat dulled. In 1949 and again in 1954 there were minor setbacks, which were first viewed as the beginning of a new disaster but from which there was a prompt recovery. These provided more reassurance. The convention which requires businessmen and politicians who are in office to say that all will always be well—that at any time prosperity is assured—has brought a rich yield of optimism. This too has had an effect. . . .

. . . The Great Depression might, conceivably, have remained the great accident if ideas had not . . . intervened. These, in their mature form, made depression, or its counterpart inflation, the normal behavior pattern of uninhibited and unmanaged capitalism. While this discouraging analysis carried with it a remedy—a remedy that was received with profound enthusiasm by many economists and much of the public at large—the remedy was unorthodox and disturbing. It is only partial comfort for a patient, who is being told he is chronically ill, to learn that there are violent and painful cures for his disease.

The ideas which interpreted the depression, and which warned that depression or inflation might be as much a part of the free-enterprise destiny as stable full employment, were those of John Maynard Keynes. A case could easily be made by those who make such cases, that his were the most influential social ideas of the first half of the century. A proper distribution of emphasis as between the role of ideas and the role of action might attribute more influence on modern economic history to Keynes than to Roosevelt. Certainly his final book, *The General Theory of Employment, Interest and Money*, shaped the course of events as only the books of three earlier economists—Smith's *Wealth of Nations,* Ricardo's *Principles of Political Economy* and Marx's *Capital*—have done. . . .

Keynes' *General Theory* could not normally be read, even by the intelligent layman, unless he was schooled in the language and, even more, in the abstractions of economics. As a result its influence on practical affairs was almost entirely by proxy. It was not from Keynes but from his interpreters at first, second or third remove that most men learned of his ideas. The interpreters were almost exclusively other economists. Keynes was also beyond the reach of those who do brokerage in fashionable thoughts and, in fact, his ideas gained their ascendancy without creating appreciable stir among intellectuals at large. In any case, millions came to accept Keynes' conclusions who had never read a word he had written. More interesting, thousands came to be advocates of his proposals who, if asked, would have indignantly denied they were Keynesians. While everyone knows that Keynes was important and influential, there has always been a remarkable uncertainty as to just how or why.

The major conclusion of Keynes' argument—the one of greatest general importance and the one that is relevant here—is that depression and unemployment are in no sense abnormal. (Neither, although the point is made less explicitly, is inflation.) On the contrary, the economy can find its equilibrium at any level of performance. The chance that production in the United States will be at that level where all, or nearly all, willing workers can find jobs is no greater than the chance that four, six, eight or ten million workers will be unemployed. Alternatively the demand for goods may exceed what the economy can supply even when everyone is employed. Accordingly there can be, even under peacetime conditions, a persistent upward pressure on prices, i.e., more or less serious inflation. . . .

For purpose of displaying the essentials of the Keynesian argument it is convenient to assume an increase in saving and to see what happens —or rather what does not happen. The important consequence is that investment does not necessarily increase in order to absorb the saving; instead total production and employment may be reduced sufficiently to bring reduced saving into line with investment. In practice, economists have almost uniformly stressed fluctuations in investment rather than changes in saving as the important factor affecting total production. What people will endeavor to save from any given volume of income is commonly supposed to be less subject to change than what business concerns may seek to invest. It has become customary, therefore, to think of changes in investment as the principal cause of changes in total production and employment. Insufficient investment has become the shorthand Keynesian explanation of low production and high unemployment. The obvious remedy is more investment and, in principle, it is not important whether this be from private or public funds. But the expenditure of public funds is subject to central determination by government, as that of private funds is not, so the Keynesian remedy leads directly to public expenditure as a depression remedy.

It is apparent that public spending is only one of the remedies implicit in the Keynesian system. Abatement of taxes in order to leave private individuals more money to spend and measures to stimulate private investment or discourage saving would have a similar effect. However, it is always for his prodigality that a man is known—Henry VIII for his wives, Louis XV for his mistresses and General Douglas MacArthur for his prose. The Keynesian has become forever associated with public spending. . . .

The time has now come to consider the political consequences of Keynes for, more than any man of the century, he reformulated attitudes on the agitated question of the relation of the state to the economy.

The United States, in the thirties, was urgently in need of a new theory of the relation of government to economic life. The American political parties had long been in the habit of assuming full responsibility for economic well-being and of campaigning with promises of prosperity for all. The inconsistency of these promises, which Republicans and Democrats had made with equal fervor, with the role assigned to the state by the competitive model was untroublesome so long as there was reasonable prosperity in any event. It was bound to be troublesome to a party which was forced to contend with a serious depression. The New Deal came to power on the usual promises and with little clearer view than predecessor administrations of how the government might intervene to bring prosperity.

It was inevitable that the attention of liberals in a liberal administration would be directed toward the structure of the economy. The preconceptions of the competitive model guided their thinking in this direction. Implicit in the rise of big business was the possibility that it had created a structure that departed so far from the competitive model that it could not work. Two courses of action were open. The incentives which, under the competitive model, were presumed to guide businessmen to a socially desirable behavior could be replaced by some kind of central guidance which would get the desired results. Perhaps businessmen could be brought together under the aegis of government and be told, or made to agree, to increase employment and stabilize wages and prices. Or, alternatively, perhaps private incentives could be rehabilitated by remaking business enterprise so that it conformed more closely to the preconceptions of the model.

Both enterprises involved the most serious difficulties. The first, which was given a trial run in the NRA [National Recovery Act], suffered from a grievous unclarity of both methods and goals. The self-interest of the businessman dictated the particular low level of employment he was offering and investment he was making in 1933. This simple fact was not altered by bringing him together with other businessmen under the supervision of a Code Authority. It seems improbable that much would have been accomplished had he been ordered directly by government to increase employment and investment outlays at his own cost and contrary to his own assessment of interest.

To remake the economy in accordance with the requirements of the competitive model was obviously a time-consuming enterprise. To take time out to break up large corporate units and re-establish the competition of the model was hardly in keeping with the temper of a country which found depression tiresome and which was not noted for its patience. To the extent that it was contemplated in the later years of the New Deal it was as a decidedly long-run reform. There remained in 1933 only the possibility of abandoning capitalism entirely. This was a project which raised the question of alternatives concerning which only a handful of Communists were in any way clear. It is hardly surprising that the early days of the New Deal were distinguished in American history for their foggy semanticism—for meaningless or incomprehensible talk about social planning, guided capitalism and industrial self-government. When stumped by a problem the American liberal rarely admits defeat. He takes the offensive with words.

It was Keynes who provided the escape from the dilemma—and the words. It would be hard, at first glance, to imagine a formula that was better designed for the American scene. The depression was overwhelmingly the important problem. The notion of an excess of savings or a deficiency of investment defined the nature of the government intervention. By public borrowing or expenditure, or the appropriate changes in taxation, the government could make up for the deficiency in private spending. By so doing it could return the economy to full employment and keep it there. To the naked eye, the scope of private business decision remained as before. General Motors still decided what cars to produce, what prices to charge, how to advertise and sell them, when to build a new assembly plant and how many workers to employ. It merely sold more cars because employees on public works projects became customers for secondhand Chevrolets, their foremen for new ones and the contractor for a Buick. . . .

Liberals almost spontaneously adopted the Keynesian formula. They were also puzzled by the reluctance of conservatives, especially businessmen, to embrace it. Here was protection from the overwhelming threat of depression, the only threat of potentially revolutionary proportions seemingly faced by capitalism. The businessman remained undisturbed in his prerogatives as an owner and manager and had the promise of better business to boot. What could he lose?

With time there has been some explicit and a great deal of implicit acceptance of the Keynesian formula by American businessmen. However, as often happens, it encountered the sharp cleavage which exists in our attitude toward technological and social change. If a man seeks to design a better mousetrap he is the soul of enterprise; if he seeks to design a better society he is a crackpot. For those who mistrust social change it was not an argument that profits might be increased, even that disaster might be avoided. They were opposed to change and they could not be bought. They were men of principle.

There were also more positive grounds for business opposition to

Keynes than liberals have been inclined to suppose. The Keynesian system, though it perhaps involved a less than revolutionary change in the relation of the government to the economy, implied, nonetheless, an important one. For a doctrine that excluded government it substituted one that made government indispensable. Keynes was sufficiently unpalatable when he made depression and inflation not adventitious or war-induced misfortunes but normal occurrences. He went on to make government the indispensable partner of business. In failing to recognize the prestige that goes with power and decision-making in American life, American liberals failed to recognize that, for some businessmen, the Keynesian remedy was at least as damaging as the depression it presumed to eliminate. Even though the businessman might profit in a narrow pecuniary sense from the new role of government there was no chance that his prestige would survive intact. Where, in economic life, people had previously looked upon business decisions as the ones that had shaped their destiny, now they would have regard for government decisions as well, or instead. Those of an Assistant Secretary of the Treasury on interest rates were now of more importance than those of any banker. Those of a regional administrator of public works on investment attained a significance greater than those of a corporation president. To share the prestige of decision-making is to lose prestige. The Keynesian remedies thus represented an assault on a valued possession. Those who were losers could hardly be expected to embrace the ideas that brought this loss. Much of their dissatisfaction was expressed in personal terms— it was directed against the Administration and against the public servants who implemented the new ideas. But a good deal was directed at Keynes. His American followers, taking at face value our conventional disavowal of any interest in power, failed to understand the discontent over its impairment.

The Keynesian system also, though unobtrusively, opened the way for a large expansion of government services and activities. This was the result of a new and very important concept of social waste which followed in its train. If the normal tendency of the economy is toward full employment, then the use of labor and other economic resources by government is at the expense of their use by the private economy. Dams and post offices are built at the cost of private consumption or investment. If there is full employment in the first place, something must be given up. But if unemployment is chronic, the dams and post offices require no sacrifice of private production or consumption. The labor, plants and materials that are used would otherwise have been unemployed. They are wasted if someone does not employ them. Again ideas had produced a topsy-turvy world. Government spending, long the mark of profligacy, was now sanctioned in the sacred name of avoiding waste.

It was inevitable also that wild men would draw from this paradox, and the substantial truths on which it is built, a sanction for any and all expenditures at any and all times. Here was further discomfort for the conservative.

The Keynesian ideas had other new, heterodox and even threatening corollaries. Thrift, an ancient and once an absolute virtue, was brought into question; it suffered from the guilt of association with redundant saving and depression. A doctrine which cast doubt on so conventional a good was bound to be suspect. We commonly bring a deep theological conviction to the defense of our chosen principles. Those who dissent are not wrong, they are evil. Nothing could better prove that a man was secretly in the service of the devil or communism than that he should raise his voice against thrift. . . .

The disagreements arising out of Keynes' proposals should not be magnified. He was not a divisive figure; on the contrary his work was solidly in the Anglo-American tradition of compromise which seeks progress by reconciling the maximum number of conflicts of interest. But it is also easy to see how his formula, and the speed with which it was accepted, provided its own ground for uneasiness. . . .

The Keynesian concepts have continued to exert their influence on the formulation of American governmental policies and even such basically conservative statesmen as Richard Nixon have accepted some of Keynes' prescriptions. Governmental intervention in the economy has been increasingly exercised during this century in the United States, and similar trends have been noticed in western European countries as well. Considering that in addition to the American laws mentioned earlier, the United States has enacted price subsidies and acreage control in agriculture, federal deposit and mortgage insurance, old-age pensions and Medicare, peacetime prices and wage controls, and other programs of an economic nature, it is clear that the pendulum has indeed swung back from the period when nonintervention of the state in the economic order was the key principle of industrial society.

These programs and others designed to alleviate poverty have frequently evoked an apprehension in the United States that the country is moving toward the welfare state, which would be the first step in socialism. The term "welfare state" is ambiguous. While some take it to suggest economic security from the cradle to the grave, others give it a less extensive meaning. In the opinion of the latter, it implies state functions to raise the standard of living, work toward full employment, and assure minimum sustenance, shelter, and health. Certainly this interpretation is compatible with capitalism, perhaps even a necessary corollary to a healthy capitalistic system whose basic objectives include an economy of ever increasing abundance and equality of opportunity. On the other hand, this interpretation of the welfare state does not necessarily imply an enhancement of socialism, whose major objectives are social control of economic power and substantial social equality.*

Government-Dominated Economic Systems

So far we have directed our attention mainly toward the degree of governmental intervention in the economy exercised in capitalistic systems. Now we will examine briefly some of the economic systems which are completely dominated by the state or in which the state has a controlling influence.

The concept of the corporate state was the underlying economic philosophy for Benito Mussolini's Fascist Italy and to a lesser degree also for Adolf Hitler's Nazi Germany. The corporate state was perceived as being composed of associations representing every form of economic activity such as industry, commerce, agriculture, and others. These associations had their own pyramidal structure ranging from local through regional to central organizations on the national level. At the top, the central organizations were joined into one large body, which was dominated by the state and the ruling party. This body and its subordinate associations served as devices for full governmental control of every aspect of the national economy, as was brought out in the chapter on dictatorship.

According to the doctrine of Fascism (derived from the Italian word *fascio*, literally a bundle, also meaning political groups) † the economy was not the only concern of the state. Rather, the state was viewed as a living organism which held a pivotal position in every social activity and was endowed with the utmost authority. The brief excerpt from Mussolini's writings— our next selection—enlarges on this concept and highlights the state's function in the economy. Much of what Mussolini has to say in this selection was also accepted by the ideological advocates of Nazi Germany.

---

* See N. S. Preston, *Politics, Economics, and Power* (New York: Macmillan Co., 1967), pp. 43, 100.

† The term "Fascism" can also be related to the Latin word "fasces," meaning a bundle of sticks tied around an axe, which was the symbol of authority in ancient Rome.

THE POLITICAL AND SOCIAL DOCTRINE OF FASCISM

BENITO MUSSOLINI

The foundation of Fascism is the conception of the State, its character, its duty, and its aim. Fascism conceives of the State as an absolute, in comparison with which all individuals or groups are relative, only to be conceived of in their relation to the State. The conception of the Liberal State is not that of a directing force, guiding the play and development, both material and spiritual, of a collective body, but merely a force limited to the function of recording results: on the other hand, the Fascist State is itself conscious, and has itself a will and a personality—thus it may be called the "ethic" State. In 1929, at the first five-yearly assembly of the Fascist régime, I said:

> For us Fascists, the State is not merely a guardian, preoccupied solely with the duty of assuring the personal safety of the citizens; nor is it an organization with purely material aims, such as to guarantee a certain level of well-being and peaceful conditions of life; for a mere council of administration would be sufficient to realize such objects. Nor is it a purely political creation, divorced from all contact with the complex material reality which makes up the life of the individual and the life of the people as a whole. The State, as conceived of and as created by Fascism, is a spiritual and moral fact in itself, since its political, juridical, and economic organization of the nation is a concrete thing: and such an organization must be in its origins and development a manifestation of the spirit. The State is the guarantor of security both internal and external, but it is also the custodian and transmitter of the spirit of the people, as it has grown up through the centuries in language, in customs, and in faith. And the State is not only a living reality of the present, it is also linked with the past and above all with the future, and thus transcending the brief limits of individual life, it represents the immanent spirit of the nation. The forms in which States express themselves may change, but the necessity for such forms is eternal. It is the State which educates its citizens in civic virtue, gives them a consciousness of their mission and welds them into unity; harmonizing their various interests through justice, and trans-

Reprinted from Benito Mussolini, "The Political and Social Doctrine of Fascism," International Conciliation (January, 1935), No. 306, pp. 13–15, by permission of the Carnegie Endowment for International Peace.

mitting to future generations the mental conquests of science, of art, of law and the solidarity of humanity. It leads men from primitive tribal life to that highest expression of human power which is Empire: it links up through the centuries the names of those of its members who have died for its existence and in obedience to its laws, it holds up the memory of the leaders who have increased its territory and the geniuses who have illumined it with glory as an example to be followed by future generations. When the conception of the State declines, and disunifying and centrifugal tendencies prevail, whether of individuals or of particular groups, the nations where such phenomena appear are in their decline.

From 1929 until today, evolution, both political and economic has everywhere gone to prove the validity of these doctrinal premises. Of such gigantic importance is the State. It is the force which alone can provide a solution to the dramatic contradictions of capitalism, and that state of affairs which we call the crisis can only be dealt with by the State, as between other States. Where is the shade of Jules Simon, who in the dawn of Liberalism proclaimed that, "The State must labor to make itself unnecessary, and prepare the way for its own dismissal"? Or of McCulloch, who, in the second half of the last century, affirmed that the State must guard against the danger of governing too much? What would the Englishman, Bentham say today to the continual and in-evitably-invoked intervention of the State in the sphere of economics, while according to his theories industry should ask no more of the State than to be left in peace? Or the German, Humboldt, according to whom the "lazy" State should be considered the best? It is true that the second wave of Liberal economists were less extreme than the first, and Adam Smith himself opened the door—if only very cautiously—which leads to State intervention in the economic field: but whoever says Liberalism implies individualism, and whoever says Fascism implies the State. Yet the Fascist State is unique, and an original creation. It is not reactionary, but revolutionary, in that it anticipates the solution of the universal political problems which elsewhere have to be settled in the political field by the rivalry of parties, the excessive power of the parliamentary régime and the irresponsibility of political assemblies; while it meets the prob-lems of the economic field by a system of syndicalism which is con-tinually increasing in importance, as much in the sphere of labor as of industry: and in the moral field enforces order, discipline, and obedience to that which is the determined moral code of the country. Fascism desires the State to be a strong and organic body, at the same time reposing upon broad and popular support. The Fascist State has drawn into itself even the economic activities of the nation, and, through the corporative social and educational institutions created by it, its influence reaches every aspect of the national life and includes, framed in their respective organizations, all the political, economic and spiritual forces of the nation. A State which reposes upon the support of millions of individuals who recognize its authority, are continually conscious of its power and are ready at once to serve it, is not the old tyrannical State of the medieval lord nor has it anything in common with absolute governments either before or after 1789. The individual in the Fascist State is not annulled but rather multiplied, just in the same way that a soldier in a regiment is not diminished but rather increased by the number of his comrades. The Fascist State organizes the nation, but leaves a sufficient margin of liberty to the individual; the latter is deprived of all useless and possibly harmful freedom, but retains what is essential; the deciding power in this question cannot be the individual, but the State alone.

Although the era of Fascism ended in Italy and Germany in 1945, modifications of its economic doctrine have found their way into other countries. In Argentina the regime of Juan Perón from 1946 to 1955 borrowed several of Fascism's authoritarian features to control the economy to some degree. In Spain and Portugal, the extreme rightist governments of Franco and Salazar often employed economic policies which in both form and substance are reminiscent of the Fascist practices, and in both countries many of these policies continue.

While Fascism produced a very high degree of control of the economic order by the government, the domination of the state over the economy is considerably more comprehensive in communist countries. This can be seen from the operating principles of the communist system: state ownership of all means of industrial production and distribution, state or collective ownership of agricultural productive resources, total government planning and control of the economic order, and a system of rewards (and punishments) to maximize productive effort.* A prominent feature of the communist economic system until the latter part of the 1950s was the central decision-making with respect to planning and executive functions. However, a measure of decentralization has been introduced since then in order to improve the efficiency of industrial production and the quality of the goods produced, especially those for the consumer. As a consequence, plant managers in the Soviet Union and other East European communist state now have some freedom of decision, but the amount of discretion allowed is still very small when measured against the standards of the capitalist systems. Moreover, the communist plant manager remains subject to checks of the efficiency and effectiveness of his plant by a full apparatus of government and party agencies.

---

* See Preston, *Politics, Economics, and Power,* p. 162.

The incentive system in the Soviet Union is tied to the achievement of planned output targets for managers and to increased productivity for workers. Since concentration upon output goals by managers has often led to the ignoring of cost factors, and since the quality of produced goods has frequently suffered, the incentive system for plant managers was reorganized in 1965. Targets were set not merely in terms of output that managers actually produce but in terms of their ability to sell the produced goods at a "profit" for the enterprise. In addition interest charges were introduced on investment capital used by individual plants. The man largely responsible for these changes was a Russian economist by the name of Yevsei Liberman, and so the new methods used have been labeled "Libermanism" by Western students of the Soviet system. A discussion of his system by Liberman himself is found in our next selection.

THE RUSSIAN REVOLUTION—FIFTY YEARS AFTER/
The Soviet Economic Reform

YEVSEI LIBERMAN

. . .

The Role of Profit in the Soviet Union

The question of profit has been widely discussed in recent times in the U.S.S.R.—not because profit was previously unknown there or was being introduced for the first time, but because prior to the reform profit was not employed as the chief criterion or overall indicator of the effectiveness of an enterprise. Profit was only one of many required indicators which were set as goals. Those indicators established as targets for the enterprise included gross volume of output, an excessively detailed list of the items to be produced, cost reduction, number of employees, output per employee, average wage, etc. The number of obligatory targets fettered initiative. Often the enterprises concerned themselves primarily with increasing gross volume of output, since their performance was

Excerpted by permission from Foreign Affairs, October 1967. Copyright 1967 by Council on Foreign Relations, Inc.

judged above all by that and not by the amount of output sold, as is now the case. In addition, enterprises gave little heed to the utilization of production assets. Trying to find the easiest way to meet the assigned volume of output, they asked and received from the state, free of charge, a great deal of equipment and new structures which they did not always use rationally and fully.

Much of this is explained by the fact that for a long time the Soviet Union was the world's only socialist country. It was faced with the task of creating industry as fast as possible and providing for the country's defense. No thought was given at that time to the quality or attractiveness of goods, not even to production cost or profit. This was entirely justified, for the Soviet Union not only withstood the war of 1941–1945 but played a decisive role in ridding the world of fascism. This was worth any price. It was our "profit" and, if you please, the "profit" of the whole civilized world.

But, as Lenin said more than once, our virtues, if carried too far, can turn into faults. This is what happened in our country when the practices of management by administrative fiat were continued into the period after our country had entered the state of peaceful economic competition with the developed countries of the West.

Success in this competition cannot be gained by the old methods of administrative and excessively centralized management. It was necessary to change so as to give the enterprises themselves a material stake in the better utilization of their assets and in providing the best possible service to their consumers. To do this the enterprises obviously had to be relieved of the excessive number of planned targets and their work had to be judged, first, by how they fulfilled the contracts for deliveries of commodities and, if they did this, secondly by their profit level.

Profit sums up all the aspects of an enterprise's work, including quality of output, since the price for better goods is correspondingly higher than for outmoded or relatively inefficient items. But it is important to note that profit is neither the only nor the chief goal of production. We are interested above all in output of specific commodities to satisfy consumer and producer needs. Profit is used as the chief index of, and incentive to, efficiency of production, as a mechanism for appraising and stimulating the work of an enterprise and also as a source of accumulation and investment.

By means of bonuses drawn from profits we wish to encourage enterprises to draw up their own plans which would be good—that is, advantageous—alike for society and themselves; and not only to draw up such plans, but to carry them out, something which should be encouraged at the expense of the profits. It is not a question of weakening or discarding planning, but, on the contrary, of reinforcing and improving it by drawing the enterprises themselves into the planning process, for they always know better than anyone their own real potentialities and should study and know the needs of their clients. . . .

What is the difference between "capitalist" and "socialist" profit, in my opinion? The difference will be best understood if we consider: (1) how the profit is formed; (2) what it indicates; and (3) how it is spent.

From the viewpoint of private enterprise, all profit belongs to the capitalists alone. To justify this, there was long ago devised a theory that three factors—capital, land and labor—create value. Joseph A. Schumpeter, in his "Theory of Economic Development," wrote that profit is the excess over production cost. But this "cost" includes "payment" for the entre-preneur's labor, land rent and interest on capital, as well as a premium for "risk." Over and above this, profit should reward the entrepreneur if, by a fresh combination of production elements, he reduces the pro-duction cost below the prevailing average level of expenditures.

The nature of this "combination of elements" can be perceived from the fact that in the private enterprise system most profit is now derived from redistribution of income in the market in the process of exchange. It is common knowledge, for instance, that big profits are most easily obtained by the advantageous purchase of raw materials, by a monopoly-controlled raising of retail prices, by unequal exchanges with underdeveloped countries, by the export of capital to countries with low wage levels, by a system of preferential duties and tariffs, by the increase in stock-market prices through capitalization above profit, and, finally, by military orders.

In our country all these sources of profit are precluded by the very nature of socialism, under which there is neither private ownership of the means of production nor holding of stock (and hence no stock market). The level at which labor is paid depends on the productivity of the labor and is regulated by law. Prices of raw materials and supplies are planned; the market cannot be taken advantage of in purchasing raw materials or hiring labor. Nor is it possible to take advantage of market conditions to raise the prices of finished goods. Exchange with other countries is conducted on a basis of equality and by long-term agreements.

In the Soviet Union, by virtue of the very nature of the mode of production and distribution, profit indicates only the level of production efficiency. Profit is the difference between production cost and the factory sale price. But since in our country the price represents, in principle, the norms of expenditure of socially necessary labor, any increase in profit is an index of relative economy in production. Higher profits in the Soviet Union are based solely on economized hours of working time, economized tons of raw materials and supplies and fuel, and economized kilowatt hours of electricity. We do not justify profits obtained from chance circumstances, such as excessively high prices, and do not regard such profits as being to the credit of the enterprise. Rather do we consider such profit the consequence of insufficiently flexible price setting. All profits of this kind go into the state budget; from such profits no bonuses are granted to the enterprises.

Now let us see what is done with profit in the U.S.S.R., that is, what it is spent on. First of all, no private individual and no enterprise as a group of private individuals may acquire profit. Profit may not be invested arbitrarily by any persons or groups for the purpose of deriving personal income.

Profit in our country belongs to those who own the means of production; that is to say, to society, to all the working people as a whole. All profit in our country goes first of all into the planned expansion or improvement of social production, and next into providing free social services to the public, such as education and science, public health services, pensions and stipends. A part is spent on the administrative apparatus and, unfortunately, quite a large part on defense requirements. We would be happy to dispense with the latter expenditures if a program of universal disarmament were adopted.

Profit used to be given insufficient importance in our country because of a certain disregard of the law of value. Some Soviet economists incorrectly interpreted this economic law as an unpleasant leftover of capitalism; they held that the sooner we got rid of it the better. Disregard of the requirements of the law of value led to the establishment of arbitrarily planned prices—prices which, moreover, remained in force for overly long periods. Prices thus became divorced from the real value of goods; profit varied greatly from enterprise to enterprise and even from article to article within the same general group of goods. In these circumstances profit did not reflect the actual achievements of the producers. Because of this, many economists and managers began to regard profit as something totally independent of the enterprise and therefore an unreliable barometer of economic management. It is this mistake that many of our economists, including the author, are now trying to eradicate. And our economic reform is aimed at this. We have no intention of reverting to private enterprise; on the contrary, we want to put into operation the economic laws of socialism. Central planning is entirely compatible with the initiative of enterprises in managing the economy profitably. This is as far from "private enterprise" as the latter is from feudalism.

The law of value is not a law of capitalism, but of any form of production for the market, including planned commodity production, which is what socialism is. The difference from capitalism is that ends and means are reversed. Under capitalism, profit is the basic aim, whereas satisfaction of the needs of the public is the means of attaining that aim and is secondary. Under socialism, on the contrary, the aim is to satisfy the needs of the public, and profit is the means toward that end. This is not a verbal distinction but the crux of the matter, since in our conditions profit does not work counter to social needs but helps to satisfy them.

The Reform and the Problems

The first stage of the economic reform has confronted us with certain difficulties in realizing its basic principles—difficulties which appear to be inherent in this period of the reform. The transfer of the first 704 enterprises to the new system was not immediately accompanied by substantial changes in their relations with the superior agencies, with other enterprises, with agencies supplying materials and equipment, etc. . . .

The reform puts the old established relationships in industry to a severe test. The enlargement of the rights of enterprises is an important condition of the reform. In many cases, however, the superior agencies have proved insufficiently prepared for this development. Sometimes this has taken the form of the old bureaucratic ills—inflexibility, irresponsibility and lack of initiative, reliance upon the formality of issuing orders instead of working out economic as opposed to administrative methods of influencing production. . . .

The reform has not yet sufficiently permeated the administrative interrelationships between enterprises and superior agencies. This is indeed a complicated process of many steps. Complaints and mutual dissatisfactions are inevitable. First of all, the reform requires a sharp improvement in the qualifications of those engaged in the management process. If the economic and organizational level of management is low, the efficiency and profitability of the enterprise are generally low. The point of the reform is to raise production efficiency, increase labor productivity and open wide the road to rapid technical improvement. As it goes on, the reform inevitably will foster the selection and promotion of the more able, both below and at the top, to executive managerial positions. The reform will not tolerate the retention of anything that is obsolete and that has failed to justify itself in our methods of management.

It would be premature to call these changes in the Soviet economic system "creeping capitalism," as has been done by some observers. Rather, the inclusion of "profits" and "interest" in the criteria for measuring the performance of plant managers should be seen primarily as an attempt on the part of the Soviet governmental apparatus to use more sophisticated methods for the creation of an efficient, modern industrial economy considered necessary to attain long-range communist goals. In Poland, Czechoslovakia, and Hungary even greater managerial discretion is allowed than under Liberman's methods in the Soviet Union, but it would be again an error to see in these developments the slow abandonment of governmental control over the economy and a gradual approach to a free market system. The greatest significance of the Liberman methods does not lie in their bearing upon the question of private versus public ownership of the means of production nor their possible impact upon industrial efficiency in the Soviet Union. Their major significance lies in the fact that these methods could be evolved as the result of frank criticism of long-standing governmental policies and planning operations, an open and uninhibited debate which would have been unthinkable in the days of Stalin.

We should note that the new schemes have been only a mixed blessing for the communist countries. Many managers, accustomed to receiving strict directives from governmental sources, have great difficulty in using properly the newly won freedom of decision, and as a consequence the operation of the economy in many instances has been suffering rather than gaining greater efficiency.

One of the East European communist countries, Yugoslavia, has introduced radical changes into its formerly traditional communist economic system by seeking to create a "socialist market" economy during the last few years. In this system the state continues to set the general target and engages in overall planning, but the plants themselves determine through joint decisions by the managers and the workers' councils future production plans, most prices, and the use of profits for reinvestment or employee compensation. Of course, the government and the Communist Party seek to retain a measure of control over the plant decisions, but in the determination of what and how much to produce the market conditions play a decidedly greater role than the announced goals of the government.

It is evident that Yugoslavia is moving economically in a different direction from that taken by the Soviet Union. Her economic order now seems to be headed toward concepts under which democratic socialism attempts to operate. The basic operating principles of the socialist system are state ownership or state control of basic industries and financial establishments, subjection of the market to government planning and controls, and conscious use of governmental policies to bring about economic and social equality.* Some of these principles have been put into practice in a number of countries of Western Europe and the developing world. Great Britain under the Labor Party government has nationalized a number of basic industries, among them the important iron and steel enterprises. The socialist governments of Sweden,

---

* Preston, *Politics, Economics, and Power*, p. 104.

Norway, and Britain have introduced planning schemes that curtail operation of the free market economy to the extent perceived necessary to obtain certain social and economic goals. In addition, the three countries have established national health and welfare services which, in terms of comprehensiveness, exceed materially those existing in such basically capitalistic countries as the United States and West Germany.

Democratic socialism does not seek to attain its goals through revolution but through the democratic process, the ballot box. While the preceding examples suggest some progress toward its goals, democratic socialism as practiced at present has not succeeded fully in transferring control over all basic industries from private hands to the government. Moreover—and this is confusing—some of the activities asserted to be typical of socialism are also practiced under capitalistic systems. Certain social welfare measures are now found in all capitalistic countries; in fact, national health insurance was introduced in Germany by Bismarck as early as the 1880s. Economic planning by the government is to varying degrees carried out in practically all capitalistic countries and is especially developed in France. And even various kinds of state ownership exist in many capitalistic countries, ranging from state-owned railroads and public utilities in all West European democracies to the hydroelectric plants of TVA in the United States.

There can be little doubt that today the notion of laissez-faire is virtually dead and that capitalist and socialist economic systems have much in common as far as governmental intervention in the economy is concerned. Yet there remain significant differences in concept and emphasis. In the modern capitalistic system the free play of market forces remains the basic principle, but the government is given the responsibility of placing restraints on private economic despotism and of ensuring a reasonable balance of power among the participants in the economic order. Government support for education, retraining programs, employment services, assistance to depressed areas of the economy, and social welfare measures are seen as ways to ensure equality of opportunity in the economic struggle rather than as social values in themselves. In the contemporary socialist economic system, the government is committed to the development of substantial economic equality requiring intervention considerably more extensive than that seen necessary under the capitalist system. In addition, the social objectives of the state have a much broader range and greater depth. Finally—and here lies perhaps the greatest difference—the state under the socialist system is committed to restructuring the bases of the economy through the nationalization of certain industries and services.

The Performance of Governmental Intervention

With governmental intervention an accepted fact in all modern economic systems, although the degree of intervention varies considerably, we must raise the question as to how well government has performed this function. In this connection we must understand that any time governmental intervention in the economic order is proposed as necessary for the common good of a society as well as for the development of the individual citizen, selfish and vested interests are created and political conflicts are generated. Turning something over to the government to do, no matter how high its moral purpose, makes it political, and all aspects of politics will play their roles in evolving governmental policies and administrative decisions. And considering the tremendous growth of government everywhere, it increases the complexity of an already very complex structure operated by an immense bureaucracy with its own personal and institutional goals.

We will close this chapter with a critical view of governmental performance in dealing with economic matters, but it is perceptive and constructive criticism, with hope and suggestions for the future. Our selection from Peter F. Drucker's book, *The Age of Discontinuity*, provides much food for thought in a crucial period of transition for all of us.

THE SICKNESS OF GOVERNMENT

PETER F. DRUCKER

Government surely has never been more prominent than today. The most despotic government of 1900 would not have dared probe into the private affairs of its citizens as income-tax collectors now do routinely in the freest society. Even the Czar's secret police did not go in for the security investigations we now take for granted. Nor could any bureaucrat of 1900 have imagined the questionnaires that governments now expect businesses, universities, or citizens to fill out in ever-mounting number and ever-increasing detail. At the same time, government has everywhere become the largest employer.

Government is certainly all-pervasive. But is it truly strong? Or is it only big?

There is mounting evidence that government is big rather than strong; that it is fat and flabby rather than powerful; that it costs a great deal but does not achieve much. There is mounting evidence also that the citizen less and less believes in government and is increasingly disenchanted with it. Indeed, government is sick—and just at the time when we need a strong, healthy, and vigorous government.

There is certainly little respect for government among the young—and even less love. But, the adults, the taxpayers, are also increasingly disenchanted. They still want more services from government. But they are everywhere approaching the point where they balk at paying for a bigger government, even though they may still want what government promises to give.

The disenchantment with government cuts across national boundaries and ideological lines. It is as prevalent in Communist as in democratic societies, as common in white as in nonwhite countries. . . .

The Fabians in Great Britain or the German Social Democrats started their love affair with government before 1900. It became general with World War I when government, using taxation and the printing press, mobilized social resources way beyond what anyone earlier would have thought possible. The German war economy, the War Production Board in the United States, and the United States propaganda machine dazzled contemporaries. It convinced them that government could do anything. . . . World War II reinforced this belief. Again government proved itself incredibly effective in organizing the energies of society for warfare.

But now our attitudes are in transition. We are rapidly moving to doubt and distrust of government and, in the case of the young, even to rebellion against it. We still, if only out of habit, turn social tasks over to government. We still revise unsuccessful programs over and over again, and assert that nothing is wrong with them that a change in procedures or "competent administration" will not cure. But we no longer believe these promises when we reform a bungled program for the third time. Who, for instance, believes any more that administrative changes in the foreign aid program of the United States (or of the United Nations) will really produce rapid worldwide development? Who really believes that the War on Poverty will vanquish poverty in the cities? Or who, in Russia, really believes that a new program of incentives will make the collective farm productive? . . .

What explains this disenchantment with government?

We expected miracles—and that always produces disillusionment. Government, it was widely believed (though only subconsciously), would produce a great many things for nothing. Cost was thought a function of who did something rather than of what was being attempted. . . .

But the greatest factor in the disenchantment with government is that government has not performed. The record over these last thirty or forty years has been dismal. Government has proved itself capable of doing only two things with great effectiveness. It can wage war. And it can inflate the currency. Other things it can promise but only rarely accomplish. Its record as an industrial manager, in the satellite countries of Eastern Europe as well as in the nationalized industries of Great Britain has been depressing. Whether private enterprise would have done worse is not even relevant. For we expected perfection from government as industrial manager. Instead we only rarely obtained even below-average mediocrity.

Government as a planner has hardly done much better (whether in Communist Czechoslovakia or in de Gaulle's capitalist France).

But the greatest disappointment, the great letdown, is the fiasco of the welfare state. Not many people would want to do without the social services and welfare benefits of an affluent modern industrial society. But the welfare state promised a great deal more than to provide social services. It promised to create a new and happy society. It promised to release creative energies. It promised to do away with ugliness and envy and strife. No matter how well it is doing its jobs—and in some areas in some countries some jobs are being done very well—the welfare state turns out at best to be just another big insurance company, as exciting, as creative, and as inspiring as insurance companies tend to be. No one has ever laid down his life for an insurance policy. . . .

The best we get from government in the welfare state is competent mediocrity. More often we do not even get that; we get incompetence such as we would not tolerate in an insurance company. In every country there are big areas of government administration where there is no performance whatever—only costs. This is true not only of the mess of the big cities, which no government—United States, British, Japanese, or Russian—has been able to handle. It is true in education. It is true in transportation. And the more we expand the welfare state the less capable even of routine mediocrity does it seem to become. . . .

During the past three decades, federal payments to the big cities have increased almost a hundredfold for all kinds of programs. But results from the incredible dollar flood into the cities are singularly un-impressive. What is impressive is the administrative incompetence. We now have ten times as many government agencies concerned with city problems as we had in 1939. We have increased by a factor of a thousand or so the number of reports and papers that have to be filled out before anything can be done in the city. . . .

But in other areas, the welfare state does not perform much better. Nor is the administrative mess a peculiarly American phenomenon. The daily press in Great Britain, in Germany, in Japan, in France, in Scandi-navia—and increasingly in the Communist countries as well—reports the same confusion, the same lack of performance, the same proliferation of agencies, of programs, of forms, and the same triumph of accounting rules over results. Everywhere rivalry between various agencies is replacing concern with results and with responsibility.

Modern government has become ungovernable. There is no government today that can still claim control of its bureaucracy and of its various agencies. Government agencies are all becoming autonomous, ends in themselves, and directed by their own desire for power, their own rationale, their own narrow vision rather than by national policy and by their own boss, the national government.

This is a threat to the basic capacity of government to give direction and leadership. Increasingly policy is fragmented, and policy direction becomes divorced from execution. Execution is governed by the inertia of the large bureaucratic empires, rather than by policy. Bureaucrats keep on doing what their procedures prescribe. Their tendency, as is only human, is to identify what is in the best interest of the agency with what is right, and what fits administrative convenience with effectiveness. As a result the welfare state cannot set priorities. It cannot concentrate its tremendous resources, and therefore does not get anything done. . . .

Yet never has strong, effective, truly performing government been needed more than in this dangerous world of ours. Never has it been needed more than in this pluralist society of organizations. Never has it been needed more than in the present world economy.

We need government as the central institution in the society of organizations. We need an organ that expresses the common will and the common vision and enables each organization to make its own best contribution to society and citizen and yet to express common beliefs and common values. We need strong, effective governments in the international sphere so that we can make the sacrifices of sovereignty needed to give us working supranational institutions for world society and world economy.

The answer to diversity is not uniformity. The answer is unity. We cannot hope to suppress the diversity of our society. Each of the pluralist institutions is needed. Each discharges a necessary economic task. We cannot, as I have tried to show, suppress the autonomy of these institutions. Their task makes them autonomous whether this is admitted by political rhetoric or not. We therefore have to create a focus of unity. This can only be provided by strong and effective government.

Certain things are inherently difficult for government. Being by design a protective institution, it is not good at innovation. It cannot really abandon anything. The moment government undertakes anything, it becomes entrenched and permanent. Better administration will not alter this. Its inability to innovate is grounded in government's legitimate and necessary function as society's protective and conserving organ.

A government activity, a government installation, and government employment become immediately built into the political process itself. This holds true whether we talk of a declining industry such as the nationalized British coal mines or the government-owned railroads of Europe and Japan. It holds equally true in Communist countries. No matter how bankrupt, for instance, the Stalinist economic policies have become in Czechoslovakia, Hungary, or Poland, any attempt to change them immediately runs into concern for the least productive industries which, of course, always have the most, the lowest paid, and the least skilled—and, therefore, the most "deserving"—workers.

The inability of government to abandon anything is not limited to the economic sphere. We have known for well over a decade, for instance, that the military draft that served the United States well in a total war is immoral and demoralizing in a "cold war" or "limited war" period. No one defends our present system, yet we extend it year after year on a "temporary" basis. The same inability to abandon applies to research projects supported by government. It holds true as soon as government supports the arts. Every beneficiary of a government program immediately becomes a "constituent." He immediately organizes himself for effective political action and for pressure upon the decision maker. . . .

We have built elaborate safeguards to protect the administrative structure within government against the political process. This is the purpose of every civil service. But while this protects the going machinery from the distortions and pressures of politics, it also protects the incumbents in the agencies from the demands of performance. Of course, we maintain officially that civil-service tenure is compatible with excellence. But, if we had to choose, we would probably say that mediocrity in the civil service is a lesser evil than politics. . . .

The purpose of government is to make fundamental decisions, and to make them effectively. The purpose of government is to focus the political energies of society. It is to dramatize issues. It is to present fundamental choices.

The purpose of government, in other words, is to govern.

This, as we have learned in other institutions, is incompatible with "doing." Any attempt to combine governing with "doing" on a large scale, paralyzes the decision-making capacity. Any attempt to have decision-making organs actually "do," also means very poor "doing." They are not focused on "doing." They are not equipped for it. They are not fundamentally concerned with it.

There is good reason today why soldiers, civil servants, and hospital administrators look to business management for concepts, principles, and practices. For business, during the last thirty years, has had to face, on a much smaller scale, the problem which modern government now faces: the incompatibility between "governing" and "doing." Business management learned that the two have to be separated, and that the top organ, the decision maker, has to be detached from "doing." Otherwise he does not make decisions, and the "doing" does not get done either.

In business this goes by the name of "decentralization." The term is misleading. It implies a weakening of the central organ, the top management of a business. The purpose of decentralization as a principle of structure and constitutional order is, however, to make the center, the top management of a business, strong and capable of performing the central, the top-management, task. The purpose is to make it possible for top management to concentrate on decision making and direction by sloughing off the "doing" to operating managements, each with its own mission and goals, and with its own sphere of action and autonomy.

If this lesson were applied to government, the other institutions of society would then rightly become the "doers." "Decentralization" applied to government would not be just another form of "federalism" in which local rather than central government discharges the "doing" tasks. It would rather be a systematic policy of using the other, the nongovernmental institutions of the society of organizations, for the actual "doing," i.e., for performance, operations, execution.

Such a policy might be called "reprivatization." The tasks which flowed to government in the last century because the original private institutions of society, the family, could not discharge them, would be turned over to the new, nongovernmental institutions that have sprung up and grown these last sixty to seventy years.

Government would start out by asking the question: "How do these institutions work and what can they do?" It would then ask: "How can political and social objectives be formulated and organized in such a manner as to become opportunities for performance for these institutions?" It would also ask: "And what opportunities for accomplishment of political objectives do the abilities and capacities of these institutions offer to government?"

This would be a very different role for government from that it plays in traditional political theory. In all our theories government is *the* institution. If "reprivatization" were to be applied, however, government would become *one* institution albeit the central, the top, institution.

Reprivatization would give us a different society from any our social theories now assume. In these theories government does not exist. It is outside of society. Under reprivatization government would become the central social institution.

Political theory and social theory, for the last two hundred and fifty years, have been separate. If we applied to government and to society what we have learned about organization these last fifty years, the two would again come together. The nongovernmental institutions—university, business, and hospital, for instance—would be seen as organs for the accomplishment of results. Government would be seen as society's resource for the determination of major objectives, and as the "conductor" of social diversity. . . .

The next major development in politics, and the one needed to make this middle-aged failure—our tired, overextended, flabby, and impotent government—effective again, might therefore be reprivatization of the "doing," the performance of society's tasks. This need not mean "return to private ownership." Indeed, what is going on in the Communist satellite countries of Eastern Europe today—especially in Yugoslavia—is reprivatization in which ownership is not involved at all. Instead, autonomous businesses depend on the market for the sale of goods, the supply of labor, and the supply of capital. That their "ownership" is in the hands of the government is a legal rather than an economic fact—though, of course, important. Yet to some Yugoslavs it does not appear to be incompatible with that ultrabourgeois institution, a stock exchange.

Reprivatization, therefore, may create social structures that are strikingly similar, though the laws in respect to ownership differ greatly from one country to another and from one institution to another. What they would have in common is a principle of performance rather than a principle of authority. In all of them the autonomous institution created for the performance of a major social task would be the "doer." Government would become increasingly the decision maker, the vision maker, the political organ. It would try to figure out how to structure a given political objective so as to make it attractive to one of the autonomous institutions. It would, in other words, be the "conductor" who tries to think through what each instrument is best designed to do. And just as we praise a composer for his ability to write "playable" music, which best uses the specific performance characteristic of French horn, violin, or flute, we may come to praise the lawmaker who best structures a particular task so as to make it most congenial for this or that of the autonomous, self-governing, private institutions of pluralist society.

Business is likely to be only one, but a very important, institution in such a structure. Whether it be owned by the capitalist, that is, by the investor, or by a cooperative or a government, might even become a secondary consideration. For even if owned by government, it would have to be independent of government and autonomous—as the Yugoslavs show—not only in its day-to-day management, but, perhaps more important, in its position in the market, and especially in a competitive capital market.

What makes business particularly appropriate for reprivatization is that it is predominantly an organ of innovation; of all social institutions, it is the only one created for the express purpose of making and managing change. All other institutions were originally created to prevent, or at least to slow down, change. They become innovators only by necessity and most reluctantly.

Specifically business has two advantages where government has major weaknesses. Business can abandon an activity. Indeed, it is forced to do so if it operates in a market—and even more, if it depends on a market for its supply of capital. There is a point beyond which even the most stubborn businessman cannot argue with the market test, no matter how rich he may be himself. Even Henry Ford had to abandon the Model T when it no longer could be sold. Even his grandson had to abandon the Edsel.

What is more: of all our institutions, business is the only one that society will let disappear. . . .

Reprivatization is still heretical doctrine. But it is no longer heretical practice. Reprivatization is hardly a creed of "fat cat millionaires" when black-power advocates seriously propose making education in the slums "competitive" by turning it over to private enterprise, competing for the tax dollar on the basis of proven performance in teaching ghetto children. It may be argued that the problems of the black ghetto in the American city are very peculiar problems—and so they are. They are extreme malfunctions of modern government. But, if reprivatization works in the extreme case, it is likely to work even better in less desperate ones.

One instance of reprivatization in the international sphere is the World Bank. Though founded by governments, it is autonomous. It finances itself directly through selling its own securities on the capital markets. The International Monetary Fund, too, is reprivatization. Indeed, if we develop the money and credit system we need for the world economy, we will have effectively reprivatized creation and management of money and credit which have been considered for millennia attributes of sovereignty.

Again business is well equipped to become the "doer" in the international sphere. The multinational corporation, for instance, is our best organ for rapid social and economic development through the "contract growing" of people and of capital. In the Communications Satellite Corporation (COMSAT) we are organizing worldwide communications (another traditional prerogative of the sovereign) as a multinational corporation. A Socialist government, the Labour government of Britain, has used reprivatization to bring cheap energy to Britain—in contracts with the multinational oil companies for the exploration and development of the natural gas fields under the North Atlantic Ocean.

And the multinational corporation may be the only institution equipped to get performance where the fragmentation into tribal splinter units such as the "ministates" of Equatorial Africa makes performance by government impossible.

. . .

We do not face a "withering away of the state." On the contrary, we need a vigorous, a strong, and a very active government. But we do face a choice between big but impotent government and a government that is strong because it confines itself to decision and direction and leaves the "doing" to others. We do not face a "return of laissez-faire" in which the economy is left alone. The economic sphere cannot and will not be considered to lie outside the public domain. But the choices for the economy—as well as for all other sectors—are no longer *either* complete governmental indifference or complete governmental control.

In all major areas we have a new choice in this pluralist society of organizations: an organic diversity in which institutions are used to do what they are best equipped to do. This is a society in which all sectors are "affected with the public interest," while in each sector a specific institution, under its own management and dedicated to its own job, emerges as the organ of action and performance.

This is a difficult and complex structure. Such symbiosis between institutions can work only if each disciplines itself to strict concentration on its own sphere, and to strict respect for the integrity of the other institutions. Each, to use again the analogy of the orchestra, must be content to play its own part. This will come hardest for government, especially after the last fifty years in which it had been encouraged in the belief of the eighteenth-century organ virtuoso that it could—and should —play all parts simultaneously. But every institution will have to learn the same lesson.

Reprivatization will not weaken government. Indeed, its main purpose is to restore strength and performance capacity to sick and incapacitated government. We cannot go much further along the road on which government has been traveling these last fifty years. All we can get this way is more bureaucracy but not more performance. We can impose higher taxes but we cannot get dedication, support, and faith on the part of the public. Government can gain greater girth and more weight, but it cannot gain strength or intelligence. All that can happen, if we keep on going the way we have been going, is a worsening sickness of government and growing disenchantment with it. And this is the prescription for tyranny, that is, for a government organized against its own society.

THE INTERNATIONAL SOCIETY

7

POINT

View of the United Nations Charter.

We the peoples of the United Nations determined . . . to practice tolerance and live together in peace with one another as good neighbors, and to unite our strength to maintain international peace and security, and to ensure, by the acceptance of principles and the institution of methods, that armed force shall not be used, save in the common interest, and to employ international machinery for the promotion of the economic and social advancement of all peoples, have resolved to combine our efforts to accomplish these aims.*

COUNTERPOINT

View of the "realists."

International politics, like all politics, is a struggle for power. Whatever the ultimate aims of international politics, power is always the immediate aim. Statesmen and peoples may ultimately seek freedom, security, prosperity, or power itself. They may define their goals in terms of a religious, philosophic, economic, or social ideal. They may hope that this ideal will materialize through its own inner force, through divine intervention, or through the natural development of human affairs. . . . But whenever they strive to realize their goal by means of international politics, they do so by striving for power.†

---

* Preamble to the United Nations Charter.

† Hans J. Morgenthau, *Politics Among Nations: The Struggle for Power and Peace*, 5th ed. (New York: Alfred A. Knopf, Inc., 1973), p. 27.

The point and counterpoint presented above put into stark contrast the hopes of mankind about international society as so eloquently expressed in the Charter of the United Nations and the realities of international interaction as we witness them every day. In these interactions considerations of power, displayed openly or concealed, often play a major role. History has shown that nations active in international politics seek to maintain the power they possess, to increase power, or at times to demonstrate their power for purposes of prestige.

We now turn to the international scene, where the sovereign nation-state is the basic unit and the major actor. Although during the twentieth century international organizations such as the United Nations, the Organization of American States, NATO, the European Common Market, and many others have played and continue to play an increasingly important role in the international society, their constituent members are nation-states, and their activities are largely determined and controlled by these states.

International society as a whole lacks the institutional framework of the state. Under this framework, peaceful changes can be initiated and carried out through legislation and enforcement of laws by the state government. There is a body of rules called international law, which is to guide the behavior of states in the international arena, but no effective enforcement machinery exists. States follow these norms usually in areas of minor significance such as commercial and diplomatic intercourse because they derive mutual benefits from the orderly conduct of such relations. For fear of retaliation, other international rules—for example, those pertaining to the treatment of prisoners of war—are also adhered to in most cases. But when vital stakes of a state are involved, considerations of what is perceived as the national interest may prompt governments to disregard international law and pursue courses of action that, in their opinion, will best serve their own interests. In such cases, the legal machinery for the settlement of international disputes as provided by the United Nations is largely ignored.

The rejection by national governments of binding international laws for the resolution of essentially political and strategic problems should not be surprising, so long as the concept of sovereignty prevails. It suggests freedom from external control for as long as the sovereign state is the kingpin of international society. Sovereign states and an international law possessing effective sanctions as found in national law are logically incompatible. Either the states are truly sovereign and recognize no superior, in which case no enforcement of any norm from the outside can be accepted, or enforcement against the will of the states is recognized, and then the states are no longer sovereign.

As a consequence of this difficulty, international society has not progressed much beyond the time when the sovereign nation-state emerged in the sixteenth and seventeenth centuries. It is a competitive and in many respects anarchical society in which power is more important than justice, survival is often menaced, and the threat of violence is commonplace. Thomas Hobbes' description of the nature of man characterized by competition, diffidence, and glory set forth in 1651, is unfortunately even today applicable to the relations between the nation-states. To realize the truth of this statement one needs only to think of the many smaller and larger wars that have occurred in all parts of the globe since 1945 when World War II, the greatest of all holocausts, ended. For this reason it is instructive to recall Hobbes' vivid description of the nature of man in his *Leviathan,* a small excerpt of which is included as the first reading in this chapter.

OF THE NATURAL CONDITION OF MANKIND AS CONCERNING THEIR FELICITY, AND MISERY

THOMAS HOBBES

Men by nature equal. Nature hath made men so equal, in the faculties of the body, and mind; as that though there be found one man sometimes manifestly stronger in body, or of quicker mind than another; yet when all is reckoned together, the difference between man, and man, is not so considerable, as that one man can thereupon claim to himself any benefit, to which another may not pretend, as well as he. For as to the strength of body, the weakest has strength enough to kill the strongest, either by secret machination, or by confederacy with others, that are in the same danger with himself.

And as to the faculties of the mind, setting aside the arts grounded upon words, and especially that skill of proceeding upon general, and infallible rules, called science; which very few have, and but in few things; as being not a native faculty, born with us; nor attained, as prudence, while we look after somewhat else, I find yet a greater equality amongst men, than that of strength. . . .

From equality proceeds diffidence. From this equality of ability, ariseth equality of hope in the attaining of our ends. And therefore if any two men desire the same thing, which nevertheless they cannot both

Reprinted from Thomas Hobbes, Leviathan, *ed. Michael Oakeshott (Oxford: Basil Blackwell, Publisher, 1957), pp. 80–84.*

enjoy, they become enemies; and in the way to their end, which is principally their own conservation, and sometimes their delectation only, endeavour to destroy, or subdue one another. And from hence it comes to pass, that where an invader hath no more to fear, than another man's single power; if one plant, sow, build, or possess a convenient seat, others may probably be expected to come prepared with forces united, to dispossess, and deprive him, not only of the fruit of his labour, but also of his life, or liberty. And the invader again is in the like danger of another.

From diffidence war. And from this diffidence of one another, there is no way for any man to secure himself, so reasonable, as anticipation; that is, by force, or wiles, to master the persons of all men he can, so long, till he see no other power great enough to endanger him: and this is no more than his own conservation requireth, and is generally allowed. Also because there be some, that taking pleasure in contemplating their own power in the acts of conquest, which they pursue farther than their security requires; if others, that otherwise would be glad to be at ease within modest bounds, should not by invasion increase their power, they would not be able, long time, by standing only on their defence, to subsist. And by consequence, such augmentation of dominion over men being necessary to a man's conservation, it ought to be allowed him.

Again, men have no pleasure, but on the contrary a great deal of grief, in keeping company, where is no power able to over-awe them all. For every man looketh that his companion should value him, at the same rate he sets upon himself: and upon all signs of contempt, or undervaluing, naturally endeavours, as far as he dares, (which amongst them that have no common power to keep them in quiet, is far enough to make them destroy each other), to extort a greater value from his contemners, by damage; and from others, by the example.

. . . [In] the nature of man, we find three principal causes of quarrel. First, competition; secondly, diffidence; thirdly, glory.

The first, maketh men invade for gain; the second, for safety; and the third, for reputation. The first use violence, to make themselves masters of other men's persons, wives, children, and cattle; the second, to defend them; the third, for trifles, as a word, a smile, a different opinion, and any other sign of undervalue, either direct in their persons, or by reflection in their kindred, their friends, their nation, their profession, or their name.

Out of civil states, there is always war of every one against every one. Hereby it is manifest, that during the time men live without a common power to keep them all in awe, they are in that condition which is called war; and such a war, as is of every man, against every man. For WAR, consisteth not in battle only, or the act of fighting; but in a tract of time, wherein the will to contend by battle is sufficiently known: and therefore the notion of *time*, is to be considered in the nature of war; as it is in the nature of weather. For as the nature of foul weather, lieth not in a shower or two of rain; but in an inclination thereto of many days together: so the nature of war, consisteth not in actual fighting; but in the known disposition thereto, during all the time there is no assurance to the contrary. All other time is PEACE.

The incommodities of such a war. Whatsoever therefore is consequent to a time of war, where every man is enemy to every man; the same is consequent to the time, wherein men live without other security, than what their own strength, and their own invention shall furnish them withal. In such condition, there is no place for industry; because the fruit thereof is uncertain: and consequently no culture of the earth; no navigation, nor use of the commodities that may be imported by sea; no commodious building; no instruments of moving, and removing, such things as require much force; no knowledge of the face of the earth; no account of time; no arts; no letters; no society; and which is worst of all, continual fear, and danger of violent death; and the life of man, solitary, poor, nasty, brutish, and short. . . .

But though there had never been any time, wherein particular men were in a condition of war one against another; yet in all times, kings, and persons of sovereign authority, because of their independency, are in continual jealousies, and in the state and posture of gladiators; having their weapons pointing, and their eyes fixed on one another; that is, their forts, garrisons, and guns upon the frontiers of their kingdoms; and continual spies upon their neighbours; which is a posture of war. But because they uphold thereby, the industry of their subjects; there does not follow from it, that misery, which accompanies the liberty of particular men.

In such a war nothing is unjust. To this war of every man, against every man, this also is consequent; that nothing can be unjust. The notions of right and wrong, justice and injustice have there no place. Where there is no common power, there is no law: where no law, no injustice. Force, and fraud, are in war the two cardinal virtues. Justice, and injustice are none of the faculties neither of the body, nor mind. If they were, they might be in a man that were alone in the world, as well as his senses, and passions. They are qualities, that relate to men in society, not in solitude. It is consequent also to the same condition, that there be no propriety, no dominion, no *mine* and *thine* distinct; but only that to be every man's, that he can get: and for so long, as he can keep it. And thus much for the ill condition, which man by mere nature is actually placed in; though with a possibility to come out of it, consisting partly in the passions, partly in his reason. . . .

Nationalism

While Hobbes focused on the nature of man as being responsible for the anarchy in international society, another powerful force often disturbing the peace in international relations during the last two centuries has been the phenomenon of nationalism. Although a destructive factor inasmuch as it has been producing international tension and hostility, it has also been a constructive element by providing the prerequisites for the emergency of the newly independent states in Asia and Africa since 1945. It has transformed the political map of the world during the last 180 years and at the same time has been gaining in importance as an element in social solidarity as other social ties such as those of the family, the church, and the local community have been weakening.

Nationalism arose as a mass movement following the French Revolution when the national feelings of the common man became an immensely important factor in the relations between states. From then on, wars were fought by common men who proudly called themselves citizens but no longer felt themselves subjects. The battle flags were deployed in the name of freedom and equality, as well as for the sacred and inalienable rights of nations. Thus, the common man was entering on his new political career both as a citizen and as a patriot. The French example of genuine mass patriotism infected the whole continent of Europe, and mass nationalism began to spread all the way from Spain to Russia. The idea that man owed his highest allegiance to his nation was taking hold among all European peoples, reinforcing political structures that had previously come into existence.

To offer an insight into the elements of nationalism, whose nature is extremely complex, we present as the second selection an abbreviated chapter of Carlton J. H. Hayes' book, *Nationalism: A Religion.*

WHAT NATIONALISM IS

CARLTON J. H. HAYES

Bases of Nationality: Language and Traditions

Nationalism is an obvious and impelling movement in the modern and contemporary world. It is so obvious, indeed, and so frequently mentioned in the news, that it is apt to be taken for granted, like the rising and setting of the sun, and its importance overlooked.

Nationalism, as we know it, is a modern development. It has had its origin and rise in Europe, and through European influence and example it has been implanted in America and all other areas of Western civilization. But it is now no longer peculiar to the Christian West.

It has recently become an outstanding feature of states and peoples throughout the vast expanses of Asia and Africa, amid the traditional civilizations of Muslim, Hindu, Confucian, and Buddhist. It is especially evidenced across the whole breadth of the Muslim world: in the Turkey of Ataturk, in the Iran of Riza Pahlevi, in the Egypt of Nasser, in the separation of Pakistan from India, in the successful revolt of Indonesia against the Dutch, in the recently won independence of Libya, the Sudan, Somalia, Tunis, and Morocco, and in the Algerian rebellion. It is basic to the conflict between Arabs and Israelis.

Moreover, to a fully developed nationalism in Japan have now been added the nascent and militant nationalisms of India, Burma, Ceylon, Malaya, Vietnam, Cambodia, Laos, Thailand, and, most recently of colored peoples almost everywhere in Africa. In its latest stage, nationalism is proving the dissolvent of overseas colonial empires of Britain, France, the Netherlands, and Belgium, and probably too, before long, that of Portugal. And we should not overlook the fact that nationalism, as well as communism, is a mark of contemporary Russia and China.

What actually is this nationalism which is now so universal? It may best be understood, I think, by concentrating attention on Europe, and at first on western Europe. For here is its original home; here, its roots

Reprinted with permission of The Macmillan Company from Nationalism: A Religion by Carlton J. H. Hayes. Copyright 1960 by The Macmillan Company.

demonstrably reach far back into the past; and here, for at least five centuries, it has been an increasingly important factor in the evolution of our historic civilization.

In simplest terms, nationalism may be defined as a fusion of patriotism with a consciousness of nationality. For proper understanding of the matter, both *nationality* and *patriotism* require some explanation.

For centuries and for millenniums—as far back as we have any historical knowledge—the world has contained a large number of different nationalities. In Europe, the smallest of the five major continents, there has long been a variety of diverse nationalities: Greek, Latin, Celtic, German, Baltic, Slavic, Magyar, and so forth, some thirty-three at least at the present time.

Now what is a *nationality?* The word derives from the Latin *natio*, implying a common racial descent, but few, if any, modern nationalities consist of a distinctive "race" in the biological sense. Frenchmen are a nationality compounded of such different types as Mediterranean, Nordic, and Alpine. Germans include long-headed blonds and round-headed brunets. Italians represent curious mixtures of Etruscans, Phoenicians, and primitive Celts, of Saracens, Goths, and Norsemen. And in the United States Negroes belong, not to any African nationality, but, along with whites and red men, to the American nationality. Every nationality of which I have knowledge has been, or is, biologically and racially, a melting pot.

Nor is nationality determined simply by physical geography. To be sure, certain cultural features of Arctic peoples are bound to differ from those of tropical peoples, and both from life in temperate zones. For geographical reasons Czechs can hardly be expected to become a seafaring nationality, or the English not to become such. Yet, something other than geography has to explain why Englishmen from their island built up in modern times a great navy and merchant marine, while Irishmen from their adjacent island didn't. Or why similar habitats, climates, and pursuits failed to weld Frenchmen and Germans into a single nationality. Or why the mountainous ruggedness of Scotland and Switzerland is supposed to explain the proverbial thriftiness of their inhabitants, but fails utterly to do so in the case of Dutchmen or of the French peasantry.

No, a nationality receives its impress, its character, its individuality, not, unless very incidentally, from physical geography or biological race, but rather from cultural and historical forces. First and foremost among these I would put *language.*

Language is peculiarly human, and at least ever since the legendary Tower of Babel there has been a wide, fluid, and baffling variety of languages. Anthropologists have shown that primitive tribes are marked off from one another by differences of speech. And alike to scholars and laymen it should be obvious that language is the surest badge of nationality. It is the one thing which all persons of a particular country have in common, whether they be rich or poor, good or bad, intelligent or stupid; and it is the one thing which distinguishes them from all other persons. It is common, for example, to all Germans, whether they be long-headed or round-headed, whether they live on the Alpine heights of the Tyrol or at sea level in Hamburg; and it differentiates them from all Frenchmen, including those who may be just like Germans in race and habitat.

Likewise, language is a tangible tie between the present generation of a nation and preceding generations. The English language ties the subjects of Elizabeth II with those of Elizabeth I, and Americans of the twentieth century with those of the seventeenth and eighteenth. Similarly the German language joins people who heard Martin Luther with those who have more recently listened to Adolf Hitler and [still later heard] Konrad Adenauer. Of every nationality, language bespeaks both the solidarity and the continuity of a people. And national literature, in its many forms of prose and poetry, history, and romance, does much to emphasize what is supposedly peculiar to a nationality rather than what is fundamentally common to mankind.

Along with language, and a close second to it in importance in constituting a nationality and distinguishing it from others, are *historical traditions.* These comprise an accumulation of remembered or imagined experiences of the past, an accumulation differing in content and emphasis from one linguistic group to another.

There are several kinds of historical tradition and background. There is (a) a people's religious past, whether, for instance, it was traditionally Christian, and if so whether Catholic like Italy or Spain, or Protestant like Sweden, or Eastern Orthodox like Greece or Russia, or divided between different forms of religion, like Germany and the United States. Religious traditions, it should be stressed, have been very important in shaping human culture, not merely by providing certain beliefs, but by establishing and maintaining particular social *mores,* observances, and habits, and by influencing literature and law.

There is also (b) a people's territorial past, its ancestral soil, involving a popular, sentimental regard for a homeland where one's forebears lived and are buried, a homeland that, though perhaps now fallen somewhat from a once high estate, still evokes memory and emulation of past greatness and glory. I need only mention, by way of illustration, the appeal of Jerusalem and Palestine to Jews, the "auld sod" to Irish, the Hellenic lands and isles to Greeks.

Then there is (c) a people's political past, whether their nation was detached from a big empire or expanded from a tribal state, whether it dominated other peoples or was long subject to alien rule, what government it has traditionally had—monarchical or republican, absolutist or constitutional, or democratic. There is (d) a people's fighting past, its exploits of valor and prowess, whether chiefly by land or by sea, whether victorious or vanquished. A people may be more united and nationalistic through grief over defeat than through celebration of triumph. Serbs for centuries have recalled in glowing verse and fireside folk tales their valorous but disastrous defeat by the Turks at Kossovo in 1389. The epic fate of the "Invincible Armada" in 1588 stirred and spurred vanquished Spain scarcely less than victorious England.

There is, besides, (e) a people's industrial and economic past, whether it has been more or less advanced—"progressive" or "backward," to use a contemporary dichotomy—in agriculture, or trade, or manufacturing, or in all three, or has been famous for some specialized industry, and whether, too, it has had greater or less class wealth and distinctions. Lastly we may mention (f) a people's cultural past, what distinctive and distinguished literature and architecture and pictorial arts and music it has produced, and what scholarship and learning and degree of popular literacy.

Fluidity and Complexity of Nationality

All the foregoing and similar *historical traditions* are matters of culture, and so is *language*. Together, they constitute the cultural bases of nationality. Hence I would define nationality as "a cultural group of people who speak a common language (or closely related dialects) and who possess a community of historical traditions (religious, territorial, political, military, economic, artistic, and intellectual)." When such a group—such a nationality—cherishes in marked degree, and extols, its common language and traditions, the result is *cultural nationalism*.

Cultural nationalism may exist with or without political nationalism. For nationalities can and do exist for fairly long periods without political unity and independence. A notable example has been the Jewish or Israeli nationality; and scarcely less notable have been the Gaelic or Irish, the Polish, and the several Balkan nationalities. A nationality may be partitioned among two or more states, like the German or the Italian or the Basque, or it may be incorporated with others in a single state, like Switzerland or Belgium. Switzerland includes portions of three nationalities: German, French, and Italian. Belgium contains parts of two: French and Dutch-Flemish. If we are to grasp what a nationality is, we must avoid confusing it with state or nation. There is a Swiss state and nation, but, strictly speaking, no Swiss nationality. In like manner, there is a Belgian state and nation, but not a Belgian nationality.

The tendency has been, of course, for cultural nationalism to lead to political nationalism, and for each nationality to strive to establish an independent national state of its own. Yet, even in Europe, this goal has not yet been completely achieved. Countries which are usually thought of as possessing long-established national states, such as Great Britain, France, and Spain, still harbor national minorities with dissident languages and traditions. Besides Englishmen, Britain has Scots, Welsh, and some Irish. Besides Frenchmen, France has Provençals, Bretons, and Flemings. Besides Castilians, Spain has Catalans, Basques, and Portuguese-Galicians.

We should recognize, moreover, the fluidity of nationalities in the long run of history, and the existence of what may be called "subnationalities" or "secondary nationalities." Nationality has always existed throughout human history, just as there has always been differentiated human culture with variety of languages and customs and traditions. But specific nationalities have appeared and disappeared, risen and fallen. We know that in antiquity there were Hittite and Phoenician and Etruscan nationalities, Elamite and Edomite nationalities, but where are they now? They are gone, quite swallowed up long ago; only their names and some of their monuments remain. On the other hand, when they throve, where then were the French and English nationalities? These were nonexistent; their distinctive languages were not formed in antiquity, but only in the Middle Ages.

Since the sixteenth century, members of European nationalities have migrated overseas, carrying with them their languages and traditional culture. Thus the American continents were partitioned among Spanish, Portuguese, French and English nationalities, and South Africa became the home of a segment of the Dutch nationality. All this developed when America and South Africa—to say nothing of Australasia and the Philippines—were far more remote from Europe than they are today. Then there were only sailing vessels and no cables or radio or airplanes. The remoteness of the overseas settlers from Europe and the novel frontier life they led, coping with strange lands and strange peoples, gradually served to qualify and add to the historical traditions which they had originally brought with them from the mother country.

Eventually, as we know, the widening differences were accentuated by the forceful revolutionary breaking of political ties, so that in the Americas an independent United States of English-speaking people emerged, and likewise a group of independent republics of Spanish-speaking peoples, an independent Portuguese-speaking Brazil, and an independent Haiti and autonomous Quebec of French-speaking peoples, while in South Africa the Dutch acquired practical independence. And political independence, it is hardly necessary to point out, has operated to provide the new nations with special historical traditions at variance not only with one another's but those of parental or primary nationalities in Europe.

Wherefore the nationalities in America—English, Spanish, Portuguese, French—may conveniently be described as secondary, or subnationalities. They have the same languages as their counterparts in Europe, with only dialect differences; but they possess and cherish divergent historical traditions, and a firm will to maintain free and sovereign national states. Special bonds of culture and sympathy survive, of course, between secondary nationalities and their respective primary nationalities. Common language means that Shakespeare, Milton, and Keats are as much a heritage of the people of the United States as of England, and, vice versa, that modern American novels find a large market among Englishmen. It also helps to explain why for almost a century and a half there has been no war between Britain and the United States, why, rather, they have fought side by side in the World Wars of the present century, and are likely to stand together in "cold" or "hot" wars of the future. Likewise, common language, with common literature and customs, contributes to a continuing sympathetic feeling between European Spaniards on the one hand and Spanish Americans and Filipinos on the other, and between Portuguese and Brazilians; and this despite marked racial differences.

The Dominion of Canada contains two secondary nationalities: French Canadian, and English-speaking Canadian; and the latter may conceivably consist of such "tertiary" nationalities as British Canadian and Irish Canadian, for example. Among other self-governing members of the British Commonwealth, Australia and New Zealand have come to comprise a secondary nationality each, while the Union of South Africa includes at least three: Dutch, English, and indigenous Negro.

Further illustrative of the fluidity and complexity of nationality, is the existence of sectionalism, with its tendency to create and preserve separatist variations of dialect and historic tradition and to threaten the unity of a people. In the United States we have had a glaring spectacle of sectionalism and of its issue, a century ago, in a long bloody struggle to break an American "secondary" nationality into two: a Northern States' and a Southern States'; and though political union was preserved and fortified, we all know that a kind of peculiar and "tertiary" American nationality has survived to this day in Dixie.

Furthermore, we should remark here that nationalism as an exalting of nationality is somewhat more artificially stimulated, though no less potent, in a country like the United States than in a European country such as England or France or Sweden or Germany. It is naturally so. In Europe everyone is aware of belonging to a particular nationality with distinguishing language and traditions; and one's nationalism is a relatively normal outgrowth and expression of it. In the United States, on the other hand, where the population consists of descendants of immigrants from a great variety of European nationalities, to say nothing of Negroes and Asiatics and indigenous Indian tribesmen, nationalism is invoked and pressed into service as creator and assurer of a novel and unifying American nationality—a national "melting pot."

Patriotism

Nationality is a fact, and from the dawn of history there has been a multiplicity of nationalities in various stages of development or decline. But until people are conscious of nationality and make it the prime object of their *patriotism,* they do not produce cultural or political nationalism.

What, then, is patriotism? It is "love of country," yes. As "love" it is an emotion, involving fondness, sympathy, fidelity, loyalty. In one form or another, it appears to be instinctive with man, a natural part and essential prop of his gregariousness. It is basic to human life in family, in locality, in society.

Love of country is an aggregate of several kinds of loyalty. It involves a "feline" loyalty to familiar places, a "canine" loyalty to familiar persons, a distinctively human loyalty to familiar ideas and usages. There may be various objects of these combined loyalties—of this patriotism. It may be family or clan or tribe. It may be village or town. It may be a province or an empire or any sort of state. It may be a club or a Masonic lodge or a church. It may be a nationality.

Loyalty to familiar places is relatively natural, but it requires artificial effort—purposeful conscious education and training—to render man loyal to the sum total of places, unfamiliar as well as familiar, in an entire country inhabited by his nationality. In French, distinction is usefully made between *patrie* (one's whole nation or "fatherland") and *pays* (one's immediate homeland). Everybody, besides having a *patrie,* has a *pays.* My own *pays* is New York, particularly the south central part of Upstate New York. Here I was born and spent my youth. Here five generations of both paternal and maternal ancestors lived and are buried. Here is my true home, along the gently flowing Susquehanna and amid the smiling wooded hills. Hither I resort whenever I can. This *pays* is for me a primary and most natural stimulus of patriotic sentiment and

loyalty. Yet I have been taught—and am expected—to extend this senti-
ment and loyalty to such unfamiliar places as Alaska, North Dakota,
Oklahoma and Utah, and at the same time to withhold them from
Canada and Mexico.

Similarly, loyalty to familiar persons—to family, friends, and neighbors—is natural and usual. But special civic training is required to make
a man loyal to the sum total of persons, familiar and unfamiliar, who
constitute his whole nationality. And it takes additional training for a
man to learn that he should respect and obey, and be patriotic about,
national officials who carry on remote from him.

Furthermore, man being man, it is natural for him to be loyal to
some ideas and ideals which occur to him and which he thinks good.
But most such ideas do not germinate spontaneously within him. Rather,
they are carried to, and seeded in him by his fellows. And it necessitates
systematic and repeated efforts to implant in the masses of an extended
nationality a community of national thought and ideals to which they
will be loyal.

Patriotism, therefore, while instinctive in its origin and root, is
much more naturally and readily associated with a small community in
a restricted area than with a large nationality in a broad expanse of territory. Only through an intensive and extensive educational process will
a local group of people become thoroughly aware of their entire nationality and supremely loyal to it.

The cultural bases of nationality, let me repeat, are a common language and common historical traditions. When these by some process of
education become the objects of popular emotional patriotism, the result
is nationalism.

There are degrees of nationalism, as of any emotion. Our loyalty
to nationality and national state may be conditioned by other loyalties—
to family, to church, to humanity, to internationalism—and hence restricted in corresponding degree. On the other hand, nationalism may
be a paramount, a supreme loyalty, commanding all others. This usually
occurs when national emotion is fused with religious emotion, and nationalism itself becomes a religion or a substitute for religion.

It is interesting to note that nationalism can coexist with any ideology, as the
history of the nineteenth and twentieth centuries has demonstrated. It has been
liberal-democratic in several Western countries such as the United States, Britain, and France, where popular attachment to democratic ideals is prevalent.
It also prospered under all sorts of authoritarian and Fascist regimes, especially

Hitler's Germany and Mussolini's Italy. In the Soviet Union and Communist China, nationalism has been wedded to the Marxist-Leninist ideology, which originally was truly cosmopolitan.

A frequent result of nationalism is ethnocentrism, which consists in regarding one's own country as the center of the world and as the only measure of the accomplishments and failures of foreign nations. One's own nationality is viewed as intellectually and morally superior to other nationalities, and other countries are labeled as backward, evil, or unenlightened communities. Most modern nation-states are guilty of ethnocentric bias to varying degrees, and for this reason international understanding between different countries has often suffered. In addition, the meaning of terms such as "democracy" and "liberation" varies between the Western and communist worlds, giving rise to confusion and conflicts and thereby further accentuating the differences between the nations of the world.

Perhaps the most striking example of destructive nationalism in recent times has been the Germany of Adolf Hitler. Nationalism was shaped by Hitler into a force bent on aggression, territorial expansion, and the subjugation of other nationalities. The German nation was deified while other countries were vilified as decadent societies. Hitler and his associates manipulated and exploited the frenzied nationalism they had created and turned the German rank and file into blind and fanatical worshippers of a nearly "divine" leader. Marching abroad to make slaves of the populations of foreign countries— France, Russia, Poland, and others—the Nazis offered one of the most horrible spectacles of nationalism degenerating into contempt and hatred.

The best example of recent constructive nationalism has been the fight of Asian and African peoples against colonialism and for national self-determination. The main goal of national self-determination is the freedom of a nationality to determine its own political fate and to manage its own affairs. A second purpose is to unite all members of this nationality within the borders of their own nation-state.

The triumph of national self-determination does not necessarily mean that the members of the nationality who have won their own state will enjoy democratic freedoms as understood in Western terms. Many of the new African states have one-party legislatures and only thinly veiled dictatorial governments. This is due mainly to the lack of political maturity in countries where societies are still tribal and where political values are not commensurate with the ideals and practices of Western democracy. Moreover, self-determination for one nationality may have unfortunate consequences for people of another nationality, as was the case for Englishmen in East and Central Africa and for Frenchmen in North Africa when the countries of these areas received their independence.

The triumph of self-determination has not been an unmixed blessing for the new Asian and African states. They have found it difficult to replace foreign administrators with their own people because trained native personnel are in short supply. They have had to face expenditures formerly borne by the colonial powers and have been confronted with a variety of economic difficulties. We will return to this problem later.

The Future of the Nation-State

The loyalties that citizens attach to their state are based at least in part on the implied assumption that the state will provide certain services in return. Among these services are protection from hostile external forces, military as well as economic, and assurance of the necessary conditions for economic well-being and for steady improvement of living standards. Traditionally, protection from external forces presupposed that the government had full control over the state's territory and could prevent hostile penetration of the territorial boundaries. Economic well-being was closely linked to economic self-sufficiency in terms of supply and markets and to assured lines of transportation for needed raw materials.

The tremendous advances made by technology during the twentieth century and especially since World War II cast doubt on the continuing validity of these assumptions. Consequently, the frontiers of a state have been losing their meaning as lines delineating a territory under the complete sovereignty of its government. The main challenges have come from technological developments in warfare—from bombers, long-range ballistic missiles, and orbiting space platforms possibly linked with nuclear weapons. The interior of states can now be effectively struck from outside; even the superpowers, the United States and the Soviet Union, cannot prevent such intrusions into their territory. Other challenges to the sovereign control of territories have come from psychological warfare and changing economic conditions. Radio is extensively used for propaganda, and even the best jamming devices have not been capable of fully silencing the intruding radio voice, no matter how unwelcome it may be. Industrialization and mass production have greatly increased the economic vulnerability of states because of their dependence on external sources of supplies and markets which can be cut off by military and economic warfare.

In a brilliant analysis, Professor John Herz has examined the elements leading to the decline of the nation-state. Although Herz's cogent observations were made in the late 1950s, they are even more applicable today, since technological developments have increased the capabilities of external forces to intrude into the territories of individual nation-states. Our next selection reproduces parts of Professor Herz's book, *International Politics in the Atomic Age.*

THE DECLINE OF THE TERRITORIAL STATE

JOHN H. HERZ

In view of the tremendous role nation-states—or at least several of them—play in the world today, talking about the "decline" of states manifestly would be absurd. What is referred to in the title of this [reading] is the decline of that specific element of statehood which characterized the units composing the modern state system in its classical period, and which I called their "territoriality" or "impermeability." The "model-type" international system built upon units of this structure was that of a plurality of countries—at first all European—bound together by certain common standards, different but not too different in power, all enjoying a certain minimum of protection in and through that system. They would quarrel, try to diminish each other, but they would hardly ever suffer one of theirs to be extinguished. In their quarrels, which they called wars, they would attack each other, but their fortress-type shells of defense could be breached only by frontal assault and thus even the smaller powers had a goodly chance to resist and survive. Self-contained, centralized, internally pacified, they could rely on themselves for a high degree of external security.

Beginning with the nineteenth century, certain trends emerged which tended to endanger the functioning of the classical system. Directly or indirectly, all of them had a bearing upon that feature of the territorial state which was the strongest guarantee of its independent coexistence with other states of like nature: its hard shell, that it, its defensibility in case of war.

Naturally, many of these new trends concerned war itself and the way in which war was conducted. But it would be a mistake to identify them with what is often referred to as the shift from limited war, the war typical of the duel-type contests of the eighteenth century, to the more or less unlimited wars that developed with conscription, "nations in arms," and the increasing destructiveness of weapons in the nineteenth century. For by themselves these developments were not inconsistent with

Reprinted from John H. Herz, International Politics in the Atomic Age *(New York: Columbia University Press, 1959), pp. 96–108, by permission of the publisher.*

the "classical" aim of war in the era of territorial states: the attempt by one state to enforce its will on that of the opponent by defeating the latter's armed forces and overcoming its defense installations through frontal attack. Instituting universal military service, putting the state's economy on a war-footing, and similar measures served to enhance a country's capacity to defend itself in the traditional way. Rather than endangering the territorial state they served to bolster it. This kind of "unlimited war" must be regarded simply as a more developed form of traditional warfare.

Total war, as distinguished from both kinds of traditional war, limited and unlimited, is involved with developments in warfare which enabled belligerents to overlap or by-pass the traditional hard-shell defense of states. As soon as this happens, the traditional relationship between war, on the one hand, and territorial sovereignty and power, on the other, is altered decisively. Arranged in order of increasing effectiveness, these new factors may be listed under the following headings: (a) possibility of economic blockade; (b) ideological-political penetration; (c) air war; and (d) atomic war. It is true that even outside and in some cases prior to the emergence of these factors, growth in offensive power and increase in range and destructiveness of conventional weapons, such as was witnessed in the second half of the nineteenth century, tended by itself to render the smaller among the traditional units of territorial power obsolete because they became too easily "breachable." Countries like Holland or Belgium, once defensible through fortresses and a corresponding military setup, became simply minor obstacles, unable to resist with their own defensive strength when attacked by the concentrated offensive power of a "big" one. . . . Overrun with no possibility of offering effective resistance, their only hope lay in eventual "liberation" by their more powerful allies. . . . On the other hand, exceptional geographic location, combined with exceptionally favorable topography, might still enable small countries such as Switzerland to survive, if only because of the deterrent effect of their resistance-readiness.

Turning now to the factors which, more generally, have tended to affect old-style territoriality, let us begin with *economic warfare*. It should be said from the outset that "economic blockade" so far has never enabled a belligerent to force another into surrender through "starvation" alone. In the First World War, Germany and her allies were seriously endangered when the Western Allies cut them off from overseas supplies, particularly foodstuffs. Countering with the submarine, the Germans posed a similar threat to Britain for a while. But German post-war propaganda efforts to blame defeat solely on *Hungerblockade* (plus alleged enemy-instigated subversion), with its companion slogan "im Felde unbesiegt" (undefeated on the battlefield), ran contrary to the fact that a very real effort had been required to defeat the Central Powers on the military fronts. The same thing applies to the Second World War. But blockade was an important contributing factor in both instances. Its importance for the present analysis lies in its unconventional nature, which permits belligerents to by-pass the hard shell of the enemy. Its use reflects an entirely untraditional approach to warmaking; its effect is due to the changed economic status of industrialized nations.

Prior to the industrial age the territorial state was largely self-contained ("self-sufficient"), economically as otherwise. Although one of the customary means of conducting limited war was to try to starve fortresses into surrender, this applied only to the individual links in the shell, and not to entire nations in order to avoid breaching the shell. . . . The Industrial Revolution changed all this, for it made countries like Britain and Germany increasingly dependent on imports. This meant that in war they could survive only by controlling areas beyond their own territory, which would provide them with the food and raw materials they needed. The Germans managed by overrunning food-surplus and raw material producing areas in the initial stages of both world wars, and the British, of course, by keeping the sea lanes open through superior naval power.

In peacetime, economic dependency became one of the causes of a phenomenon which itself contributed to the transformation of the old state system: imperialism. Anticipating war, with its new danger of blockade, countries strove to become more self-sufficient through enlargement of their areas of control. I do not mean to imply that the complex phenomenon of imperialism was exclusively or even chiefly caused by economic interdependence and its impact on war. Clearly, the earlier stage of capitalist industrialism as such had already supplied various motives for expansion, especially in the form of colonialism. But an economic determinism which sees the cause of imperialist expansion only in the profit motive and the ensuing urge for markets or cheap labor overlooks the additional, and very compelling, motivation that lies in power competition and the urge for security in case of war. To the extent that the industrialized nations lost self-sufficiency, they were driven into expansion in a—futile—effort to regain it. Today, if at all, only the control of entire continents enables major nations to survive economically in major wars. This implies that hard-shell military defense, if it is to make any sense, must be a matter of defending more than one single nation; it must extend half way around the world. This, in turn, affects the status of smaller nations, whether they are included in the larger defense perimeter or not. If they are, they tend to become dependent on the chief power in the area; if they are not, they may become "permeable" precisely because of the possibility of economic blockade.

Psychological warfare. The attempt to undermine the morale of an enemy population, or to subvert its loyalty, shares with economic warfare the effect by by-passing old-style territorial defensibility. Like economic blockade, such "ideological-political" penetration is not entirely new, but it was formerly practiced, and practicable, only under quite exceptional circumstances. Short periods when genuine "world-revolutionary" propaganda was circulated, such as in the early stages of the French Revolution, scarcely affected the general practice under which dynasties, and later governments, fought other dynasties or governments with little "ideological" involvement on the part of larger masses or classes. With conscription for military service, loyalty to the cause of one's country of course became more important, but since this new approach to mobilization for war coincided with nationalism (of which it was one expression), it served to increase, rather than to detract from, national coherence and solidarity. Only in rare cases—for instance, where national groups enclosed in and hostile to multinational empires could be appealed to—was there an opening wedge for what we today call "fifth column" strategies. Even then, to take advantage of such opportunities was considered "ungentlemanlike" and "not to be done" (as, for instance, in the case of Bismarck's appeal to certain nationality groups in Austria-Hungary during his war of 1866).

With the emergence of political belief systems and ideological creeds in our century, however, nations have become susceptible to undermining from within. Although, as in the case of economic blockades, wars have not yet been won solely by subversion of loyalties, the threat has affected the coherence of the territorial state ever since the rise to power of a regime that claims and proclaims to represent not the cause of one particular nation, but that of all mankind, or at least its exploited or suppressed "masses." Bolshevism from 1917 on has provided the second instance in modern history of world-revolutionary propaganda. Communist penetration tactics were subsequently imitated by Nazi-Fascist regimes, and eventually even by the democracies. To be sure, neither Nazi-Fascist propaganda directed to the democracies nor democratic counterpropaganda directed to populations under totalitarian regimes were by themselves sufficient to defeat an enemy in the Second World War; but individual instances of "softening up" countries and then gaining control with the aid of a subversive group within occurred even then. Such tactics have, of course, become all to familiar during the cold war. It is hardly necessary to point out how a new technological development and a new technique of penetration—radio broadcasting—has added to the effectiveness of political penetration through psychological warfare. The radio has rendered units accessible to propaganda and undermining from abroad, which formerly were impenetrable not only in a political but also in a technical sense. . . .

Thus, new lines of division, cutting horizontally through state units instead of leaving them separated vertically from each other at their frontiers, have now become possible. Under such political-ideological alignments, "aliens" may turn out to be friends, citizens, more treacherous than "enemy aliens"; "friendly" prisoners of war may have to be distinguished from hostile ones, as, in the Second World War in the case of German or Italian PW's, or, more recently, in Korean prison camps; "refugees" may be revealed as spies or "agents," while "agents" may deliver themselves up as refugees; the Iron Curtain is crossed westward by those who feel that this is the way to escape "slavery," while others cross it eastward to escape "oppression" or "discrimination." How even in peacetime such a new type of loyalties (or disloyalties) can be utilized to weaken the internal coherence and therewith the "impermeability" of nations is vividly portrayed by the statements of French and Italian Communist leaders calling upon their compatriots to consider the Soviet Union a brother instead of an enemy in case of war. And during actual war, political-ideological fissures can be utilized to counter the effects of newly developed means of attack by rendering it more difficult to "pacify" territory "conquered" in the traditional manner of breaching the outer defense wall. Guerrilla warfare then becomes another means of rendering obsolete the classical way of defeating an enemy through defeating his traditional armed forces. Using planes to establish communication with guerrilla forces behind enemy lines, or to drop them supplies or advisers, illustrates the combined effect which political-ideological strategy and air war may have upon the customary type of classical warfare.

Air war, of all the new developments and techniques prior to the atomic age, is the one that has affected the territoriality of nations most radically. With it, so to say, the roof blew off the territorial state. It is true that even this new kind of warfare, up to and including the Second World War, did not by itself account for the defeat of a belligerent, as some of the more enthusiastic prophets of the air age had predicted it would. Undoubtedly, however, it had a massive contributory effect. And this effect was due to strategic action in the hinterland, rather than to tactical use at the front. It came at least close to defeating one side "vertically," by direct action against the "soft" interior of the country, by-passing the "fronts" and other outer defenses. By striking against cities, "morale," supplies, industries, etc., it foreshadowed the "end of the frontier," that is, the demise of the traditional impermeability of even the militarily most powerful states. . . .

The process has now been completed with the advent of the atomic weapon. With it, whatever remained of the impermeability of states seems to have gone for good. . . . Now that power can destroy power from center to center everything is different.

What have been the responses of the nation-states to meet the new challenges? The most prominent device to overcome the military deficiencies and vulnerabilities inherent in the new technology has been the formation of regional units, either in the form of traditional alliances or through the establishment of regional international organizations endowed with a variety of institutions for common decision-making. While alliances between states date back to the beginning of recorded history, regional organizations are of much more recent origin and have become especially conspicuous in the wake of the ideological and strategic struggles between the communist and anti-communist blocs since World War II.

Within the Free World, it is the North Atlantic Treaty Organization (NATO) which is the most important defense unit. Concerned with the defense of Western Europe, its members include the United States, Canada, Great Britain, and a number of other European allies. NATO has not superseded national controls over defense, and employment of nuclear weapons remains within the authority of those states that possess them. Nevertheless, common defense programs are negotiated by the members of NATO, and a beginning has been made in the coordination of nuclear policies. As a consequence, the independence of the participating governments in the formulation and execution of their military policies becomes somewhat restricted, although final decisions remain within the sphere of their national competence. Other Free World military organizations include the South East Asia Treaty Organization (SEATO), a modified version of NATO with responsibilities mainly in Asia; the Organization of American States (OAS), concerned with inter-American defense problems; and the Central Treaty Organization (CENTO), whose major interests lie in the Middle East and western Asia.

The communist counterpart of NATO is the Warsaw Pact Organization, which includes the Soviet Union and her East European satellite countries such as Poland, Czechoslovakia, Hungary, Romania, and others. While within NATO the views of the United States, by far the greatest contributor, often prevail, the remaining members are not coerced. The Soviet Union has consistently dominated the Warsaw Pact Organization, as seen in the Czechoslovakian developments of late 1968. It is interesting to note that divergent attitudes are coming increasingly to the fore in both NATO and the Warsaw Pact Organization—France has withdrawn from the comprehensive NATO military organization but continues to adhere to the NATO Treaty, and Romania shows signs of independence—and for this reason the future of both organizations remains somewhat uncertain.

In order to meet their responsibility for the economic well-being of their citizens, a number of states have also formed regional organizations of an economic nature. The most prominent of these is the European Economic Community, better known as the Common Market. It is composed of France, West Germany, Italy, Great Britain, Ireland, Denmark, and the Benelux countries. Sweden, Norway, Switzerland, Austria, Portugal, Greece, and Turkey are associate members of the Community. The main objective of these organizations—the formation of a larger market than is offered by the individual member states—is accomplished through the elimination of all tariffs between the participating countries. The European Economic Community has materially raised the levels of economic activity and the standard of living of the citizens in the member states. There was hope that the Common Market would lead eventually to the political unification of all of Western Europe, perhaps in the form of a United States of Europe. This hope was based on the initial restrictions of sovereignty of the member states that were stipulated in the Common Market treaty and on the authorization in certain instances to take decisions by majority vote, precluding any veto of a member state.

The success of the European Economic Community in the creation of a mass market has been contagious, and attempts have been made in Latin America and Africa to emulate it. For a number of reasons, however, the Latin American Free Trade Area (LAFTA) and the Central American Common Market have not come up to the expectations of their founders. Various endeavors in Africa to create larger trading units have been even less successful.

Despite these extensions of existing nation-states into regional organizations for military and economic reasons, no "region-state" has yet developed. The most promising and advanced unit, the European Common Market, has failed to progress on the path to political unification during the last few years and may in fact have slipped back. General de Gaulle's exaltation of nationalism appears to have killed the fledgling European enthusiasm for a united state. Thus we must recognize that the nation-state persists as the supreme unit in international society and is likely to continue to do so at least within the foreseeable future. The fires of nationalism, which seemed to be banked during the first 15 years after World War II, have been rekindled in Western Europe and continue to burn brightly in other parts of the world as well. Man has not yet accepted a compass of loyalties more extensive than the customary one to his national state, and most governments of nation-states appear to view extensions into regional units more as a buttress of their own sovereignty than as a possible transition into a larger political entity.

The Third World

One of the most difficult problems facing international society is the continuing gap between the economically advanced countries and the underdeveloped countries of the world. The plight of the latter, which prefer to call themselves the "developing" rather than the underdeveloped countries, is basically that they cannot find the capital they need for improving their desperate economic position. With approximately 70 percent of the world's population, their contribution to total world production is only 10 percent. This imbalance has not only economic, but also serious political implications. Most of the developing countries are located in Asia, Africa, and Latin America, and virtually all of the newly independent countries belong to this group. They are frequently referred to as the "Third World." * Eugene Staley, in our selection for this chapter, succinctly describes the economic, social, and political characteristics of the developing areas and identifies the countries that fall into this classification.

THE VIEWPOINT OF UNDERDEVELOPED COUNTRIES

EUGENE STALEY

The economy of every country is "underdeveloped' in the sense that more can be done to build up its productive power and to improve the economic well-being of its people. The term has come to be used, however, to refer—more politely than by the old word "backward"—to those countries which stand very low in relative income. The usage is loose, the distinction between more developed and less developed countries is one of degree, and there is no point in trying to be very precise in the matter. For those who like their concepts as clear as possible, however, I offer the following definition of an underdeveloped country: A country characterized (1) by mass poverty which is chronic and not the result of some temporary misfortune, and (2) by obsolete methods of production and social organization, which means that the poverty is not entirely due to poor natural resources and hence could presumably be lessened by methods already proved in other countries.

Reprinted from Eugene Staley, The Future of Underdeveloped Countries (New York: Harper & Row, Publishers, for the Council on Foreign Relations, 1961), pp. 13–26, by permission of the Council on Foreign Relations, Inc.

---

* This is an ambiguous term inasmuch as it implies that the globe can be divided into Free World, communist, and uncommitted countries. While perhaps most of the developing countries fall in the third category, they also are found in the first two categories. See the listing in our selection by Staley.

Two-Thirds of the World's Population

Table I classifies the countries of the world as highly developed, intermediate, or underdeveloped, mainly on the basis of the best available indices of national income per person. The underdeveloped group includes almost all of the countries of Asia and Africa, most of Latin America, and some of Europe. . . . Countries falling in the intermediate range include seven in Europe, five in Latin America, plus Japan, the U.S.S.R., Israel, and the Union of South Africa. . . . The highly developed group consists entirely of countries in northwest Europe plus the United States, Canada, Australia, and New Zealand, all settled by northwest Europeans. . . . Thus, two-thirds of the world's population of 2,400,000,000 live in underdeveloped countries, a little more than one-sixth in countries of the intermediate range, and a little less than one-sixth in highly developed countries.

Two facts stand out. One is the great disparity in income levels over the world. At one end of the scale are the United States and Canada with national incomes of more than $1,000 per person (in the case of the United States, more than $1,500). At the other end are the under-

COUNTRIES GROUPED BY LEVEL OF ECONOMIC DEVELOPMENT

A. HIGHLY DEVELOPED

Americas	Europe	Oceania
Canada	Belgium	Australia
United States	Denmark	New Zealand
	France	
	Germany	
	Netherlands	
	Norway	
	Sweden	
	Switzerland	
	United Kingdom	

B. INTERMEDIATE

Africa	Americas	Asia	Europe	Eurasia
Union of South Africa	Argentina	Israel	Austria	U.S.S.R.
	Chile	Japan *	Czechoslovakia	
	Cuba		Finland	
	Puerto Rico		Hungary	
	Uruguay		Ireland	
	Venezuela		Italy	
			Poland	
			Portugal	
			Spain	

C. UNDERDEVELOPED

Africa	Americas	Asia	Europe
Algeria	Bolivia	Afghanistan	Albania
Angola	Brazil	Borneo	Bulgaria
Belgian Congo	British West Indies	Burma	Greece
Cameroons	Colombia	Ceylon	Rumania
Egypt	Costa Rica	China	Yugoslavia
Ethiopia	Dominican Republic	Formosa	
French Equatorial	Ecuador	India	
Africa	El Salvador	Indo-China	
French West Africa	Guatemala	Indonesia	
Gold Coast	Haiti	Iran	
Kenya	Honduras	Iraq	
Liberia	Mexico	Jordan	
Libya	Nicaragua	Korea	
Madagascar	Paraguay	Lebanon	
Morocco	Peru	Malaya	
Mozambique		Nepal	
Nigeria		New Guinea	
Northern Rhodesia		Pakistan	
Nyasaland		Philippines	
Ruanda-Urundi		Saudi Arabia	
Sierra Leone		Syria	
Southern Rhodesia		Thailand	
Sudan		Turkey	
Tanganyika		Yemen	
Tunisia			
Uganda			

---

* Japan would now be considered as a "highly developed" country (Eds.).

Sources

For income data: United Nations, *Monthly Bulletin of Statistics,* June, 1952, pp. viii–ix; United Nations, Department of Economic Affairs, *National Income and Its Distribution in Under-Developed Countries* (New York: 1951. XVII.3).

The grouping is based mainly on per capita national income, as of 1950 or thereabouts. In Group A the estimated annual income is $450 per capita or more; in Group B, $150 to $450; in Group C, less than $150. However, degree of urbanization and proportion of the working population engaged in nonagricultural occupations were also taken into account, especially to classify countries for which income data are lacking, but also in a few instances to determine that a country should be in a lower or higher group than the one in which income estimates alone would place it. Germany was placed in Group A, although on the basis of 1950 income alone it would fall in Group B. Japan was placed in Group B, although on the basis of 1950 income alone it would fall in Group C. Venezuela was placed in Group B, although on the basis of 1950 income alone it would fall in Group A.

developed countries, comprising two-thirds of the world's population, where incomes average less than $150 per person. According to the United Nations Statistical Office, half the people of the world live in countries that have per capital incomes of less than $100, some of them much less. Countries with more than $600 annual income per person include only one-tenth of the world's population. The United States alone, with slightly more than six percent of the world's population, accounted for forty percent of the world total of national income in 1950. Europe, with twenty-five percent of the population, generated another forty percent. Although Asia, Africa, and Latin America together have more than sixty-five percent of the world's population, they produced only seventeen percent of the world's national income.[1]

The other outstanding fact is political. While population is obviously not the only or even the main factor in world power and in the relative influence of nations on trends in world civilization, the sheer numbers of people in the underdeveloped countries give them a potential influence that cannot be overlooked. Their ability to make themselves heard in world affairs has already grown enormously in the last few decades. As they acquire more of the tools of modern production, higher levels of education, and more experience in modern management and government—as seems inevitable—it is likely that they will exert more and more influence on issues both of peace and of war. Given their numbers and their growing technological competence, the underdeveloped countries may in fact hold the balance of the future as between the political system and the way of life which have been evolving over several centuries in the West and the modern reversion to tyranny represented by Communism and other totalitarian systems. Whether most of these countries take a democratic or a Communist or other totalitarian path in their development is likely to determine the course of civilization on our planet.

The Revolution of Rising Expectations

The poverty of underdeveloped countries means that their people, on a broad average, have a life expectancy only about half that of the people of the highly developed countries. They suffer much of the time from malaria, dysentery, tuberculosis, trachoma, or other ills. They have the services of less than one-sixth as many doctors in proportion of population. Their food supply is about one-third less, measured in calories, than that of developed countries, and when account is taken of the needs of the human body for the relatively expensive "protective" foods, such as milk and meat, the extent of malnutrition is found to be very great indeed. The opportunity to attend school is limited to a small minority in most underdeveloped countries, even for the lower grades.

---

[1] All figures are for 1950, based on the United Nations *Monthly Bulletin of Statistics,* June, 1952, pp. vii–xi and Table 54.

High school, college, and professional training is even less available. Only one person in four or five, again on a broad average of underdeveloped countries, knows how to read and write. The supply of cloth for clothing, home furnishing, and other purposes is about one-fourth as great per person in underdeveloped as in highly developed countries. Nonhuman energy to supplement the labor of human beings in industry, agriculture, transport, and household tasks is less than one-twentieth as plentiful, measured in horsepower-hours per person. Incomes, on the average, are less than one-tenth as high.

These disparities in living levels between underdeveloped and highly developed countries appear to have been growing wider, rather than narrowing, in recent years. According to the statistical services of the United Nations, the developed countries are not only far ahead but are pulling further ahead. Their rates of economic progress, on the whole, continue to be more rapid than those of the underdeveloped countries.

Poverty and the hunger, disease, and lack of opportunity for self-development that it implies have been the lot of the ordinary people in the underdeveloped countries for centuries past. The new thing is that now this poverty has become a source of active political discontent. Of course, no statement can be unqualifiedly true of underdeveloped countries so diverse in culture, history, and present situation as those of Asia and Latin America, Africa and Southeastern Europe. . . . But, speaking broadly, it is one of the most profoundly important political facts of the mid-twentieth century that among the people of the underdeveloped countries a ferment is at work which has already produced in some, and is bound to produce in others, irresistible demands for a stepped-up pace of economic and social change. The evidence is overwhelming. . . .

Testimony . . . by journalists and university scholars whose business it is to follow political and economic movements in the principal underdeveloped regions is emphatic and impressive. . . . Justice Douglas talked with hundreds of people in the rural areas of the Middle East and found that the complaints of the peasants were specific: The absence of medical care comes first, then absence of schools. Next comes land reform; they have a passion for land ownership. Next is the desire to learn how to farm the modern way. The right to vote, to elect a representative government, to expel and punish corrupt officials are also important claims. Finally, the people of the area have a new sense of nationalism which expresses itself in many ways. "There are professional agitators who stir this brew of discontent; but the rebellious drive comes from the masses. I have not seen a village between the Mediterranean and the Pacific that was not stirring uneasily."

Nearly all of the underdeveloped countries have within the past decade set up official agencies charged with planning and promoting economic development. Many of the plans, especially at first, were little more than dreams on paper, but now there is a noticeable trend toward sober, concrete, feasible projects. All this activity indicates a strong social demand for economic advancement.

The need for economic development, and for international assistance to hasten it, is the constant theme of spokesmen for underdeveloped countries in the economic and social organs of the United Nations and the specialized agencies.

In short, a "revolution of rising expectations," as it has been called, is sweeping the underdeveloped nations of the world. Political leaders who nowadays aspire to popular support in underdeveloped countries (and even modern dictators want popular support) must at least talk in favor of economic modernization. Failure to achieve practical, visible improvement in the lot of the ordinary people is more and more going to provoke unrest and bring political extremists to power.

Why is this happening now, not fifty years ago or fifty years hence? The answer lies chiefly in two factors: (1) the examples set by Western nations, which have proved that general poverty is not inevitable, and (2) the miracles of twentieth-century communication, through movies, the press, radio, and travel, including the travel of armies (for example, the demonstration of the fabulous American living standards by GI's on every continent in World War II). Poverty is old, but the awareness of poverty and the conviction that something can be done about it are new. . . .

It is worth stressing that the social stirrings in underdeveloped countries are basically a reflection of the revolutionary technological and economic progress of the Western world, and in considerable part reflect Western ideals. The Soviet revolution and the work of Communist agitators and organizers, however, are influencing the form which discontent takes. Communists turn the discontent to their own purposes and use it to seize power where they can. But revolutionary economic, social, and political changes would be under way in the underdeveloped countries today had there never been a Moscow or a Communist.

Political and Psychological Motives

It is my conviction that in the United States discussion of the driving forces behind the new demands for economic development generally pays too exclusive attention to desires for more food, clothing, health, and education and neglects the motives that may be labeled political and psychological. These motives are just as strong as desires for improved economic well-being, and in many underdeveloped countries they are even more decisive in their immediate effects on attitudes and government policies.

Factors in the demand for economic modernization in underdeveloped countries, other than the desire to overcome poverty, include:

1. The desire of new, self-conscious nationalisms to attain or preserve independence, and to be free of foreign political or economic dominance, real or imagined.

2. The desire for the means of national defense and security. In some cases there may be an unavowed or latent desire for expansion at the expense of neighbors.

3. The desire for national and personal respect, status, prestige, and importance in the world, which experience shows not to be readily accorded to "backward," weak countries or their citizens.

Of course, state policy in most countries is more concerned today than formerly with economic well-being for the citizens. Even so, considerations like national power for defense or offense and psychological imponderables, such as a respected and important position in the world, have by no means lost their compelling force. An Indian economist, after describing traditional social obstacles which impede economic development, writes that the "most important" factor at work to break through barriers is "the wave of national feeling that is sweeping the backward areas of the world. Nationalism is everywhere associated with a twofold objective. Firstly, to be able to order one's own affairs, and secondly, to attain a position of dignity and importance in the community of nations."

The lesson that a country with backward technology and a poor economy is militarily weak and politically uninfluential has not been lost upon the leaders of today's underdeveloped countries. Many have only recently gained political independence or still aspire to attain it, and one of the strongest compulsions for economic development is the desire to build up economic power as a foundation for independence.

Ambition for a respected status in the world must not be underrated among the driving forces behind economic development programs. Many, perhaps most, of the present-day leaders of underdeveloped countries have known in bitter personal experience the humiliation of "colored" peoples exposed to the arrogance of some members of the white race. In some areas there are resentful memories of the social discrimination that characterized the old colonialism—clubs for the white rulers only, no "natives" allowed—and of other tokens of inferiority and exploitation. These things, which Westerners tend to forget, combine with conditions of appalling human need and the passions of new nationalisms to produce attitudes and demands which would hardly be human if they were always sweetly reasonable. As a Pakistani put it, "We want freedom from contempt."

Prestige is involved in development, as well as living levels, independence, and security. The experience of an international agency in one of the Latin American countries is not uncommon: when the organization's engineers were asked to advise on construction of a steel mill they showed how to design one that would cost about 12 million dollars, but the country's representatives wanted a much larger and more complex one to cost about 80 millions. Prestige, not economic calculation, was the ruling factor. There is a strong feeling, not entirely rational but powerful none the less, which associates export of raw materials and import of manufactured goods with "colonial" status. Sensitive national pride rebels against the thought that raw materials producers are "hewers of wood and drawers of water" for the industrially advanced countries. Here is one of the roots of the demand for industrialization, as distinct from the improvements in the efficiency of agriculture and commerce which in some circumstances may be more immediately helpful in a country's economic development. . . .

Societies in Motion

The new nationalisms of the underdeveloped countries and their passion for equality, respect, and status, like their new awareness of poverty, have some of their roots in the West's own cultural contributions. The ideas and ideals which produced the struggles for parliamentary rule in Britain, the American Declaration of Independence, the liberty, equality, fraternity, and the rights of man of the French Revolution, and the national unifications of Germany and Italy are now at work in new places. Not only mechanical inventions like radio, the airplane, and improved roads are having their impact on underdeveloped countries; so are social inventions like the free public school, universal suffrage, business corporations, trade unions, and social insurance. In lands with different cultural settings and historical backgrounds, where recent relations with the West have been tinged with inferiority and resentment, the effects of these cultural borrowings are not readily predictable.

Also available and being borrowed in some places are social inventions of the Communists, such as new strategy and tactics in revolution, comprehensive five-year plans, and methods of rule by police and propaganda. What the end results will be no one can tell, though we may be sure they will be important not only for the people of these countries but also for us.

The underdeveloped countries are in motion, and economic modernization of some kind, accompanied by drastic social and political changes as well, is on the way in practically all of them, though at different speeds and in a variety of directions. This does not mean that the resistance to change, which has kept some of these countries static for centuries, has entirely disappeared. The inertia of long-established habits and institutions is still a very important fact. So is the open or secret opposition of powerful individuals and groups that fear to lose their present privileged positions. . . . But the impact of the industrial revolution has now become so overwhelming that few of the underdeveloped countries are likely to delay for long their switch to the more feasible response of adaptation.

As a measure of the changed climate of opinion in most underdeveloped countries we may recall that in China only about a century ago the first railway had to be torn up because of popular opposition; people threw their bodies in front of the engine. Conservatives of that day opposed the establishment of schools to teach the youth of China science and technology. Still further back, Emperor Ch'ien Lung had sent the famous message to Britain's King George III: "Our Celestial Empire possesses all things in prolific abundance, and lacks no product within its own borders; there is no need to import the manufactures of outside barbarians." The technical assistance officials of the United States or the United Nations would be much surprised to receive a communication in this tenor from any government today!

It is obvious from Staley's description that the countries of the Third World have great difficulties in solving their problems by their own efforts. They must rely on outside food supplies, at least in years of poor harvests, and on outside advice regarding the means of birth control if they wish to curb the population explosion, so much more extensive and much more serious in the developing countries than in the economically advanced areas of the world. They depend on outside financial and technical help for industrialization, which is indispensable to increase their national incomes and make them less susceptible to the fluctuations of the prices for their agricultural and mineral export commodities on which they presently rely for the bulk of their revenues. Finally, they need infusions of modern technology and proper schooling for their inhabitants in order to provide the underpinnings for a stable political order.

Unfortunately, aid to the Third World is often tied up with political considerations emanating from the global struggle between the Free World and communist forces. Yet aid should be dispensed according to economic need and economic promise and should eventually become a cooperative enterprise in which all economically advanced countries should participate in accordance with their national incomes. Such aid is not a matter of charity, but needs to be regarded as the fulfillment of enlightened economic and political self-interest. Without adequate financial aid and technical assistance, the population explosion in the Third World may well become a political revolution whose dimensions and direction nobody can foresee.

Before leaving the subject of the Third World, it would be useful at this point to look at some recent data and to compare it with Staley's categories. You will notice that many countries have advanced their positions since 1952, for example, Japan and Mexico. Reprinted below is a ranking of countries according to gross national product per capita in dollars.[1]

Rank	Country	GNP Per Capita in $	Rank	Country	GNP Per Capita in $
1	United States	3575	20	Soviet Union	1357
2	Kuwait	3390	21	Austria	1287
3	Sweden	2549	22	East Germany	1260
4	Canada	2473	23	Puerto Rico	1154
5	Iceland	2469	24	Italy	1104
6	Switzerland	2333	25	Hungary	1094
7	Denmark	2120	26	Ireland	980
8	Australia	2002	27	Poland	978
9	New Zealand	1980	28	Venezuela	882
10	Luxembourg	1979	29	Japan	861
11	France	1924	30	Bulgaria	829
12	West Germany	1901	31	Romania	778
13	Norway	1890	32	Argentina	770
14	United Kingdom	1818	33	Cyprus	695
15	Belgium	1804	34	Greece	687
16	Finland	1749	35	Trinidad and Tobago	646
17	Czechoslovakia	1561	36	South Africa	611
18	Netherlands	1554	37	Uruguay	573
19	Israel	1422	38	Chile	565

[1] Sources: United Nations, Statistical Office, *Yearbook of National Account Statistics, 1966* (New York, 1967); United States, Arms Control and Disarmament Agency, Economic Bureau, *World-Wide Defense Expenditures and Selected Economic Data, Calendar Year, 1965;* United States, Arms Control and Disarmament Agency, Economics Bureau, *World Military Expenditures and Related Data, Calendar Year 1966 and Summary Trends, 1962–1967;* International Bank for Reconstruction and Development, *World Bank Atlas;* and *Gross National Product: Growth Rates and Trend Data by Region and Country,* RC-W-138 (Washington, D.C.: U.S. Government Printing Office, 1967); supplemented by *Selected Economic Data for the Less Developed Countries,* W-136 (Washington, D.C.: U.S. Government Printing Office, 1967).

Rank	Country	GNP Per Capita in $	Rank	Country	GNP Per Capita in $
39	Spain	561	87	Bolivia	164
40	Libya	542	88	Philippines	160
41	Malta	502	89	United Arab Republic	159
42	Singapore	500	90	Sierra Leone	154
43	Jamaica	497	91	South Viet Nam	150
44	Panama	485	92	Ceylon	144
45	Mexico	455	93	Cambodia	136
46	Mongolia	453	94	Thailand	129
47	Yugoslavia	451	95	Cameroon	128
48	Lebanon	437	96	Southern Yemen	125
49	Hong Kong	421	97	Mauritania	121
50	Costa Rica	413	98	China	109
51	Portugal	406	99	Pakistan	109
52	Cuba	393	100	South Korea	105
53	Barbados	373	101	India	101
54	Peru	367	102	Sudan	100
55	Albania	366	103	North Viet Nam	100
56	Nicaragua	343	104	Angola	100
57	Guatemala	318	105	Indonesia	99
58	Guyana	306	106	Yemen	98
59	Malaysia	306	107	Togo	95
60	Ghana	285	108	Kenya	90
61	Colombia	282	109	Central African Republic	90
62	Turkey	282	110	Malagasy Republic	90
63	Gabon	281	111	Uganda	87
64	El Salvador	271	112	Laos	87
65	Brazil	267	113	The Gambia	85
66	Dominican Republic	265	114	Nigeria	84
67	Mauritius	262	115	Afghanistan	83
68	Jordan	256	116	Congo—Kinshasa	82
69	Iran	251	117	Niger	75
70	Ivory Coast	251	118	Haiti	74
71	Rhodesia	240	119	Mozambique	74
72	Iraq	231	120	Guinea	73
73	Taiwan	227	121	Nepal	73
74	Saudi Arabia	225	122	Chad	72
75	Algeria	222	123	Tanzania	71
76	Honduras	221	124	Burma	71
77	Paraguay	218	125	Dahomey	70
78	Ecuador	216	126	Mali	65
79	Tunisia	214	127	Botswana	61
80	Zambia	214	128	Somalia	60
81	Syria	212	129	Lesotho	59
82	North Korea	207	130	Upper Volta	53
83	Liberia	199	131	Rwanda	50
84	Morocco	196	132	Malawi	47
85	Senegal	195	133	Ethiopia	45
86	Congo-Brazzaville	164	134	Burundi	44
			135	Papua/New Guinea	38

The Quest for Peace and the Balance of Power

In our international society, characterized by competition and conflict of national interests and devoid of an enforceable legal order, war has been a frequent intruder. Yet, since 1648, when nation-states became the principals of international society, there have also been prolonged periods of peace, which often were the result of a precarious balancing of powers between the various states.

Although all sovereign states could theoretically participate in a balance-of-power system, the balance was maintained in fact by only a few larger states in Europe. Whenever one state made a bid for dominant power, other states tended to join in an alliance which opposed the first state's quest for ascendancy and the challenge to the status quo. As a consequence, the major challenges in Europe by Louis XIV, Napoleon, and the German Kaiser ultimately ended in defeat at the hands of opposing coalitions.

The balance-of-power system attained its greatest success between 1815 and 1914 when the stability of Europe was developed from the Congress of Vienna, in which the main participants were Great Britain, Austria, France, Prussia, and Russia. Wars were mostly localized, were of relatively short duration, and did not spread into general conflagrations. Aware of the benefits of the system, the victors refrained from eliminating any of the major opponents, even if they were capable of annexing the territory of the defeated country. On the other hand, smaller countries were occasionally gobbled up, as the division of Poland—in three stages—between Russia, Prussia, and Austria demonstrates.

The main elements making up the power of a state permitting it to play a role in the balance-of-power system are the size and location of its territory, its economic strength, the size and skills of its population, its political traditions, and last, but obviously not least, its military force. During the nineteenth century, the stability of the system was enhanced by the fact that industrialization and colonial expansion could be undertaken with relative ease and great profitability, and the pursuit of these activities was much more promising in enlarging the power of a country than military subjugation of a neighbor. Moreover, no dramatic changes in technology, such as the invention of nuclear weapons, upset the power relationship of the member states. However, some gradual changes in the system did take place, which eventually created difficulties. Foremost among them was the unification of both Germany and Italy and the aspirations of these countries for a greater role in world affairs.

Following the traumatic experiences of World War I, which some observers thought of as having been caused by the imperfections of the balance-of-power system, mankind searched for a new device to maintain the peace of the world. The answer seemed to be a system of collective security, which simply means that an attack on any one state would be regarded as an attack on all states participating in the collective security system and requires repulsion of the attack by the combined forces of these states. The resort to collective security was based on the assumption that it would do for international society what police action does for the domestic community. The early organization for collective security was the League of Nations, founded in 1919, which was to replace the insecurity of fluctuating national alliances.

The failure of the League to develop an effective peace-keeping machinery caused widespread disillusionment with the concept of collective security. Of course, contributing in no small measure to this failure was the unwillingness of the United States to join the League. In the meantime, the United States and Japan, two non-European powers, had begun to play increasingly important roles on the world scene. As a result, balance-of-power considerations were gradually shifting from the European plane to the global level.

The end of World War II saw a new effort to establish a collective security system in the form of the United Nations. Founded basically on the concept of co-sovereign equality among the member states, the United Nations Charter nevertheless accords veto rights to the five permanent members of the Security Council, the central organ for collective security. As a consequence, collective security action by the United Nations proved to be impossible unless the great powers—the United States, the Soviet Union, Great Britain, France, and the Republic of China—could come to an agreement.

Another reason for the difficulties of the United Nations in its efforts for peace was the emergence of two superpowers at the end of World War II —the United States and the Soviet Union. When the Russians mastered the secrets of the atomic bomb in the late 1940s, the world moved in the direction of a bipolar balance of power. The two main protagonists of the struggle sought to maintain this balance by building up two tightly controlled blocs of military alliances in which NATO was the main device for the free world camp and the Warsaw Pact for the communist camp. What kept the world from sliding into another tragedy of a general conflagration during that time was not the United Nations or collective security, but the "balance of terror." Both parties were fully aware that in a nuclear holocaust nobody would be a victor. To maintain the necessary deterrent to restrain either the Soviet Union or the United States from initiating a first nuclear strike, the other superpower had to have a credible retaliatory counterstrike nuclear force to rain vast destruction on the people and weapons of the initiator of nuclear warfare.

There is much argument about exactly what it takes in the way of "assured destruction capability" in order to deter, but it is generally accepted that only a few hundred warheads exploding over population and industrial centers would be sufficient for the purpose. In fact, a strong "overkill" is likely, especially since in the future all or most missiles will have so-called MIRV (Multiple Independently Targeted Re-entry Vehicles) warheads which can deliver several individually targeted nuclear weapons carried by one missile. To enlarge on these problems, we present as our next selection certain pertinent excerpts from Professor Morton H. Halperin's book, *Defense Strategies for the Seventies.*

THE ROLE OF FORCE IN THE NUCLEAR AGE

MORTON H. HALPERIN

Through the ages, the evolution of technology for warfare has been marked by a search for, as well as a fear of, the absolute weapon, which, depending upon one's point of view, either would enable one state to dominate the world or would force all men to live in peace. Men have thought the crossbow, the machine gun, and the airplane to be such a weapon. The destruction of Hiroshima and Nagasaki led some people to describe the atomic bomb as the absolute weapon, but clearly the atomic bomb was not the ultimate weapon, and the search for it has proceeded to intercontinental missiles and submarine-launched missiles.

We are never likely to devise anything that can accurately be called an absolute weapon, but it is important to understand some of the changes in weapon technology that have followed the development of the atomic and then the hydrogen bomb—namely, changes in the destructive power of weapons and in the ability to deliver them. Unless one understands, at least generally, what changes technology has brought about, one cannot understand how the political problems of using or controlling force have changed.

The destructive power of a weapon should be thought of as a yield to weight ratio—that is, the amount of destruction caused for each pound of explosive material. The base taken for comparing the destructive power of nuclear weapons is the weight of a TNT bomb that would

From Defense Strategies for the Seventies, *Morton H. Halperin, pp. 1–9, 20–24. Copyright © 1971 by Little, Brown and Company (Inc.). Reprinted by permission.*

cause the same amount of destruction as the nuclear weapon. The yield of an atomic bomb is expressed in the equivalent of one thousand pounds of TNT (kilotons) or one million pounds of TNT (megatons); that is, a two-megaton bomb has the equivalent destructive power of two million tons of TNT.

Twice during the nuclear age the destructive power of weapons increased enormously. The first atomic weapons, the so-called fission bombs, had a destructive power a thousand times greater per pound than traditional TNT and other high explosive weapons. The hydrogen or fusion bomb was a thousand times more powerful per pound than fission weapons. Thus, these two revolutions in fire power have produced a millionfold increase in power for a given weight.

Another way to indicate this changed magnitude of destruction is to say that one American bomber now carries more destructive power than that of all weapons used in all wars in human history. The largest bombs of World War II were the equivalent of approximately five tons of TNT, and the Hiroshima bomb was equal to approximately twenty thousand tons of TNT. Currently American nuclear weapons have yields from tenths of a kiloton to one million tons on the warhead of the Minuteman intercontinental missile and several million tons in large intercontinental bombers. Soviet warheads appear to have a similar range; the largest Soviet missile has a five-megaton warhead.

The fantastic increase in the destructive power of weapons has almost been matched by improvements in the ability to deliver these weapons. ICBMs possessed by the Soviet Union and by the United States can reach any point on the globe from any other point within thirty to forty minutes with incredible accuracy. This accuracy is expressed in terms of Circular Error Probability (CEP). The number identified as the CEP is the radius of a circle within which half of the fired weapons land. For example, if four missiles with a CEP of two miles were fired at a target, two of the missiles would land within two miles of the target. American and Soviet missiles appear to have a CEP of considerably less than two miles. Superpowers thus can fire missiles five thousand miles or more and have half of their missiles land within two miles of their target. The effectiveness of ICBMs will be further enhanced by the deployment of Multiple Independently Targeted Re-entry Vehicles. These warheads, known as MIRVs, enable each missile to carry several warheads, each of which can be accurately directed at a different target. The United States began deploying MIRVs in 1970, and the Soviets are believed to be working on MIRVs.

The Soviet Union has deployed a small Anti-Ballistic Missile (ABM) system around Moscow to shoot down incoming missiles and the United States began deploying a small ABM system in 1969. These systems could somewhat reduce the number of missiles that can reach their target, but they would not alter the basic facts; both of the superpowers have thermonuclear weapons a million times more powerful than World War II weapons, and both can deliver these weapons with intercontinental missiles in about thirty minutes. These two general quantitative developments are important for understanding the impact of thermonuclear weapons on international politics.

In the period immediately after World War II these changes in technology were accompanied by a bipolar distribution of power between the United States and the Soviet Union. By the end of the 1960's, bipolarity had somewhat broken down; the substantial nuclear capability of the two superpowers was proving less revelant to the course of events than factors such as the conflict between the Soviet Union and China, the growing economic and political power of West Germany and Japan, and persistent nationalism in developing countries.

The Military Balance

Although analysts have argued about whether military force still has a role to play, governments have feared the results of inadequate military capability. Both the United States and the Soviet Union have spent large sums of money, perhaps exceeding the combined total of $100 billion, to develop nuclear forces and their delivery systems. To assess the role of nuclear weapons, it is important to have some understanding of the nuclear and conventional forces on both sides.

Strategic Nuclear Forces

Through the 1960's the American strategic nuclear force consisted of a large missile force and a moderate number of intercontinental bombers in addition to shorter range, fighter-bomber aircraft and missiles in Europe and perhaps elsewhere. The number of missiles in the American strategic nuclear arsenal has remained constant since the early 1960's and is likely to remain unchanged until at least the late 1970's. The United States has 1,000 Minuteman ICBMs and 54 Titan ICBMs. The Minuteman is a small solid-fueled missile kept in well-protected underground silos. Originally the Minuteman had one one-megaton warhead, but in 1970 the United States began to equip many of its Minutemen with a small number of MIRVs. The Titan is an older, larger liquid-fueled missile; it cannot be fired as quickly nor can it be as well protected as the Minuteman. The United States also has 41 submarines, each equipped with 16 missiles. In the late 1960's the original one-megaton warheads on some of the 656 Polaris missiles were replaced with three Multiple Re-entry Vehicles (MRV), which unlike MIRVs cannot be separately targeted. In 1970 the United States began to install *Poseidon* MIRV missiles in most of its missile-firing submarines. The United States also maintains a fleet of B-52 bombers, which has been gradually declining in numbers since the mid-1960's. In addition to these offensive forces American strategic capability includes an air defense system, and in 1970 the United States began to deploy a limited ABM system.

Soviet nuclear forces grew steadily during the 1960's. As of September 1969 the Soviet Union had surpassed the United States in number of land-based ballistic missiles and was producing *Polaris-type* submarines with 16 missiles each. The Soviets also had about 150 intercontinental bombers and an extensive air defense system as well as the small ABM system centered on Moscow.

Tactical Nuclear Forces

Since the mid-1950's the United States has built up an impressive array of so-called tactical nuclear weapons—that is, nuclear weapons designed to support land forces—in Europe and Asia. The United States has a capability in the form of nuclear weapons from extremely low yields—below that of the largest conventional weapons—to a kiloton and larger weapons for attacking air bases and other large targets. American stockpiles of tactical nuclear weapons in Europe grew steadily during the 1970's to a force of over seven thousand; these weapons are carried by a variety of delivery systems. The Soviets are reported to have a much smaller and less varied arsenal of tactical nuclear weapons consisting mainly of short-range rockets with warheads in the kiloton range. The Soviets also have over seven hundred medium-range missiles targeted against Western Europe.

Conventional Forces

Despite the growth of nuclear power and the increasing sophistication of the arsenals of the two superpowers, the United States and the Soviet Union as well as their allies have maintained large conventional ground forces. These forces might be employed along with tactical nuclear weapons, but they are also able to fight alone. All the major powers spend more than half of their military budget on conventional forces, much of it on salaries. Thus, along with their nuclear capabilities, the superpowers have a very real ability to fight conventionally.

The Effect of Military Power

We can consider the effect of military power on peacetime diplomacy, crises, conventional war, and nuclear war.

Peacetime Diplomacy

The great expense involved in developing large, sophisticated thermonuclear capabilities has been one of the prime reasons for the continuing of bipolarity. Only the United States and the Soviet Union have been able to afford many of these weapons. The United States, for example, spends on defense approximately three times the total United Kingdom budget and six times the British defense budget. Similar, perhaps greater, disparities exist between the Chinese and the American and Soviet budgets. Thus, although France, Great Britain, and China have begun to develop nuclear capabilities, the Soviet Union and the United States are—and are likely to remain for quite a while—the two superpowers.

Thermonuclear weapons have forced the two superpowers to take a new view of their relations. In a classic balance of power situation the two main powers would be in total conflict with each other and would seek support from other countries in an effort to tip the balance. However, particularly in the last several years, the two superpowers have come to see that although many things separate them, they are joined by a common desire to avoid thermonuclear war. This insight has led to pressure for détente in both the United States and the Soviet Union. The search for disarmanent and arms-control agreements has changed in focus and emphasis from the attempt of idealists to create a world of total peace to an attempt by realists to improve the nature of the military balance and to reduce the likelihood of general nuclear war. Thus, in a world situation in which disagreement between the superpowers remains great, a partial test ban treaty and other measures, including the "hot line" agreement linking the United States and the Soviet Union with a high-speed, reliable communication system have been agreed to. The Strategic Arms Limitation Talks (SALT), which began in 1969, are the most dramatic and important manifestation of this trend. The greater emphasis on agreement between the two superpowers, particularly in arms control, must be attributed almost entirely to their destructive potentialities. Former Soviet Premier Nikita Khrushchev said, "The atom bomb recognizes no class differences."

Fear of thermonuclear war has led the superpowers to try to avoid situations of intense international political crisis. Both sides have refrained from pressing political advantages that might upset the military balance and have been extremely cautious in the use of conventional military forces. Thus, the Soviet Union has never employed its conventional capabilities to seize Berlin, and the United States has been restrained in its use of military force against Cuba. Various restraints on both sides have been operative, but fear of setting in motion a chain of events that might lead to general nuclear war has been dominant.

The same pressures have compelled the superpowers to become directly involved in local conflicts throughout the world. The Soviet Union and the United States believe that any conflict might precipitate general nuclear war. There has been a tendency, particularly on the part of the United States, to intervene quickly at the first sign of local conflict in order to isolate the conflict and to halt the fighting before it spreads to general war.

Crises

Caution has marked the approach of the superpowers to crises as well as to peacetime diplomacy. Both sides have sought to contain quickly any spontaneous crisis, such as the Hungarian uprising of 1956 and the Arab-Israeli wars. Even in crises induced by one of the superpowers—for example, the Cuban missile crisis in 1962—both sides have acted in a cautious way designed to reduce the likelihood of general war and to end the conflict as quickly as possible. It is not that the superpowers and their allies have not sought to get political advantage from a crisis, but rather that their willingness to maneuver and to seek advantage has been severely limited by the overall military balance. In fact, the history of postwar crises suggests that the probability of nuclear war has been exaggerated and has tended to dominate the thinking of decision-makers during a crisis. One has only to recall Khrushchev's statements during the Cuban missile crisis about the world being close to thermonuclear war or to read memoirs of American leaders at that time to realize the extent to which top leaders will allow this problem to influence their views. Because of the fear of a general nuclear war and the desire to end the conflict quickly, local conventional military power, which can be brought to bear quickly, has tended to be critical in crises such as those in Hungary and in Cuba.

Conventional War

Thermonuclear weapons have made extremely unlikely another large-scale military conflict of the order of World War I or World War II. Although neither of the superpowers has ruled out such a conflict in developing its military capabilities, neither seems to attach high priority to the probability of such a war. Nor if such a war were to occur, would it be likely to remain conventional and limited. Further, with the improbability of worldwide general war has come an increase in local conventional wars—both international and, more frequently, civil—for example, in Vietnam, Laos, Greece, and Korea. Such wars have all been fought under the shadow of the nuclear deterrent capability of the two superpowers; that is, the actions of the superpowers in these conflicts have been influenced by their belief that local conflicts could explode into general nuclear war. Though this phenomenon has led to the exercise of restraint on the part of the superpowers in the exploitation of success in local conflict, local conventional military forces and local political factors have nevertheless tended to dominate and determine the outcome of any particular military clash. Limited local wars, including guerrilla wars, have been an instrument of international political change and have become to a large extent the ultimate arbitrator of political conflict because nobody wants to use the real "ultimate" weapons—the nuclear weapons.

Nuclear War

The United States and the Soviet Union have been willing to allow conventional and local political factors to determine the outcome of much conflict in the postwar period precisely because this conflict does not threaten their vital interests. However, it is clear that nuclear weapons would remain the final arbiter when and if their vital interests were challenged. The major powers compete with each other in nonmilitary ways and in the use of conventional military force but with no hope of total military victory. We must try to live in peaceful coexistence with potential adversaries because we live in a world in which war cannot be abolished because there is no other means to settle issues that men feel are worth fighting for. But war—at least general nuclear war—can lead only to such complete destruction that, in the final analysis, the war will not have been worth fighting. This paradox provides the challenge and the setting for consideration of the role of military strategy in the nuclear age. . . .

General Nuclear War

Five alternative strategies for deterring or fighting a general nuclear war can be identified. Two of these strategies, *minimum deterrence* and *credible first strike,* have advocates outside the government but have never been seriously considered by the American government. The other three strategies are variations of the strategy of *assured destruction,* which has formed the basis of American policy during the postwar period.

When a country employs a strategy of minimum deterrence, it uses a relatively small strategic force to attack enemy population centers in order to convince the enemy that it will only use the force in retaliation for an enemy first strike. The strategic forces are used, if at all, in a second strike; little concern is given to the actual fighting of a general nuclear war.

The strategy of a credible first strike calls for the development of a large strategic offensive force—two or three times more than that called for by an assured destruction strategy—capable of destroying most of the enemy's strategic forces. It also requires a large ABM system designed to shoot down enemy missiles that survive a first strike. By using the strategy of a credible first strike, a country would convey to its enemy that here is a significant probability that a first strike will be launched in the event of various kinds of provocation. In the event of war, this strategy prescribes a large first strike directed at all the enemy's strategic forces.

Assured deterrence strategies rest on the basic assumption that what is necessary to deter a nuclear war is the ability without question to destroy the enemy society after receiving an all-out attack. The variations in the strategy depend on two questions of capability: (1) how much force is necessary to deter and (2) whether some additional capability to seek to limit damage in the event of war should be purchased. The effort in employing this strategy is to convince the potential enemy that one is not threatening his deterrent by developing a first strike capability and that in the event of nuclear war both countries will be destroyed. In the event of war an effort would be made to use nuclear forces in a controlled way but with little expectation that a nuclear war could be limited.

These alternatives raise a number of specific issues, which can be considered in terms of capability, communication, and action.

A major issue of American defense policy in the postwar period has been how much of a strategic force is enough. Or, as the critics of current policy put it: How much "overkill" do we need? The answer to this question depends on a judgment about how much is necessary to deter an attack and whether nuclear forces should be brought for other purposes—for example, to try to limit damage in the event of war. Some analysts have suggested that a small strategic force, perhaps one hundred intercontinental missiles, is sufficient: at the other extreme, some have argued that the United States should produce as many strategic forces as it can. The decisions in between are much more complicated. Most analysts now accept that Soviet forces are so large that it is not feasible for the United States to prevent the Soviet Union from inflicting massive damage on American cities in the event of nuclear war. Thus the recent debate has largely centered on how much is enough to deter.

Just as important as the quantity of the strategic forces is the quality of those forces: their accuracy and their ability to survive an enemy attack, to penetrate enemy defenses, and to be used in controlled and sophisticated ways. During the 1960's the United States—and apparently to some extent the Soviet Union—spent large sums of money improving the quality of strategic forces, in particular, command and control systems and the ability to use the force.

American communication policy about general nuclear war has been ambiguous throughout the postwar period. On the one hand, American officials emphasize the traditional American reluctance to begin a general nuclear war and state that the United States would never be the "aggressor." On the other hand, it is clear that American policy for the defense of Europe includes the threat to launch a nuclear attack on the Soviet Union in response to a Soviet attack in Europe.

A second major issue in communications has been what sort of attack the United States should threaten to launch. Should the United States indicate that it will bomb cities as well as strategic forces? The United States has stated that it might not strike Soviet cities, particularly if the Soviet Union refrained from attacking American cities. Soviet statements, on the other hand, have implied that cities as well as strategic forces would be struck in the event of a nuclear war.

Deterrence of a deliberate attack would appear to be strengthened by emphasis on the hair-trigger nature of, or loosely controlled, strategic forces, because if strategic forces are only loosely controlled, they can more readily react to early signs of an enemy attack and consequently, are less likely to be destroyed. On the contrary, however, American communication policy has stressed that American strategic forces are under tight command and control, would not be used in provocative ways, and would not be launched until after a number of Soviet missiles had exploded in the United States.

Since the development of an American atomic arsenal, military planners have produced plans for the employment of nuclear weapons, should they be ordered into use by the President. There has been considerable reluctance in the United States and elsewhere to think about what would occur in the event of general nuclear war.

A major question, which now appears to have been answered, is whether the United States should contemplate preemptive nuclear war. American leaders apparently have enough confidence in the ability of

United States strategic forces to survive a Soviet first strike that they are determined to be sure that the strike has occurred, by waiting for a significant number of missiles to hit the United States, before launching American forces. In this way American forces would not be triggered by "geese on the radar screen," the accidental firing of a few Soviet missiles, or an attempt by a local Soviet commander or a third country to simulate an all-out Soviet attack. Although the United States has retained the option of striking first in response to massive Soviet aggression in Europe, it has emphasized the desire not to be faced by this dilemma by increasing its own ability to respond to Soviet aggression in kind or at levels below a general nuclear strike.

Perhaps the most significant question that would face the United States in the event of a nuclear war would be how large a strike to employ. If American action were in response to a Soviet strike, the magnitude of the strike would very likely be influenced by the nature of the Soviet attack. At one extreme, the United States might launch all its strategic forces against military targets and population centers in the Soviet Union. At the other extreme, it would launch a limited strike against a few targets in the Soviet Union, withholding the great bulk of its force to threaten city destruction. In the 1950's American strategy seemed to call for the destruction of Soviet cities as quickly as possible in the event of war. From this perspective one talked about the "bonus damage" received from attacking strategic targets: the United States would get added value from an attack in which a weapon that struck an airbase would through its fallout or blast kill a large number of civilians, for destruction in the Soviet Union would be increased. Another approach to city damage is essentially to ignore it—that is, to launch strategic forces against Soviet military installations without reference to whether this brings on large-scale civilian destruction—neither desiring civilian destruction nor taking any steps to avoid it. A third approach suggests launching a sizable attack against strategic forces but avoiding city damage.

The withholding of strategic forces that could be used in city destruction rests on the belief that deterrence can continue even after general nuclear war begins. It is assumed that there will be communication, perhaps on the so-called hot line between Moscow and Washington, and also that both sides will communicate by the way in which they use their strategic forces. Because we need to communicate only if we want to negotiate an end to the war, communication would suggest willingness to stop the war short of the all-out use of strategic forces, combined with a threat to attack cities if the war continues. The problem of how to terminate a general nuclear war is one that has been given little attention in the United States. . . .

The SALT talks to which Professor Halperin has referred in the preceding selection have been concluded with an initial agreement in May 1972. It limits ABMs to very low levels, including a commitment not to build a nationwide ABM defense which would upset the maintenance of mutual deterrence. Agreement was also reached to stabilize the level of strategic offensive weapons, giving both sides an opportunity to proceed to a second stage of negotiations for further limitations and controls.

Toward the end of the 1950s the tight control of the two superpowers over their blocs began to loosen. Some of the West European states, their economies restored and imbued with a new spirit of independence, became reluctant to follow the demands of American policy. In the communist camp, an ideological and strategic struggle between the Soviet Union and Communist China broke out that created an increasingly wider rift between the two chief communist powers. At the same time, the East European satellites began to show signs of independent national aspirations, which slowly began to reduce the tight control that the Soviet Union had initially exercised over these countries. In addition, the two superpowers lost their nuclear monopoly. Britain, France, and Communist China were able to become members of the nuclear club, with other countries also approaching the threshold. Instead of a strictly bipolar world, a number of power centers are beginning to emerge in international society. These centers of power, which include not only blocs but also single states, play an increasingly important role in the international arena, and new balance-of-power systems may be in the making. The establishment of friendly relations with the People's Republic of China has given the United States increased feasibility in dealing with both China and the Soviet Union and has created a triangular relationship susceptible to balance-of-power diplomacy. The government of each of the three countries may throw its support to the government of one of the other two countries in the pursuit of its national interests or to balance the dominant position of another country in the triangle. If one takes into account the emergence of the European Community of Nine and Japan as major independent economic and political powers, a five-cornered balance-of-power system could be visualized that might play a key role in the maintenance of international peace. In any case, the nature of international society that seems to be developing can thus best be labeled polycentric, but the full implications of this system for the future are still obscure at this time. While deterrence continues to keep nuclear danger at bay, the spread of nuclear weapons to more and more countries portends serious hazards. Although the concept of balance of power may still be relevant in the emerging polycentric world, the clear and continually present danger of a nuclear debacle makes it more and more imperative that the United Nations be made into a more effective instrument for achieving the peace and well-being of the world.

New Forces in the International Society

During the last 25 years new influential forces have entered the international arena which are either nongovernmental entities or flow from technological advances and environmental concerns. Among the nongovernmental entities the multinational corporation or enterprise (MNE) has created the greatest impact on world politics. This should not be surprising when one considers that corporations such as General Motors (GM), IBM, Standard Oil of New Jersey, or Philips of Holland possess much greater material resources than many nation-states, which enables them under certain conditions to exert more powerful influences in the international sphere than the governments of many middle-sized and small states. A striking example is General Motors, which in 1970 on a worldwide basis produced goods and furnished services amounting to nearly $19 billion and which employed globally approximately 700,000 people. While it is not possible to compare the General Motors figure for goods and services produced with the gross national product (GNP) of nation-states because the former includes double counting of intermediate goods bought from other firms and the latter includes investment expenditure on new machines and construction, it is interesting to point out that Switzerland's GNP is almost $2 billion less than the goods and services furnished by General Motors. If one equates GM's 700,000 employees with the total civil service, national and local, of a state, General Motors compares favorably with New Zealand. Looking beyond the giantism of GM, one finds that in 1970, 197 American and European multinational corporations each produced goods and provided services amounting to over $1 billion while more than half of the 140-odd countries of the world had a GNP below that figure. To give further insights into the activities of MNEs and their impact on the international society, short excerpts from Professor Werner J. Feld's book, *Nongovernmental Forces and World Politics,* constitute our next reading selection.

MULTINATIONAL BUSINESS ENTERPRISES:
Transnational Initiatives

WERNER J. FELD

. . . The rise of the MNE [Multinational Enterprises] and its world-wide expansion have indeed been spectacular. The dynamic nature of the MNE is dramatically demonstrated by the claims of some authors, though contested by others, that goods currently produced under international investments amount to over $400 billion. In 1968, half of this amount (about $200 billion) had been produced by foreign subsidiaries of American MNEs, an impressive figure when compared with United States export sales of only $34.6 billion that year and a GNP of $360 billion for the whole EEC area. American industry abroad had thus become the third largest economy in the world, outranked only by those of the domestic United States and the Soviet Union. Since over the last two decades foreign investments of MNEs and the resulting output of goods have been growing approximately twice as fast as world GNP, the world economy could well be more than half internationalized by the end of the century provided that these rates are maintained. It has been estimated by some observers that by as early as 1980, 75 percent of the world's production capacity will be controlled by a small group of 300 multinational corporations. In turn, these 300 corporations might employ as much as 20 percent of the labor force on this planet. Although other students of the MNE seem to consider these assertions as exaggerated, Howard V. Perlmutter advances several reasons which make such a development very plausible. Among these reasons are the ability of giant firms such as Unilever, IBM, Nestlé, Standard Oil of New Jersey, or Philips to obtain capital from anywhere in the world if they need it, although many of these giants not only generate sufficient revenue to be self-financing, but on occasion lend money to banks. Moreover these large MNEs have developed world-wide production and distribu-

From Werner J. Feld, Nongovernmental Forces and World Politics: A Study of Business, Labor, and Political Groups *(New York: Praeger Publishers, 1972), pp. 21–22, 37–38, by permission of the author and the publisher.*

tion systems which make it possible to launch new products anywhere in the world and reach several billion customers all over the globe. They have the financial resources to undertake research and development activities necessary to make and exploit breakthroughs in science and technology. They can diversify their risks by global investment patterns reducing their vulnerability to the economic and political cycles of a given state and to takeovers or acquisition moves by other companies. . . .

Transnational Aspects of Foreign Investments

International investments are potentially powerful agents of economic, social, and political change regardless of whether they are made in developed or developing, Free World or Communist, countries. Their manifold effects on states, IGOs [Intergovernmental Organizations], and indirectly on the international system can offer advantages or create conflicts as the following examples illustrate. The investments influence the balance of payments of the countries involved, may lead to the control of strategic industries often considered undesirable by national governments of the host countries, may add to the export totals of the countries in which new factories are built, and provide investing corporations with bargaining leverage regarding prospective host country laws and regulations, particularly if the infusion of capital can be shifted to a neighboring country without impunity as is possible in a customs union or free trade area. Moreover, they may affect domestic politics because wage scales and working conditions are likely to be improved in the countries where investments are made and perhaps job opportunities impaired in the countries where the parent company is located. Also, bidding up labor costs may cause inflation and borrowing of multinational companies in countries with weak currencies may tend to weaken these currencies further. Finally, investments abroad may reduce the control over the corporation that can be exercised by the parent government and thus give management greater operational latitude such as circumventing export embargoes through shipment from foreign subsidiaries. At the same time, a multinational corporation may appeal to its parent government to intervene through diplomatic channels or even stronger means in order to obtain protection against unfriendly action by host governments. But international investments may also supplement the foreign policy goals of the parent government through helping developing countries to achieve a higher economic level and thereby attain greater political stability, or promoting national security by ensuring the flow of needed raw materials. . . .

The forces of change in international society stemming from technological advances are primarily (1) the need to develop large-scale generation of power to meet the expanding requirements of industrial and domestic users, (2) the growth of telecommunications by means of global satellites ringing the world, (3) the increased ability to exploit the hitherto untapped marine resources of the earth, and (4) the refinement of weather prediction and the expanded capability of climate modification. We should note that the cost of developing these new technological areas is enormous and only giant industrial nation-states or combinations of these states will be able to afford to do so. To explore briefly the significance of these developments for international society is the purpose of our next reading, which consists of an article written by Professor Victor Basiuk.

THE IMPACT OF TECHNOLOGY
IN THE NEXT DECADES

VICTOR BASIUK

. . . Historically, technology has always played a major role in creating new resources or helping to exploit the traditional ones, but in most instances it tended to be tied down to its physical resource base. Major industrial centers were built around coal-iron ore complexes, such as those in the Durham-Cleveland, Great Lakes-Pennsylvania, Ruhr, and Krivoi Rog-Donbas regions. The development of railroads was fairly closely tied to the availability of resources—either mineral or agricultural —on the land the railroads crossed. Electricity made water power a significant source of energy, but hydroelectric stations and the economic

From Victor Basiuk, "The Impact of Technology in the Next Decades," Orbis, Spring 1970, pp. 17–42, by permission of the author and the publisher. (This article is based in part on research sponsored by the U.S. Arms Control and Disarmament Agency under contract with the Institute of War and Peace Studies, Columbia University, and in part on research sponsored by the Institute for the Study of Science in Human Affairs, Columbia University. The judgments expressed are those of the author and do not necessarily reflect the views of the U.S. Arms Control and Disarmament Agency or any other agency of the U.S. government.)

activity stimulated by them were narrowly confined to rivers and their vicinity.

What is noteworthy today is the decline in importance of the location of raw materials and sources of energy as a determining factor in economic development and the rise of new power centers. No single invention was responsible for this decline, but the most significant technologies initially responsible were chemistry and transportation. By combining and recombining elements and thus converting them into more useful products, chemistry undertook to make "resources" out of the most ubiquitous materials, such as air, water and sand. Substitution of raw materials became relatively easy and prevalent; e.g., if natural rubber was not locally available, snythetic rubber could be produced from coal, oil or foodstuffs.

Technological advance in transportation, resulting in the reduction of costs, greatly increased the mobility of raw materials. Perhaps the most striking example in this respect is the post-World War II development of the steel industry in Japan, which by 1964 had become the third largest in the world (after the United States and the Soviet Union). In 1965, Japan imported 88 percent of her iron ore and 64 percent of her coking coal at an average distance of 5,500 miles. The magnitude of Japan's achievement (aided, besides transportation, by other technological improvements) was driven home in April 1969 when the merger of the two largest Japanese steel companies generated serious concern on the part of both American and European steel manufacturers about their ability to compete with the Japanese. It has been estimated that if the two companies, Yawata Iron and Steel and Fuji Iron and Steel, merge and continue to grow at their present rate, they will overtake United States Steel by the middle 1970's, thus becoming the largest steel company in the world.

In brief, the availability of superior technology—and not the location of raw materials or sources of energy—has become the principal factor in the emergence of new industrial centers and the economic viability of nations and regions. The extent of this trend is illustrated by the nuclear agro-industrial centers which have been proposed for the 1970's.[1] These centers, located on the coast of a water-deficient area,

---

[1] See Oak Ridge National Laboratory, *Nuclear Energy Centers-Industrial and Agro-Industrial Complexes; Summary Report* (Oak Ridge, Tenn., July 1968). *The concept* was developed at Oak Ridge and the feasibility study undertaken produced encouraging and economically attractive results. The Indian government was sufficiently interested to participate in the Oak Ridge study. At present, Oak Ridge National Laboratory is conducting a detailed study of uses for large energy centers in the Middle East, and a study has been undertaken for a large energy center for Puerto Rico. See also Edward A. Mason, "Nuclear Reactors: Transforming Economics as Well as Energy," *Technology Review*, March 1969, pp. 32–33.

would combine desalinization of water for irrigation purposes with large-scale production of those chemicals, fertilizers and metals which require cheap and abundant electricity. Seawater and air would provide the raw material for such chemicals as hydrochloric and nitric acids and ammonia, while other raw materials (e.g., bauxite and phosphorus) would be imported. These centers would offer many millions of people new sources of food and employment. . . .

The Integrative Effect of Technology

With the freeing of technology from a resource base has come a different trend: the integrative effect of technology on society and the integrative process within technology itself. Many loose statements have been made in this connection: e.g., progress in transportation and tele-communications has "shrunk" the world; the peoples of the world or a given region have become inter-dependent. In fact, the integrative influence of technology is a highly complex and multifaceted phenomenon that has not been fully understood and probably will not be for some time. It operates on different levels, and its impact on society frequently runs at cross currents.

One level is the integration of human activity and spatial units into one global geo-technical system. The advanced industrial societies are highly interrelated, technologically and politically. The three remaining areas which, have not been fully—or at all—integrated into the global system are the underdeveloped regions, the scarcely inhabited regions (the Amazon, the Arctic), and the ocean floor. Technological developments in the next decade or so will contribute significantly toward the integration of these areas.

Thanks largely to satellites, costs of telecommunications are rapidly decreasing; by 1980 it may be possible to telephone anywhere in the world for one dollar during off-business hours. The drop in telecommunications costs will be a major factor in the process of integrating the less developed countries internally and with the world system. A satellite-based television network for less developed nations as large as India could be developed, built, and made operational in about four years. To construct a comparable terrestrial network would take perhaps as long as two or three decades and the cost would be about twice as great. Provided the government of the receiving state cooperates, such a network would make possible direct transmission of programs from an advanced nation into community receivers of the less developed countries. If the presently available receivers are appropriately augmented (at a cost of at least $40 each), a global television network, involving direct transmission through satellites into home receivers, could be operational by the late 1970's. . . .

The nuclear agro-industrial complexes described above will contribute to the integration of arid and hitherto sparsely inhabited areas. Even now, conventional means of desalinization of water combined with controlled-environment greenhouses of air-inflated plastic are beginning to be used successfully to convert deserts into economically productive areas. The techniques for controlling rainfall will improve significantly by 1989, thus helping to increase geographic areas capable of sustaining agricultural productivity and possibly to expand the areas of human habitat in general. It appears that by diverting the flow of ocean currents, large-scale changes in climate are economically feasible even at the present cost of energy. As the cost of energy declines projects designed to implement such changes will become increasingly more attractive; eventually, they may lead to freeing huge areas of permafrost for agriculture and other economic activity and improve the means for converting present deserts into productive regions.

The use of the earth resource survey satellites, to be introduced in the early 1970's, is expected to facilitate the discovery of mineral resources, thus generating economic activity in geographic regions hitherto not considered to be economically attractive and perhaps not even habitable.

Exploitation of oil and gas from the sea bed has advanced rapidly in recent years; the present gross annual revenue of the U.S. offshore oil industry exceeds $9 billion. Human underwater missions of long duration at a depth of 600 to 1,000 feet are expected to take place in the near future. It has been predicted that commercial capability for extensive and prolonged engineering operations on continental slopes as deep as 3,000 feet will take place by 1980, while commercial deployment of vehicles and machines at 6,000 feet and beyond is expected sometime in 1980–1990. . . .

Last but not least, integration proceeds within science and technology itself. The combination of computers, satellites, atmospheric sciences and oceanography opens up broad vistas for weather prediction and modification. Transplantation of body organs and their increasing substitution of synthetic items—which is revolutionizing medicine—represents the meeting of medicine, mechanics and chemistry. The combination of electronics and chemistry, electronics and physics, biological sciences and chemistry are further examples of the growing trend. It appears that the synergistic effect resulting from the meeting and integrating of two or more sciences and technologies produces the most rapid progress. . . .

The integrative trend of technology creates an appreciable measure of global, regional and local interdependence, but it does not necessarily create unity. Indeed, in a number of its forms this trend can create or exacerbate conflict. A growing settlement and integration of Northern

China and Eastern Siberia may increase rather than diminish conflict between the USSR and China, and the better integrated instruments of military force are likely to intensify a clash. There is no conflict for the sea bed in the deep ocean areas at this time, but such a conflict looms as a definite possibility in the future as the ocean floor begins to be integrated into global activity. . . .

Global Projection of Influence Through Technology

The integrative impetus of technology is accompanied by the increasingly versatile, global projection of national influence and power through technology. In the nineteenth century this phenomenon was manifested by Great Britain's global projection of power, first through the Royal Navy and later through telecommunications (cable and radio). In the post-World War II period, the United States eclipsed all other powers by a wide margin in the magnitude of its global projection and the multiplicity of its instruments. After the massive display of U.S. military power in both Europe and Asia during World War II the United States made an effort to withdraw, but was compelled to stay. The forms of its military power grew in variety and size—from bombers to ICBM's and Polaris IRBM's trained on various targets in Eurasia. Global military operations have been improved—and are continuously improving—through nuclear propulsion in naval vessels, better communications systems, more effective logistics support, worldwide surveillance through satellites and other means, and long-range airlift.

On the nonmilitary level, the Voice of America provides another form of projection of global influence. Physically, the recent lunar landings were aimed at the moon, but politically they were aimed at Earth. Foreign aid is, in part, a means of extending America's influence through more advanced technology into the less developed world. The multinational corporation—primarily a subsidiary of the technologically and managerially superior American companies—is a projection mainly into industrialized nations.

The Kremlin imitated the American global strategic nuclear projection, and now the Soviets are expanding their global capability in subnuclear military technology. The Soviet Union is roughly equal to the United States in global extension of its influence through outer space technology (but not communications satellites), broadcasting and oceanology. In other respects, its efforts at projecting Soviet power are less significant than those of the United States.

In comparison with the United States and the Soviet Union, Western Europe has not scored conspicuously in the global projection of its power and influence. In the first place, Western Europe lacks the unified political will required for such an undertaking. . . . Europe participates in Intelsat, the Europeans have an outer space program of their own, and Great Britain and France have a nuclear striking capability; but, on the whole, the present capability of Western Europe to project its power and influence globally is small when compared with U.S. and Soviet capabilities. . . .

The Rapidity of Technological Change

The continuously accelerating growth of technological innovation and change constitutes another major trend. Over half of the products manufactured by American industry today did not exist twenty years ago. Only ten years ago it used to take from five to seven years for a chemical product to advance from the laboratory to the production stage; the process has now been shortened to from one to three years. When the Communications Satellite Corporation was established, it was viewed as an investment in a technology several years away; its operational capability and earnings potential proved to be much faster and greater than originally anticipated. Only a year ago it was expected that commercial use of controlled thermonuclear reaction would be available sometime after the year 2000; now nuclear scientists are thinking in terms of an operational prototype reactor in the late 1970's. . . .

Implications for American Policy

Technology of the future will bring both great benefits and serious perils to society. The problem is to *control* it and its impact; the alternative is to be controlled by it. Control of technology requires a systematic effort by society to maximize its benefits and minimize its harmful effects in the context of social goals and purposes. As a corollary, it also requires analytical insights into the nature of the technological impact and the existence of appropriate institutions capable of generating and implementing the needed policies.

Since the dimensions of the technological impact range from local to global, in the last analysis its control can be effective only if it is undertaken on a worldwide scale. The political organization of the contemporary world does not permit effective control on such a scale at present. This suggests at least two criteria for American policy. (1) It is important that the United States be earnest and persistent in its efforts to subject technology and its impact to control in cooperation with other nations. (2) It is even more important that we as a society concentrate on improving our own capability in this regard. There can be little hope of being able to control technology globally if we are incapable of providing the requisite instruments of control within our own nation. . . .

In the past the United States had adequate resources to develop and take full advantage of practically the entire spectrum of potentially available technology. Because of the rapid proliferation of sciences and technologies and their initially high costs, the United States in the future will have the resources to develop and effectively utilize only a part of the spectrum. This will require a careful selection of priorities. In the postwar decades, priorities for the federally-supported development of science and technology were primarily determined by competition from the Soviet Union (nuclear-missile and outer space technologies) and by the interplay of various constituencies, inside and outside the U.S. government, competing for resources in support of their interest in particular development (e.g., nuclear energy, marine science and technologies). A more rational and comprehensive approach to the determination of priorities in science and technology, which would consider the interests of the nation as a whole and anticipate the future, is needed.

A new look at nonmilitary technology, from the point of view of both control of its impact and priorities for support, might be in order. This is the technology which is not only growing in importance for national security, but is and will remain the principal instrument for increasing the nation's productivity and hence its ability to solve the multiple internal social and environmental problems contingent on the availability of resources. . . .

Last, there is a need for a clearer understanding of how technological development can serve as a functional instrument of foreign policy and how to apply it wisely. In particular, the direct and indirect impact of technology as an independent variable on the future world order deserves close examination. The next step would be the formulation of a conscious policy, involving the use of technological instruments, to steer the development of the world order in a desirable direction.

The advances in technology suggested by the preceding selection imply the continuation and perhaps acceleration of economic growth at least in the industrially advanced countries and the need to curb the harmful effects which the progression of technology and economic growth may have on the environment. Worldwide concern over these problems led a group of scientists and intellectuals in North and South America as well as Europe to search for ways to avert a breakdown of society that was felt to be intrinsic in the uncontrolled growth of technology, population, and industrial output. A study made in 1972 by M.I.T. entitled "The Limits of Growth" and based on computer simulation warned that mankind probably faces uncontrollable and disastrous collapse of its society within 100 years unless it moves speedily to establish global equilibrium in which growth of population and industrial output are halted. The study contends slowing of growth constitutes the primary task facing humanity and will demand international cooperation on a scale and scope without precedent. Unless the warning is heeded, it is argued that the world's natural resources would be largely exhausted by 2100 and pollution would become intolerable.

Many economists doubt that given human motivation and diversity a no-growth world is possible. Moreover, it would lock in the people in the developing countries at roughly their present standards of living, which would be politically indefensible. The opponents of the M.I.T. study also argue that the known resources of nonrenewable raw materials have been underestimated and the record since World War II indicates that in many instances the discovery rate of known reserves has increased faster than the rate of consumption. Moreover, the way in which new technology can increase available reserves—for example, the extraction of manganese from the sea, of sulphur from salt domes, or quantities of metals from previously dumped materials (recycling)—seem to have been ignored. On the issue of pollution the opponents claim that advanced industrial societies can choose to spend extra money on pollution control and that, while pollution is an acknowledged danger, pollution build-up and world collapse are not necessarily inevitable with continued economic growth.

Whatever the outcome of the debate between the advocates of a no-growth world and a growth economy, it is obvious that changes in technology, the exhaustion of raw materials, and the problems of pollution have worldwide implications. They affect the economies and politics of advanced and developing countries alike and the question of whether the cost of pollution control should be paid from the private resources of the polluters or from public funds has ramifications bearing on competition in international trade. For these reasons it is not surprising that demands have been advanced to subject these problems and perhaps also the activities of multinational corporations to regulation by international organizations. Indeed, the United Nations took an initial step in this direction by organizing in Stockholm in the summer of 1972 the *first* United Nations Conference on the Human Environment. Our next reading focuses on politics associated with this conference by presenting relevant excerpts from an evaluation by Dr. Jon McLin.

STOCKHOLM:
The Politics of "Only One Earth"

JON McLIN

. . . . As planned, the Conference adopted three sets of decisions: (1) a group of recommendations to governments and international organizations, collectively constituting the Action Plan; (2) recommended arrangements for a set of institutions and a fund which will provide a focus for future environmental action on a global scale; and (3) a Declaration on the Human Environment, embodying a set of principles intended to form a basic corpus of international environmental law and to stimulate further concrete action. That these measures resemble so closely in form and in substance the proposals submitted to the Conference by the Secretariat—and that they were taken on schedule within twelve days—is a tremendous tribute to the quality of the preparatory work that had been done under the leadership of [Conference Secretary General] Maurice Strong and his staff.

It does not follow that the Conference was a hollow, rubber-stamping affair or that its outcome was foreordained or without suspense. On the contrary, it was marked by a political debate which, though not always of high quality, was about genuine and important global issues: the fixing of responsibility for environmental conservation; and the *distribution*, as well as the preservation, of the planet's limited amenities. Hard, constructive, and imaginative work by several national delegations as well as Secretariat members was necessary to keep the agenda from getting bogged down in extraneous political questions or in the national-ego or personal-ego problems of delegates from 110 countries. . . .

The absence of the Soviet Union and most of its allies, though ritually regretted by all, probably made the work of the Conference easier; and it is reasonable to hope that they may nonetheless not be alienated from future United Nations environmental activities.

From Jon McLin, Stockholm: The Politics of "Only One Earth" *[JM–4–'72] Fieldstaff Reports, West Europe Series, Vol. VII, No. 4, 1972.*

The most striking feature of the committee work which ground out the 106 recommendations comprising the Action Plan was the large measure of support which the original proposals enjoyed. It was evident that the Preparatory Committee and the Secretariat had done their work well. Debates were largely concerned with slight changes in the language of the proposed recommendations. Motives varied: strengthen the wording; weaken it; take account of some national peculiarity which the original form overlooked; take account of some domestic political problem of the delegation proposing the amendment; or simply render the language more logical or felicitous. Major amendments usually took the form of additions, rather than deletions; very few of the recommendations originally proposed did not survive in some form, while several new ones were added. . . .

The failure of the much-heralded polarization between industrialized and less developed countries (LDCs) to materialize, at least with the sharpness that had been expected, is one manifestation of governments' converging positions. The developed countries were not disposed to challenge the view that the symptoms of underdevelopment may be considered among the gravest problems of the human environment, though they were reluctant to open their purses further in order to allow the LDCs to pursue both sets of goals. The LDCs were somewhat more hesitant to acknowledge the other point of view. They stressed their fears that anti-pollution standards adopted by the industrialized countries might restrict their exports; or that increased recycling might diminish their sales of raw materials; or that inappropriate pollution control technology might be conveyed to them. . . .

The principle of national sovereignty, the right of a nation to exploit its natural resources as its government sees fit, was obsessively asserted by Brazil, among others. Yet these stances were by and large tough positions taken in defense of concrete interests, and as such they were combatable with constructive deliberation. There was no attempt by Brazil to wreck the Conference, as had been feared, and if that was China's goal (see below) which is not certain, then it failed to reach it. As for massive and continuing confrontations between rich and poor countries, both groups were too divided internally for that danger to materialize; coalitions shifted from issue to issue. Interests—and voting patterns—diverged for example between states with long coastlines and those with large merchant marines; between oil-producing states and the other LDCs; between producers of oil with low sulfur content and those with high content.

The content of the measures adopted by the Conference may best be discussed by considering separately the three groups of decisions already referred to.

The Action Plan

The recommendations comprising the Action Plan were considered and drafted within the framework of five subject areas:

1. *Planning and management of human settlements for environmental quality.* In a subject area which, because of its vastness, scarcely lent itself to dramatic action by the Conference, the stress was laid on urban problems of developing countries. The 19 recommendations adopted in this area are quite varied. . . .

One very mildly worded recommendation deals with the principle that was a sticking point in the drafting of the Declaration (see below), namely the responsibility of states to consult their neighbors about environmental actions which could affect them. A new recommendation was added (with only Sudan opposed and six countries, including the United States, abstaining) calling for an investigation of the feasibility of international standards for measuring and limiting noise emissions from motor vehicles and certain kinds of working equipment. . . . Other recommendations set out long lists of priority areas for United Nations agencies and governments to follow in both their research and operational programs dealing with human settlements. These broad, general and hortatory recommendations seem likely to prove the least consequential.

2. *Environmental aspects of natural resources management.* This most voluminous of all the subject areas resulted in no fewer than 44 recommendations running to 24 single-spaced pages. They cover soils, forests, fish, genetic resources, water, energy, wildlife, parks and other protected areas, and minerals. Most recommendations spell out at some length the methods and responsible agencies for achieving the stated objectives. . . .

3. *Identification and control of pollutants of broad international significance.* Perhaps the most impressive body of recommendations to emerge from the Conference is that arrived at through the happy combination of talent that was enjoyed by Committee III. . . .

The *headline-grabber* in this subject area was a resolution condemning "nuclear weapon tests, especially those carried out in the atmosphere," and calling for their discontinuance. In its final form, it was voted against by France, Gabon, and—in one of the few instances in which its delegation participated in the voting—China, while the United States and several other Western delegations abstained.

Another recommendation calls upon governments to "use the best practicable means available to minimize the release to the environment of toxic or dangerous substances such as heavy metals and organochlorine compounds, until it has been demonstrated that their release will not give rise to unacceptable risks or unless their use is essential to human health or food production, in which case appropriate control measures should be applied." Others counsel caution and consultation to governments in introducing pollution control measures, or in conducting large-scale weather activities, that could affect their neighbors or result in climate modification. A Scandinavian proposal aimed at preventing commercial SST flights was the victim of Common Market politics. First the Danes and Norwegians withdrew their support for the proposal which was opposed by the United Kingdom and France as an uncomradely act aimed at the *Concorde* project by two would-be future partners in the E.E.C. Then Sweden, not wishing to stand alone, withdrew also.

4. *Educational, informational, social, and cultural aspects of environmental issues.* Although it was one of the less glamorous subjects, this agenda item produced one of the Conference's most important specific decisions: that an International Referral Service for sources of environmental information should be established. The Service is envisaged not as a collection of primary data but as a clearing house able to direct a variety of inquirers—all of which would be governmental authorities or United Nations bodies—to sources of information and expertise on specific environmental problems. It will probably make use of the International Computing Centre, a United Nations facility located in Geneva.

The more important points deal with the trade effects of environmental measures. There was general agreement that countries would not "invoke environmental concerns as a pretext for discriminatory trade policies or for reduced access to markets" and that "the burdens of the environmental policies of the industrialized countries should not be transferred, either directly or indirectly, to the developing countries." The United Nations system generally, and GATT (General Agreement on Tariffs and Trade) and UNCTAD (UN Conference on Trade and Development) specifically were asked to monitor the threats to exports that arise from environmental concerns and to help develop "mutually acceptable common international environmental standards" which might avert such problems. . . .

The Declaration on the Human Environment

The major element of suspense in the Conference was provided by the Chinese in reopening discussion on the draft declaration of principles on the human environment which came to the Conference from the Preparatory Committee, on which China was not represented. That draft was the fragile result of a prolonged negotiation over many months, which had resulted in a compromise with which no one was entirely happy but in which the dissatisfactions were somewhat evenly balanced. It was commonly believed, therefore, that if the Chinese insisted not only on making their views known but on formally reopening the drafting process, everyone's desiderata would emerge from the Pandora's Box and the Conference would end with no agreement. . . .

The working group on the Declaration sat for long hours privately —though news of its deliberations did not long remain confidential— until the day the Conference ended. The drafting process was reopened, and for some time it appeared that the prediction of failure would be fulfilled. An initiative by the Secretariat to involve directly in this negotiation at a late stage the heads of delegations, on the supposition that they had the authority to accept compromises which their subordinates could not, broke the logjam, and at the last moment an agreement of sorts was reached. A Declaration consisting of a preamble and 26 principles was endorsed by acclamation, although the Chinese delegation chose not to participate in the voting in protest against the retention of a principle to which it objected dealing with nuclear weapons (and implicitly with their testing). . . .

The changes made in the draft at Stockholm contain mainly political points of interest to the LDCs, such as reaffirmations of the importance of development and condemnation of apartheid and other forms of discrimination and domination. As a basis for legal rights and obligations, few of the principles—three, to be specific—appear to have sufficient force and clarity to provide a possible basis for enforceable claims. These are the following:

" 1.   Man has the fundamental right to freedom, equality and adequate conditions of life, in an environment of a quality which permits a life of dignity and well-being, and bears a solemn responsibility to protect and improve the environment for present and future generations.

" 7.   States shall take all possible steps to prevent pollution of the seas by substances that are liable to create hazards to human health, to harm living resources and marine life, to damage amenities or to interfere with other legitimate uses of the sea.

"21.   States have, in accordance with the Charter of the United Nations and the principles of international law, the sovereign right to exploit their own resources pursuant to their own environmental policies, and the responsibility to ensure that activities within their jurisdiction or control do not cause damage to the environment of other States or of areas beyond the limits of national jurisdiction."

For a description of the concepts that will be guiding those located at the new focal point for global environmental concern, let Maurice

Strong speak for himself (quoted from his opening speech at the Conference):

> I believe we must build on these foundations:
>
> New concepts of sovereignty based not on the surrender of national sovereignties, but on better means of exercising those sovereignties collectively and with a greater sense of responsibility for the common good.
>
> New codes of international law to give effect to the new principles of international responsibility and conduct which the environmental age requires, and new means of dealing with environmental conflicts.
>
> New international means of managing the world's common property resources—the oceans and atmosphere beyond national jurisdiction—for the benefit of all mankind.
>
> New means of universalizing the benefits of technology and directing it towards the relief of those pressing problems which continue to afflict the great majority of the human family.
>
> New approaches to more automatic means of financing programmes of international co-operation, including use of levies and tolls on certain forms of international transport or on the consumption of certain non-renewable resources.

The Conference on Human Environment was only the first of other conferences to follow in the area of ecology dealing with such diverse functional subjects as marine pollution and whaling. A permanent Secretariat on the Environment has been established by the United Nations, marking an important milestone in the UN activities regarding social and economic welfare. Successes in this field are especially significant for the weaker states of the world for which the United Nations has become a favorite forum. But, of course, concern with bringing about a more effective peace-keeping machinery remains the urgent task for the 1970s, and it is for this reason that we close the chapter with an address by Dean Rusk which evaluates the first 25 years of the United Nations and looks at what the next decade may hold for the organization, and a more recent letter to the American public written by Ambassador George Bush upon his retirement as Permanent United States Representative to the United Nations.

THE FIRST TWENTY-FIVE YEARS OF THE UNITED NATIONS—
From San Francisco to the 1970's

DEAN RUSK

My assignment—to talk about the first 25 years of the United Nations—is unusual punishment for a Secretary of State. It is difficult enough to be a reasonably accurate historian of world affairs years later, after all the evidence is in. It is nothing short of foolhardy to foretell the future—especially when you are trying to tinker with the future to make it come out the way you think it should.

. . . I decided to try to look ahead as well as to look back. For, if we are to act wisely in world affairs, we must have some sense of direction, some conviction about the way human events are moving, some expectations about the forces and counterforces just over the horizon. I do have some expectations for the United Nations over the next five or ten years, and I might as well state them straightaway.

I believe that the influence of the United Nations will be even greater in the 1970's than it is today.

I believe also that the executive capacity of the United Nations to act in support of the purposes of the charter will be greater in the 1970's than it is today.

I hold these convictions despite valid cause for concern and some necessary reservations. I shall try to explain why.

The U.N.: A Necessity for Our Times

Let me begin by observing that it means little to study the performance of an institution against abstract standards without reference to the realities—and even the illusions—of the total environment in which

Department of State Bulletin, *Vol. L, No. 1283, Jan. 27, 1964. (The Dag Hammarskjold Memorial Lecture, prepared for delivery by Secretary of State Dean Rusk and read by Harlan Cleveland, Assistant Secretary for International Organization Affairs, at Columbia University, New York, N.Y., on Jan. 10, 1964).*

it must operate. In that context the first thing that strikes one about the United Nations is that international organization is a plain necessity of our times. This is so for both technical and political reasons.

The technical reasons stem, of course, from the headlong rush of scientific discovery and technological advance. That process has over-run the hypothetical question as to whether there is to be an international community that requires organization. It has left us with the practical question of *what kind* of international community we have the wit to organize around the scientific and technical imperatives of our time. In the words of Ogden Nash:

> When geniuses all in every nation
> Hasten us towards obliteration,
> Perhaps it will take the dolts and geese
> To drag us backward into peace.

World community is a fact

    —because instantaneous international communication is a fact;
    —because fast international transport is a fact;
    —because matters ranging from the control of communicable disease to weather reporting and forecasting demand international organization;
    —because the transfer of technology essential to the spread of industrialization and the modernization of agriculture can be assisted by international organizations;
    —because modern economics engage nations in a web of commercial, financial, and technical arrangements at the international level.

The advance of science, and the technology that follows, creates an insistent demand to build international technical and regulatory institutions which lend substance to world community. Few people seem to realize just how far this movement has gone. The United States is now a member of 53 international organizations. We contribute to 22 international operating programs, mostly sponsored by these same organizations. And last year we attended 547 international intergovernmental conferences, mostly on technical subjects. We do these things because they are always helpful and often downright essential to the conduct of our national and international affairs.

It is obvious that in the 1970's we shall require more effective international organization—making for a more substantial world community —than we have today. We already know that in the next decade we shall become accustomed to international communication, including television, via satellites in outer space. We shall travel in aircraft that fly at speeds above a thousand, and perhaps above two thousand, miles per hour. Industrialization will pursue its relentless course. Cities and their suburbs will keep on growing. The world economy will become increasingly interdependent. And science will rush ahead, leaving to us the task of fashioning institutions—increasingly on the international level—to administer its benefits and circumscribe its dangers.

So, while nations may cling to national values and ideas and ambitions and prerogatives, science has created a functional international society, whether we like it or not. And that society, like any other, must be organized.

Anyone who questions the *need* for international technical organizations like the United Nations agencies dealing with maritime matters, civil aviation, telecommunications, atomic energy, and meteorology simply does not recognize the times in which we live.

In a world caught up in an urgent drive to modernize areas containing two-thirds of the human race, there is need also for the United Nations specialized agencies dealing with health, agriculture, labor standards, education, and other subjects related to national development and human welfare. A massive effort to transfer and adapt modern technology from the more to the less advanced areas is a part of the great drama of our age. This sometimes can be done best through, or with the help of, the institutions of the international community.

And the international organizations concerned with trade and monetary and financial affairs are important to the expanding prosperity of the world economy.

Adjustment to Reality of Political World

The need for political organs at the international level is just as plain as the need for technical agencies.

You will recall that the decision to try to form a new international organization to preserve peace grew out of the agonies of the Second World War. The United States took the lead in this enterprise. President Franklin D. Roosevelt and Secretary of State Cordell Hull sought to avoid repeating what many believed to have been mistakes in political tactics which kept the United States from joining the League of Nations. They consulted at every stage the leaders of both political parties in both Houses of Congress. They insisted that the formation of this organization should be accomplished, if possible, *before* the end of the war.

Most of our allies readily endorsed this objective and cooperated in achieving it. You will recall that the charter conference at San Francisco convened before the end of the war against Hitler and that the

United States Senate consented to ratification of the charter in July 1945, before the end of the war in the Pacific. The vote in the Senate was 89 to 2, reflecting a national consensus bordering on unanimity. The significance of that solemn action was especially appreciated by those of us who were in uniform.

The commitment of the United States to the United Nations was wholehearted. We threw our best efforts and some of our best men into getting it organized and moving. We set about binding the wounds of war. We demobilized our armed forces and drastically reduced our military budget. We proposed—not only proposed but worked hard to obtain agreement—that atomic energy should be put under control of an agency of the United Nations, that it should be devoted solely to peaceful purposes, that nuclear weapons should be abolished and forever forbidden.

What happened? Stalin refused to cooperate. Even before the guns were silent, he set in motion a program of imperialistic expansion, in violation of his pledges to the Western Allies and in contravention of the principles of the United Nations.

You will recall that the United Nations was designed on the assumption that the great powers in the alliance destined to be victors in the Second World War would remain united to maintain the future peace of the world. The United Nations would be the instrument through which these powers, in cooperation with others, of course, would give effect to their mutual determination to keep the peace against any threats that might arise from some future Mussolini or Hitler. World peace was to be enforced by international forces carrying the flag of the United Nations but called into action and directed by agreement among the major powers. Action without big-power agreement was not ruled out by the charter, but such agreement was assumed to be the prior condition of an effective peace organization. Indeed, it was stated repeatedly by early supporters of the United Nations that the organization could not possibly work unless the wartime Allies joined in collective action within the United Nations to exert their combined power to make it work.

That view of the postwar world rapidly turned out to be an illusory hope. One might well have expected—as many good people did—that when the conceptual basis for the United Nations fell to the ground, the organization would fall down beside it.

But all great institutions are flexible. The United Nations adjusted gradually to the political and power realities of the quite different world that came into being. In the absence of major-power agreement in the Security Council, it drew on the charter's authority to balance that weakness with a greater reliance upon the General Assembly.

By adapting to political reality the United Nations lived and grew in effectiveness, in prestige, and in relevance. It could not act in some of the ways the founding fathers intended it to act, but it went on to do many things that the founding fathers never envisaged as being necessary. The most dramatic reversal of its intended role is seen in the fact that, while the United Nations could not bring the great powers together, it could on occasion keep them apart by getting between them—by becoming the "man in the middle"—as it did in differing ways in the Middle East and in the Congo.

In short, the political organs of the United Nations survived and did effective work under the shadow of a nuclear arms race of awesome proportions, despite the so-called cold war between the major powers whose unity was once presumed to be its foundation.

This was not bound to happen. It is evident that in the political environment of the second half of the twentieth century both technical and political reasons dictate the need for large-scale and diversified international organizations. But it does not necessarily follow that the United Nations was destined to work in practice—or even to survive. Indeed, its very survival may be more of an achievement than it seems at first blush. That it has steadily grown in its capacity to act is even more remarkable.

It has survived and grown in effectiveness because a great majority of the nations of the world have been determined to make it work. They have repulsed those who sought to wreck or paralyze it. They have remained determined not only to keep it alive but to improve and strengthen it. To this we owe in part the peace of the world.

Preserver and Repairer of World Peace

Indeed, it is difficult to avoid the conclusion that the existence of the General Assembly and the Security Council these past 18 years was a plain necessity for the preservation and repair of world peace. The failures would still have been failures, but without the U.N. some of the successes might not have been possible. . . .

With half a dozen international disputes chronically or repeatedly at the flash point, with forces of change bordering on violence loose in the world, our very instinct to survival informs us that we must keep building the peace-keeping machinery of the United Nations—and keep it lubricated with funds and logistical support.

And if we are to entertain rational hopes for general disarmament, we know that the U.N. must develop a reliable system for reconciling international conflict without resort to force. For peace in the world community—like peace in smaller communities—means not an end of conflict but an accepted system of dealing with conflict and with change through nonviolent means.

"Switchboard for Bilateral Diplomacy"

Traditional bilateral diplomacy—of the quiet kind—has a heavier task today than at any time in history. But with the annual agenda of urgent international business growing apace, with the birth of more than half a hundred new nations in less than two decades, an institution that can serve as an annual diplomatic conference becomes almost a necessity. As a general manager of our own nation's diplomatic establishment, I cannot imagine how we could conduct or coordinate our foreign affairs if we were limited to dealing directly through bilateral channels with the 114 nations with which we have diplomatic relations tonight.

At the last General Assembly representatives of 111 countries met for more than 3 months to discuss, negotiate, and debate. Two more countries became U. N. members, to make it 113.[1] When the tumult and the shouting had died, the General Assembly had adopted, curiously enough, 113 resolutions. This is what we have come to call parliamentary diplomacy.

But outside the formal agenda the General Assembly also has become the world's greatest switchboard for bilateral diplomacy. For many of the young and small nations, lacking a fully developed diplomatic service, the United Nations is the main, sometimes the only, general mechanism available for the conduct of their diplomacy.

Without formal decision the opening of each new Assembly has turned into something like an informal conference of the foreign ministers of the world community. In New York last fall, in a period of 11 days, I conferred with the foreign ministers or heads of government of 54 nations.

The need for an annual diplomatic conference, the need for a peacekeeping deterrent to wars large and small, and the need for an international monitor of peaceful change are plain enough. They seem to me to warrant the conclusion that the political organs as well as the technical organs of the United Nations have been very useful to the world at large for the past decade and a half. Common sense informs us that they can be even more useful in the years ahead.

---

[1] At present the United Nations has 135 members.

Recognizing the Peacekeeping Capacity of U.N.

I suspect that the near future will witness another period of adjustment for the United Nations. Some adjustments are, indeed, required—because the political environment is changing and so is the structure of the U.N. itself.

For one thing the cobweb syndrome, the illusion that one nation or bloc of nations could, by coercion, weave the world into a single pattern directed from a single center of power, is fading into limbo. That other illusion, the bipolar theory, of a world divided permanently between two overwhelming centers of power with most other nations clustered about them, is fading too. The reality of a world of great diversity with many centers of power and influence is coming into better focus.

Meanwhile, a first brake has been placed on the nuclear arms race, and the major powers are searching for other agreements in areas of common interest. One is entitled to hope that the major power conflicts which so often have characterized U.N. proceedings in the past will yield more and more to great-power cooperation; . . .

As long as a member possessing great power was intent on promoting conflict and upheaval—the better to coerce the world into its own image—that member might well regard the United Nations as a threat to its own ambitions. But suppose it is agreed that all members, despite their deep differences, share a common interest in survival and therefore a common interest in preventing resort to force anywhere in the world. Then the peacekeeping capacity of the United Nations can be seen realistically for what it is: an indispensable service potentially in the national interest of all members—in the common interest of even rival states.

If this reality is grasped by the responsible leaders of all the large powers, then the peacekeeping capacity of the United Nations will find some degree of support from all sides, not as a rival system of order but as contributor to, and sometimes guarantor of, the common interest in survival.

It would be a great service to peace if there could develop common recognition of a common interest in the peacekeeping capacity of the United Nations. That recognition is far from common now. My belief that it will dawn is based on the fact that it would serve the national interests of all nations, large and small, and because sooner or later nations can be expected to act in line with their national interests. . . .

The radical expansion of the membership raises problems for the newer and smaller nations. They rightly feel that they are underrepresented on some organs—notably the Security Council and the Economic and Social Council—whose membership was based on the U.N.'s original size and composition.

The growth of membership also raises problems for the middle-range powers, who were early members and have reason to feel that they are next in line for a larger voice.

And it raises problems—or potential problems—for the larger powers too.

The rapid and radical expansion of the General Assembly may require some adaptation of procedures if the U.N. is to remain relevant to the real world and therefore effective in that world.

Theoretically, a two-thirds majority of the General Assembly could now be formed by nations with only 10 percent of the world's population, or who contribute, altogether, 5 percent of the assessed budget. In practice, of course, this does not happen, and I do not share the dread expressed by some that the General Assembly will be taken over by its "swirling majorities."

But even the theoretical possibility that a two-thirds majority, made up primarily of smaller states, could recommend a course of action for which other nations would bear the primary responsibility and burden is one that requires thoughtful attention.

There are two extreme views of how national influence should be expressed in the work of the United Nations. At one extreme is the contention that no action at all should be taken by the United Nations without the unanimous approval of the permanent members of the Security Council. This is a prescription for chronic paralysis. The United Nations was never intended to be kept in such a box. The rights and duties of the General Assembly are inherent in the charter. The United Nations has been able to develop its capacity to act precisely because those rights were not blocked by the requirement of big-power unanimity.

At the other extreme are those few who feel that nothing should matter except the number of votes that can be mustered—that what a majority wants done must be done regardless of what states make up the majority. This notion flies in the face of common sense. The plain fact of the matter is that the United Nations simply cannot take significant action without the support of the members who supply it with resources and have the capacity to act.

Some have suggested that all General Assembly votes should be weighed to reflect population, or wealth, or level of contributions, or some combination of these or other factors. I do not believe that so far-reaching an answer would be realistic or practical. The equal vote in the General Assembly for each member—however unequal in size, wealth, experience, technology, or other criterion—is rooted in the idea of "sovereign equality" And that idea is not one which any nation, large or small, is eager to abandon. . . .

I would hope that the discussions which lie ahead will not only strengthen the financial underpinnings of the U.N. but, among other things, develop an acceptable way for the General Assembly to take account of capacity to act, of responsibility for the consequences, and of actual contributions to the work of the U.N. Such a way must be found if the United Nations machinery is to be relevant to the tasks that lie ahead—in peacekeeping, in nation building, and in the expansion of human rights.

All adjustment is difficult. Adaptations of the U.N. to recent changes in the environment may take time. It will require a shift away from some hardened ideas and some rigid patterns of action and reaction— perhaps on all sides. It will require—to come back to Hammarskjold's worlds—"perseverance and patience, a firm grip on realities, careful but imaginative planning, a clear awareness of the dangers. . . ."

To ask all this may seem to be asking a great deal. But I am inclined toward confidence because the U.N. already has demonstrated a capacity to adapt under the flexible provisions of the charter to the realities of international politics.

I am further persuaded that all, or most, of the smaller members are realistic enough to know:

> —that their own national interests lie with, not against, an effective United Nations;
> —that the U.N. can be effective only if it has the backing of those who have the means to make it effective;
> —that the U.N. is made less, not more, effective by ritualistic passage of symbolic resolutions with no practical influence on the real world;
> —that only responsible use of voting power is effective use of voting power;
> —that true progress on behalf of the world community lies along the path on which the weak and the strong find ways to walk together.

The Greatest Goal—Extending Human Rights

These are some of the reasons, derived from analysis of the current state of world affairs, why I expect the United Nations to evolve and to grow in executive capacity to act in support of its goals.

And apart from the issue of human survival, the greatest of these goals is, of course, the steady extension of human rights.

Dedication to the principle of the universality of fundamental human rights collides in practice with dedication to the principle of national sovereignty. For most violations of human rights are committed within the confines of national societies, often by the very governments that have ratified the charter's prescription for "fundamental freedoms for all." Yet securing equal rights for all individual members of the human race is the ultimate goal of world community—and the ultimate challenge to the United Nations as the elementary but principal expression of that community. Somehow the United Nations must learn how to increase respect for the rights of the human person throughout the world.

It is here that we sense the permanent value and the final force of the basic principles of a charter which dares to speak for "We the people of the United Nations." Sometimes I feel that we talk too much about the universality and brotherhood of man and too little about the valuable and interesting differences that distinguish all brothers. But the lessons of recorded history, and the teachings of the world's great teachers, make clear the basic wants of mankind.

Men and women everywhere want a decent standard of material welfare for themselves and their children. They want to live in conditions of personal security. They want social justice. They want to experience a sense of achievement, for themselves and for the groups with which they identify themselves.

But men and women everywhere want more. They want personal freedom and human dignity.

Individuals and societies place differing values on these aspirations. But surely these are universal desires, shared by all races in all lands, interpreted by all religions, and given concrete form—or lip service—by leaders and spokesmen for every kind of political, economic and social system.

Peace and security, achievement and welfare, freedom and dignity —these are the goals of the United Nations for all peoples. And any nation which questions for long *whether* we should seek these aims is destined to become a pariah of the world community.

Because the kind of world projected in the charter is the kind of world we want, the United Nations—despite its quarrels and its shortcomings—commands our continuing support. As President Johnson said to the General Assembly on December 17: ". . . more than ever we support the United Nations as the best instrument yet devised to promote the peace of the world and to promote the well-being of mankind."

And because the kind of world projected in the charter is the kind most people everywhere want, I believe that others will join with us in improving and strengthening the United Nations. That is why I am confident that the executive capacity of the United Nations—its machinery for keeping peace, building nations, and promoting human rights— will be greater on its 25th birthday than on its 18th.

The letter from the former United Nations Ambassador George Bush reprinted below should give the reader some insights into problems facing the United Nations today and serve as a basis for making some judgments about the validity of the predictions made by Dean Rusk.

LETTER TO THE AMERICAN PUBLIC UPON HIS RETIREMENT AS UNITED STATES PERMANENT REPRESENTATIVE TO THE UNITED NATIONS

GEORGE BUSH

February 2, 1973

Dear Fellow American:

I have had a unique vantage point of the world during my two years here at the U.N.—a picture window view of major events and occurrences that are now written into history. I've enjoyed it thoroughly. I've loved every moment of it. I came here both as a strong supporter of the U.N. and as its strong critic. My sense of criticism remains with me; in some ways it has been sharpened. But my support at the same time is far stronger than when I came here as a new ambassador.

During my tenure we've lost some battles, but we've achieved victory, too. We lost in our effort last year to keep a seat for Taiwan in the U.N., although we welcomed at the same time the admission of Peking. This year we won on the issue of keeping the two Koreas talking peace between themselves by not dragging the subject into the international debating forum. We won on the crucial issue of reducing the United States assessment rate in the U.N. budget to a ceiling of 25 percent. We lost on the issue of making the U.N. take a responsible role in curb-

Letter written to the American public from Ambassador George Bush upon his retirement as United States Permanent Representative to the United Nations.

ing international terrorism. If you want to keep score, we haven't done too badly.

Meanwhile, we've been able to keep in touch informally and meaningfully with just about all the rest of the countries of the world, including the People's Republic of China. With others, too, that perhaps have only one ambassador at large and that one at the U.N.

This may sound defensive. Certainly we have to listen to an awful lot of criticism of both what we do and what the U.N. does. Let's look at the record of the positive side, the side that's less often presented.

Over nearly 25 years, U.N. peacekeeping operations—sometimes just a few dozen men, sometimes thousands—have served again and again to keep the peace, or restore it when it was broken—in such chronic trouble spots as Kashmir, Cyprus, and the Middle East. There is no way to estimate how much tragedy the world was spared by these operations.

A major U.N. peacekeeping operation in the Congo a decade ago prevented that new nation from collapsing in civil war or becoming a battleground between the major powers. Today the Congo is peaceful, independent, united, and making progress.

When South Korea was the victim of massive aggression in 1950, the U.N. joined in a successful collective action against the aggressor; and today South Korea is one of the major political and economic success stories of Asia.

To write off the U.N.'s achievements in keeping the peace because of its inability to be effective in Czechoslovakia or Vietnam would be like writing off medical science because it has not yet found a solution for cancer. It is worthwhile curing pneumonia and hepatitis—while new breakthroughs are sought—and it is decidedly in mankind's interest to use existing U.N. peacekeeping, whatever its limitations, while striving to develop its capacities further.

But peace is of course much more than the absence of war. What has the U.N. done to build peace by making the world a better place to live? Again, I have discovered it has done some very impressive things—far more than is generally realized or appreciated.

U.N. health programs are within sight of wiping malaria from the face of the earth, and in just three years have reduced the number of countries in which smallpox is prevalent from 27 to 17.

U.N. Development Program surveys have turned up mineral deposits valued at over $13 billion—copper in Mexico and Panama and Malaysia, limestone in Togo, iron ore in Chile, coal in Pakistan.

The World Bank and the IDA are providing loan capital to the low-income countries at an unprecedented rate. Last year such credits exceeded $2 billion, more than twice the level of two years ago. For the five-year period beginning last year the Bank's President, Robert

McNamara, has projected a target of $12 billion—a figure exceeding its loans to low-income countries during its first 20 years of existence.

The U.N. Declaration of Human Rights, adopted over 20 years ago without any force of law, has served as a source book for the constitutions of over 40 new nations.

The U.N. has had a hand in the writing of a series of important treaties to curb the arms race and strengthen international law—the Test Ban Treaty, the Outer Space Treaty, the Non-Proliferation Treaty and most recently the treaty against emplacement of weapons of mass destruction on the seabed.

The U.N. has helped to ease the transition of almost a billion people—a third of mankind—from colonial status to independence—to make that transition peaceful—and to help over 60 new and struggling nations with the aid of protection of the international community.

Those are a few proven examples of what the U.N. can do when its Members cooperate. And, of course, the bigger and more powerful the Member, the more important is its cooperation—or lack of it. This means both a heavy responsibility and a great opportunity for the United States.

Given this instrument, given this proven capability and still greater potential—what do we want it to do in the future? What interests or desires of the American people do we want it to serve? What needs does the world have in which the U.N. can be helpful?

I think the answer to that question must proceed from two fundamentals: our own national purposes and the kind of world that we live in at this point in history.

As for our national purposes, I believe we are a nation with a very deep commitment to building a better life for our own people and to living as good neighbors with other nations. That is not only the American vision; I think it is also the vision of most of the peoples of the world—and that's why it is such a powerful force. By itself it would be a sufficient reason for our best efforts to make a success of the U.N.—so that the unavoidable tensions and collisions between nations can never erupt once more into a world war.

But there is another reason, too, which must shape our policy in the U.N. This is a whole new set of facts about the kind of world we live in, and it can be summed up in one word: technology. In the past generation the scientists and engineers and medical men—in this country and abroad—have put into our hands these incredible new powers—to heal, to lengthen life, to communicate and travel at unheard of speeds, to go to the moon, to mine the bottom of the sea, to abolish hunger and poverty or to blow each other off the face of the earth. And the research that gave us these powers is continuing to give us more—so that the world of the year 2000 may well be more completely transformed from today than we are from the world of 30 years ago—when there was no atomic energy, no penicillin, no commercial television, no transistors, no jet power. The world is already suffering a bit from what one writer has named "future shock," and there is going to be more.

Not all the results of progress have been good. Along with the lengthening of life comes overpopulation. Along with peaceful nuclear power comes the nuclear arms race. Along with new industries, new cars and jet planes, comes the pollution and wounding of our environment and the deterioration of the cities we live in.

And—perhaps the most significant fact of all—the world is now so linked together by trade and investment, by radio and television and jet travel, that we simply have to try to tackle our problems together. Nations may be capitalist or communist, black, brown or white, rich or poor, big or little—but never in history have people been so aware that this is one world with one human species living in it, and having common hopes and common problems.

The United Nations is one important place in which we can do that. As President Nixon pointed out in a recent Foreign Policy Report to Congress:

> The march of technology has pressed upon the world an increasing number of exigent problems which can only be solved by collaboration among governments. As a result, the United Nations' role in facilitating international cooperation has taken on a new importance.

This is the future, then, as we see it. By the time these lines are read, I shall have moved on to another position and will no longer be carrying our ball at the U.N. But insofar as the U.N.'s destiny is bound up with the destiny of our country, and I believe it is, I shall constantly be conscious of it in my future work.

Yours very truly,

/S/ George Bush

INDEX